The Middle East
in Global Perspective

The Middle East
in Global Perspective

edited by Judith Kipper
and Harold H. Saunders

Westview Press

American Enterprise Institute for Public Policy Research

Published in 1991 in the United States of America by Westview Press, Inc., 5500 Central Avenue, Boulder, Colorado 80301, and in the United Kingdom by Westview Press, 36 Lonsdale Road, Summertown, Oxford OX2 7EW

Library of Congress Cataloging-in-Publication Data
The Middle East in global perspective / edited by Judith Kipper and
    Harold H. Saunders.
        p. cm.
    Includes bibliographical references and index.
    ISBN 0-8133-0296-X
    ISBN 0-8133-0295-1 (Pb.)
    1. Middle East—Politics and government—1979–   . I. Kipper,
Judith.   II. Saunders, Harold H.
DS63.1.M4887 1991
320.956—dc20   91-4042
                                                                                CIP

Printed and bound in the United States of America

The paper used in this publication meets the requirements
of the American National Standard for Permanence of Paper
for Printed Library Materials Z39.48-1984.

10   9   8   7   6   5   4   3   2   1

Contents

Preface and Acknowledgments

This book has evolved over a period of five years. This extended period of preparation reflects the complexity of producing a multiauthored volume across miles and cultures. Institutional growth, retrenchment, and change also took time, as did conflicting demands in the lives of all involved. The passage of time has required some painful rewriting, but it has also made the overall purpose of the book sharper and even more compelling than when we began.

We owe far more than the usual thanks to our authors for their patience and personal support and for going more than the extra mile in helping us to bring their chapters up to date—even to reflect in some way the Iraqi invasion of Kuwait and the war in the Gulf. They have been more than gracious, and we are deeply grateful to all of them.

We also express our thanks to two administrations of the American Enterprise Institute. President William J. Baroody, Jr., provided the environment and leadership to launch this project, and President Christopher DeMuth provided a context for following through the preparation of the final manuscript. Edward Styles managed the production and editorial processes with patience and skill through both administrations. Dana Lane edited with the careful yet sensitive hand so important in a book for which some of the authors are kindly writing in English as a second language. We also appreciate the patience and interest of Fred Praeger and his colleagues at Westview Press and the gentle, careful editing of Ida May B. Norton in the especially difficult task of preparing the manuscript for press.

The project has been principally funded by a grant to the American Enterprise Institute from the Rockefeller Foundation. This grant not only covered the normal expenses of producing the chapters but provided support for a trip by several of the authors, traveling as a group, to host institutions in the Middle East in January 1986. We are grateful for the hospitality of the Al Ahram Strategic Studies Center in Cairo, Egypt; the Arab Thought Forum in Amman, Jordan; the Arab Council for Public Affairs in East Jerusalem; and the Leonard Davis Institute at the Hebrew University and the Dayan Center at the Tel Aviv University in Israel.

Finally, while preparing the final manuscript, both of us have been visiting scholars at The Brookings Institution, and we want to express our thanks for its support of our broader work.

Hal Saunders expresses his thanks to Thomas R. Smerling for helping in the initial articulation of assumptions underlying his approach to international relationships. During a year of work at the American Enterprise Institute as a Bush Foundation Leadership Fellow in 1985–1986, Tom Smerling distilled from conversation the assumptions underlying Hal Saunders's approach and contrasted them to the current literature in the field of international relations. Although he bears no responsibility for the evolution of later formulations, his research and the conversations surrounding it helped launch this line of inquiry, which provides some of the larger thinking about the themes in this book.

Finally, we hope that the new concepts, perspectives, and vocabulary suggested here will help generate thinking that can accelerate progress toward peace—whether in the Arab-Israeli arena, in Lebanon, or in the Gulf. We write with no partisan purpose and only with a keen commitment to a peaceful resolution of the conflicts that burden the lives of those who find their destiny in the Middle East. What motivates us is our heartfelt concern for this very human dilemma.

Judith Kipper
Harold H. Saunders
Washington, D.C.

1
Introduction:
The United States, the Middle East, and Our Changing World

Judith Kipper and Harold H. Saunders

Our dramatically changing world demands new perspectives to bring our experience into focus, new vocabulary for describing what shapes that experience, and new political tools for changing it creatively and peacefully. The new century before us demands a new way of thinking about how the world works and how peoples and nations relate. In few places is that need greater or more urgent than in the Middle East following the Gulf crisis and war of 1990–1991.

The concepts developed over almost five centuries to explain a world of nation-states amassing military and economic power to pursue objectively defined national interests do not adequately explain how peoples and nations act today. The instruments of force, economic pressure, diplomacy, negotiation, and propaganda that leaders have used to initiate and direct change do not reliably produce expected results. Neither these familiar concepts nor the potential of those instruments seems to inspire leaders today to guide change with imagination and direction. It may one day be said that the Gulf war was among the last wars of a traditional era, not among the first of the crises handled in the perspective that will have to govern as the nuclear age matures beyond the East-West rivalry that has begun fading away.

Nowhere have events taught this lesson more sharply than in the Middle East. The lesson is a global one, but focusing on this one area makes vivid the need for new approaches and the price of continuing to live with old perspectives and stalemates. Until we develop new perspectives, we have little chance of dealing creatively with these intractable problems. Yet in this area where more than half the inhabitants are still in their formative years, an unusual opportunity exists to help a new generation find more constructive ways to live. Just as the period following the 1973 war became a period of political change—sometimes creative, sometimes destructive—the years following the Gulf crisis and war could bring historic changes to the region. How leaders and people alike interpret what they are experiencing will determine in large part how they direct the course of change.

This book addresses the compelling need to redefine the concepts we use to bring our rapidly changing world into focus so that we may act more effectively, peacefully, and creatively in it. The book is rooted in the experiences of the Arab-Israeli peace process after the 1973 war and written against the background of a fading cold war and dramatic global change. It is presented in the wake of another war in the Middle East. It reflects the concepts and vocabulary we were learning to use in the Arab-Israeli arena, but it offers insights for coping with the aftermath of conflict and the changes that will follow in the Gulf. It is an effort to conceptualize experience, not to recount it. It is intended both to transcend particular moments and to offer a wider framework for working effectively within them.

Refocusing our thinking about how nations relate is not an abstract theoretical exercise—whether in the Middle East or on the global stage. How people and governments perceive what they do heavily influences how they do it. Our assumptions about how our world works could determine whether nuclear, chemical, or biological war destroys us or peace flourishes. They could determine whether most of the world's people continue to live in grinding poverty or share in economic and technological change. They could determine whether conflicts such as those in the Middle East give way to peaceful political processes or to fanatical violence. They could determine whether great powers pursue conflicting interests in the developing world or work in complementary ways with people there for peaceful development. This discussion is not about theories and ideologies but about how leaders will use the instruments of peacemaking and economic progress or destruction in a nuclear and still poverty-plagued world. A shift in how leaders and publics think about international relationships could focus attention on a broad array of political—and therefore peaceful—instruments that have been too often neglected but may now have become more usable.

This rethinking reflects the beginnings of what scholars have called a paradigm shift. Clearly, sovereign states and military or economic power remain central on the world scene. The Gulf war left us in no doubt of that. This rethinking does not suggest otherwise. It does suggest that we need to understand familiar concepts such as states and power in new ways. Most of us do not yet see the decline of sovereign states, but many of us observe that national sovereignty is increasingly limited in what it can accomplish by itself and argue that genuine influence in the third millennium will not come alone from the use of raw power. Others argue that any "great power" will steadily decline over the next century if it does not recognize that the nature of power and genuine influence has changed.

Three observations about international relationships today are worth setting down briefly because they set a global perspective for our discussion of the Middle East. They reflect the analysis of our authors and establish a link connecting that analysis to the larger task of reconceptualizing relationships among nations around the world.

First, more and more events confront nations that no one nation can deal with alone. Only in active relationships with others and only by cooperating can nations deal with events that cut across borders. Nations are confronted by the nature and limits of national power outside a relationship with others who have interests or influence in any particular situation.

Borders have become so permeable that nations define part of their own identity in relationship to their larger environment, and they define their larger environment partly as a projection of their own experiences and perceptions. On the level of perception, there is an intertwining of one nation's experience and its relationships with others. Robert Pranger, citing Professor Carl Brown of Princeton, writes in Chapter 2 of the "domestication of the international and internationalization of the domestic in the Middle East."

In the past, nation-states have been pictured as rational systems in which leaders amass power to pursue interests in a strategic chess game with other states. In that picture, states resolve problems by the unilateral use or threat of military or economic power and by formal negotiation. Today unilateral action seems less and less effective. As Ghassan Tuéni advises in Chapter 12, "The United States must renounce its determination to solve problems alone."

Governments acting alone, for instance, may no longer be able to meet one of their most basic responsibilities—providing security for their peoples with their own military power against external threat. Most dramatically, in a nuclear world one government's drive to build superior military force may tempt a preemptive attack by an adversary that would inflict the unacceptable losses the drive is committed to prevent. In East-West relations, the concept of "common security" has come to connote the paradoxical recognition that each party to a conflict has an interest in the other party's sense of security and that neither may be able to provide security without some cooperation with the other.

This point is not limited to East-West relations. The destructive capacity of sophisticated nonnuclear weaponry—including chemical and biological—amassed in regions such as the Middle East may make war prohibitively costly. The Gulf war underscored the point. As General Avraham Tamir notes in Chapter 9, these nations, too, are on the threshold of facing nuclear weapons on their battlefields. Many people in these nations, including those writing in this book in one way or another, also understand that real security may come only from building new relationships with neighbors. Although no military planner can lessen the efforts of a nation to strengthen itself, our authors write in agonizing awareness that military power alone cannot ensure security. Even while a state of war continues, as Ahmed S. Khalidi and Hussein Agha point out in Chapter 8, Israel and Syria depend in some part on unwritten understandings that establish limits of military action between them in Lebanon and on the Golan Heights. Whatever their strength, it seems unlikely by itself to resolve their conflict or prevent war.

Finally, mounting attention to the rights of individual human beings has steadily become a factor affecting relations among states. When asked in conversation why he gave priority to the Israeli-Palestinian conflict, former President Jimmy Carter responded that he "saw it as a human rights problem." Crown Prince El Hassan bin Talal of Jordan writes in Chapter 13 of the centrality of an effective U.S. commitment to the right of self-determination for the Palestinians as an important factor affecting U.S. influence in the Middle East.

Governments still jealously guard the principle of noninterference by others in relations between them and their people. Yet the legitimacy of one government's concern for the rights of individuals in another sovereignty has been established in such interstate agreements as the Helsinki accords and in the watchfulness of such nongovernmental organizations as Amnesty International. Nations can and do choose to ignore these new norms of international behavior, but the existence of such norms and international attention can serve as a brake on abuses of human rights. Whatever governments may get away with, they will be judged in some way by those standards. Their stature and credentials for leadership will be affected. Military and economic power are no longer the only standards.

Second is a broadening popular participation both within and between nations. Change seems often to swell from the bottom up rather than to come from the state institutions down. Focusing on the political energies and interaction of communities of people—not just on state institutions—causes us to think in different ways about concepts such as the national interest, national policy, and the causes and resolution of conflict. Key chapters that follow focus on the intercommunal character of the Arab-Israeli conflict—Meron Benvenisti in Chapter 3—and on the dynamics of policymaking within those communities—Rashid Khalidi on the Palestinians in Chapter 4 and Naomi Chazan on Israel in Chapter 5.

There are two aspects to this observation. One relates to the larger participation of people in some nations in policymaking. The other relates to the wider role of communities of people as significant elements of whole nations interacting across national boundaries.

As Robert Pranger writes: "This means that the tasks of foreign policy now include much more than the traditional management of a nation's foreign relations: Successful policy also involves an ability to forge domestic consensus about ends and means in conditions that grow steadily more complex for every nation and to take advantage of the diversity of interests and actors in other countries as well as in one's own."

Pranger goes beyond focusing on the decisionmaking institutions of states and beyond the conflicts of state-defined interests to bring into focus the fact that conflict, especially in a region like the Middle East, is often not between states but between communities of people. He does not lay aside insights into the formal policymaking of states but says rather that the effectiveness of that policymaking requires a capacity to show sensitivity and understanding for the communal aspects as well as the state dimensions of conflict. He argues that the capacity of governments to make foreign policy involves the skillful mixing of key international and domestic variables for peaceful achievement of nations' vital interests. In establishing this focus, he points to the need of those who govern nations to show an ability both to understand interests as they are defined by domestic constituencies in the give-and-take of the internal political arena and to explore ways of pursuing those interests peacefully in the interaction with other nations. Facing a broad regional Middle East agenda following the Gulf war, leaders will have to reexamine the capacity of their bodies politic to develop and conduct a political process large enough to deal with such an agenda.

Meron Benvenisti—as Pranger notes—also draws attention in Chapter 3 to the implications of regarding the Israeli-Palestinian conflict not as a traditional state-to-state conflict within the international system but rather as a communal conflict between two peoples with claims in the same land. He believes that a peace process designed in the context of traditional diplomacy does not address fundamental issues of communal identity that must be dealt with if two peoples are to live together in peace. Formulas for negotiation do not produce movement toward peace until the fundamental resistance of peoples to negotiate at all can be addressed and removed. In short, Benvenisti adds a range of issues and of devices for pursuing intercommunal peace that are not normally found on the agenda of governmental diplomacy. If we are to think of a broader Middle East process in the years following the Gulf war, taking into account the needs and identities of the different communities in the region will add a critical dimension to the peacemaking.

Rashid Khalidi provides a vivid picture of the texture of policymaking in the Palestinian movement, in which the conventional attributes of sovereignty and state decisionmaking are not present but intensive and often coherent political life is possible. In discussing the evolution of the policy of the Palestine Liberation Organization (PLO), he provides insight into the way an internationally significant movement can have attributes of self-government even without the normal attributes of statehood. This view provides a basis for considering some of the problems Palestinian leaders must deal with in moving toward consolidation of Palestinian politics and a normal relationship with Israel. As Khalidi points out, the choices made by the PLO leadership during the Gulf crisis will have a "profound and lasting impact on the Palestinian polity" and on how others deal with it.

In a chapter that complements both Benvenisti and Khalidi, Naomi Chazan paints a detailed picture of Israeli politics and society in transition by reviewing the four stages through which Israeli government passed in the 1980s. Throughout Chapter 5, she emphasizes that "the foreign policy orientations of Israel and its responses to external actions and initiatives are directly related to domestic social and political currents."

Whereas Israel had responded decisively to the 1973 war, Israel's responses to external events were far more hesitant in the 1980s because they "highlighted contradictions in the Israeli body politic." As she explains, "The Palestinian-Israeli conflict, progressively internalized on the societal level, has remained external to the political system that has primary responsibility for coming to terms with its various manifestations. The policy aspects of the Palestinian question and its relationship to the Arab-Israeli conflict have continued to be seen as a matter of security and foreign affairs, handled according to the principles guiding the determination of external relations in the past."

Chazan makes clear that domestic change in Israel and steps toward an Israeli-Palestinian settlement are intimately intertwined. Analysts of the present situation in Israel, she says, "have raised doubts about the possibility of reorienting or unifying the diverse strands of Israeli political culture without bringing about basic changes in the political conditions that have allowed these opinions and constellations to flourish. In this view, a negotiated political solution to the ongoing conflict is a precondition for real change in the Israeli body politic."

Chazan's point about Israel if more generally stated could apply to a number of bodies politic around our changing world, including the Palestinian movement: "Because Israel's external outlook and the possibilities open to the international community in relating to Israel are determined to no mean degree by domestic configurations, a more careful look at Israeli political dynamics is vital to any projection of prospects for change in the Middle East." If relations between nations are indeed a political process of continuous interaction between significant elements of whole bodies politic, the analyses of Benvenisti, Khalidi, and Chazan in effect urge a much broader focus on the peace process as a political process essential in changing relationships between peoples in conflict, whether in the Arab-Israeli arena or in the wider Middle East.

William Green Miller points out in Chapter 6 that in a large, constitutionally established government such as that of the United States, policymaking is influenced not only by the political dynamics of the body politic at large but by the dynamics of the relationship between major branches within the government itself. He describes how in some circumstances members of the U.S. Congress have over the years become almost more personally familiar with the problems of a region such as the Middle East than have members of an incoming presidential team in a new administration. He describes the active relationship that developed between President Anwar Sadat of Egypt and members of the Congress, as well as the more familiar relationship with prime ministers of Israel. In both these cases, ambassadors and their staffs have spent almost as much time cultivating relationships with the members of Congress as they have with members of the executive branch. All of this is an evolution beyond the traditional diplomatic view that heads of government deal only with heads of government, not with their political constituencies or with other elements of their government except for the appropriate ministries.

Although they are more difficult to analyze, the revolutions in communication and transportation open the door to a wide range of relationships among these communities. What one leader says or does one day in his or her own country will be heard, seen, and assessed within hours by another leader's constituencies. In addition, peoples in many nations are more aware of each other as human beings and not just as institutional abstractions. Nowhere is this more evident than in the breadth and intensity of media coverage during a crisis such as that in the Gulf in 1990–1991. It is also physically possible today for many more people to experience international relationships by visiting back and forth. Those who cannot yet travel are still in touch with the world beyond them by transistor radio and, increasingly, by television. Groups of people in distant places can experience the same event and each audience's interaction with the other via communications satellites.

It is the potential of these relationships that has only barely begun to be introduced into the process of peacemaking. As Robert Pranger states in Chapter 2: "Successful negotiations may seek more than one track: Although participants must never neglect the opportunities provided by official state-to-state relations or ignore the limitations of these techniques, they must also make an effort to get *communities* involved through negotiating methods quite different from those of formal diplomacy." The proliferation of Israeli-Palestinian meetings provides a ready opportunity.

Governments have encountered the consequences of an increased popular role in other ways. Both the Soviet Union and the United States, for instance, have seen aims thwarted by popular movements in Vietnam and Afghanistan. They saw the strategic balance between them shift following the popularly based Khomeini revolution in Iran, and each experienced the difficulties of relating to the governing authority that emerged. Soviets worry about the potential interaction between Islamic movements in Iran and Afghanistan and the Islamic peoples of Soviet Central Asia. People in the United States worry about a potential flood of refugees from south of their border if economic, social, or political conditions become intolerable for large numbers of people there. In Lebanon in 1982 and in the West Bank and Gaza since 1987, we have seen the capacity of armed and unarmed resistance to change the character of the Israeli-Palestinian relationship.

As more people experience or affect international relationships, incentives have mounted to understand nations and governments at least partly as collections of people. Increasingly, the world demands that we deinstitutionalize and humanize our analysis of how nations relate. The growing involvement of people in domestic and world politics demands new awareness of the human roots of interests, priorities, and conflict in international relationships. Fear, suspicion, rejection, mistrust, hatred, and misperception are often greater obstacles to peace between nations than is the inability to resolve technically definable problems. In this century, the behavioral sciences have deepened our insight into what moves human beings and what influences their interaction. In his speech to the Israeli Knesset on November 20, 1977, Egyptian President Sadat captured the point: "It is this psychological barrier which I described in official statements as constituting 70 percent of the whole problem."

Third, traditional instruments of statecraft often do not reliably accomplish what is expected of them. As we observe the broadening involvement of publics, we focus on the instruments used in the political arena for changing political environments so that publics will encourage and sustain new approaches.

We have normally thought of the instruments of statecraft as including the exercise of various forms of military and economic power to gain what nations want or, as a nonviolent alternative, negotiation. In more recent times, we have come to think also of those opinion-shaping programs which fall under the rubrics of "information" or "propaganda."

Today the most powerful weapons the world has ever known cannot be used by leaders of conscience, and even when force is still used, it has not produced expected results. The U.S. experience in Vietnam and the Soviet experience in Afghanistan are not unique. Israel learned that neither sophisticated combat aircraft nor superior armored ground forces could exterminate the Palestinian national movement in Beirut—a city mainly defended not by the armed forces of Lebanon but by the armed men of the PLO and local political militias. In the winter of 1987–1988, change in the Israeli-Palestinian relationship came not from the armed power of a state but from the civil disobedience of an unarmed people under Israeli military occupation. Television screens pictured Palestinian youths throwing stones at Israeli youths in the uniform of the Israeli Defense Force and those Israeli soldiers not using planes and tanks but beating Palestinian youths on the ground with sticks and stones. These scenes dramatized the limits of traditional state military power in today's world.

Anthony H. Cordesman in Chapter 7 makes the case for tighter interaction between military and political thinking. Leaders have not formulated their objectives with precise understanding of what military instruments can and cannot achieve. "The end result is almost constant abuse of military power," he writes. "Military adventure and civil struggles are sustained without any clear grand strategic objective or 'end game.' Short-term tactical advantage is confused with long-term victory, and the purchase of arms is confused with the purchase of political power and military effectiveness."

From the perspective of the United States, he points out that it is important to preserve a distinction between our political commitments to a nation like Israel and our strategic interest in the stability of oil-producing countries in the Gulf. "The war between the U.S.-led United Nations coalition and Iraq showed that the United States had little hope of avoiding continuing regional entanglements," he writes. "The challenge the United States faces is to shape its strategic relations around" oil and lines of communication—the "only two features which are of vital strategic importance to the United States and the West"—instead of its historical and political ties to the Levant. "The issue is not one of choosing between Israel and its Arab neighbors—it is one of ensuring Israel's security while recognizing that the primary U.S. strategic interests lie in the Gulf and not along the coast of the eastern Mediterranean."

Whatever the strategic reasoning and military capability, Cordesman points out that the U.S. ability to intervene in the region depends on careful attention to the interaction between military and political policies. The naval intervention at the end of the Iran-Iraq war and the military action against Iraq in 1990–1991, for instance, "showed that the United States can play a powerful role if it has the support of regional states, but it cannot act alone." In the Arab-Israeli area, "the United States also needs to work closely with Israel on the development of improved warning, surveillance, and low-level conflict technology of the kind that will allow Israel to withdraw from territory like the southern part of Lebanon and from as much of the West Bank as possible."

One comes away from Chapter 8 by Ahmed S. Khalidi and Hussein Agha with a clear sense that neither Israel nor Syria can force a solution of their conflict by military means. These authors present a broad picture of all the factors at play in Syria's pursuit of strategic parity with Israel in order to force negotiation of the Arab-Israeli conflict. The analysis of the imbalance of power reaches across the full spectrum of quantitative and qualitative differences in military forces, through the respective economic and technological foundations, to the character of each nation's relationships with the great powers and the regional military-political context in which each operates. They point out that the Arab nations over the past forty years since the establishment of Israel have attempted a variety of political, social, diplomatic, and military means of redressing the Arab-Israeli imbalance. They explain that Syria has, in a unique way, reflected in its national experience and policies each of these approaches. In that context, the authors describe the Syrian doctrine of attaining strategic parity with Israel as, in Syria's view, the only way of forcing Israel to take Syria seriously and to make a genuine effort to achieve a settlement. They also make clear that Syria is still groping to define the exact nature and purpose of that parity, given the changing arms supply relationship with the Soviet Union and the new regional security regime that may emerge from the Gulf war.

The authors' discussion of Syria's search for a strategic doctrine that can make possible a settlement with Israel leads them to conclude that "a policy of containment may ultimately seem the most rational and effective means by which 'parity' can be put to use against Israel." Their chapter points to the possibility of Syrian recognition that "the prime purpose of its military buildup is not so much to force Israel to the negotiating table as it is to instill confidence in Syria's own capability to resist Israeli aggrandizement. This may lead," they suggest, toward "a Syrian readiness to concede certain politico-territorial points within an overall policy of containing Israeli power and restricting its influence and fields of action." Their conclusion underscores the need in our changing world to look to the underlying politics of moving conflict toward resolution, even when we are considering the implications of military strategy.

General Avraham Tamir has been a central figure in the establishment of peace between Egypt and Israel through the political process that evolved after the 1973 Arab-Israeli war and was defined in part at Camp David in 1978 and in the Egyptian-Israeli peace treaty. In Chapter 9 he writes from his long experience as one of Israel's senior military planners. Surrounding his straightforward description of how Israelis must think about their own defense is his recognition—both explicit and implicit—that Israel's security depends on regional and global factors well beyond the reach of any traditional military capability Israel can develop for itself. Starting with an understanding that great powers play a role, Tamir acknowledges that the threat to Israeli security ranges from terrorist acts to the grave problem that will be posed for regional powers if their adversaries acquire nuclear weapons—a concern brought to the world's attention by the Gulf crisis. He points out that even in the more familiar realm of conventional warfare, the defense of a country like Israel will depend on how it deals with the larger political constraints which flow from its relationship with the United States and with other elements of the world community. He also cites as a primary objective of Israel's military strategy "deterring Arab confrontation states from continuing the war and bringing them to the negotiating table to resolve the Arab-Israeli conflict."

Turning to economic instruments in his study of the use of oil as a political weapon in the 1970s, Robert D. Hormats in Chapter 10 underscores the complexity of political and security interests as well as economic concerns which affect the consequences of using an economic resource such as oil as a political weapon. In today's highly interdependent world, measuring the consequences requires an integration of political, economic, and security considerations which goes well beyond simple economic calculations. In addition to raising questions about the utility of economic leverage—whether in 1973–1974 or during the Gulf crisis of 1990–1991—he makes a strong argument for the need to integrate more fully insights from both the fields of international economics and analysis of security and political concerns.

Focusing on the Arab-Israeli peace process, Stanley Hoffmann in Chapter 11 argues that the task of pursuing an Arab-Israeli peace "far exceeds the dimensions of traditional state-to-state diplomacy." He points out that the politics of a region like the Middle East are not easily explained by the familiar theories of international relations, but two important insights do emerge. One is that nations interacting in an essentially anarchic system—"no central power, few compelling common values"—will experience deep suspicion that blinds them to understanding the real motives and fears at work in their relationship. This misunderstanding imposes "sharp limits on cooperation and on diplomatic settlements whenever important issues of security arise."

Underlying the importance of the suspicion and fear at work in a relationship, Hoffmann argues, is the fact that "relations among countries can no longer be analyzed as if they take place among rational 'unitary actors,' as if statesmen were merely, to use Clausewitzian language, the 'personified intelligence of the state.' We know now that international relations is a concept encompassing the encounters, bonds, and collisions of societies. . . . A state determined to influence another . . . must try to move not only the policymakers with whom it deals officially but also those domestic forces from which the policymakers derive their support."

In that context, Hoffmann concludes, the task of pursuing an Arab-Israeli peace "calls for remarkable skill and for the art of playing on the domestic underpinnings of states" and of the Palestinian movement. "Thus, two prenegotiations, in which unofficial personalities may play an important role, appear necessary: one between the United States and Arafat's PLO to define as much as possible in advance the assurances the PLO would give to Israel in exchange for self-determination, and one between the United States and the more moderate Israeli politicians to make sure they would accept and exploit a U.S. initiative for peace along the lines suggested here." Hoffmann argues for an active U.S. role, although the circumstances have become even more difficult as a result of developments in 1990–1991.

Ghassan Tuéni in Chapter 12 describes the U.S. role in four major developments during the Lebanese civil war to argue that Washington was not clear in its objectives and used instruments of statecraft too narrow and too legalistic to accomplish the results expected of them. "The U.S. intervention in the Lebanese crisis," he writes, "even more than in Iran, demonstrated the uselessness of power when not at the service of a consistent, feasible, and credible policy." In Lebanon, "success will require a realistic recognition of new forces and factors and of new problems and aspirations, particularly those emerging from the development of the crisis and the war. . . . War has been a universal failure. Peace should still present a valid option for all."

Crown Prince Hassan of Jordan in Chapter 13 highlights—through the eyes of a Middle Eastern friend of the United States—the contradictions that result from U.S. "difficulty in producing a policy that integrates the traditional diplomacy of global power politics with the fact that its security often depends on the ability to involve itself with understanding and sensitivity in the political dynamics of postcolonial nations in a region such as the Middle East." Similarly, he continues, "U.S. scholars have themselves recognized the difficulty U.S. citizens have had in integrating their deep historical commitment to the ideals of the U.S. Declaration of Independence with the conflict they feel between the requirements of traditional power politics and the aspirations of nations that have themselves recently emerged from colonial status." Crown Prince Hassan particularly focuses on the U.S. commitment to the right of peoples to self-determination and says, as a friend, that "the challenge facing the United States at the end of the twentieth century is to find some way to integrate these contradictory factors and to produce a clear vision of its role and purpose in the world. Nowhere have these contradictions been more apparent than in the Middle East." He also notes that these contradictory philosophical tendencies are sometimes reflected in the divisions within the policymaking community in Washington and the interplay between elements in that community and foreign nations such as Israel.

Looking to the postwar future, the Crown Prince calls for a new effort in a truly international perspective reflecting the needs and commitment of East, West, South, and North in launching a political process for rehabilitation, reconstruction, and reconciliation in the Middle East. His framework encompasses many of the concepts developed in this book.

Negotiation—normally considered the peaceful alternative to force—depends more on political leaders working to change the political environment than on the skills of negotiating teams in finding technical solutions. The following observation is as relevant to the summit talks between Soviet and U.S. leaders as to the Arab-Israeli peace process: Negotiation does not initiate change. Change is initiated and shaped in the political arena. Negotiation may define, capture, crystallize, and consolidate change already begun. But until political leaders have transformed the political environment, negotiators are unlikely to succeed. Or, if they do reach a technically sound agreement, it may not be fully implemented or have the intended consequences.[1]

As Robert Pranger points out in Chapter 2: "Efforts to encourage peacemaking must use not only the usual methods of diplomacy but also approaches that bring one culture together with another." More than conventional negotiation will be needed to move the Arab-Israeli peace process, he argues: "Not only the hurdles of dramatically divergent national interests but the barriers to agreement caused by communal and psychological interests must be surmounted."

In the concluding chapter, Harold Saunders examines the Arab-Israeli peace process in the context of global change as a step toward laying the foundations for a broader Middle East peace process in the wake of the 1991 Gulf war. He explains why experience in the Middle East and on the world stage caused U.S. participants in the Arab-Israeli peace process in the 1970s to see it as a series of negotiations embedded in a larger political process. He argues that viewing the peace process in a global perspective strengthens the argument for a broader, political approach to it. He then goes on to suggest how we might begin to think about a larger regional peace process that includes dealing with the Arab-Israeli-Palestinian conflict but goes beyond it to address the larger Middle Eastern agenda in the 1990s.

In examining the Arab-Israeli peace process, Saunders draws together two themes that flow through this book and applies them to the peace process. First, our changing world—including a changing Middle East—opens the door to a richer way of understanding and changing relationships among peoples in conflict and peoples in cooperation. He characterizes the peace process as a political process in which communities and societies in conflict can build new problem-solving relationships. Second, from his intensive involvement in the peace process during the 1970s—and from comments on an earlier version of this chapter during a 1986 tour of the Middle East—he acknowledges that many of those involved in conflict are not yet willing to commit themselves to an open-ended political process. Such a commitment requires some shared understanding about a common goal and solid working relationships within which to achieve it.

Reflecting on the last three decades of U.S. experience in the Middle East and in the larger world, Saunders offers the following thought: It is not adequate in today's world to see only states amassing military and economic power to pursue objectively defined interests in competition with other states. Relations between nations today may increasingly be a continuous political process of complex interaction among policymaking and policy-influencing communities on both sides of a relationship. As more people participate, change often takes place through that interaction on many levels at once rather than mainly through a linear series of government actions and reactions. Beyond the power and policymaking of individual states acting on each other, we need to focus on the total pattern of interaction—the overall relationship—between two nations. He contrasts the assumptions underlying this approach to a more mechanistic view of state-to-state relations.

Shifting focus to that political process of interaction incorporates two important dimensions of experience into our thinking about foreign affairs. First, we pay more attention to the larger political environment in which people reach fundamental value judgments about peace, war, negotiation, and economic change and trade. Second, when we turn to that political environment, we introduce ways of influencing those judgments and therefore the course of change by political action rather than only by contests of force. This is the art of high politics. If power is the ability to influence the course of events, power today may emerge as much from the political ability to conduct that interactive process creatively as it does from wielding military or economic power or being an unyielding negotiator. It is around more active use of political instruments that Saunders feels a reconstituted Arab-Israeli peace process must be built.[2]

Looking beyond the Arab-Israeli peace process, he suggests that experience in that process may offer insight into developing a political process large enough to encompass the wide range of issues that the 1990–1991 Gulf crisis and war put on the regional agenda. The Arab-Israeli peace process was itself born in the aftermath of war. As a political process, it addressed issues ranging from lifting an oil embargo, restoring diplomatic relations, and establishing joint commissions for economic cooperation through arranging and monitoring military disengagement, instituting confidence-building measures, and laying the foundations for a peace treaty and normalization of relations to addressing the fundamentals of the Israeli-Palestinian conflict and the longstanding state of belligerency between Israel and neighboring Arab states. Some post–Gulf war thinking has turned to the Helsinki process in Europe as a model for addressing the Middle East's complex agenda, and although that analysis will be instructive, Saunders urges that we not neglect the model already in place in the Middle East.

A shift from one way of understanding how the world works to another does not happen neatly or swiftly. The past does not give way quickly, and the shape of the future does not easily come into sharp focus. The authors in this book are standing on the bridge between two paradigms—recognizing that old words do not describe what they experience and reaching for new thoughts to describe the world that is emerging. The purpose of this book is to offer in the words of those writing about the Middle East today a context for the rethinking that is taking place.

Notes

1. These thoughts on our changing world and the conduct of international relationships today were developed initially in Harold H. Saunders, "Beyond 'Us and Them'—Building Mature International Relationships," a draft monograph prepared in 1987–1988 under a grant from the United States Institute of Peace

in collaboration with the Kettering Foundation, and in "International Relationships—It's Time to Go Beyond 'We' and 'They,' " *Negotiation Journal*, vol. 3, no. 3 (July 1987), pp. 245–274. Saunders applies these thoughts to the Middle East in "The Arab-Israeli Conflict in a Global Perspective," chap. 8 in John D. Steinbruner, ed., *Restructuring American Foreign Policy* (Washington, D.C.: Brookings Institution, 1988), written with support from the Carnegie Corporation of New York and the MacArthur Foundation. A fuller presentation written with the support of the Ford and MacArthur foundations appears as his "An Historic Challenge to Rethink How Nations Relate," in Vamik D. Volkan, Demetrios Julius, and Joseph V. Montville, eds., *The Psychodynamics of International Relationships—Vol. 1: Concepts and Theories* (Lexington, Mass.: Lexington Books, 1990), chap. 1. He also applies this approach to "The Soviet-U.S. Relationship and the Third World," in Robert Jervis and Seweryn Bialer, eds., *Soviet-American Relations After the Cold War* (Durham, N.C.: Duke University Press, 1991), chap. 6. It provides a global setting for detailed analysis of the obstacles to an Arab-Israeli peace in *The Other Walls: The Arab-Israeli Peace Process in a Global Perspective* (Princeton, N.J.: Princeton University Press, 1991 printing with new introduction, epilogue, and appendixes). In each case, these observations and the concept of relationship are stated in more or less the same—often verbatim—form as the necessary starting point for analysis of a particular question. Each publisher has agreed to this practice.

2. To capture the totality of this dynamic interaction, Saunders suggests the concept of relationship. That concept is explained and developed in Saunders, "An Historic Challenge to Rethink How Nations Relate."

PART ONE

New Perspectives

2
Foreign Policy Capacity in the Middle East

Robert J. Pranger

The capacity to design foreign policies adequate for protecting and pursuing peaceful achievements of vital interest in contemporary dynamic environments is a critical factor in a nation's effectiveness. In today's world, that capacity involves the skillful mixing of key international and domestic variables. With the rising importance of domestic communal participation in international relationships, governments must develop expertise and organization to devise policies which stand as bridges between domestic constituencies and the requirements within a regional or global system of interaction among nations. This means that the tasks of foreign policy now include much more than the traditional management of a nation's foreign relations: Successful policy also involves an ability to forge domestic consensus about ends and means in conditions that grow steadily more complex for every nation and to take advantage of the diversity of interests and actors in other countries as well as in one's own.

On the one hand, adequate foreign policy capacity today requires understanding interests as defined in domestic political give-and-take; on the other hand, these interests must be pursued with capabilities effective in relationships among nations and among communities that reach across national borders. This interaction of domestic and international factors challenges the capacity of those who make policy and demands of them a perspective which embraces not only the institutions of states but the needs of communities within and across those states' borders. In some instances, peace can be made only if the road toward peace involves both the institutions of nations and the communities in which their people live.

The idea of foreign policy capacity, though of very recent vintage conceptually, has already been explored in some depth. For example, two students of third world security have proposed a three-dimensional model for expressing this idea, composed of threat, capability, and capacity itself. Most third world states, it is argued, are relatively insecure and fall in the intermediate range of policy capacity because their feelings of a high degree of threat and their strong military capability are offset by a rigid policy capacity for making the adjustments necessary to achieve national interests without resort to armed conflict. The authors of this view see Israel and Lebanon standing as polar opposites in the Middle East, of strong and weak policy capacity respectively, with most of the other states in the region lying somewhere between in relative impotence.[1]

Once military hostilities take place, of course, the very nature of such conflict brings considerable unpredictability to the protection of vital interests in a crisis management environment.[2] Neither a state of war nor a condition of "no war, no peace" provides much ground for expecting a foreign policy adequate to defend national interests by essentially peaceful means. Were it not for international intervention and mediation in Arab-Israeli wars since 1948, the Middle East would be a good deal more unstable than it is now.

In the field of foreign relations, peace may be defined as a process in which the tools of international conflict—diplomacy, military power, and economics—are employed in such a way as to create a stable system secured against significant armed struggle among the powers that constitute the system. This definition may be applied at the regional as well as the global level. In the Middle East, as in all third world regions to some extent, the two levels interact with each other and with the domestic environments of the nations involved. Peace seems impossible without the practical use in foreign relations of instruments that may just as conveniently be used for creating instability and war.

The ideologies most important for modern nationhood move in the direction of instability rather than stability in the international order. They seek always to divide humankind into specific identities, to distinguish "us" from "them." As a result, peacemaking is always a battle against entropy—the threat of fragmentation and disaster. It is important, therefore, to view the foreign policies of regional and global powers in light of their capacities to avert such disaster so as to stabilize their policies toward one another.

This task involves skillful mixing of key international and domestic variables that impinge on the capacity of states to make foreign policies adequate for peaceful achievement of their vital interests. Because the demands placed on national interests by international and domestic environments differ in ends and means, foreign policy adequacy is more complicated than domestic policy adequacy and requires areas of expertise not normally available in any abundance to leaders whose legitimacy usually depends on domestic political authority.[3]

This chapter explores the interaction of international and domestic factors in the making of foreign policy among the key regional actors in the Arab-Israeli conflict—Egypt, Israel, Jordan, Syria, and the Palestine Liberation Organization (PLO). It gives special attention to the important power of domestic bodies politic in foreign policies that also need to fit these popular pressures into imperatives of regional and global environments, where an adaptation at considerable variance with domestic constituencies may be demanded if national interests are to be fulfilled. Foreign policy presents a cruel political paradox for decisionmakers: Sometimes the interests of the nation, reflecting the pluralistic demands of a given body politic, require compromises between these demands and the necessity for international adaptation to achieve these interests in regional and global environments.

What is evident in the Middle East today, though not confined to the Middle East or to the third world more generally, is the rising importance of domestic communal participation in foreign policy even as demands for greater regional and international interdependence grow as well. Already hampered by inadequate expertise and organization, foreign policy capacity is further weakened by escalating pressures from ethnic, religious, and economic divisions within the national societies of regional parties involved in the Arab-Israeli conflict. Cross-pressures from domestic and international sources of policy engender considerable confusion about appropriate ends and means. Under these circumstances the demands of peacemaking are both complicated and difficult to meet, the future seemingly bleak. A sophistication that even the great powers lack is required to weld competing priorities and methods.

Domestication of the International Environment in the Arab-Israeli Conflict

Two striking features of the foreign policies of the main parties in the Arab-Israeli conflict date back to the origins of the "Eastern Question game," as Carl Brown calls it, during the expansion of European imperialism into the Ottoman Empire: domestication of the international and internationalization of the domestic in the Middle East.[4] This interaction of domestic and international factors has been both objective and subjective: The reality of foreign policy in this region has involved a perceptual field where the tangible and the symbolic are so closely connected that negotiation must engage in forms of political dramaturgy to achieve results. An important contemporary example of this problem in political symbolization is the question of Palestinian representation at an international peace conference for settling the Arab-Israeli conflict.[5]

This section deals with how the international environment is seen by the regional actors as an extension of their domestic political cultures; the next section reverses the perspective so that domestic politics appear as a sublimation of international affairs. Both transferences, to adopt psychological terminology, exist in Middle East foreign policy, with extraordinary confusions of focus the result.

The Middle East is not alone in transferring domestic perspectives to foreign policy, as any student of U.S. foreign policy recognizes (nowhere more so than in U.S. Middle East policy), but in the Arab-Israeli conflict this transference has taken the character of a Manichaean struggle between cultural as well as state-centered foreign policies. Although some may see in the Arab-Israeli struggle parallels to U.S.-Soviet relations, with their strong emphasis on ideological as well as power politics, the inability of the main parties to the Arab-Israeli conflict to separate state and culture in foreign policy makes any peaceful resolution extremely difficult. The United States and the Soviet Union, for example, could successfully conclude arms control agreements even while remaining ideological adversaries, but such disaggregation of issues is virtually impossible in the Arab-Israeli conflict. Anwar el-Sadat's assassination was a reminder that not even Egypt, alone among Arab states in making peace with Israel, has successfully separated its state interests from its cultural imperatives in foreign policy.

For the Arabs, this domestication of foreign policy toward Israel inevitably takes the form of protecting the security of comprehensive Arab culture—transnational and national, secular and spiritual—from Israel's Zionist and Jewish political culture, which is seen as an extreme extension of the old Eastern Question in the Middle East. Hence Israel's most vigorous defender, the United States, becomes the imperialist power par excellence in this region, on one hand trusted for that part of its foreign policy that emphasizes international realpolitik but on the other hand suspected of transferring its domestic bias toward Zionism to its Middle East foreign policy. Small wonder then that Arab leaders see Israel as their first security threat because Israel, with its explicitly Jewish nationalism, presents not only a military but a cultural challenge. The close connection between nationalism and religion in the Middle East probably encourages this extension of domestic anxiety into international policy. Lord Palmerston's often cited aphorism that nations have no permanent friends or enemies, only permanent interests, is hardly an accurate portrayal of nations in the third world today, a number of which were created out of the wreckage produced by the European realpolitik generated by Palmerston's line of reasoning. It is precisely the permanence of national animosities that underlies the Arab-Israeli conflict, a permanence ensured by the domestication of international politics in the foreign policies of the key regional actors.

In a peace process aimed at stability and demilitarization, therefore, the persistent transference of domestic cultural anxieties, heightened by the close connection between politics and religion in the Middle East, cannot be ignored. Nor can it be simply bracketed in some novel "fractionation" wherein the more profound divisions between Israel and the Arabs can be postponed until a more practical settlement is achieved.[6] Camp David has sometimes been cited as a success story for this negotiating method, but the peace accords had a tragic denouement. The lesson drawn by other Arab leaders from Sadat's assassination in 1981 may prove instructive here: Sadat was struck down by the most militant religious zealots in Egypt as punishment for his alleged perversion of Egypt's Muslim political culture, a perversion most evident, said his assailants, in the separate peace with Israel. Others who would risk fractionating practical political steps from the main preoccupations of their domestic bodies politic, especially in the religious sphere, tempt a fate similar to Sadat's.

Domestic political culture in the Middle East may include secular as well as spiritual anxieties, also connected to the state of Israel. King Hussein's reluctance to go the Sadat route is no doubt connected mainly with the presence of a Palestinian majority in Jordan, although religious fundamentalism has also been on the increase in his kingdom. Israel's cultural exclusivity applies not only to non-Jews but to Arabs who once lived in the territory now held by the state of Israel or its defense forces in the West Bank and Gaza. A secular exclusiveness toward the Palestinian Arabs, here more akin to South African apartheid than to religious zealotry, is also seen by the Arab world, especially the Palestinians, as central to Israel's foreign policy, with a transference of cultural anxieties of a more secular kind by the Arabs to their own foreign policies. This transference is strengthened by two centuries of unhappy Arab experience at the hands of Britain and the United States. Again, a peace settlement process must somehow account for secular as well as spiritual cultural transference to foreign policy in the Middle East, with not much likelihood that these transfers can be eliminated from the process.

The strong tendencies toward domestication of foreign policy in the Middle East mean that efforts to encourage peacemaking must use not only the usual methods of diplomacy but also approaches that bring one culture together with another. Increasingly in the Middle East, as well as elsewhere in the third world where "protracted social conflict" based on ethnic, religious, and other social and economic divisions persists, efforts to settle longstanding conflicts involving cultural as well as pragmatic issues require negotiations that somehow include bodies politic as well as foreign policy elites (the importance of these bodies politic in the Middle East is discussed later in this chapter).[7] Successful negotiations may seek more than one track: Although participants must never neglect the opportunities provided by official state-to-state relations or ignore the limitations of these techniques, they must also make an effort to get *communities* involved through negotiating methods quite different from those of formal diplomacy.[8] These creative approaches constitute, at one level, simply a recognition of the domestication of the international environment that is more and more prevalent in the third world and beyond and surely is paramount in the Arab-Israeli conflict.

Internationalization of Domestic Political Cultures in the Arab-Israeli Conflict

No region has been more penetrated by outside powers, argues Carl Brown, than the Middle East. Since the effective collapse of the Ottoman Empire against Western intrusion in the Treaty of Carlowicz of 1699, the Middle East has been opened for the extraordinary internationalization seen today. As part of this opening, Israel was created out of the Zionist movement born in an environment of European, not Middle Eastern, anti-Semitism during the nineteenth and twentieth centuries. Indeed, the Arab world is unanimous in its view that Israel represents the epitome of Western imperialism in the Middle East despite Israel's own perception of its victimization at the hands of the West. This dramatic difference in perception of what Israel is, in an ontological sense, makes the Arab-Israeli conflict the perplexing international problem that it is today, unequaled by any other regional conflict for its explosive impact on global affairs.

The international community cannot agree, however, on what the Arab-Israeli conflict, a struggle among national societies, represents in international terms. Even among the Western powers there is a difference of perspective on this matter; the former European imperial powers, including the Soviet Union, have a decided ambivalence about Israel, whereas the United States has fully embraced the Israeli perception of international victimization.[9]

Within the framework of a peace settlement in the Middle East, the internationalization of domestic policy finds various expressions, from the extreme sensitivity of the Arab world about how foreign policy in this area affects the domestic legitimacy and authority of national leaders to the clash of views on the composition and role of an international peace conference. To illustrate the reverse role of international affairs in the domestic politics of the Middle East—the impact of foreign policy on domestic politics—it is useful to look first at the international environment's relationship to the legitimacy of national leaders and then turn to problems associated with an international peace conference that relate to the struggle among concepts of Israel's existence involving not only Arabs and Israelis but outside powers as well.

Brown's view on international penetration of the Middle East can be documented in the extreme centrality and sensitivity of foreign policy in the realm of domestic authority in Middle Eastern states. To Israeli leaders, for example, negotiations with the PLO become a litmus test of who is and who is not loyal to the fundamental precepts of Israel's existence. Legitimacy and authority in Israel hinge on this central international issue, as well as on certain domestic criteria, and the PLO problem has become closely connected with the domestic fabric of the Jewish state. Indeed, the PLO, as it has gained widespread international recognition, has become increasingly both "the enemy within" and "the stranger at the gates" for Israelis, thus reflecting the international origins in the 1947 United Nations partition of Israel.

On the Arab side, resistance to the 1947 partition has become central to the domestic authority of leadership in all countries except Egypt. And Sadat, the author of Egyptian deviation from this international solidarity domesticated in Arab opinion, was gunned down by his fellow countrymen in an act of domestic defiance against his secularist regime.

For the PLO, resistance to the 1947 partition, sponsored by all the international great powers, has been transferred into the very covenant of Palestinian national existence in the call for one unified, secular Palestinian state encompassing all of present-day Israel as well as the occupied territories. Within the Palestinian movement this part of the national covenant remains the key to splits between "moderates" and "radicals" within the PLO. Together with fear of terrorism, it also forms the central focus of Israel's total rejection of the PLO as a negotiating partner. In sum, the great dividing line between Arabs and Israelis in the domestic politics of the Middle East remains a 1947 *international* act of partition upon which Israel raised its flag of independence and against which the Arabs moved in the 1948–1949 war.

On both sides of the Arab-Israeli conflict are strong, subjective perceptions of international victimization that might well belong more appropriately in the realm of psychiatry than of public policy if they did not have such important policy consequences. In a sense both Israel and its Arab adversaries share a common history of origins and struggle with modern Europe—Arab nationalism a creation of Western penetration of the Middle East and Zionism a response to anti-Semitic trends in European nationalism in the nineteenth and twentieth centuries. This

common fate, however, divides rather than unifies, because for the Arabs
Israel is symptomatic of their victimization by the West while for Israelis
the Arab world is now seen as an extension of European persecution
of the Jews. In other words, the internalization of domestic opinion in
the Middle East brings with it a special kind of Manichaeism, that of
executioners and victims.[10]

The perception of the adversary as executioner raises fears in
domestic political culture of possible national extinction at the enemy's
hand, most dramatically evident in Israel's attitude toward the Arabs,
until Sadat's dramatic trip to Jerusalem, but also present in Palestinian
views of Israel. Created by the international legacy of victimization in
the Middle East, this psychology of perceiving a threatened loss of
national identity among Israelis and Palestinians must be accounted for
in peace negotiations.

I noted earlier that because of the strong tendencies toward domestication of foreign policy in the Middle East, peace negotiations may
well have to pursue more than one track to bring communities into the
peace process as participants. Given the peculiar impact of international
power on the domestic politics of the Middle East, another track for
negotiation will have to account for victims, with full understanding
that they see their negotiating partners not as morally equal to themselves
but as potential executioners. This explains why, in Middle East peace
negotiations, there is a pervasive sense that the game being played is
zero-sum, with one side seeking, through these negotiations, to eliminate
the other. This also accounts for the special symbolism the various
parties attach to who should participate in the negotiations and under
what terms.

A negotiating track that takes account of victimization and fear of
the other as executioner would necessitate a more psychological approach
than standard diplomacy requires. In some ways negotiations that account
for bodies politic or communities must also allow for the strong perception
each party has that the other side may be bent on holocaust and evil.
This is particularly true when the heart of the Arab-Israeli problem is
reached, the issue of the Palestinians or, as the PLO often puts it, "the
Palestine question."

The idea of a "Palestine question" suggests something problematic
or perhaps enigmatic in the elusive relationship between Israel and the
Palestinians. Israel's refusal to recognize the legitimacy of the question
from a Palestinian perspective is, of course, prima facie evidence for
Palestinians that Israel stands as executioner of this emergent nation.
Yet there is also on the Palestinian side a certain lack of clarity about
whether this victimization by Israel is sufficient to define Palestinianism
or whether the definition carries with it more positive identities that

can be separated from the executioner-victim *danse macabre* with Israel. If the latter definition is possible, then coexistence with Israel is also possible. On the subject of victimization versus coexistence, however, Palestinian perspectives are perhaps more ambiguous than Israel's outright rejection of the idea of a separate nation of Palestine. No doubt Israel's grand refusal continues to perpetuate the perception of victimization on the Palestinian side, whatever other nuances are present in the Palestinian movement, and the psychology of executioners and victims must somehow be incorporated in any peace settlement that takes Palestinian claims to nationhood into account.

Also present in the Middle East peace process, of course, is the pervasive sense of Israel's victimization, first at the hands of Europe in the holocaust and now repeated in Arab threats to Israel's national independence. Palestinian ambiguity about national status has been both cause and effect of Israel's own sense of foreboding about extinction. U.S. policy has concentrated on the Israeli psychology of victimization more than on the Palestinian preoccupation with the same subject. The psychology of both sides, each reinforcing the other, underlies and constantly subverts normal diplomatic efforts to reach a just and lasting settlement.

To summarize the argument so far, the peace process in the Middle East must not only account for the usual difficulties associated with tortuous negotiation but also provide for special methods to deal with the domestication of international politics and the internationalization of domestic politics in the Middle East—ways of coping with the intrusion of bodies politic or communities, along with their psychologies of victimization at the hands of outside powers, in the settlement process. Not only the hurdles of dramatically divergent national interests but the barriers to agreement caused by communal and psychological interests must be surmounted, and probably in some simultaneous rather than fractionated way.

Harold Saunders uses the analogy of racquetball to describe the complexities of Middle East negotiation, but a railroad metaphor is also useful: The attempt to move a single train on three single, nonparallel tracks simultaneously gives some idea of the complications of accounting for normal diplomacy as well as communal and psychological dimensions of the peace process. Fortunately, negotiations of this sort are political, not physical, problems, but nonetheless the metaphor indicates a complex set of operations that take into account both the domestication of foreign policy and the internationalization of domestic policy in the Arab-Israeli conflict. It is important to add, however, that the same track metaphor can be applied to a number of other protracted social conflicts in the third world from which a great deal can be learned and applied to the

Middle East. Despite its high drama, the Arab-Israeli conflict is not unique.

It should come as no surprise, therefore, that discussions about international conferences for a Middle East peace settlement might become ensnarled in controversies about participants and agendas. Not only do such conferences highlight the powerful relationships between foreign and domestic policy in the Middle East, but they raise issues on three levels of significance—national, communal, and psychological—in ways that may be difficult to deal with as the number of participants expands. This has led some analysts to advocate more intimate, communally oriented negotiations between Israelis and Palestinians.[11] Even before the Iraq-Kuwait crisis of 1990–1991, there was little doubt that either the idea of an international conference would have to be developed in more innovative ways than had so far been suggested if the conference approach was to be anything more than an aggravation of the problem or separate tracks would have to be provided—for example, a full international diplomatic conference with "delegations," supplemented by more informal dialogue among community leaders and perhaps some special group discussions of basic psychological issues. The results from these three tracks might be put together in a final agreement that might also be multifaceted or in a diplomatic document with certain protocols or understandings based on diverse tracks, especially in sections where implementation is required. The Gulf crisis of 1990–1991 further complicated the problem when Iraq proposed adding that crisis to the agenda of a conference.

The domestic and psychological dimensions of foreign relations in the Middle East, especially in the Arab-Israeli conflict but not in this area only (Lebanon and the Iran-Iraq and Iraq-Kuwait conflicts come to mind as also requiring more negotiating sophistication than has so far been demonstrated), highlight the importance of taking into account the cultural bases of foreign policy and the ways the body politic of any nation influences international affairs. They also call attention to the need for new methods in foreign relations that both account for the influence of national cultures and build forms of negotiation that will include these communities as well as formal diplomatic elites. More often than not these methods will be innovative ones and not simply appendages of standard diplomatic practices. Indeed, the capacity of any nation's foreign policy to operate in complicated international and regional environments will be determined not only by the motivation and skill of its leaders but by the strengths and limitations of the domestic political culture these leaders rule and serve.

Middle East Leadership
and the National Body Politic

Foreign policy capacity may be defined as dynamic policy adaptation by nation-states, an adaptation that involves the domestic systems of these countries as well as external factors. The focus here is on the domestic management of foreign policy in the Middle East by major regional actors, with special emphasis on the Arab-Israeli conflict, using a cybernetics "steering model" adapted from a recent analysis of the "anomalous successes" of Japan, Taiwan, and South Korea in their foreign relations by Davis B. Bobrow and Steve Chan.[12] The steering model involves a wide range of domestic actors and factors represented in the control, implementation, and information units of national foreign policy, not just public sector agencies and elites.[13] In other words, this approach to capacity is from the standpoint of the national body politic, extending from its most formal institutional expressions in organized government to its most informal noninstitutionalized groups in the realm of citizen participation.[14] Successful steering involves an ability (1) to forge domestic consensus about ends and means in conditions that grow steadily more complex for every nation and (2) to take advantage of the diversity of interests and actors in other countries as well as in one's own.

Bobrow and Chan argue that the likelihood of greater policy capacity for individual states, as well as more adaptation to changing international circumstances in the realm of the multiple "games of interdependence,"[15] will be increased when the following nine dimensions of the steering model are present.[16]

1. sensitivity to feedback from domestic and external environments that produces a wariness about unrealistic goals and about treating the world as static
2. creation of generalized goals and objectives that avoid extreme specificity
3. construction of national consensus about ends and means
4. development of "whole system," or holistic, approaches to policy formation and avoidance of artificial compartmentalization
5. maintenance of solidarity among policy implementers
6. choice of goals and implementation of means based on realistic and wide-ranging information about national capabilities and external constraints
7. advance establishment of goals and implementation with allowance for indeterminacy[17]

8. perspectives of a diverse external environment with nonunitary actors engaged in multiple games
9. belief in the efficacy of improved policy capacity for enhanced probabilities of success in foreign relations and for influence on private goals of participants as well

It is a crucial feature of cybernetic models that they pay a great deal of attention to entropy in foreign policy: problems of policy drift and possible "organized anarchy." The nine dimensions of this model are designed to provide remedies for entropy, that is, to organize foreign policy better for operation in very complicated global and regional environments. Although all nine of the criteria are important, special attention is focused here on the significance of the third dimension for facilitating the other eight: the necessity to have national consensus about ends and means so that the flexibility and adaptability implicit in the eight other dimensions are possible in the first place.

As noted earlier, however, the foreign policies of the various regional parties to the Arab-Israeli conflict may have *too much* consensus as far as the other side is concerned, thereby inhibiting the ability of any national leadership to participate creatively in the peace process. Under these circumstances the peace process must reach into the areas of communal consensus and psychological fear as well in order actually to loosen the grip of national solidarity on leadership. More creativity is required within the national political culture, most importantly at grass-roots levels among communities in constant interaction with each other. The bodies politic of the Middle East, often said to be in the grip of authoritarian leaders or, in Israel's case, to be set along the fluid lines of the U.S. electorate, may actually have too much solidarity and too much monolithic control over foreign policy in the area of Arab-Israeli relations. From the standpoint of progress toward peace in the Middle East, the leaders may well be more flexible than their constituencies, so that the constituencies themselves must become part of the negotiating process to reach a definitive settlement.[18] Precisely the opposite has more often than not been the U.S. approach, with either highly provisional results (the Henry Kissinger shuttles were, after all, only "disengagements") or speciously definitive outcomes (Camp David put the Palestinian problem to one side in such a way that it could not be retrieved for further negotiation under this agreement).[19]

The bringing of communities into the peace process has already been noted here. Meron Benvenisti is a leading advocate of this approach, and it is worth pausing for a moment to review his rationale, because his reasoning highlights the important limiting conditions between foreign policy leadership and the everyday existence of communities that must live together in the body politic the leadership claims to represent.[20]

Benvenisti contends that the very idea of a "peace process" for settling the Arab-Israeli conflict starts with a false premise about where the center of the problem lies. After some forty years of national existence and twenty years of occupation of the West Bank and Gaza, Israel has become an established entity coexisting with a Palestinian population that has not yet found its appropriate physical expression as a national entity. In other words, it is the fate of Arabs and Jews in the land of Palestine to coexist with each other as communities living side by side. Benvenisti points out that in some cases this physical proximity is in the same neighborhood, such as his own, where there also exists, unfortunately, great cultural and psychological distance even among persons who have been next-door neighbors for years.[21]

What is wrong with all approaches to the Middle East peace process so far, Benvenisti contends, is that they begin and end in a political process dominated by national governments and their orthodox conceptions of power and the powerful, rather than originate in communities that have lived together in war and must, for their survival, now learn to coexist in peace in their own political time and space. This chapter goes beyond Benvenisti's analysis to examine the importance of differing perspectives of political time and political space for peace in the Arab-Israeli struggle, because unless it is clear where the *political* problem of peace in the Middle East lies, creative foreign policy approaches to peace are impossible.[22]

Since 1967 the main continual form of war in the Middle East has been between Israel and the Palestinians under occupation in the West Bank and Gaza along with their national brethren in the so-called Palestinian diaspora. In a sense, this situation was a reversion to pre-1948 conditions when Arabs and Jews lived together, as "Palestinians," in a British mandate in a constant state of tension and war; the 1948–1967 period was one of fictional separation of Israelis and Arabs, now called Palestinians, even though many Arabs were incorporated in the new state of Israel. The 1967 war, however, shifted the struggle between the Arabs and Israel back to an internal struggle in the land of Palestine between Palestinian Arabs and, one might say, Palestinian Israelis, both claiming rights to the same land. The 1973 war, which provided the basis for Egypt's separate peace with Israel, brought the Arab-Israeli war even more into the realm of local communities within Israel and in the West Bank and Gaza, especially after the 1977 Likud electoral victories when the occupied territories were claimed by Israeli leadership as Eretz Yisrael, no longer the "land of Palestine" but the "land of Israel."

Under shifting circumstances since 1967, the political space and time of the Arab-Israeli conflict have become increasingly localized between communities largely alien to each other for many decades, even before Israel's establishment as an independent nation. This accords with Benvenisti's argument that future peace efforts must deal not only—or even primarily—with the conflicts of interest among nation-states—but with communities living side by side in a perpetual state of alienation from each other. "Peace plans" formulated in foreign ministries and supported by the resources of global as well as regional powers do not get to the heart of the matter: Arab-Israeli conflict today is local, and solutions must build on the capacities and incapacities of communal leadership.[23]

If the political space of communal leadership is local, in contrast to the regional and international levels on which peace plans for the Middle East usually operate, then the political time of communal conflict in the Arab-Israeli conflict extends back well before 1948. This is why rejection of Israel is so powerful a force in a Palestinian community that has been at war against Jewish settlement of Palestine since almost the turn of the century, with national consciousness of both Jews and Arabs escalating in the establishment by the British mandate of Palestine, the former Ottoman possession, after World War I. In a very profound sense the struggle between these two communities in the interwar period was over who was entitled to be authentically Palestinian. The space of this struggle may be local, but its time seems endless, thereby creating a paradox: What in principle should be settled at the local level, without the complications of international politics, is the most internationalized of regional conflicts in the third world.

One can see in the contemporary Israeli-Palestinian struggle, therefore, the interplay of domestic and international dimensions played out on a historical canvas broader than the rivalries between Israel, established in 1948, and specific Arab states. Approaches to Middle East peace settlement, then, must combine the political process of interstate rivalry with the politics of intercommunal struggle; Benvenisti argues, indeed, that the latter politics is the truly authentic perspective for Middle East peace. Although Benvenisti's position may seem too dichotomous to some, those seeking new directions in foreign policy in the Middle East will have to concentrate more on the importance of bodies politic— communities of everyday politics—in the foreign policy of Middle East states, forms of domestic politics that do not necessarily enhance the policy capacity of nations poorly endowed with such capacity in the first place. As noted earlier, third world foreign policies can be strengthened only to the extent that they take into account and accommodate communal conflict and consensus in these policies, a tall order indeed.

The concept of a monolithic "national interest" in today's world seems fictitious—albeit a convenient fiction—for many nations.[24]

National Power Versus Communal Power in the Middle East

The tragic downing of an Iranian Airlines airbus by the U.S. Navy cruiser *Vincennes* on July 3, 1988, with the loss of some 300 lives on board the aircraft, is one of the most dramatic examples of the decreasing utility of traditional national power, exemplified by military force, in the Middle East. With reference to this tragedy, Admiral William J. Crowe, chairman of the Joint Chiefs of Staff, described the Gulf as a "lake" so congested with military and civilian traffic that accidents are just waiting to happen.[25] The U.S. naval combatants assigned to the Gulf to safeguard civilian tankers were designed for fighting not in lakes but in the great oceans and seas of the world. Yet it is precisely the human and cultural congestion of the Gulf region, dating back many centuries before the founding of the United States, that makes the accidental killing of so many innocent people an important lesson for the future usefulness of military force in the Middle East.

Many of the passengers on board the Iranian Airlines plane were Iranians either visiting relatives in Dubai or returning to Dubai from vacations in Iran. The story of the Gulf, including the controversy over whether it should be called "Persian" or "Arab," is the story of inter-mingled communities—Arab, Persian, Indian, and others—that until this century did not know the meaning of independent nationhood. In fact, the main threat of fundamentalist Iran to its Arab neighbors has to do with the large number of ethnic Iranians and religious Shiites living among ethnic Arabs and religious Sunnis. The key to peace between Iran and Iraq probably has more to do with peace settlements among these communities than between nations, where military force, so prominently displayed in the Iran-Iraq war, will not be decisive.

In the preceding section, the same point about the importance of communal involvement was argued in the Arab-Israeli struggle, especially on the question of the future of Palestinian claims to national self-determination. Political space in the Middle East is more intimate than nation-states, most of them recently built on ancient ethnic and religious foundations. All three main areas of warfare in the Middle East today—Arab-Israeli, the Gulf, and Lebanon—provide the same lessons in the limits of national coercive action, chiefly in the form of military power, in conflicts among local communities. In each case local and indigenous pathologies resist outside intervention, either from a nation-state or from foreign powers, much as certain strains of disease become resistant to medication designed to curb them.

The highly interventionist foreign policy of the United States, which has been twice as often involved in crisis intervention during the postwar period as any other nation, reveals that policymakers have had special difficulty understanding the immunity of local, communal conflict to external treatment.[26] Nowhere has this lack of understanding in the U.S. approach to the world prevailed more than in the use of military force as a strong medicine for achieving "stability" in regions of conflict, including the Arab-Israeli conflict. Between 1967 and 1973, for example, U.S. Middle East policy concentrated on the importance of arming Israel so that the Arabs "would come to their senses" and make peace; this prescription appealed to practitioners of realpolitik in Washington and also played into the hands of Israel's leadership, which saw this as a way of maintaining the status quo in the West Bank and Gaza. Since 1973 U.S. policy has vacillated between disillusionment with Israel as a regional military superpower, as in the 1982 Lebanon invasion, and continued adherence to the idea of a strategic special relationship that would ensure Israel's primacy pending the day Arab nations and the Palestinians would come to the peace table. That Sadat succumbed to the latter view, to become strategically dependent on the United States himself, only aided the Washington delusion that traditional national means of diplomacy and force—carrots and sticks—would finally achieve that supreme objective of U.S. Middle East policy, peace.

Peace in the fundamental communal conflicts of the Middle East— Arab-Israeli, Iran-Iraq, and Lebanon—has not been achieved with much success through national efforts at mediation and the use of force. Quite the contrary, these struggles have most often been exacerbated by outside intervention or the efforts of central governments to stabilize themselves through military action. Every such intervention creates new forms of instability, and each new departure in the use of armed force gives rise to a counteroffensive from insurgents operating in the many guises of national liberation and terrorist movements. The Arab-Israeli conflict has explored an entire range of armed struggle dating back to the British mandate period, a most depressing and largely unwritten history to be sure. The space of such conflict extends from the intimacy of neighbors living together and yet psychologically far apart to the highest levels of international debate in Washington, Moscow, and the United Nations. But the Arab-Israeli conflict begins with neighbors who have never seen each other as fully authenticated human beings, no matter how intimate the spatial setting, and this must finally be where the struggle will be settled peacefully, if at all. In a very real sense, this is a struggle between two Palestinian families claiming exclusive rights to the same property:

The problem is one of getting them to share these claims in mutual recognition of the other's right to be an equal partner.[27]

As noted earlier, however, the problem of peace in the Middle East has to do with local and indigenous pathologies, of which the Arab-Israeli struggle is the most prominent in the region but in important respects like the Iran-Iraq and Lebanon conflicts. What I have described as "spasm politics" in Lebanon can also be seen in the remorseless struggle between Israelis and Palestinians:[28]

> Everyday life has assumed grotesque proportions, while major political personalities shrink in importance. What leads Lebanon after ten years of violence are not great political leaders but a myriad of events indeterminate in duration and outcome . . . [defying] solution by the governments and officials ostensibly responsible for them, and yet those caught up in everyday life are equally powerless. . . . Lebanon changes constantly but has no direction. Events have taken over and have become the leaders of Lebanese political life, but they seem to have no logic of their own. Lebanon's politics have reached a surrealistic phase, a randomness like the spasm anticipated in the aftermath of nuclear war, a political pathology in the most authentic sense, where established political institutions and practices occasionally and spasmodically appear as important, but where everyone—officials and citizens alike—drown in the powerful flood waters of chaos. . . . A spasm politics . . . has little heart for its regeneration; plans yes, will no. Survivorship becomes a cardinal virtue for officials and ordinary citizens alike, yet few can define why survival has much importance.

Communal solutions to communal struggles, while superficially attractive as alternatives to peace settlements based on national diplomacy, must contend with the intractability of conflict that creates pathological conditions in which sheer equilibrium, to say nothing of peace, seems almost impossible to achieve. This is why it is likely in the Arab-Israeli case that the realities of community strife requiring communal leadership in peace efforts also demand enlightened national and international policy that will both support and supplement local solutions. Again, the criticism of Benvenisti's approach as too dichotomous—*either* power politics *or* participation by communities—has a certain merit, if not carried to the extreme of casting doubt on the importance of everyday life experience in the continuation of the Arab-Israeli conflict. As Benvenisti notes, every Israeli and Palestinian, no matter how well intentioned about peace between the two communities, lives also in an environment where each community is under constant threat from the other and where, as in the Lebanon civil war, survivorship becomes a cardinal virtue even on the part of those who cannot identify why survival should be so important. Survival, a psychological as well as a physical imperative, may well become the primary motivating force for peace in the Middle East, a quest for spiritual renewal through maintenance of communal authenticity.

To move toward peace in the Arab-Israeli struggle, local communities must shift from crisis management mentalities to longer-term solutions. In this change of perspective the international community can be of important assistance in at least three ways.

First, by changing their policies from crisis orientation to long-range objectives in concert with one another, major outside powers can encourage similar thinking in the Middle East. This is where the influence of the United States and the Soviet Union on a peace settlement between Israelis and Palestinian Arabs will have its greatest impact, as the superpowers explore with each other the positive and negative aspects of continuing their present course of cooperation in the Middle East. What pays the greatest dividends for U.S. national interest, war or peace in the Middle East?[29] Despite often repeated observations that the Soviet Union's interests benefit more from war than peace in the Middle East, is this, in fact, the case? Even if that assessment of Soviet interests was true in the past, does it hold good for the current leadership of Mikhail Gorbachev?[30]

Second, the policies of major international actors may be used in such a way as to enhance the foreign policy capacities of both nation-states and communities in the Middle East through everything from moral support to development assistance. The nine criteria for strong foreign policy capacity itemized earlier in this chapter apply equally to nations and to communal movements struggling with each other, to the extent that the latter, as in the Arab-Israeli conflict, have international status. For example, the policy capacity of the PLO, widely recognized today as an international actor with diplomatic legitimacy, might still require some strengthening of its ability to achieve enough consensus in its own ranks to operate as an effective and reliable peace partner with Israel. At the same time, Israel's foreign policy may require stronger international guarantees from the Soviet Union as well as the United States in order for Israel to take risks in diversifying its options on the Palestinians.

Third and finally, the international community can provide valuable private support for improvement of foreign policy capacity in the Middle East among the various states and communities involved with the Arab-Israeli conflict. Because peace may well begin and end with private communities at war with each other inside Israel and in the West Bank and Gaza, it makes a good deal of sense for private outside parties to engage themselves in both mediation and consultation with these communities. A book such as this one, dedicated to exploring new directions in foreign relations, can make a genuine contribution to this badly needed private support for a peace process between communities that must ultimately find their own singular paths to survival.[31]

Notes

1. Edward E. Azar and Chung-in Moon, "Legitimacy, Integration, and Policy Capacity: The 'Software' Side of Third World National Security," in Edward E. Azar and Chung-in Moon, *National Security in the Third World* (College Park, Md.: Center for International Development and Conflict Management, 1988), chap. 4.

2. This is most evident in careful analysis of the limitations of crisis management as an instrument in controlling the escalation of violence. See Richard Ned Lebow, *Between Peace and War: The Nature of International Crisis* (Baltimore, Md.: Johns Hopkins University Press, 1981), chap. 8.

3. See Robert J. Pranger, "The President and the National Security Process," in Kenneth T. Thompson, ed., *The Virginia Papers on the Presidency*, vol. 5, White Burkett Miller Center Forums, 1981, part 1, (Lanham, Md.: University Press of America, 1981), pp. 1–21.

4. L. Carl Brown, *International Politics and the Middle East: Old Rules, Dangerous Games* (Princeton, N.J.: Princeton University Press, 1984), pp. 16–18.

5. On the concept of political symbolization, see Robert J. Pranger, *Action, Symbolism, and Order: The Existential Dimensions of Modern Citizenship* (Nashville, Tenn.: Vanderbilt University Press, 1968), chap. 5.

6. The negotiating principle of "fractionation" is developed in Roger Fisher and William L. Ury, *Getting to Yes: Negotiating Without Giving In* (London: Hutchinson, 1982).

7. The idea of "protracted social conflict" is developed in Edward E. Azar, "Protracted International Conflicts: Ten Propositions," in Edward E. Azar and John W. Burton, eds., *International Conflict Resolution: Theory and Practice* (Boulder, Colo.: Lynne Rienner Publishers, 1986), chap. 2.

8. See Meron Benvenisti, *1986 Report: Demographic, Economic, Legal, Social, and Political Developments in the West Bank* (Jerusalem: West Bank Data Project/Jerusalem Post, 1986), chap. 6; and Benvenisti, *Conflicts and Contradictions* (New York: Villard Books, 1986), chap. 5. The importance of enlisting the support of bodies politic or communities in the Middle East peace process is given very strong emphasis in the recent work of Harold H. Saunders. See his *The Other Walls: The Politics of the Arab-Israeli Peace Process* (Washington, D.C.: American Enterprise Institute, 1985), chap. 9; "Reconstituting the Arab-Israeli Peace Process," in William B. Quandt, ed., *The Middle East: Ten Years After Camp David* (Washington, D.C.: Brookings Institution, 1988), part 4, pp. 413–441; and "The Arab-Israeli Conflict in a Global Perspective," in John D. Steinbruner, ed., *Restructuring American Foreign Policy* (Washington, D.C.: Brookings Institution, 1988), chap. 8.

9. Precisely the view of President Harry S. Truman, quoted in Robert J. Pranger, "American Foreign Policy in the Middle East," in Peter J. Chelkowski and Robert J. Pranger, eds., *Ideology and Power in the Middle East: Studies in Honor of George Lenczowski* (Durham, N.C.: Duke University Press, 1988), p. 441.

10. On perceived victimization in protracted social conflicts, see Azar, "Protracted International Conflicts," p. 30.

11. See Benvenisti, *1986 Report,* pp. 92–95. Also note Saunders, "The Arab-Israeli Conflict in a Global Perspective," pp. 244–245.

12. Davis B. Bobrow and Steve Chan, "Understanding Anomalous Success: Japan, Taiwan, and South Korea," in Charles F. Hermann et al., eds., *New Directions in the Study of Foreign Policy* (Boston: Allen & Unwin, 1987), chap. 7.

13. Note the argument of Roger Hilsman on foreign-policy making in the United States in his *The Politics of Policy Making in Defense and Foreign Affairs: Conceptual Models and Bureaucratic Politics* (Englewood Cliffs, N.J.: Prentice-Hall, 1987), pp. 58–81.

14. See the treatment of politics as "a wide range of relationships, some hierarchical and others participatory, whereby humans organize themselves in common undertakings to meet and to resolve their differences with a minimization of violence," in Robert J. Pranger, *The Eclipse of Citizenship: Power and Participation in Contemporary Politics* (New York: Holt, Rinehart and Winston, 1968), p. 41 and chaps. 3–5.

15. See Stanley Hoffmann, *Primacy or World Order: American Foreign Policy Since the Cold War* (New York: McGraw-Hill, 1978), pp. 122–132.

16. Bobrow and Chan, "Understanding Anomalous Success," pp. 121–122.

17. On the difficulty of establishing goals and implementing them in an indeterminate international setting, see Robert J. Pranger, *Defense Implications of International Indeterminacy* (Washington, D.C.: American Enterprise Institute, 1972).

18. On the general tendency of international foreign policy elites to be highly sensitive to interactions among themselves, even more so in the developing than in the developed world, see Michael Brecher, *Decisions in Israel's Foreign Policy* (New Haven, Conn.: Yale University Press, 1975), chap. 9.

19. See William B. Quandt's interesting question, "Camp David: Model or Obstacle?" in his *Camp David: Peacemaking and Politics* (Washington, D.C.: Brookings Institution, 1986), pp. 329ff.

20. "PLO political maneuvering and Israeli security-oriented perceptions overshadow the slow but steady accumulations of internal Palestinian communal power." Benvenisti, *Conflicts and Contradictions,* pp. 186–187.

21. Ibid., chap. 4.

22. On "political space" and "political time," see Sheldon S. Wolin, *Politics and Vision* (Boston: Little, Brown, 1960), chap. 1; and Pranger, *Action, Symbolism, and Order,* pp. 35–53. Note Saunders's emphasis on the Middle East peace process as a political process in *The Other Walls,* chap. 9.

23. Benvenisti, *1986 Report,* pp. 92–95. Edward Azar agrees: "It follows that protracted social conflicts in multi-ethnic societies are not ameliorated

peacefully by centralized structures. For conflicts to be enduringly resolved, appropriate decentralized structures are needed. These structures are designed to serve the psychological, economic and relational needs of groups and individuals within nation-states." "Protracted International Conflicts," pp. 33–34.

24. Azar, "Protracted International Conflicts," pp. 31–32.

25. *New York Times*, July 4, 1988.

26. Michael Brecher and Jonathan Wilkenfeld, "Crisis in World Politics," *World Politics*, vol. 34 (April 1982), pp. 380–417.

27. See, for example, the unusual article by the violinist Yehudi Menuhin, "Mideast Answer: Federation," *Washington Post* (Outlook), July 3, 1988.

28. Robert J. Pranger, "Lebanon and Its Political Change Events: The Pathology of Spasm Politics and the Challenge of Reconciliation," in Edward E. Azar et al., *The Emergence of a New Lebanon: Fantasy or Reality?* (New York: Praeger, 1984), pp. 56–57.

29. On the centrality of a peace policy for reconciling U.S. interests in Israel's security and friendship in the Arab world, see Pranger, "American Foreign Policy in the Middle East," pp. 441–445, 450–454. See also Saunders, *The Other Walls*, pp. 109–114; "The Arab-Israeli Conflict," pp. 225–243.

30. A number of signs indicate that a reassessment of Soviet interests in the Middle East has been under way since President Gorbachev became leader of the Soviet Union in March 1985.

31. An example of such private support for the peace process in the Middle East is found in the work on Lebanon of the University of Maryland Center for International Development and Conflict Management. See Edward E. Azar, "The Lebanon Case," in Azar and Burton, *International Conflict Resolution*, chap. 9. Two seminars/workshops with Lebanese participants in 1984 explored issues of "intercommunal confidence."

3
Peace Process
and Intercommunal Strife

Meron Benvenisti

It is a safe assignment to serve as an analyst dealing with the Middle East. One's gloomy forecasts are almost invariably confirmed and even perceived as quite cheerful—everyone expects even worse news.

It is also a permanent job, as nothing seems to change, and no solution is in sight. Issues raised twenty or even forty years ago seem valid forever. Thus, one does not have to alter one's messages because they seem perennially relevant; nor should one suggest new remedies. The problem, once defined, remains unaltered, and the paradigm durable. After all, we are no closer to resolving the conundrum. So, why bother to redefine it?

One reason for the conservative approach to Middle Eastern problems, besides intellectual laziness, is the blinding blaze of the Israeli-Arab conflict. This perpetual conflagration dominates the horizon and eclipses all other quarrels which tear the vast region apart. The world is transfixed by the century-old tragedy of Jew and Arab fighting for the possession of the Holy Land. So profound is this tragedy that it dominates the Middle East scene and subsumes all its malaise.

Nobody can remain indifferent to the Israeli-Arab conflict. The drama of Israel, rising from the ashes; the two thousand years of Jewish-Gentile encounter; the plight of the Palestinians who have to pay for the wickedness of others; the image of the quintessential victim turned oppressor; the biblical association—all evoke powerful emotions, which turn this strife into an ideological, spiritual shibboleth, not an international conflict.

So powerful is the hypnotizing effect of the Israeli-Arab conflict that one pays little attention to fundamental changes that have transformed the situation in the Middle East since it first appeared on the international agenda. The almost axiomatic conviction that the Israeli-Arab conflict is the core trouble of the region remains an ideological precept, but it has long been overtaken by events; the perception that the Fertile Crescent is still in the era of wars that change geopolitical facts is the premise prompting diplomats and politicians to engage in a "peace process." Yet this premise is in itself obsolete after Camp David, the Israeli-Egyptian peace treaty, the Lebanon campaign of 1982, the intifada, Jordan's dissociation from the West Bank, and even the Gulf crisis and war in 1990–1991. These events ushered in a new phase for Israel and its neighbors that can be called *unstable equilibrium*. In the Arab-Israeli arena, it is an unstable yet durable geopolitical system maintained by Israel and Syria. Each needs the other as an enemy—each, for its own reasons, needs the conflict to continue unresolved, but in a manner that will not explode into an all-out war.

This equilibrium is facilitated by the cold yet durable peace between Israel and Egypt, the vulnerability of the Hashemite regime in Jordan, and the profound impact of both the Iran-Iraq war and the Gulf crisis and war. The notion that the Palestinian cause can serve as a battle cry that will shatter the unstable equilibrium is maintained only by a minority of ideologically motivated observers (in Israel and in the West), who in their despair believe in a deus ex machina that would resolve the century-old Jewish-Arab feud. The Palestinians themselves have given up that hope. The Arab states care very little about the Palestinians, as was demonstrated quite clearly during the Lebanon campaign, during the long months of the intifada, and by Iraqi President Saddam Hussein's cynical exploitation of the issue. Arab regimes believe they have done for the Palestinians what they could and keep their involvement in the Palestinian cause only when it serves their interests.

The Israeli-Arab conflict, which for forty years has been a regionwide, interstate conflict, has shrunk to its original core: the Israeli-Palestinian intercommunal strife. This major turning point—which if true renders the traditional paradigm obsolete and requires reformulation of options and choices—is not acknowledged by most observers. It is precisely in perceiving the reality of the Israeli-Palestinian relationship at the beginning of the 1990s that denial, evasion, and ideological catechism are most powerful.

To understand the new phase in the Israeli-Palestinian relationship, one must return to the formative phase of this tragic encounter. To be sure, one can fix the starting point at the end of World War I, or even earlier, when in 1882 the first Zionist settlement had been established. But it seems that the mid-1930s—and more specifically, the Arab Revolt of 1936 and its aftermath—have defined the contours of the dispute and formed the point to which we can trace back present relationships, perceptions, and even strategies. In the mid-1930s, both the Jewish and Palestinian communities had developed into cohesive and self-sustaining societies and moved irrevocably and consciously toward total confrontation. The Palestinians, aware of their growing national power, endorsed armed struggle as their strategy and launched the Arab Revolt—a tremendous effort to overthrow the British mandate and destroy the Zionist enterprise. Their primary targets were the British, because they viewed the Zionists as white-settler colonists, totally dependent on the British, a nonviable society bound to disappear once the colonial power was ousted.

The Zionist reaction to that mortal danger was just as powerful. Even the most moderate among them understood that a bloody showdown was inevitable. They had to abandon their earlier naive and self-serving perception of the conflict as an international class struggle or as a tragic misunderstanding caused by the ignorance of the natives, who would learn to accept the Jews because of the material benefits they brought. The Zionists realized that the Palestinians were in fact a national movement but could not grant it legitimacy and therefore depicted it as a fascist, reactionary gang of murderers. In the same way the Palestinians viewed them, the Zionists viewed the Palestinians as a nonviable society, an offshoot of the Arab world, not as an independent factor.

Since 1936, the perceptions of both Palestinians and Jews have been characterized by exclusionary attitudes, and the conflict has been perceived as a zero-sum game and an externally generated dispute. Each side ignored or underestimated the other side and viewed it as an object, manipulated by external forces. As a result, neither side saw any point in trying to relate to its adversary directly, but rather tried to deal with the external forces that controlled it. These perceptions persisted and were even exacerbated. The defeat of the Palestinians in 1937–1938 prompted the neighboring Arab countries to take over their cause, which confirmed Jewish perceptions of the Palestinians as an externally generated force. The 1948 war reinforced these perceptions. The total collapse and the physical destruction of the Palestinian society completed the process of externalization as objective reality caught up with the perceived reality. The intercommunal strife became a conflict between sovereign states, the Israeli-Arab conflict. The Palestinians themselves assisted the Israelis in redefining the conflict. During the pan-Arab Nasserite era, Palestinian activists perceived their national struggle in the broader anti-imperialist context. They clung to their old views of the Zionist entity as a neocolonial, nonviable phenomenon, relying for its sheer survival on imperialist power.

The 1967 war, the occupation of the West Bank and Gaza, and the 1973 war have not changed these perceptions, which by now have become a fundamental credo. They have persisted despite the gradual reduction of external interstate tensions reflected in the signing of the Israeli-Egyptian peace treaty. They have not changed despite the winding down of the cold war and the exacerbation of the intercommunal strife between Jews and Arabs in the occupied territories, for these perceptions satisfy deep-seated psychological needs and enable both sides to believe in the exclusivity of their claims.

The inability of each side to accept the legitimacy of the other side even as an enemy—let alone as a partner for peace negotiations—is central to the understanding of the failure of traditional diplomacy in its attempt to resolve the Israeli-Palestinian dispute. The diplomat's vocabulary is not designed to cope with fundamental issues of self-identity, self-expression, existential fears of annihilation, clash of symbolic interests, and absolute justice. An intercommunal dispute of such proportions is simply beyond diplomacy, and therefore the attempts to resolve it through the traditional government-to-government "peace process" approach are bound to failure.

The diplomatic peace process is a linear, means-end effort to transform war situations into peaceful conditions. It is designed to formulate answers to the questions which result from a clash of national interests in the international arena. For the peace process to be effective, certain conditions must be met. It must take place within the context of an international system that is based on a recognition of its national members as legitimate, independent actors who may interact with other members on an equal basis. Participants in the peace process must be perceived as accredited entities, who represent extraneous power structures over which other members have no authority and who report to independent constituencies. The basic right of the enemy to an autonomous and separate identity cannot be an issue for discussion; rather, the issue is the circumstances under which the right is exercised. It is only within this procedural context that the peace process can function.

Substantive issues have their own constraints. The peace process must be premised on the assumption that the conflict is not a zero-sum game. The belligerents must be prepared to participate in negotiations in which concessions and compromises can take place, and issues must be translatable into clearly defined texts and must focus on concrete issues of dispute.

It is only because these conditions were met that the peace process between Israel and Egypt was successfully concluded; it is because none of these conditions could be met that the Israeli-Palestinian dispute has not been resolved by a similar process.

In UN Security Council resolution 338, both Israel and Egypt had agreed on a means-end effort to transform belligerency into peaceful relations, within the context of the international system.[1] Sadat's visit to Jerusalem symbolized the recognition of Israel as a legitimate actor and the Israeli public as an autonomous and independent constituency. Secret Israeli-Egyptian meetings (prior to official negotiations) established a positive-sum game: the return of Sinai and an unconditional recognition of Egyptian sovereignty in exchange for security arrangements. Bilateral issues could be translated into a clearly defined text, and disputed issues could be broken down into concrete items on which concessions and compromises could be eventually reached.

The Israeli-Palestinian dispute is stuck at the critical preprocedural phase. Although objective observers would like to define the dispute as one involving a clash of national entities struggling for the same land, this definition is not accepted by the adversaries. The core of this conflict is understood by them as "survival." The struggle goes beyond the apparent physical survival of the peoples involved and encompasses basic issues of identity and integrity. The core of this dispute is therefore nonnegotiable because issues of identity are a zero-sum game.

Furthermore, the requirement that the peace process take place within the framework of the international system means that both members must be full members of that system. Negotiations take place around tables with representatives of the belligerent parties equipped with their symbols of legitimacy. Diplomats present credentials, flags are displayed, and national anthems respected. Yet the very core of the conflict is over the legitimacy of these symbols. Participation itself implies a symbolic concession too great for the opposition. In the normal peace process, enemies recognize each other's legitimacy to exist as an entity, albeit a belligerent one. The normal issue is not the right of the opposition to exist but rather mutual relationships. In the Palestinian-Israeli conflict, as we have already seen, the basis of the conflict is that very existence.

To be sure, the status of Israelis and Palestinians is asymmetrical. Israel is recognized as a sovereign state, and its legitimacy is not disputed by most countries (including some Arab countries). The Palestinians are internationally recognized as a quasi-national entity, but that status is too ambiguous to allow them participation in the international system as equal partners. Recognition is denied to them because the status of an independent and equal actor implies acknowledgment of their right to self-determination and of the existence of an autonomous and separate constituency represented by a recognized leadership.

Despite the inapplicability of the traditional diplomatic approach, it must continue because "international disputes" are handled by negotiators. The only common language diplomats share is their particular jargon; their only secure environment is "procedure"—for diplomatic jargon is clinical and procedure is antiseptic. In that sterilized environment, one converses in a dead language, the Latin of the Middle East: "242 and 338," international "forum," "umbrella," "conference," the Palestinian "issue," "freeze," "condominium," "confederation," "working groups," "redeployment," "modalities for elections." Trusted envoys come and go, brilliant draftsmen produce working papers, secret conclaves convene, information leaks. It is the subculture of the mighty shrouded in the mystique of power. "Something is going on," whisper the uninitiated. "It must be important, for otherwise important people would not be involved." But the real world speaks in the vernacular, and the environment of substance is polluted. The operation, alas, must be performed in field conditions. And in the field, alas, a bloody, cruel civil war is raging. Its arena is the entire area of former mandatory Palestine. Policies of enforced integration have completely erased the Green Line separating Israel proper from the occupied territories and created a new sociopolitical reality.

On the day after the Six-Day War, the second Israeli republic was established in the area of the former British mandate of Palestine. It replaced the first republic, which came into existence in 1948 and lasted nineteen years—a Jewish nation-state (with a small Arab minority), engaged in Jewish nation-building processes and in armed conflicts with Arab states.

The political, societal, economic, and administrative systems of the second republic took form gradually and consolidated twenty years later. Its government rules over all of mandatory Palestine and has the monopoly on governmental coercive power in the entire area under its dominion. The distinction between Israel's sovereign territory and the area in which it rules by military government has long since lost its meaning. It acts as sovereign, for all intents and purposes, in the whole area west of the Jordan River.

The second Israeli republic is a binational entity with a rigid, hierarchical social structure based on ethnicity. Jewish Israelis, numbering 3.5 million, hold total monopoly over governmental resources, control the economy, form the upper social stratum, and determine the educational and national values and objectives of the republic. The 2 million Palestinians divide into Israeli Palestinians and the Palestinians of the territories. Although the half million Israeli Palestinians are citizens of the republic, their citizenship does not assure them equality in law because one crucial test of citizenship is military service, and Israeli Palestinians are exempt.

The remaining 1.5 million Palestinians are citizens of a foreign state (in the West Bank) or altogether stateless (in Gaza). They have no political rights, on the rationale that they are under military occupation; even their rights under international conventions that govern military occupation are not assured, because the government of the republic does not recognize the application of these conventions to the territories.

The ethnic groups maintain economic interaction sometimes resembling the more familiar relationship between colonists and an indigenous population, in which one group provides both cheap labor and a market for the finished consumer goods produced by the other. The second republic is, in effect, a dual society and political system. This situation is not usually characterized in this way because the territories have not been formally annexed and are still thought of technically as in temporary status.

Communal strife rages on in the second Israeli republic. There is a perpetual conflict, not necessarily violent, between the Jewish majority group that seeks to maintain its superiority and the Arab minority group that seeks to free itself from majority tyranny. The majority community perceives the struggle as one of "law and order." The minority community, which does not regard the occupation regime as legitimate, seeks to destroy it. Each community denies the other's standing as a legitimate collective entity. Hence, the Arabs define Zionism (the expression of the collective aspirations of the Jewish people) as racism—ergo illegitimate. The Israelis in turn define Palestinian nationalism as PLO terrorism— ergo illegitimate. The delegitimization is vital for both sides, for it enables them to believe in the exclusivity of their claim and in the absolute justice of their position.

Both communities, though internally divided, outwardly present a monolithic facade. The Israeli consensus, comprising the vast majority of the Jewish group, is united in its aspiration to preserve the Jewish character of the second republic, even at the cost of democratic values. The differences between the main Jewish political factions are those of emphasis, style, and abstract moral scruples, but even these vanish utterly on the daily tactical level. The vast majority of the Arab group is united in its desire to destroy Jewish hegemony and is divided only over the most effective method—armed struggle or *sumud* (steadfastness)—for achieving their objectives. Just as all Israelis are Zionists, so too are all Arabs PLO.

The dynamic of the Israeli-Palestinian communal strife is similar to that of intercommunal strife everywhere—from Beirut to Belfast. It is waged in an endless cycle of violence, enforcement, domination, containment—fights over every piece of land, every tree. It is accompanied by the development of stereotypes, a lowering of the threshold of moral sensitivity, the loss of humanistic values, and despair leading ultimately to psychological withdrawal, anarchy, and fundamentalism. The conflict erupts periodically, usually following an unplanned provocation. Violence simmers just below the surface. It is an endemic condition, lacking a durable, "ultimate" solution.

The basic, almost primordial nature of the intercommunal Jewish-Arab strife has been masked by its international manifestations. Conceptual frameworks filtered facts and data; cozy answers sought facile questions and found them. This emerging intractable condition was too ominous for people to acknowledge and confront.

Then came the Palestinian uprising of December 1987. Reality no longer demanded confirmation and refused to be shaped by perception. The intifada was the symbolic declaration of the Israeli-Palestinian civil war. It should not have come as a surprise, least of all to the Israeli military. Israeli generals were monitoring the gathering storm; all data relating to the intensification of spontaneous expressions of violent protest were at their disposal. They should have reached the same conclusions as independent researchers who warned that a new phase of Palestinian resistance and of the intercommunal strife had begun, a phase characterized by grass-roots, uncoordinated initiative, carried out by angry young men acting on their own accord and undeterred by risks to their lives.

The dramatic increase of violent demonstrations since 1982, combined with a decrease in PLO-initiated terrorist acts, should have sounded the alarm. But Israeli generals were captive of the obsolete conception of the externally generated conflict, and the internal civil war caught them by surprise. December 1987 was Israel's second Yom Kippur. In 1973 Israeli generals misread the signs of imminent external attack; in 1987 they ignored signs of imminent internal uprising. In both cases, panic seized the generals and blunders ensued, except that in 1987 it was the Palestinians who paid with their lives. Israeli generals, however, learn fast and quickly turned the army into a powerful internal security force. It is the politicians and "peacemakers" who have yet to grasp the significance of events and their implications and who instead have absorbed them into the obsolete paradigm of the "Israeli-Arab conflict."

The Palestinian intifada was regarded as the shattering of the status quo. Now that the Green Line has been reestablished by Palestinian stone-throwers, and PLO Chairman Yasser Arafat has uttered the "Latin" phrases of the diplomatic jargon, the curtain rises on the final act of the Jewish-Arab drama. There would now come a radical change, brought on by the success of the now inevitable peace process.

This is a normative forecast, not a realistic one. Since the 1987 uprising, the internal Israeli-Palestinian conflict is even further away from a solution than it was before. The feelings of hostility, fear, and hatred have intensified rather than subsided. The dynamics of the internally generated conflict engender more violence and harsher enforcement. The intifada is itself the status quo. Anyone who wishes to estimate the time span of what I term "status quo" should remember that the current "troubles" in Northern Ireland began in 1969 and that the Sharpeville massacre, which triggered the violent racial confrontation in South Africa, happened in 1960. However, people wish to believe that what "must" happen will indeed happen.

This analysis is even more true in the wake of the Gulf crisis and war. Even apart from the war, Israeli-Palestinian relationships deteriorated markedly during the autumn of 1990, especially after the shooting by Israeli police of more than a dozen Palestinians near the mosque on the Temple Mount in Jerusalem. Individual attacks between Israelis and Palestinians threatened personal security. Even those on both sides who had maintained steady relationships withdrew from each other. The gap between the peoples widened. In that context, the support by some PLO leaders and rank-and-file for Iraqi President Saddam Hussein's invasion of Kuwait as well as for his threats and Scud missile attacks on Israel seriously worsened prospects for attempts at reconciliation between the two peoples on the Israeli side. The initial Israeli denial of gas masks to Palestinians and then the round-the-clock curfews deepened Palestinian anger.

The eruption of the intifada in the territories, now in its fourth year, marks the final act in the process of the internalization of the Israeli-Arab conflict and its transformation into overt, Jewish-Palestinian intercommunal strife. The essence of the new phase lies in the Palestinians' having at last healed their internal schisms, overcome their lack of motivation, and crossed the threshold of fear. For the first time in their history, they have succeeded in mobilizing the entire community in a sustained political struggle and in waging a controlled confrontation guided by realistic and not emotional considerations.

The leaders of the uprising have permitted no deviation from a quite rigid strategy that makes constant allowance for the population's capacity to endure hardship. This realistic strategy is manifested in the limited commercial strikes, in allowing workers to continue their employment in Israeli enterprises, and, especially, in the ban on the use of firearms against Israelis. More than two decades of intimate acquaintance with the Israeli polity have taught the Palestinians the political and moral constraints that inhibit the Israelis' freedom of action and restrict their ability to employ their immeasurably vaster physical power. The Palestinians have turned these constraints to their own benefit.

It was the realism evinced by the leaders of the uprising that enabled them to persist with the revolt and reap the political fruits of the intifada. However, it was beyond them to formulate a positive political program: That was the exclusive prerogative of PLO institutions.

Unlike in the past, though, the Arabs in the territories did not allow the PLO to remain captive to its own illusions. They sent Yasser Arafat a clear message: The uprising must be translated into an achievable political program, one rooted in reality. The illusion that Israel does not exist because the Palestinians are unable to accept its existence, or that it can be wished away, is a recipe for disaster. To go on ignoring the true power relationship would have resulted in the loss of the little that can still be salvaged.

This was the juncture at which Yasser Arafat found his calling as a leader. Submitting to the constraints of reality, he sacrificed the maximalist formulations of the Palestinian revolution in favor of a political plan that recognized the facts of life—the cardinal component of which is acknowledgment of Israel's unassailable, permanent existence.

Realpolitik is not normally considered an unusual trait in a political leader, but the historic significance of the shift in the Palestinians' posture at the PLO Algiers conference and in Arafat's Geneva speech in November and December 1988 can only be assessed against the background of the traditional Palestinian national strategy.

In contrast to Zionism, which opted for a strategy of stages and pursued attainable objectives, the Palestinian movement had refused to compromise on its ultimate objective, even if by doing so it could have made substantial short-term gains. The Palestinians always believed that no compromises should be made on matters of principle in a just cause. Had they reconciled themselves to reality and been willing to forgo the sanctity of the principle, they might already have been celebrating the fortieth anniversary of the state of Palestine in half of the homeland. In 1988, Yasser Arafat grasped that subjective will cannot overcome objective reality and forced this realism on his movement. The question was whether this new realism, which was not forthcoming when it was needed forty years ago, would now permit the rapid attainment of the new and relatively modest goals of the Palestinian national movement. PLO support for Iraq during the 1990–1991 Gulf crisis made that attainment more difficult.

The new Palestinian program lacks a vital element: It refuses to accept the fact that, unlike in 1947, the Palestinian state cannot be established by "the justice of the nations." The price of refusing to accede to the partition resolution of 1947 at the time was that Israel in the meantime became a vital independent actor, with impressive maneuverability in the international arena. If in 1947 independence was achievable from the outside world, in the 1990s that same independence is obtainable only from the Israelis, who occupy the entire land with overwhelming force.

But not even Yasser Arafat before the Gulf crisis was capable of demonstrating that level of hard-headed realism. He continued to believe that international pressure and a political campaign aimed at third parties would eventually succeed in twisting Israel's arm. Essentially, he seemed to think that the United States is a mere replica of His Majesty's government (1947–1948) and that UN intervention to implement the partition resolution—intervention which the Palestinians rejected outright in 1947—would materialize. "Israel is not a principal side in the conflict," Khaled al-Hassan, one of Arafat's principal associates, told the Egyptian paper *Al-Mussawar* in January 1989, "for it is merely a corporation turned into a state, as has been said about General Motors. . . . We are aiming at the Americans more than at the Israelis."

It is hard enough to admit, finally, that 1948 is irreversible and that the Jewish state is a fait accompli. It is unbearable, however, to admit a catastrophic error that resulted in the loss of two generations and allowed the enemy a head start of forty years. Therefore, because Israel must remain for the PLO an object, manipulatable by external forces, external diplomatic activity was seen as the means to achieve Palestinian national objectives.

It is fascinating to contemplate the reversal of roles that has occurred in Palestinian and Zionist perceptions. In 1947, mainstream Zionists felt that they had to salvage what was still salvageable. The aftermath of the holocaust forced them to agree to the partition of Palestine without western Galilee and without Jerusalem. The Palestinians, confident of their strength, refused to compromise with a minority they perceived as an alien element, doomed to extinction once the colonial power departed.

Things have come full circle. The present debates among the Palestinians are not substantially different from the debate in the Zionist movement in 1947 between revisionists who believed in "Greater Israel" and rejected the partition plan and mainstream Zionists who supported it. Now the Israelis, in their turn, are confident of their strength, believe in holding on to everything, and deny the existence of the other side as an independent constituency, capable of resisting superior power. Both sides have behaved, in 1947 and now, as one might have expected them to behave, given their subjective perceptions of the power relationships.

The intifada and the strategy adopted by the PLO have forced the Israelis to confront the Palestinian collective directly. The cherished illusion of the "Jordanian option" and the perception of the conflict as an Israeli-Arab interstate dispute have had to be abandoned. Yet most Israelis are incapable of coming to grips with the fact that they are confronted by an independent and autonomous constituency which claims symmetrical attachment to the land. For the Israelis to internalize this fact would mean forgoing the exclusivity of their moral and historical claim and redefining their national ethos. They could avoid this self-assessment as long as the Palestinians engaged in terrorism and "armed struggle," thus allowing the Israelis to perceive the conflict in terms of physical survival. The challenge posed by Palestinian realism has not been perceived as legitimate but rather as a threat—precisely because of its realism.

The new Palestinian sophistication caught Israelis by surprise, so long had they been accustomed to a rash, emotional, and unrealistic adversary. The new situation called for sophistication on the part of the Israelis. That sophistication is emerging; its initial expression was the establishment of a Likud–Labor Alignment government.

Yitzhak Shamir, like Yasser Arafat, has also found his calling as a leader. He understood that the intifada and the Algiers resolutions impelled movement on his part away from extremist ideology. He therefore rejected the option of a narrow government in which parties of the radical right would have wielded immense influence. Had he left the Labor Alignment in parliamentary opposition, the political controversy would have strengthened dovish circles in the Labor party and made the parties on the left more vocal. Moreover, the replacement of Defense Minister Yitzhak Rabin with a Likud minister would have sparked the Peace Now group to undertake activity on a massive scale, thus jeopardizing the tacit national consensus in favor of persisting with the present policy concerning the territories.

A Labor Alignment–Likud government, notwithstanding its ideological differences, could in theory adopt political positions that are seemingly pragmatic but are in fact geared to preserving the status quo. Shamir also moved to change the image of his own party by clipping the wings of the extremists and coopting a group of young ministers who were trying to find pragmatic answers for the problem of the territories. The Palestinian challenge was thus initially met by entrenchment behind the status quo and the floating of "peace plans," and although their only hallmark was their unacceptability, at the same time they created an impression of movement.

For a time, a more serious attempt at sophistication seemed to be in the offing: a redefinition of the Palestinian problem. New Israeli plans in early 1989 called for free political elections in the occupied territories, army withdrawal from populated areas, and self-rule. Beyond the wish to drive a wedge between Palestinians in the territories and the PLO, there was an attempt to reduce the problem to the fate of the residents of the West Bank and Gaza. For the rest of the Palestinians outside the territories, the 1948 exodus was irreversible.

Through 1989 into early 1990, the U.S. government worked with the Israeli proposal for elections with the aim of arranging a negotiation involving Israelis and Palestinians. That effort came to an end when the Israeli coalition government broke up because it could not agree on engaging seriously in that negotiation.

Neither PLO terrorism nor a mighty Palestinian state frightens the Israelis. What frightens them is "The Return" *(al-awdah)* of Palestinians, and the principle is even more feared than the actual return. A Palestinian state, just like the Jewish state, embodies the principle of the "Ingathering of the Exiles." It is Zionism in reverse. One of the first laws to be enacted by that state would no doubt be the "Law of (Palestinian) Return."

"The Return"—a perpetual, unremitting endeavor—would be the raison d'être of the state of Palestine, just as it is the fundamental credo of the state of Israel, no matter how many actually return. Palestinian national objectives, just like Zionist objectives, would not be completely realized by independence and would produce messianic and chauvinistic impulses as powerful as any produced by the Zionist movement—and as uncontrollable as the sharp influx of Soviet Jews into Israel again demonstrated in 1990.

Israelis believe solemn Palestinian vows to forgo claims for their lands in Israel proper, just as Palestinians may believe that the Zionists have given up their "expansionist" philosophy. Israelis of all political persuasions sense that they must cope with the two million Palestinians who have remained in the land, although that realization is growing very slowly. To acknowledge, however, that Palestine is the homeland of the entire Palestinian people, almost five million strong, is insupportable.

Such is the irony of history. It was the Zionist claim to Palestine as the homeland of the entire Jewish people and demands for unlimited Jewish immigration that incensed the Palestinians more than political demands for a "Jewish national home." That role reversal is well understood by users of the intimate Israeli-Palestinian vocabulary.

The PLO reacts vehemently to any attempt at fragmenting the Palestinians, not merely because it violates their national unity and the PLO's exclusive leadership role. The PLO understands the dangers inherent in Israeli sophistication: What if third parties—the United States in particular—view the new Israeli plans as satisfactory? After all, the occupied territories and the violence therein, not the 1948 refugees, are perceived as the core problem. It is therefore imperative to nip in the bud all attempts to begin a dialogue between Israelis and an "alternative leadership" (in PLO parlance) in the territories.

Local leaders are not tempted by Israeli overtures, because they would become traitors to the cause, and understandably so. No Palestinian can forgo the principle of the unity of the Palestinian people in the homeland and in the diaspora and disown total allegiance to the recognized leadership, the PLO. Yet local leaders must contend with the reality of Israeli coercion, the high price of the intifada, and the limits of their people's endurance. If the PLO bid for a "comprehensive solution" does not succeed soon, there will be no choice but to deal directly with the Israelis, thus threatening the united front.

Perceptive Palestinians are seized with the apprehension that they will awake to find they have driven themselves straight into a blind alley—that the diplomatic club they entered after so much travail is nothing but a prestigious debating club in which points can be scored but no concrete achievements made; that U.S. recognition is very far from being a Palestinian Balfour Declaration; that, after raising all the flags on all the Palestinian embassies around the world, they will find that Israel holds higher cards in the game of nations and that a Palestinian state will not be achieved by the "justice of the nations."

Perceptive Israelis, too, are worried about the "morning after" that would follow success in deflecting the PLO political campaign. Winning the diplomatic game would not change the realities on the ground. In the shared homeland there exist two cohesive national communities, engaged in a total civil war that by now has become a way of life, an endemic and organic condition.

Israeli success in breaking up Palestinian unity would force Israel to confront a local leadership that would be even more formidable than that of the aging PLO. These local leaders—hardened by Israeli harassment, closely acquainted with the Israeli political system, and capable of manipulating its internal weaknesses and divisions—would relentlessly continue the internal struggle, and the Israelis would find it more devastating than conventional wars.

Yasser Arafat would like to believe that he is a Palestinian David Ben-Gurion. But the "real" Palestinian Ben-Gurion now lives in a refugee camp near Nablus. He is a 22-year-old youngster—perhaps now busy trying to organize a new "shock force" after members of previous units were arrested by the Israelis. He is a realist to the marrow, and he knows what Ben-Gurion also knew in his twenties: National independence is attained by stubbornly building economic, social, educational, and military communal power and not through declarations and speeches in exclusive international clubs.

The task of the Palestinian Ben-Gurion is easier than that of the Zionist hero: Ben-Gurion had to build a society from scratch, whereas the Palestinian need only consolidate a community already living on its land. But the Palestinian leader faces a greater external challenge: Israelis are not a colonial power but a powerful, indigenous people deeply rooted in their land. No force in the world can suppress the national aspirations of a cohesive national community. But there is no law of nature guaranteeing that those aspirations must be attained. The Palestinians had an opportunity in 1947 and they missed it. Paradoxically, the fact that they are now ruled by the Israelis offers them a second chance. The de facto binational entity, created by continued Israeli occupation, and the socioeconomic and cultural interaction between Israelis and Palestinians (and confrontation is a powerful form of interaction) have brought about an internally generated conflict, waged by two intimate enemies.

With time, the reality of daily friction distances those who experience the agony from even involved outsiders—and draws the Israelis and Palestinians together. Such conflicts have two basic theoretical solutions: partition or power sharing, or a combination of both. At this point in the discourse, conflict resolvers traditionally begin to discuss draft agreements. Such devices, however, require that the parties directly involved feel compelled to make use of them, which is not the case when the protagonists consider conflict-resolution devices only through the prism of their respective gains and losses, not as means to resolve amicably their differences. The traditional technique will not work for intercommunal feuds, which, unlike international conflict, are organic and cyclical. Therefore, the linear-progression approach is inapplicable.

A new approach is clearly needed. Instead of agreeing on what is achievable, one should start with an agreement on the opposite: what is impossible, unworkable, or unachievable. That would lead to an open-ended process of problem sharing. Success of the process is not measured by approximation of results to a desired goal but by the degree of agreement, no matter how trivial the issue seems. This approach—process-oriented rather than solution-oriented—requires a careful formulation of gradual steps, with concrete and meaningful measures designed specifically not to contradict the diametrically opposed "ultimate objectives" of both sides.

Palestinian realism and Israel's realization that it confronts an unyielding Palestinian community may turn out to be the first step on a very long road to reconciliation. The parties themselves must make the journey; there are no shortcuts. The international community can play a role in containing the dispute so that it does not spill over and threaten international stability, but external forces cannot replace the communities engaged in the struggle. They must themselves realize that continued strife will bring a plague on both their houses, that nobody emerges triumphant from communal strife, and that one community cannot thrive forever on the misery of another.

Notes

A shorter version of this chapter appeared in the Journal of Palestine Studies, no. 65 (Autumn 1987).

1. Resolution 338 was passed by the United Nations Security Council on October 22, 1973, at the end of the Arab-Israeli war then raging among Egypt, Israel, and Syria. The resolution called for a cease-fire, called upon the parties concerned to begin implementation of resolution 242, and decided that negotiations between the parties to the conflict would begin aimed at establishing a just and durable peace in the Middle East. Resolution 242, passed by the Security Council on November 22, 1967, following the war of June 5–10, laid down basic principles for resolution of the Arab-Israeli conflict. The basic equation in a delicately balanced formulation included two key principles, among others: (1) "withdrawal of Israel armed forces from territories occupied in the recent conflict" and (2) "termination of all claims or states of belligerency and respect for and acknowledgement of the sovereignty, territorial integrity and political independence of every State in the area and their right to live in peace within secure and recognized boundaries free from threats or acts of force."

PART TWO

The Political Foundations
of Policymaking

4
Policymaking Within the Palestinian Polity

Rashid Khalidi

The Problem of Policymaking in a Fragmented Community

How does a community that does not have sovereignty make policy? Compounding the difficulty of an already complex problem is the fact that the Palestinian community lives not under one external authority but under several. It is physically divided into seven major areas of residence (the West Bank, Gaza Strip, and Israel proper; Jordan, Lebanon, Syria, and the Gulf) and numerous minor ones; and it is politically divided in many ways.

Despite the problems it poses, lack of sovereignty is perhaps less of a problem than some other issues, for the nonstate actor, the transnational movement, and the supranational organization are now familiar factors in international affairs. A wealth of scholarly material deals with them, showing that the absence of sovereignty does not preclude active participation in international relations or analysis of participants' behavior. Making allowances for the disparate modes of action entailed by the dissimilar circumstances of states and nonstates, it is possible to explain the policymaking processes of the latter.

In the case of the Palestinians, however, we are dealing with issues of a complexity that may be unique. A first issue is whether the Palestinians can be spoken of as an entity at all, be it as a people or even as a community. Indeed, there are theories advanced in some of the literature that in talking of Palestinians, of a Palestinian people or polity, we are dealing with a chimera, a myth being foisted on an unsuspecting world.[1]

It is easy to dismiss these views as biased outpourings from one extreme of the political spectrum in the United States and Israel. Unfortunately, although they are biased and extreme, they are buttressed by the academic credentials of some of their most prominent champions. It is of little use to point out in response that such arguments are rarely heard from scholars, whether Arab, U.S., or Israeli, who have studied the Palestinians using primary sources in Arabic and who have paid careful attention to the development and dynamics of Palestinian politics.[2]

The issue of the different political authorities under which the 4–5 million Palestinians live (it is symptomatic that there is no agreed figure as to the number of Palestinians) is also a vexed one, for at least two reasons. Aside from the difficulty of disentangling what the Palestinians themselves want from the pressures of the powers that dominate them, there is the more specific problem of the bodies established by several of these powers, which purport to speak for the Palestinians.

In recent years, these groups have included the Village Leagues, the Damascus group called the National Salvation Front, Abu Zaim's Amman-based anti-PLO insurrection, and the Fateh Revolutionary Council headed by Abu Nidal. Although each has roots in Palestinian politics and political culture and a certain independent dimension (however insubstantial in some cases), these phenomena have also been subordinate to the strategies of Israel, Syria, Jordan, and a changing cast of Arab countries, respectively. The exact degree of dependence and control in each case is often murky, but none represents truly independent expressions of Palestinian popular sentiment.

It would be unnecessary to mention these groups if the Palestinians speaking with an Israeli or Syrian or Jordanian voice appeared solely in response to tactical conjunctures or as isolated phenomena. They must rather be understood against a background of persistent attempts to deny, eliminate, or dominate independent expressions of Palestinian national existence by Israel in the first place and also by various Arab states. This dual struggle of the Palestinians to assert themselves against unremitting Israeli resistance and Arab state–created obstacles ranging from indifference to outright opposition is mirrored in the careers of all major Palestinian politicians of this generation.[3]

There are more subtle examples of the problems posed for the Palestinians by living under different political authorities. Palestinians in what was mandatory Palestine (the area under the British mandate from 1922 to 1948 which now constitutes Israel and the occupied territories) live today under three different systems of law: Those in Israel are Israeli citizens subject to Israeli law; those in the West Bank were at one time Jordanian citizens and are governed by Israel using Jordanian law, supplemented by the regulations of the military occupation; those in the Gaza Strip are subject to Israeli occupation regulations and those of the former Egyptian military administration. Israelis in these three areas are little affected by these various regulations, but they affect

Palestinians in myriad ways. Newspapers published in Jerusalem, which was occupied and annexed to Israel in 1967, for example, are banned from circulating in the rest of the occupied West Bank or in Gaza.

Similarly, Palestinians from Lebanon or Gaza with refugee passports issued by the Lebanese and Egyptian governments often have difficulty traveling because their documents are not accepted by many states. Members of the same family may have different travel documents or may not all be allowed to enter Israel or an Arab country and thus must meet in some neutral location, such as Cyprus. In view of these difficulties and of the historical circumstances causing the major Palestinian communities to develop differently over nearly four decades, it is not surprising that they are at best a disparate and at worst a fragmented polity.

Centrifugal tendencies like dispersion, the obstacles erected by the various sovereignties under which Palestinians live, and the effect of almost four decades of social, educational, and economic development under different systems have not been the only influences on the Palestinian community. Countervailing centripetal tendencies include the shared history of the Palestinians before 1948 and the mobilizing effect of the relatively developed nationalism that had emerged by then. Also important have been a number of transnational political movements, some broader than the Palestinian polity and some restricted to it, that have unified Palestinians in different regions and under different systems. These include the Muslim Brotherhood, the Communist and Baath parties, the Movement of Arab Nationalists (MAN), the Islamic Liberation Party, and finally Fateh (a reverse acronym for Palestinian National Liberation Movement) and other armed resistance groups that emerged in the 1960s and took over the PLO.

Although the adherence of Palestinians to these and other competing movements increased the already great diversity of Palestinian politics, it brought together individuals of disparate backgrounds in modern political organizations under circumstances that produced a different kind of politics than had existed before 1948. It also broke down some of the new barriers that had grown up in the years of exile, dispersion, and occupation after 1948. This was particularly the case after the founding of the PLO. The group became the primary arena for Palestinian political integration, most notably after the changes in the organization following the late 1960s takeover by the new resistance groups, which have dominated it ever since.

Literature, especially poetry, has also played an integrative role, with writers such as Mahmoud Darwish, Ghassan Kanafani, Samih al-Qassem, Emile Habibi, Fadwa Touqan, and many others elaborating themes of patriotism and love of homeland, which have reinforced

Palestinian national sentiment and created images and symbols common to Palestinians from Kuwait to North America. Other artists have played a similar role, from painters, graphic designers, and cartoonists to those active in theater and music. The role of educators, journalists, and scholars in this respect is also important.

These seemingly diffuse activities—similar to those that operate in the formative phases of any national movement—are particularly significant in the Palestinian case because of high levels of literacy and mobility and because this community's overt political expression is frequently impinged on, if not totally denied. Even in literature, art, journalism, education, and scholarship, the political sovereignties that govern the Palestinians often interfere, censor, or impose harsh restrictions.

We are left with a checkered picture. In situations of stress, the Palestinians have demonstrated intense fellow-feeling and solidarity—*asabiyya,* to use Ibn Khaldun's term for the group bonds he argued were the prerequisite for state formation in the Arab dynastic states of the first six centuries of Islam. At other times, the Palestinians have shown strong divisiveness and little sense of direction.

An overview of modern Palestinian history makes it apparent that for the past two decades the PLO has increasingly provided a unifying focus for Palestinian policymaking. The Palestinian members of the Ottoman Parliament before 1914, the Arab Executive of the 1920s, and the Arab Higher Committee from 1936 until 1948 only intermittently played such a unifying role, while there were long periods, for example the years after 1948, when no clearly defined arena for Palestinian political activity seems to have existed.

What follows deals primarily with the PLO. It must be remembered, though, that the involvement of Palestinians with the PLO in different areas has by no means been uniform. Inside Israel, for example, it has only been over the past decade that the patriotism of most of the Arab population has focused on the PLO. In the West Bank and Gaza, traditional leaderships in the past often looked to Jordan as an alternative source of guidance, support, and authority, while in the diaspora there are some who see no contradiction with their Palestinian patriotism in accepting the dictates of various Arab regimes, even when this runs counter to the interests of the Palestinians themselves.

With these caveats in mind, we will assess how the PLO acts as a focus for Palestinian policymaking, operating as a nonstate actor with numerous attributes of a state and integrating many facets of Palestinian politics, while facing grave difficulties in the accumulation of power and the exercise of authority over a people spread over their homeland, the states of the Arab world, and even farther afield.

The PLO as a Focus of Policymaking

In assessing how a political entity makes its decisions, it is necessary to determine the worldview of its leaders and their perceptions of their situation, the primary inputs into the decisionmaking process, and the political environment within which they operate. In analyzing the Palestinian community, with its peculiarities, the question arises as to which leaders or leadership group should be examined and during which period.

Even if we follow the analysis of the preceding section and concentrate primarily on the PLO, we still must take into consideration more than two decades of its existence and its numerous member groups, not to speak of other bodies under occupation and in the Palestinian diaspora, some not linked formally to the PLO. It is possible to exclude from consideration the first three years of the PLO's existence and the 1967–1971 Amman period and to ignore both the smaller groups and those that were primarily an emanation of the will of various Arab regimes. Nevertheless, we are still left with a bewildering array of material and data.

Palestinian policymaking, however, is simpler than it may seem. Fateh has been at the core of Palestinian politics since at least 1965.[4] It is thus possible to focus on its leaders, who have worked together closely since the early 1950s, while taking into account their relationship with four other leading segments of the Palestinian polity. These are the men who founded and led the MAN in the 1950s and 1960s and who today constitute the top ranks of the first two of these, the Popular Front for the Liberation of Palestine (PFLP) and the Democratic Front for the Liberation of Palestine (DFLP); traditional and new leaders in the occupied territories; and the influential Palestinian bourgeoisie made up of business leaders, contractors, entrepreneurs, and bankers, based in Amman, the Gulf, the occupied territories, and Lebanon. Also important are union and student leaders, academics and intellectuals, and the military forces.

To grasp how the different groups within the PLO operate, it is useful to consider them not primarily as military organizations but as the functional equivalent of political parties. This is true of at least Fateh, the PFLP, and the DFLP, to which can be added the Palestinian Communist Party (PCP) in the occupied territories. Each group performs conventional political functions of aggregating demands, representing interest groups, and serving as platforms for broader groups within the polity, in addition to its less conventional ones.

Within limits, each has an ideology, a strategy, and a vision of the Palestinian society of the future, although like many formal organizations, each group must be seen more in terms of what it actually does politically than of what it says it is. Thus statements and doctrinal pronouncements must be examined, but only in close relation to day-to-day political practice. This is essential to avoid the trap of assuming that the PFLP and the DFLP are in fact the Marxist-Leninist protoparties they claim to be or that Fateh is actually motivated in its daily actions by the radical principles of its formal political program. The reality is much more mundane, and in practice the three groups are far more similar than a reading of their literature would indicate.

The idea that these groups are in some respects similar to political parties requires two major qualifications. The first is a function of the peculiar situation of the Palestinians: Having no sovereignty and no territory under their control, they obviously do not have a traditional political process through which normal interaction between parties can take place. The second is that, historically, the most important of these groups were formally founded as armed resistance groups rather than as political parties—Fateh secretly in the 1950s, emerging into the open in 1965, and the PFLP and the DFLP in the wake of the 1967 war.

Even here an important point emerges: The core leadership group of Fateh already existed in the early 1950s, controlling the Union of Palestinian Students in Cairo at one point and otherwise acting as a political group well before the commencement of armed attacks on Israel in 1965. Similarly, the leaders of the PFLP and the DFLP headed the influential MAN, first at the American University of Beirut in the wake of the 1948 war and later in its involvement in the politics of numerous Arab countries.

The successful transformation of the MAN into the PFLP and the DFLP (and a number of smaller groups) was not matched by that of other parties. In the late 1960s, the Palestinian branches of the Syrian and Iraqi wings of the divided Baath party founded the now politically moribund al-Saiqa and Arab Liberation Front respectively, while the Jordanian Communist Party established the abortive al-Ansar group. Like Fateh, all of these political groups underwent a major transformation into commando organizations directed at the liberation of Palestine by armed action. That change of form did not, however, entirely efface their nature as formations playing many of the roles of a political party.

With the 1970–1971 defeat in Jordan and the failure of an offensive military strategy from bases in Lebanon in the early 1970s came two important developments. The first was the growing emphasis on a political solution to the conflict with Israel by many groups increasingly working within the framework of the PLO. This was visible in the resolutions of the Palestine National Council (PNC) calling for a Palestinian state alongside Israel, a stance that became increasingly explicit from 1974 onward. Other evidence of this tendency included the growing favorable response of the PLO to the idea of an international peace conference on the Middle East, with the organization formally welcoming the October 1, 1977, U.S.-Soviet statement calling for its reconvening.[5]

A second development was the greater part played by parastate activities of a nonmilitary nature in the overall operations of the PLO. The causes for this extended beyond the failure of the cross-border offensive strategy. They included the PLO's involvement in the morass of the Lebanese war from 1975 onward, with the attendant need to provide emergency services and ultimately many others to the population.[6] Another cause was the need to offer something more than rhetoric and a symbolic national presence to Palestinians both under occupation and in the diaspora. A third was the increasing consciousness on the part of the PLO leaders that showing themselves and their organization to be the functioning and responsible nucleus of a Palestinian state was a powerful argument in favor of its establishment.

Within this increasingly institutionalized parastate structure, as it developed in Lebanon in the years before the PLO's defeat and expulsion in 1982, there were changes of another sort. Although the various groups maintained their existence, with only the PFLP, DFLP, PCP, and Fateh retaining any sort of popular following or ability to win substantial numbers of votes in union elections, the importance of all the groups declined in relation to the PLO as a whole. In the process, key members of the Fateh Central Committee imperceptibly became the core PLO leadership, including individuals with no formal PLO post, such as Salah Khalaf (known by his nom de guerre, Abu Iyyad) and Kahlil al-Wazir (Abu Jihad). Neither, for example, was ever a member of the PLO Executive Committee, but both were more powerful and spoke more authoritatively than most of its members.

The decline of the individual groups has continued since 1982. It was signified among other things by the decision of Fateh alone to hold the seventeenth PNC in Amman in November 1984, by the submission of the PFLP to the will of the majority in voting on resolutions of the nineteenth PNC in Algiers in 1988, and by the grouping together of many smaller groups in such bodies as the now defunct Democratic Alliance (DFLP and PCP) and National Salvation Front (PFLP and small Syrian-line factions). The preeminence of Fateh was little diminished by the split in its ranks that occurred in 1983, by the fierce opposition to it at that time of the National Salvation Front and the Abu Nidal group, both of which were strongly backed by Syria, or by the Jordanian-inspired rebellion of the cashiered Fateh officer, Abu Zaim.

Although the overall fortunes of the PLO have certainly not prospered during this period, in relative terms those of Fateh do not seem to have suffered. Most Palestinians apparently regard the simultaneous opposition of Israel, Jordan, and Syria to manifestations of Palestinian nationalism as a natural conjuncture. Peculiar as it may seem, this is a basic component of their worldview and one that is shared by PLO leaders. It is important to understand it because it helps explain the limited political expectations that most Palestinians have and the basis on which they judge the PLO and its leadership.

Since the beginning of the British mandate, Palestinian nationalists have operated with an awareness that they were in conflict with forces more powerful than they. Britain was seen correctly as a great imperial power, although the strength of the support of British politicians and strategists for Zionist objectives in Palestine was probably overestimated. So was the strength of the Zionist movement and of its position in Palestine. Nevertheless, there was a broadly accurate assessment before 1948 that the Palestinians were fighting an uphill battle, one borne out by the results.

Similar conclusions were drawn, with even sounder reasons, by those who revived Palestinian nationalism after 1948. The support for Israel of the dominant powers in the Middle East, of Britain and France, and later of the United States was not balanced by the weight of the Soviet Union, which did not begin to take a favorable view of the Palestinian movement until the mid-1970s. The power of Israel continued to grow relative to that of the Arab states, while the latter were increasingly divided and their regimes generally unfavorable to Palestinian irredentism before 1967, to the commando movement after that year, and to independent Palestinian nationalism at any time.

Palestinians have thus always felt that they were waging a struggle on many levels, with results measured in terms of the long odds against them. Without taking this into account, it is impossible to explain the long-term survival as popular political leaders of men like Yasser Arafat and George Habash. Without any major successes to show, they have been able to retain their standing as the most prominent Palestinian leaders for well over two decades, operating against the wishes of the governments of most states they have been based in and without significant means of coercion at their disposal. The highly politicized and relatively sophisticated polity they lead has accepted them in spite of their manifest flaws and their failures, at least in part because it is aware of the massive difficulties any Palestinian nationalist leaders would have had to overcome in this period.

Thus Palestinian political leadership operates against a background of low expectations on the part of its domestic constituency. This may seem peculiar, but it is not totally illogical: Palestinians could not have expected the PLO to defeat the Israelis during the 1982 war or believed that any Israeli government would withdraw easily from the occupied West Bank and Gaza Strip.

The dark worldview on which these low expectations are based can occasionally border on a sort of political paranoia. A study of the speeches of Palestinian leaders at the outset of the 1975–1976 phase of the Lebanese war reveals the recurrence of the word "conspiracy" to describe the situation facing the Palestinians in Lebanon. It is considered axiomatic that many of the Arab regimes (but not the Arab peoples) oppose the PLO, that they are unwilling to confront the United States or Israel on its behalf, and that most would accept a political settlement with Israel at the expense of Palestinian rights if their domestic public opinion, the inter-Arab balance of power, and the PLO would allow them to get away with it.

Other important elements of the worldview of PLO leaders include their attitude to Israel and the superpowers. There have certainly been changes regarding Israel over the decades these leaders have been active in politics. Some developments in PLO strategy have already been touched on. The importance of a shift from a goal of total liberation of Palestine and rejection of any form of compromise in the 1950s and 1960s to the current approach has not been fully appreciated. To understand how inaccurate are the claims by some that the PLO has never changed its goals, it is necessary only to read the critiques of PLO policy in the press of the radical opposition, whether it is located in Damascus, Tripoli, or Baghdad. Even making allowances for their rhetoric, no one reading such material carefully can seriously assert that the PLO leadership is still committed to the goals and methods of the 1950s and 1960s to which these radical groups still cling. With the outcome of the nineteenth PNC in Algiers in November 1988 and the later declarations of Yasser Arafat, some of the skepticism on this score has dissipated.

These changes have been evidenced in other ways. Leaving behind a policy of no compromise, no negotiations, and no contact with the "Zionist entity" and its representatives, the PLO leaders have engaged in timid and limited but nevertheless significant contacts with Israelis. In recent years, Arafat and other senior PLO officials have met with prominent Israelis such as Knesset members Matti Peled, former Director General of the Ministry of Finance Ya'kov Arnon, journalists Uri Avneri and Amnon Kapeliouk, and others. They have held other meetings at lower levels. All contacts have been with members of parties at the left end of the political spectrum, but it is worth recalling that the two mainstream Israeli political groups, Maarach and Likud, forbid their leaders from meeting PLO members and indeed that any meetings with members of the PLO are against Israeli law.[7]

The PLO has shown itself to be increasingly sensitive to the nuances of Israeli politics and to the growth in the numbers of Israelis who accept the principle of Palestinian self-determination, although PLO policies and practice do not always reflect this. A turning point in this regard was the 1982 war, when the efforts of the Peace Now movement for the first time made an impression on Palestinian opinion. Since then, Palestinians in the occupied territories in particular have had occasion to witness the opposition of influential segments of Israeli opinion to further settlement activity or continued occupation. With the Palestinian uprising, the views of these Palestinians gained more weight and were duly reflected in the resolutions of the nineteenth PNC.

The problem is that in assessing these phenomena as representing a minority trend within Israel, Palestinians are being realistic, but in so doing are effectively ruling out policies that could change the situation there. This skepticism is at the root of Palestinian unwillingness to change certain policies or approaches, rather than a belief in their efficacy. The use of violence is an example of this, for although most Palestinians believe that armed resistance to occupation is justified in principle, most would probably also accept that it has not been notably effective. Halting it, however, would require a belief that doing so would lead to positive developments in return, which this skeptical assessment of Israeli political realities does not allow. The uprising, in which there has been little use of firearms or explosives by Palestinians, but which has often involved forms of violence, shows both the ability of Palestinians to transcend this skepticism and its hold on them.

Attitudes toward the United States differ among Palestinians at all levels. Some believe that the United States is irremediably hostile to Palestinian national aspirations and linked to Israel so tightly that any differences between them are tactical and fleeting. Much persuasive evidence, drawn from the policies of the past five administrations, can be adduced to support this strongly held view. Another argument holds that it is possible for the PLO either to impose itself on or ingratiate itself with the United States and that doing so is imperative because the United States will inevitably play a central part in any peace settlement. Before the uprising, this thesis found few spirited defenders, if only because the idea that it is possible to change U.S. policy on the Palestinians seemed hard to sustain, particularly in view of the experiences of the Reagan years. However, after the shift in U.S. public opinion in the wake of the uprising and the attendant launching of a U.S.-PLO dialogue, such views gained more support, at least for a time.

The Soviet Union, on the other hand, is generally seen as supportive, if ineffectual. There is much less disagreement about perceptions of the Soviet Union than about the United States. But much less attention is paid to the Soviet Union as well, in line with the consensus that it is a less important Middle East power. None of this makes PLO leaders any less insistent on Soviet involvement in the settlement process. They have a profound mistrust of the United States and its intimate relations with Israel and a belief that a power with some history of sympathy for the Palestinians must be involved to counterbalance the United States (and also to side with the Palestinians against Arab states such as Syria if necessary).

Given their negative perceptions of the Arab environment (rooted in unpleasant memories of the day-to-day treatment accorded them by various Arab regimes and the equally jaundiced outlook of PLO leaders, many of whom have spent time in Arab jails), given their skepticism as to the possibility of Israel's ending its occupation and accepting Palestinian self-rule in the near future, and given their assessment of the international balance, it can be seen why most Palestinians have limited expectations.

PLO Policymaking in Operation

Policymakers within the Palestinian community face obstacles to ordinary interaction with one another that may be unique. Although they have more contact today than they used to, there is no way in the occupied territories to meet regularly and in a structured way with others living in the diaspora. They have always been banned by the Israeli military occupation authorities from attending meetings of the PNC or of other formal PLO bodies and must obtain permission to travel abroad for any other purpose, which is frequently denied. Moreover, contact with PLO officials—indeed with anyone connected with what Israel defines as "terrorist organizations"—can be cause for prosecution by the occupation authorities.

Palestinians living outside their homeland also face difficulties in maintaining regular contacts with one another. In many cases their movement for purposes of PLO meetings is forbidden or restricted by Arab governments. On a more mundane level, the distances and expense often make frequent meetings difficult for those in the more distant parts of the diaspora. This situation has grown considerably worse since the 1982 war, which deprived the PLO of a fixed site for meetings, planning sessions, and informal encounters. No Arab capital where meetings have been held since 1982—Tunis, Amman, Baghdad, Algiers, Damascus, and Aden—has taken the place of Beirut in this respect, and the very multiplicity of headquarters and meeting sites has further complicated the situation.

In spite of these obstacles, Palestinian leaders have managed to make policy. It took ten months of preparatory meetings during 1984 in three different Arab capitals for the PLO to decide to hold the seventeenth PNC in Amman in November 1984, from which many groups and numerous independents abstained. Similarly, nearly four months of deliberations were necessary before the historic nineteenth PNC could be convened in Algiers in November 1988. The Amman PNC was the most decisive expression of the PLO's intention to try the abortive "Jordanian option." This strategy of focusing on Jordan and the occupied territories did not achieve its main objective, which was on the diplomatic level. But this meeting and the more intensive PLO presence in Jordan that followed, which in some measure survived King Hussein's February 1986 repudiation of his accord of a year earlier with Yasser Arafat, had other dividends. These included more extensive contact between PLO officials based in Jordan and people from the occupied territories, who can visit Amman with greater ease than any other Arab capital. Another was a tightening of links between the PLO and the over 1 million Palestinians in Jordan, the largest single concentration outside of Palestine.

The PNC is not the only policymaking forum of the PLO and is often not the most important. Although its approval is essential for major changes—such as the shift to a bistate solution in 1974 or in favor of the Jordanian option in 1984, or the historic declaration of independence of 1988—other levels of decisionmaking are more important for other sorts of issues.[8] The PLO has a three-tiered structure, with the large PNC at the base and above it the sixty-odd-member Central Council and the cabinet-sized Executive Committee, which is nominally responsible for supervising the organization's day-to-day business. The Executive Committee is often paralyzed or impelled to accept compromises unsatisfactory to all concerned by the divisions inherent in its nature as a sort of "coalition cabinet."

The same ills affect the PLO Central Council, which meets between the infrequent sessions of the PNC (nineteen PNCs were held over the first twenty-four years of the PLO's existence). Its task is to deliberate on policy, make recommendations, and assess the work of the Executive Committee. Although its political pronouncements can be significant at moments when a clear stand is required of the PLO, such as during the critical negotiations with the Carter administration in summer 1977, the Central Council has relatively limited importance.[9]

In fact, both the Central Council and the Executive Committee are less important than the Fateh Central Committee, currently composed of six members (of an original fifteen) elected in 1980, together with eight newly elected in 1989. This body has at its core a group of individuals around Yasser Arafat who founded the movement and who have been close collaborators since the late 1940s and early 1950s. Because of the power of Fateh and their strong cohesiveness, they have been the decisive leadership group in Palestinian politics for over a decade.[10] The Fateh Executive Committee sits atop a three-tiered structure analogous to that of the PLO; below are the large Fateh Conference (which has met only five times in the more than two decades of the movement's existence) and the smaller Revolutionary Council (which meets every few months to debate programs and strategy). Several of the elected members of the Revolutionary Council have influenced policy in the past, particularly during the pre-1982 war period. Many of them later joined the Fateh dissidents. Other groups like the PFLP and DFLP have similar structures.

How do these formal structures relate to the other leadership groups? Some of these groups intersect with the bodies just discussed. The PNC, the PLO Central Council, and the leading bodies of Fateh and other groups include a large number of union leaders, military officers, and student leaders as well as businesspeople, intellectuals, and community leaders. Many members of the last three categories do not actually belong to any of the constituent groups of the PLO and are described as "independents." Their input can at times be decisive, especially in PNC debates, where their attendance or absence is of great importance and their interventions are more eagerly awaited and listened to than the speeches of many leaders of the major organizations.

The biggest gap in all of this was the absence of formal representation of the over 1.5 million Palestinians living under occupation in the West Bank and Gaza Strip, because of the restrictions imposed upon them by the Israeli military authorities. Leaders expelled from these areas were frequently elected to posts in PLO bodies, but this representation could not substitute for full representation of their compatriots at every level of the PLO's structures. The inevitable result was a bias in favor of the interests of those living in the diaspora, who naturally had more numerous spokespersons than their counterparts from "the inside," as occupied Palestine is called by those in exile.

PLO leaders, notably those of Fateh, attempted in various ways to make up for the lack of balance resulting from the absence of representatives of the occupied territories. It can be argued that the "Jordanian option" and the holding of the seventeenth PNC in Amman, where the televised proceedings could be seen in the occupied territories, were in large measure devised to make up for this absence, although it is questionable whether they achieved much in this regard. Whatever the success of these and other attempts to achieve a better balance between the demands of their constituents "inside" and those "outside," there can be no doubt that this is an intractable structural problem facing leaders of the PLO, although the Unified National Leadership of the Uprising, which has emerged since late 1987, has apparently had considerable input into PLO decisionmaking since then.

There are other problems. Although much of the radical social content of the original ideologies of some PLO groups has diminished— the result of the increased responsibilities of power and the profound social transformations of the past two decades as the region has been affected by new oil wealth—social tensions still exist.[11] The wealthy Palestinian bankers, contractors, and business leaders, who are influential in the councils of the PLO and its constituent groups (including some of the ostensibly Marxist ones), are resented by union leaders, leftist students and intellectuals, and others committed to an egalitarian social philosophy. Conversely, the sometimes radical rhetoric of the PLO, adopted to placate the latter groups, can be offensive to some prosperous Palestinians as well as to a segment of the large middle class. This is another continuing problem in a broadly based national movement that seeks to avoid alienating any major element of its popular constituency.

In addition to such serious and enduring contradictions within the Palestinian polity, there are others. They include personality disputes between leaders, some of them going back for decades, and others between PLO leaders and the rulers of some Arab states. These often mask real conflicts of interest, whether between different Palestinian groups or between the PLO and certain Arab regimes. At other times nothing substantial is involved. Conflicts between PLO groups, especially those involving the very small ones with no base of popular support, can sometimes be explained by looking at the position of their Arab-state patrons. The dissidence within the PLO since 1983 owes much, but of course not all, of its persistence to the support of Syria and Libya. Palestinian history is full of such cases, an important earlier one being Amir Abdallah's support for the Nashashibi faction against the mainstream of the nationalist movement during the British mandatory period.

Key PLO Policy Decisions

Given such a complex of obstacles, restraints, and divisions, how do the Palestinians manage to make policy? The easiest way to answer this question is to examine briefly a number of policy decisions of recent years: the 1973–1974 shift toward accepting a bistate solution, as enshrined in the twelfth PNC resolutions of 1974; responses to military pressures from the Maronite right-wing parties and from Syria during the two-year Lebanese war of 1975–1976; the south Lebanon cease-fire decisions of 1978 and 1981; and the 1984 convocation of the PNC in Amman with the shift to the Jordanian option this implied. Although it is not possible to discuss each in depth, I sketch here the key factors contributing to the policy that eventually emerged.[12]

The PLO Shift Toward Accepting a Bistate Solution

The debate leading to the 1974 modification of the PLO's aims and objectives is often described as having been provoked by the 1973 war and by the prospects for a regional settlement that it opened up. In fact, this debate preceded the war by many months, with an intensive dialogue taking place in public forums, at universities and in refugee camps in Lebanon, in publications like *Shu'un Filistiniyya* and *Filistin al-Thawra*, and within the leaderships of various groups throughout 1972 and 1973.[13]

What concerns us is not the terms of the debate but the roles played by the various parties to it. Publicly, the first proposals were made by the DFLP, with a number of intellectuals and cadres affiliated with Fateh taking up the call for a more flexible strategy for addressing the problem of the West Bank and Gaza Strip. In this they were supported by the Syrian-backed al-Saiqa group, particularly after the 1973 war, which signaled Syria's shift toward a strategy of negotiation with Israel for evacuation from the territories occupied in 1967.

Much of the opposition to this new approach was predictable, including that of the PFLP and other groups backed by the then-uncompromising Iraqis (which were later to form the core of the Rejection Front opposing the bistate solution adopted by the PNC in 1974). Perhaps the most significant opposition, however, came from within Fateh. Leading intellectuals and writers like Naji Alloush and Munir Shafiq, as well as officials in the Fateh information branch and many military officers, opposed any deviation from the idea of total liberation of Palestine without any compromise with Israel.

The Fateh leadership, which was fully committed to the new approach, finessed the internal Fateh opposition by aligning itself with other groups such as the DFLP; by removing many opposing officials from positions of influence, especially in the Fateh information department, which was merged with that of the PLO; and finally by appealing directly to broader Palestinian public opinion. This approach culminated at the twelfth PNC after the 1973 war had transformed the diplomatic situation in the region, opening up the prospect of a negotiated settlement of the Arab-Israeli conflict.

At the twelfth PNC in Cairo in June 1974, the Fateh leadership still had to deal with the PFLP and other smaller groups opposed to the new approach, but Fateh had by then thoroughly established the primacy of the new political line within its own organization. As a result, the leaders were able to obtain resolutions that allowed the PLO to move toward playing a role in a negotiated settlement, an idea that would have been anathema only four years earlier. The need to compromise with the PFLP and its allies meant, however, that the resolutions were far more equivocal than advocates of the new line would have wished. The efforts to placate the PFLP dissidents later proved futile when they formed the Rejection Front, abandoning temporarily their Executive Committee seat.

As for Fateh, most critics remained within the movement, some coming to accept the *sulta wataniyya* (national authority) concept for a bistate solution put forth by the twelfth PNC, and others continuing to reject it, but keeping their dissent within limits. The most notable exception was Sabri al-Banna (Abu Nidal), who openly split with Fateh and the PLO early during this debate, calling the new policy treasonous from his base in Baghdad. Much later, in 1983, other prominent Fateh critics rebelled against their leadership, this time with Syrian backing. In the interim, they continued to play important roles in the movement, their dissent notwithstanding.

The key achievement of the Fateh leaders in overcoming powerful dissension within their organization and in other PLO groups was to deal first with the opposition in their own power base, Fateh, without overt repression and later to take a unified movement into larger forums like the PNC where it had many allies. Among them were a number of independents, who approved the new flexible strategy. Their argument was that such a strategy was imperative so as to show the population of the West Bank and Gaza Strip that the PLO was concerned with their problems and also to prevent King Hussein from speaking for these territories in post–1973 war negotiations. The twelfth PNC resolutions were of help in getting Arab support at the Rabat summit of 1974 for the declaration that the PLO is the sole legitimate representative of the Palestinian people because these resolutions brought the PLO into step with the diplomatic strategy of the then-paramount Arab states, Egypt, Syria, and Saudi Arabia, and with that of the USSR.

PLO Responses to Right-Wing and Syrian Military Pressures

If the 1973–1974 policymaking process satisfied large numbers of Palestinians without alienating most others and improved the PLO's diplomatic position, the critical decisions about how to respond to the first phase of the Lebanese conflict in 1975–1976 had far less satisfactory results on all levels. In fact, the PLO was in a no-win situation. It had decisively alienated the Maronite parties of the Lebanese Front (LF), which dominated Lebanon and saw the PLO as a threat to the status quo. In self-defense, the PLO had allied itself with the leftist and Muslim factions of the Lebanese National Movement (LNM), headed by Kamal Jumblatt, which were not able or willing to overturn that status quo.[14]

The LF would not rest until it had defeated the PLO-LNM coalition or dragged in the Lebanese army, the Western powers, Israel, or Syria to do the job. Although it failed in its own attempts to achieve decisive military results, the LF did provoke repeated rounds of the war in 1975 and early 1976. In the end, most of the forces it tried to win over as allies against the PLO and the LNM did become involved, but that story goes far beyond 1975–1976.[15]

Against the Maronite right wing, weak in demographic and military terms but strong in external allies, was pitted the LNM, supported by a large majority of Lebanon's population but much less united or well organized than the LF. The Lebanese left and Muslims could not agree on whether to seek an advantageous political compromise with their conservative Maronite adversaries or to attempt to achieve a victory on the battlefield, hoping to enlist the PLO (and at an early stage, Syria) on their side in this effort.

In this situation the PLO faced a dilemma. On the one hand, Fateh leaders and those of their advisers who had some understanding of the realities of Lebanon realized that to fight alongside the LNM would drag the Palestinians into an endless morass. On the other, vocal elements among the populace in the camps, many cadres, fighters and officers, and some elements of the Fateh leadership, as well as the PFLP and some of the smaller groups, were firmly convinced that only the resolute use of force would solve the problem.

In the end the PLO chose the worst possible course, employing some feeble diplomacy with the Maronites and later with the Syrians when they began to move toward intervening against the PLO and the LNM on behalf of the beleaguered LF. It was not enough, however, to overcome the deep mistrust that had grown up in the years preceding the conflict. Worse, it was mixed with instances of the employment of force in a way that conveyed conflicting signals but was in turn not sufficient to achieve decisive results.

The most striking example of all these factors was the spring 1976 offensive, launched first by Jumblatt but later joined by the PLO, which brought to it the seasoned forces, the artillery, and the logistics necessary for an advance through well-defended mountainous terrain along a

limited number of road axes. Although the PLO leaders supported
Jumblatt in this initially successful attack, which put an end to hopes
of a Syrian-mediated political solution, they did not commit sufficient
forces to sustain the momentum of the drive. And although they tried
to avoid alienating the Syrians, mediating between them and Junblatt,
they failed to assuage the Assad regime's concern or to deter it from
intervening militarily in June 1976 against them and their LNM allies.

The pressures that forced the top PLO leadership (which tended
toward avoiding involvement) to take this course of equivocation were
primarily internal and Lebanese, and by and large they converged. A
hard line was advocated by most PLO military officers, militia leaders,
and full-time cadres (who were mobilized militarily and whose numbers
increased during the fighting) and by much of the population of the
camps, whose morale became a primary consideration as the war dragged
on. As the conflict grew increasingly savage, and especially after atrocities
like Black Saturday in December 1975 and the Karantina/Maslakh and
Dbaye massacres in January 1976, it became hard to justify a policy of
conciliation with the LF.

At the same time, many Lebanese leftist and Muslim leaders and
many of the Lebanese media pressured the PLO to become more deeply
involved in the struggle and were unwilling to contemplate a political
resolution of the conflict. Thus the PLO leadership was caught between
its knowledge that little positive could come from further escalation and
the belief of many elements among its organized Palestinian political
base in Lebanon and its Lebanese allies that the contrary was the case.

Some leaders, especially Arafat and Abu Jihad, remained unen-
thusiastic about the idea of a military solution and feared Syria's reaction.
They were balanced by others, such as Abu Iyyad, who were located
in Beirut where political pressures to act decisively were most intense.
And all were pushed by more radical PLO groups and by the LNM,
which saw the LF attacks on the PLO as an opportunity to cooperate
with the PLO in a struggle to restructure the Lebanese system. The
result was a policy that fully satisfied no one, failed to prevent continuation
of the war or to achieve victory, and left the PLO much weakened. It
should be added, however, that although full conciliation or total war
would have produced different results, it is unlikely they would have
been much better.

The South Lebanon Cease-Fire Decisions
of 1978 and 1981

Although made under intense military pressure, both cease-fires
were easier decisions than those we have already examined. In March

1978, UN Security Council resolution 425 calling for a cease-fire and Israeli withdrawal from Lebanon was accepted by the PLO after some initial hesitation, in spite of the strong opposition of some within the movement. This was the first time the PLO had accepted a cease-fire with Israel, and the idea was heresy to those who believed that the PLO should seek to engage Israel constantly and that compromise with it was out of the question.

It was an indication of how far the leadership had moved its followers in the direction of compromise since 1973–1974 that most of the PLO rank and file accepted this revolutionary departure from orthodoxy without demur. The only dissidents (two of them Fateh leaders) were a group linked to Abu Nidal that attempted to organize violations of the cease-fire, but this group was suppressed by Fateh security forces.[16] For most Palestinians, the benefits of being treated as a full-scale belligerent by the UN and of seeing the PLO's situation in south Lebanon regularized outweighed any disadvantages. Given this background, it is easy to understand how in the wake of fierce Israeli attacks on targets in Lebanon, the PLO leadership was able to accept a July 1981 cease-fire after UN and Saudi mediation with the United States and Israel. In this case there was even less opposition than in 1978, with none from within Fateh and only the insignificant PFLP–General Command headed by Ahmed Jibril refusing to abide by the cease-fire. After a "very frank" discussion at a meeting with Arafat, Jibril backed down.[17]

In both of these instances, the PLO leadership had tried to parlay its military position into a diplomatic asset, in effect winning recognition by the UN as a full belligerent alongside Israel, in the wake of indirect contacts with the United States. These results were sufficient for the PLO to justify to its rank and file followers breaking off a military engagement with Israel. But in both cases it is questionable whether the PLO was in any position to do otherwise without grave consequences, given the military realities on the battlefield. Moreover, recognition as a belligerent and indirect contacts with the United States still left the PLO far from its objectives of recognition by the United States and involvement in negotiations as a full party. The convoluted negotiations during the 1982 war had the same disappointing results for the PLO.[18]

The 1984 PNC in Amman

The results of holding the seventeenth PNC in Amman were the same. The PLO failed to achieve U.S. recognition or to become an equal party to the Middle East settlement process as was hoped when the Jordanian option was first proposed. In spite of intense opposition within Fateh when the idea was first raised in early 1982 and again in April

1983 when it helped provoke a major split in the movement, the core Fateh leadership was single-minded in pursuing this course to its unsuccessful end. It was deterred neither by the threat of a split, which took place in mid-1983, nor by Syrian opposition.

Arafat showed great flexibility in dealing with his Central Committee colleagues who had doubts about the feasibility or political wisdom of the approach. He also showed himself willing to make concessions to other groups, as in the 1984 Aden-Algiers accords with other PLO factions, which broke down in the end because of Syrian pressure. The seventeenth PNC was thereafter held in Amman without these groups, primarily because it was felt that a large majority of Palestinians, notably those under occupation and in Jordan, were in favor. The failure of this PNC and of the 1985 Arafat-Hussein accord to achieve U.S. recognition doomed the Jordanian option, which in any case was torpedoed by Hussein's abrogation of the accord in 1986 in the face of U.S.-Israeli rejection of this approach.

The 1987 and 1988 Algiers PNCs and Beyond

The flexibility of the core PLO leadership was clearly demonstrated in the wake of the fiasco of the Jordanian option. Reversing course, Arafat and his colleagues set about reunifying the PLO, helped in this by the strong sense of solidarity felt by most Palestinians because of the Syrian-backed Amal movement's siege of the camps in Lebanon.

The result was the eighteenth PNC, held in April 1987 in Algiers, where the Jordanian option was formally buried and where the PFLP and the DFLP rejoined the leading bodies of the PLO. Although some attempt was made at this PNC to move toward a political posture that might involve the PLO in negotiations for a Middle East settlement, the hostile attitude of the Reagan administration to the PLO precluded any progress along these lines. The major achievement of the eighteenth PNC was that it reunified the PLO after four years of dissension and signified the failure both of a majority within the movement to align it with Jordan and of a minority to align it with Syria.

This reunification in turn made it possible for the PLO to respond politically in a relatively coherent, if belated, fashion to the uprising that erupted in the occupied territories in late 1987. The PLO's response was precipitated both by pressure from the new Unified National Leadership of the Uprising, representing all the local organizations of the PLO factions in the occupied territories as well as some Islamic groups, and by King Hussein's July 1988 decision to sever his country's links with the West Bank. The PLO now had to fill a potential vacuum and to respond to the demands of its supporters in the occupied territories who had achieved new legitimacy through their successful launching of the uprising.

The nineteenth PNC, held in Algiers in November 1988, issued a declaration of independence proclaiming Palestinian sovereignty over the occupied territories, intended to fill the vacuum created by Hussein's move. It also approved a new political program meant to provide a platform for the PLO to join settlement negotiations and to make possible the opening of a dialogue with the United States. These documents were remarkable in a number of ways: in accepting the 1947 partition resolution as a basis in international law for a Palestinian state (and thereby formally and explicitly accepting partition for the first time); in not mentioning the Palestinian National Covenant of 1964 or armed struggle; and in calling for "a political settlement of the Arab-Israeli conflict," involving an independent Palestinian state and "arrangements for the security and peace of all states in the region."[19]

These resolutions provided the basis for the moves made by Yasser Arafat in the following month in Stockholm and Geneva, which resulted in the U.S.-PLO dialogue. Unfortunately, the resolutions of the nineteenth PNC and Arafat's subsequent statements, amounting to what the Palestinians came to call their "peace initiative," resulted in little more of substance than this abortive U.S.-PLO dialogue. This dialogue of the deaf, whose lack of progress had increasingly frustrated a PLO leadership which had committed its political prestige to a breakthrough in the negotiating process, was broken off after eighteen fruitless months by President Bush in June 1990 in response to the May 30 attack on Tel Aviv by a Baghdad-based Palestinian group.

The impasse in the Arab-Israeli peace process symbolized by the break-off of this dialogue provided the somber backdrop against which the crisis in the Gulf degenerated into war. This crisis put the PLO's leaders into one of the most difficult dilemmas of their political careers. It imposed on them choices they clearly did not want to make between aligning the PLO with the United States and its Arab clients or with Iraq and between responding either to the cold dictates of caution in the face of the lopsided balance of power in favor of the former or to overwhelming Palestinian popular sentiment against the United States and Israel.[20] The choices they made (which were more equivocal and nuanced than they were made to appear by U.S. media already in the grip of war fever) may have cost the life of one of the PLO's historic leaders, Abu Iyyad, assassinated in Tunis in January 1991. These choices will in any case have a profound and lasting impact on the Palestinian polity—whether in the occupied territories, Jordan, the Gulf, or Lebanon—and perhaps on the PLO leadership itself.

A Concluding Word

It is fitting to end a discussion of Palestinian policymaking by noting that what is lacking in this process is not the will to make decisions or to carry them through. There have been instances when this was the case, but it is important in each to assess the domestic factors restraining PLO leaders and the benefits or drawbacks for them of a given course. Often, their choices have been among a range of bad options. Above and beyond this, however, are the problems of policymaking in a physically fragmented polity involved in a halting process of reconstruction after a series of reverses going back a half century. Given this background, it is a not inconsiderable achievement that coherent policymaking has been possible for the Palestinians.

Notes

1. Joan Peters, in *From Time Immemorial* (New York: Harper and Row, 1984), enunciates this theory. Such views are also expressed in such publications as *The New Republic, Commentary, Midstream,* and *Orbis,* as well as by the American Professors for Peace in the Middle East.

2. Scholars who have done so include Yehoshua Porath, Abdel Latif Tibawi, Moshe Ma'oz, Joel Migdal, Mark Heller, Laurie Brand, Emile Sahliyeh, and William Quandt.

3. Three recent biographies are Alan Hart, *Arafat: Terrorist or Peacemaker?* 2d ed. (Bloomington: Indiana University Press, 1989); Abu Iyyad with Eric Rouleau, *My Home, My Land: A Narrative of the Palestinian Struggle* (New York: Times Books, 1981); and Fu'ad Matar, *Hakim al-Thawra: Qissat hayat al-doktor George Habash* (Wise man of the revolution: The biography of Dr. George Habash) (London: Highlight, 1984). See also Walid Kazziha, *Revolutionary Transformation in the Arab World: Habash and His Comrades from Nationalism to Marxism* (London: Charles Knight, 1975).

4. This is the thesis of the work of Helena Cobban, *The Palestinian Liberation Organization: People, Power and Politics* (Cambridge: Cambridge University Press, 1984), and is sustained by others such as Alain Gresh, *The PLO, The Struggle Within: Toward an Independent Palestinian State* (London: Zed, 1985); and David Hirst, *The Gun and The Olive Branch: The Roots of Violence in the Middle East,* 2d ed. (London: Faber, 1984).

5. This underrated episode is covered by Cobban, *The Palestinian Liberation Organization,* p. 90.

6. For more details, see Rashid Khalidi, "Le Liban et les Palestiniens," in Bassma Kodmani-Darwish, ed., *Le Liban: Espoirs et Réalités* (Paris: Institut Francais de Relations Internationales, 1987), pp. 135–152.

7. Interview with former Labor party Knesset member Abd al-Wahhab Darawsheh, New York, June 1986.

8. Cheryl Rubenberg, *The PLO: Its Institutional Infrastructure* (Belmont, Mass.: Institute for Arab Studies, 1983).

9. Cobban, *The Palestinian Liberation Organization,* pp. 89–92.

10. This leadership is described by Cobban, ibid.; Hart, *Arafat;* and Gresh, *The PLO;* as well as by Rashid Khalidi, *Under Siege: PLO Decisionmaking During the 1982 War* (New York: Columbia University Press, 1985).

11. On this subject, see Nadine Picadou, "La bourgeoisie palestinienne et l'industrie. Étude socio-historique," in *Industrialisation et changements sociaux dans l'Orient arabe* (Beirut: CERMOC, 1982); on the impact of oil wealth generally, see Rashid Khalidi, "Social Transformations in the 'Radical' Arab States," in I. William Zartman and A. I. Dawisha, eds., *Nation, State, and Integration in the Arab World,* vol. 3 (Syracuse, N.Y.: Syracuse University Press, 1988), pp. 203–219.

12. For an in-depth discussion of another set of decisions—the response to pressures on the PLO to evacuate Beirut during the 1982 war—see Khalidi, *Under Siege.*

13. This is well explained, with substantial documentation, in Gresh, *The PLO,* parts 2–4, pp. 59–175.

14. The 1975–1976 phase of the Lebanon war is covered by Kamal Salibi, *Crossroads to Civil War: Lebanon 1958–1976* (New York: Caravan, 1976); Walid Khalidi, *Conflict and Violence in Lebanon* (Cambridge, Mass.: Harvard Center for International Affairs, 1979); A. Dawisha, *Syria and the Lebanese Crisis* (London: Macmillan, 1980); and Itamar Rabinovich, *The War for Lebanon, 1970–83* (Ithaca, N.Y.: Cornell University Press, 1984).

15. See Jonathan Randal, *Going All the Way,* rev. ed. (New York: Vintage, 1983).

16. Cobban, *The Palestinian Liberation Organization,* pp. 94–97.

17. Ibid., p. 112.

18. Khalidi, *Under Siege.* Chap. 1 deals with the 1978–1981 period; the remaining chapters show how the PLO tried to achieve the same end during the 1982 war and failed.

19. For texts of these resolutions, see *Journal of Palestine Studies* 18, no. 2 (Winter 1989), pp. 213–223.

20. Evidence of this reluctance can be seen in the PLO statement of August 19, 1990, in *Journal of Palestine Studies* 20, no. 1 (Autumn 1990), pp. 165–168, which sets forth the reasoning for the PLO's stand in the Gulf crisis and has received little of the attention it deserves.

5
The Domestic Foundations of Israeli Foreign Policy

Naomi Chazan

The Changing Political Arena

Israeli politics in the 1980s has been viewed in several distinct and often contradictory manners. Because the view other countries take of the politics of Israeli foreign policymaking significantly affects their policies toward Israel, it is vital to review prevailing perspectives and to explore more fully the dynamics of Israeli politics and the elements which produce change in Israel.

One approach sees the political arena, despite its internal diversity, in essentially monolithic terms. From this perspective, Israeli society is said to have congealed through historical experience and situational circumstances into an intransigent entity totally preoccupied with its own survival. Policymaking is therefore inherently inflexible and static; changes in personae or party alignments cannot be expected to alter what is fundamentally a unidimensional picture with few prospects for change.

A second approach speaks of a political arena in a state of constant flux. It suggests that in a highly fragmented society wracked by fractious disputes, unity on critical issues is well-nigh unobtainable. From this vantage point fluidity has stamped Israeli politics with a dreary immobility marked by procrastination and programmatic stalemate. In the eyes of the upholders of this position, a more conciliatory Israeli policy must await a prolonged process of domestic reorientation and consolidation.

Neither of these images holds forth the promise of substantial change in the foreseeable future; neither is distinguished by empirical precision or analytical subtlety; neither is particularly helpful to understanding the structures and variations that exist in the Israeli context; and neither provides an accurate indication of concrete policy options.

In fact, recent Israeli political history has been characterized not only by a basic coherence but also by significant changes in form, content, and direction. Any serious attempt to come to terms with the dynamics of political life must address both the framework and the mutations that make up the contemporary political experience in the country.

This task is particularly urgent at the beginning of the 1990s in light of substantial changes in the geopolitics of the Arab-Israeli conflict (the Palestinian uprising which began in December 1987, the renunciation by Jordan of claims to the occupied territories, the revised Palestine Liberation Organization stance in the aftermath of the Algiers summit of November 1988, the change in the U.S. position toward the PLO, and the Iraqi invasion of Kuwait and the Gulf crisis). The time is therefore ripe to review the fundamental components that influence Israeli decisionmaking, to examine how they have altered during the 1980s, and to outline their implications for foreign policy formulation and interaction.

The conduct of Israel's international relations and the capacity of its leaders to respond to initiatives from abroad have been consistently molded by three domestic factors: (1) the structure and composition of political institutions; (2) social differentiation and the concern of specific groups; and (3) the substance of political debates and their relation to fundamental ideological concerns. The purpose of this chapter is to examine each of these elements for continuities, areas of change during the course of the 1980s, and ramifications for foreign policy orientations. Because the interactions among these forces help to define the dynamics of Israeli politics and by extension Israel's regional and international stance, it will be possible to offer several alternative scenarios for the direction of Israel's external relations in the near future.

The main contention of this analysis is that Israeli responses to external stimuli are filtered through a domestic political lens which operates according to its own distinctive rules. The degree of cooperation among coalition members and officeholders, the extent of social friction, and the scope of ideological polarization have an important bearing on foreign policy decisions. Because domestic considerations are predominant, and these in turn determine the mind-set of decisionmakers, the capacity of Israeli foreign policy to go beyond the reactive depends on the amount of consensus in decisionmaking circles.[1] Although shifting constellations in the international arena and significant changes in the policies of regional actors may narrow the range of options available to Israeli leaders, the substance of these overtures may be less significant than the way in which they impinge on domestic political processes.

Thus, Israel responded decisively to the 1973 war because the issue of survival is an unshakable pillar of the Israeli worldview. The Israeli-Egyptian peace negotiations (which subsequently had an important impact

on internal political developments) could be conducted relatively expeditiously because they took place at a major turning point in Israeli
political history. In contrast, official reactions to the repercussions of the
1982 invasion of Lebanon or to the Palestinian uprising (intifada) were
far more hesitant because these events highlighted contradictions in the
Israeli body politic and impeded the elaboration of innovative Israeli
initiatives.

Indeed, the Palestinian-Israeli conflict, progressively internalized
on the societal level, has remained external to the political system that
has primary responsibility for coming to terms with its various manifestations. The policy aspects of the Palestinian question and its relationship to the Arab-Israeli conflict have continued to be seen as a
matter of security and foreign affairs, handled according to the principles
guiding the determination of external relations in the past.

Israeli politics underwent four separate stages during the 1980s.[2]
The first Likud government (1977–1981) was characterized by diplomatic
achievements coupled with the emergence of profound domestic schisms;
the second Likud administration (1981–1984) coincided with a period
of domestic stagnation and external adventurism in the form of the
Lebanese invasion; the first national unity government (1984–1988) was
marked by a modicum of domestic stabilization coupled with ambiguity
on the external front; and the second national unity government (1988–
1990) magnified uncertainty in policymaking quarters and accentuated
the extent of divisions within the Israeli polity.[3] A right-wing coalition
led by the Likud assumed office in May 1990; its orientation, at the
time of this writing, was still unclear.

By the end of the decade Israeli society, far more contentious and
conflict-ridden than in the past, was also less capable of influencing
decisions in the realm of security and foreign affairs.[4] Moreover, despite
shifts in the structure of political alignments and in the relative autonomy
of cabinet members, the ability of state institutions to implement their
own policies was severely curtailed. A process of power deflation had
set in, with serious consequences for foreign policy.

Delving into the intricacies of contemporary Israeli politics is a
precondition for comprehending the direction of change within Israel
and constitutes the crucial first step in the formulation of original
measures for the resolution of conflict in the area. Because Israel's external
outlook and the possibilities open to the international community in
relating to Israel are determined to no mean degree by domestic configurations, a more careful look at Israeli political dynamics is vital to
any projection of prospects for change in the Middle East.

Domestic Determinants of Foreign Policy

The 1980s were an unsettling decade in Israel's political history. Shifts in the domestic balance of power altered the contours of social alliances and fostered uncertainty on the party scene. The unpredictability of electoral support and the precariousness of ruling coalitions reduced the inclination of political leaders to depart from declared positions and adversely affected their innovative capacities in matters of security and foreign affairs.

Political Structures

Israeli foreign policy initiatives and responses to external overtures are mediated by a complicated network of internal mechanisms. The heterogeneous interests of the various segments of Israel's population are channeled through the democratic institutions that have evolved since the creation of the state in 1948. These structures provide a clearinghouse for competing factions, their operations define the norms of political behavior, and their composition helps determine policy guidelines.

Israel's parliamentary democracy is based on the sovereignty of its national assembly, the Knesset.[5] Its 120 members are elected by a method of proportional representation, the entire country constituting a single constituency. Ballots are cast for parties, not for individuals. Each party sends to the Knesset a number of representatives (drawn from an ordered list of candidates compiled on the eve of elections) in direct proportion to the percentage of the total vote it receives. Although this system faithfully reflects diverse strands in the population, it also discourages individual competition and nurtures a multiplicity of parties (only 1 percent of the vote is needed to obtain a Knesset seat).

It is hardly surprising under these circumstances that no party has received an absolute majority in any of the twelve elections held since 1948. The creation of a government has relied on delicate coalitions cemented by trade-offs between potential partners. Consequently, most cabinets have been overinflated in size, and smaller parties have frequently been allotted disproportionate favors in return for the parliamentary backing necessary to maintain the balance of power. Such a system is inherently precarious and unwieldy.

The makeup of the coalition, the strength of its leading party, the cohesion of its members, and the capacities of its leaders have therefore dictated both the thrust and the effectiveness of the policy decisions of any government. This has been particularly true in the sphere of foreign affairs because although international issues have rarely impinged on elections and external orientations have usually not hampered coalition building,[6] the party composition of individual governments has traditionally constrained foreign policy options and clearly delimited the boundaries of the possible at any juncture.

In this setting, major policy decisions, particularly those relating to peace and security issues, have been the domain of a small inner circle of cabinet members. The prime minister (who, in the past, often also held the position of either minister of defense or minister of foreign affairs) has been ultimately responsible for foreign relations. The concentration of foreign policy has therefore gone hand in hand with its personalization: Each prime minister, from David Ben-Gurion to Shimon Peres and Yitzhak Shamir, has placed his or her own peculiar stamp on Israel's external alliances. The relationship between the prime minister, the minister of defense, and the foreign minister has dictated the room for maneuverability available in the foreign policy sphere. As long as prime ministers maintained control over key officeholders and by extension over their coalition partners, they could conduct the country's foreign relations without curtailment by the Knesset (especially through its Defense and Foreign Affairs Committee), the professional diplomatic corps, the growing number of vociferous extraparliamentary groups, or external actors. Their incorporation of demands stemming from any of these sources has depended on immediate political exigencies, ideological preferences, personal relationships, and (perhaps most significantly in recent years) some evaluation of the repercussions of particular measures on their electoral constituencies, on powerful and potentially recalcitrant segments of the social order, and on public opinion more generally. The mechanisms for foreign-policy making have been less institutionalized than virtually any other sphere of Israeli politics.

The factors governing the foreign policymaking process have been particularly mutable since 1977. On the external front, the pace of changes in the geopolitics of the region presented pressing challenges to Israeli policymakers, beginning with the Sadat initiative and culminating with the intifada and the Gulf crisis. Domestically, the party scene, the composition of ruling coalitions, and the political leadership underwent substantial transformation and vacillation (partly as a result of processes set in motion by decisions on security and foreign affairs). As the prospects for some resolution of the Arab-Israeli conflict, viewed from outside, improved, the ability of Israeli policymakers to respond creatively to changing conditions diminished.

The first sign of a more profound reordering of the structure of Israeli politics occurred in 1977, when the thirty-year hegemony of the Labor party was brought to an end with the victory of the Likud in the May elections. The Labor Alignment (Maarach), the founding establishment of the Israeli polity, lays claim to the socialist-Zionist tradition. Its members have propagated welfare-state principles on social and economic matters, defended the need for security while exploring ways for a negotiated resolution of the conflict, and generally favored the exchange of territories for peace in the post-1967 period. During the first three decades of Israeli independence, Labor relied on the electoral support of the urban professional and middle class, the cooperative agriculture sector, older voters, citizens of European (Ashkenazi) origin, and new immigrants. By 1977, however, the Labor party had lost much of its initial zeal and hence electoral appeal. The original founders of the state had been replaced by a second generation of leaders (Yitzhak Rabin, Shimon Peres, Yitzhak Navon) who did not succeed in rejuvenating the party, enhancing its responsiveness to social currents in the country, increasing its efficiency, or designing a cohesive political agenda. In the 1977 elections, Labor suffered from the disaffection of some of its traditional voters, many of whom turned to the newly formed Democratic Movement for Change, a centrist agglomeration which ran on a platform of electoral reform.

The Likud, a composite of various parties (especially Herut and the Liberals), is an outgrowth of revisionist Zionism. During its decades on the political sidelines, its leaders refined their liberal economic outlooks and the theoretical basis for their support of the notion of a "Greater Land of Israel" encompassing the West Bank and the Gaza Strip. This hawkish position on questions of peace and security, coupled with an increasingly vocal attack on the Labor establishment, fell on the receptive ears of residents of development towns and the poorer neighborhoods of the larger cities, largely drawn from lower socioeconomic groups, small-business owners, youth, and citizens of oriental and African (Sephardi) extraction. In the 1977 elections, the Likud received 43 mandates (up from 39 in 1973), which, given Labor's drop from 51 to 32 seats, sufficed to make it the largest party in the Knesset and to enable it to form the first non-Labor government in the history of the country.

The cabinet formed by Menachem Begin in 1977 consisted of a coalition of the Likud, the Democratic Movement for Change (DMC), the National Religious Party, and several small factions. Although this government represented a clear swing to the right, it was fairly heterogeneous in composition and consisted of a large group of ministers unfamiliar with the tasks of governance. To enhance governmental effectiveness, Menachem Begin appointed the experienced Moshe Dayan as minister for foreign affairs and Ezer Weizman as minister of defense, thus adding to the political diversity of the new ruling alliance. The personal relationship between the top three members of the first Likud administration was tenuous at best, but for a variety of different reasons, each had an interest in promoting substantial policy changes during his first year in office.

Anwar Sadat's dramatic visit to Jerusalem in November 1977 provided this opportunity. To be sure, the commencement of the Camp David negotiations in spring 1978 aroused considerable domestic dissent.[7] But Labor was effectively neutralized because the Likud proposals were substantially in line with its own platform, and within the Likud, ultranationalists were caught between their desire to retain the power they had only just achieved and their adherence to their political principles. Extraparliamentary movements, galvanized at this juncture, proved that their actual impact on the decisionmaking process was much more limited than they claimed. Gush Emunim (the Bloc of the Faithful), established in 1974, had acted as the main impetus for the acceleration of Jewish settlement in the West Bank and in Gaza. Together with the Committee Against the Withdrawal from Sinai and Rabbi Meir Kahane's Kach movement, it lobbied against the proposed agreements. On the other hand, in early 1978 a group of young reserve officers formed Peace Now, which became one of the strongest proponents of the accords.

Menachem Begin and his top ministers withstood these pressures not only because they canceled each other out to a large extent but also because, united in their understanding of the historical significance and the political implications of achieving a peace treaty with Egypt, they were able to maneuver deftly within a rare set of domestic political circumstances conducive to their cause. The negotiation process was prolonged and at times difficult, however, precisely because of the separate agendas of the key Israeli bargaining partners.[8] The agreements reached at Camp David consequently included phraseology and principles designed to address local concerns.

The Knesset ratification of the Egyptian-Israeli peace accords in 1979[9] brought this responsive phase of Israeli foreign policymaking to a close. First, the major coalition partners were wracked by internal schisms. The DMC split and bolted the government. The opponents of the agreements in the Likud formed the Tehiya. The National Religious Party (NRP) lost some of its strength to dissident factions. And Labor was substantially enfeebled. Second, both Ezer Weizman and Moshe Dayan resigned following disputes on the conduct of the autonomy talks. Their replacements, Yitzhak Shamir in the foreign ministry and Ariel Sharon in the defense ministry, had opposed the Egyptian-Israeli accords and were not disposed to pursuing the peace momentum. And third, the numerical base of the first Likud administration in the Knesset narrowed considerably. With the strength of the leading party precarious, the stability of the cabinet dependent on parochial parties, and key cabinet members firmly committed to nationalist-revisionist orientations, a period of entrenchment on the foreign policy front ensued.

This phase lasted through the 1981 elections, which were preceded by an acrimonious campaign punctuated by blatant ethnic mobilization and militaristic adventurism in the form of the bombing of the Osirak, the Iraqi nuclear reactor. The Likud succeeded in garnering 48 seats to Labor's 47, but it lost votes to right-wing parties (Tehiya and Morasha, a nationalist-religious NRP breakaway faction formed by key Gush Emunim personalities) and to ethnic factions (Tami). Because the 1981 ballot highlighted the polarization between the two major electoral alignments,[10] parliamentary support for the second Likud administration (based on a narrow coalition of religious and hawkish parties) was confined and the government was far less accessible than its predecessor. For the making of foreign policy, this fact, coupled with the high degree of ideological cohesion within the narrow coalition, meant that the government enjoyed a particularly large measure of decisionmaking autonomy. Because Menachem Begin came to rely increasingly on Ariel Sharon, both strategically and politically, it was possible for the top leadership to bypass cabinet procedures on the assumption that approval would be forthcoming retroactively.

The second Likud administration was therefore, in all probability, simultaneously the least responsive and the most externally aggressive of all Israeli governments. In late 1981 the new government flaunted international conventions and imposed Israeli law on the Golan Heights. In June 1982 Sharon and Begin launched the invasion of Lebanon, attempting to alter the balance of political power in that country, eradicate the military base of the PLO, remove Syria from the Lebanese equation, and, not coincidentally, consolidate Israel's hold over the West Bank.[11] Initial domestic support for the Israeli venture, as in previous wars, was high, but opposition grew when the political objectives of the operation were revealed and it became increasingly apparent that the Lebanese incursion, far from achieving its declared goals, actually exacerbated the situation and embroiled Israel in a morass beyond its control.[12]

The insulated and militaristic configuration which had initiated the Lebanon operation broke up in the aftermath of the Sabra and Shatila massacres, the subsequent hearings of the Kahan commission, the forced resignation of Ariel Sharon from the defense ministry following the publication of the commission's findings, and the sudden retirement of Menachem Begin.[13] Yitzhak Shamir as Begin's replacement and Moshe Arens in the defense ministry were unwilling, if not incapable, of undertaking any serious initiatives in the foreign policy arena. With public tensions on the rise, the economy in disrepair, and the coalition in disarray, they were hard-pressed to retain a modicum of domestic order, let alone formulate decisive positions on the external front.[14]

The last year of the second Likud administration magnified the extent of political fragmentation in the country. Because parties and movements faithfully mirror social divisions, the plethora of partisan groups revealed not only the depth of internal disagreements brought to the fore by the Lebanon war but also the extent of structural transformation which had taken place on the partisan political scene. The far right was buttressed by increased activities of Gush Emunim, Kach, and several clandestine groups formed to ensure the maintenance of Israeli control over the occupied territories. Peace Now experienced a resurgence at this time, emerging as the largest extraparliamentary group espousing a peace platform. The war also spurred the creation of a multiplicity of protest movements which, together with existing organizations such as the Association for Civil Rights in Israel and the Committee for Solidarity with Bir-Zeit University, formed the core of a growing number of organizations concerned with progressive political issues.

These movements strengthened smaller political parties located to the left and to the right of the two major alignments. Kach, Tehiya, and Morasha gained momentum on the ultranationalist side of the political spectrum, as did the newly created Tzomet, headed by the former chief of staff Raphael Eitan (Raful). To the left of Labor, the Citizens' Rights and Peace Movement (CRM) headed by Shulamit Aloni, the Democratic Front for Peace and Equality (the mostly Arab-backed and non-Zionist successor of the Communist party), and the new Progressive List for Peace (PLP) garnered additional support. With the growth of ultra-Orthodox parties (especially Agudat Israel) and the formation of the Sephardi Torah Guardians (Shas), only the center of the political map remained underpopulated. The successor of the short-lived Democratic Movement for Change, Shinui, was the sole party to have maintained a liberal-democratic parliamentary presence since 1977. The Independent Liberals were incorporated into Labor, and Ezer Weizman attempted to capitalize on middle-class votes traditionally supportive of liberal causes by establishing the centrist Yahad faction.

The explosive and indeterminate political climate prevalent at the time was expressed in the results of the 1984 elections (called a year ahead of schedule after Aharon Abu-Hatzeira, at the head of the Tami faction, bolted the coalition and effectively brought down the government). Both Likud and Labor lost votes to splinter groups of their own ideological complexion. Fifteen parties gained seats in the Knesset, more than the number represented in any previous parliament. Fringe groups—Kach on the extreme right and the PLP on the left—won enough votes to

obtain representation in the Knesset. The religious bloc, though fragmented internally, saw its electoral appeal revived. Neither Labor, with
its 44 mandates, nor Likud, with its 41, was in a position to form a
coalition with its satellite parties.[15] By overestimating the desire for
change, undervaluing the quest for predictability and security, soft-
pedaling burning political issues, misreading the allure of parties that
offered lucid and simplistic solutions to the dilemmas of the Israeli
condition, and conducting a futile campaign for an elusive swing vote,
both major blocs were substantially weakened in the polls.[16] The result
was an effective parliamentary deadlock.

The main parties were faced with two options: to call for new
elections or to join forces. Both parties feared that a return to the ballot
box would merely replicate the outcome of the July vote. They were
therefore compelled to work out a formula for the construction of a
national unity cabinet. The carefully balanced twenty-five-member Peres-
Shamir cabinet established in September 1984 brought together traditional
archrivals who lacked a unifying policy orientation. The provisions for
the allocation of cabinet portfolios and for the rotation of the premiership
between Shimon Peres and Yitzhak Shamir highlighted the power
considerations that motivated the molders of this construct and underlined
the frailty of the Israeli political system in the face of severe differences
of opinion within the electorate.

The creation of the national unity government incorporated contrasting forces within a particularly heterogeneous ruling coalition that
lacked both cohesion and direction. Its formation introduced major shifts
in the Israeli political scene, with the cumulative effect of impeding
concerted action on those issues which lacked cabinet consensus (mostly
in the realm of security and foreign affairs).

The first set of changes related to the relationship between the
cabinet and major political institutions. On the party front, the coming
together of Labor and Likud in a governing alliance blurred the differences
(although hardly the tension) between the two major blocs while mag-
nifying the ideological discrepancies between them and the opposition
on the right (Tehiya, Kach, and Morasha) and the left (CRM, Mapam,
PLP, and the Communist bloc). The Labor party suffered some defections
as Yossi Sarid bolted the party to join Citizens' Rights Movement and
Mapam reasserted its independence, refusing to participate in the coalition. At the same time, Ezer Weizman and his Yahad group were
effectively absorbed into Labor, and Shinui became part of the government
coalition. The Likud, shaken by the loss of votes to the right and to
religious parties, made plans for the complete unification of Herut and
the Liberals, which resulted in the formal consolidation of the two
parties in 1986. A breakaway faction of the Liberals withdrew from the

negotiations and formed the new Center party. By the midterm of the first national unity government, the separation between pragmatically oriented coalition parties and ideologically propelled opposition groups became even more apparent.

Within each of the major parties, internal ideological divisions were accentuated. The loose distinction between doves and hawks within Labor was institutionalized with the emergence of an activist faction of younger party members (known as Chug Mashov) espousing progressive perspectives on peace issues.[17] The Likud, and particularly Herut, was rocked by especially acrimonious disputes along ideological and personal lines. The conflict over the future leadership of the party among David Levy, Moshe Arens, and Ariel Sharon came to a head at the Herut convention in early 1986, when the party hierarchy was unable to avert violent confrontations over appointments to central party organs. Thus, if the national unity arrangements clarified the distinctions between government and opposition, they also introduced new sources of tension within each of the major coalition partners.

Indeed, as time progressed, the anomalies inherent in this situation became more manifest. On the one hand, by 1988 the relations between the Likud and Labor in office were routinized; on the other hand, informal transparty alliances among Knesset members of similar political persuasions surfaced. Thus, on critical peace and security issues, the left wing of Labor, Mapam, CRM, and at times the PLP joined forces in opposition to the more conservative segment of Labor and the moderates of the Likud, who in turn were challenged by the ultra-nationalist faction of Herut in concert with Tehiya and portions of the NRP and Morasha.

At the end of the tenure of the first national unity government, the general party picture was both less coherent and more confusing than in the past. Workable arrangements on the relations between the main parties had been ironed out, but each major bloc was subjected to pressures from within. The structure of political alignments was thus in the midst of a process of reordering. The dual basis for the mobilization of support on any given issue suggested that although traditional limits were still placed on the decisions of any party, the possibilities of forging transparty coalitions, for either ideological or opportunistic reasons, had been enhanced. In real terms, the impact of political parties on the policymaking process was circumscribed.

On the parliamentary front, therefore, the ruling coalition, with its overwhelming majority, could expect to receive Knesset approval for virtually every program it brought before the legislature. Because the cabinet no longer depended on the confidence of small factions, it was not subjected to extortion from them. From its inception it possessed a great deal of autonomy. Despite or perhaps because of its sprawling nature, the national unity government was less beholden to parliamentary or social controls than were its predecessors.

In these conditions the principle of parliamentary accountability was severely eroded. The policymaking function of the Knesset, especially on foreign and defense matters, was effectively downgraded. If in the past the Knesset provided at least a forum for serious and frequently heated debate on critical issues, during the Peres and Shamir phases of the national unity government it was relegated to a watchdog role. The members of the national assembly used their sessions to articulate concerns and to air the opinions of their constituencies; they became a monitoring device with supervisory responsibilities bereft of the capacity to impose their will on a cabinet composed of nearly one-fifth of their membership.

On the extraparliamentary front, too, the national unity structure ultimately limited the impact of large nonparty groups. Members of the major political movements, such as Gush Emunim and Peace Now, were either co-opted by the ruling coalition or lost their access to key policymakers. A variety of specific interest groups which formed single-issue lobbies applying pressure on individual politicians became far more effective than the large political movements.[18] In these circumstances, political access was more circumscribed than in the past, and the center of political gravity shifted squarely to the cabinet. The national unity government structure therefore endowed the government with greater independence vis-à-vis other institutions than previous coalitions possessed in the past.

Whether this autonomy could be translated into decisionmaking capacity depended on a second major group of changes, which revolved around the structure and dynamics of the government itself. The size and diversity of the national unity government inevitably highlighted the problem of internal cohesion. The personal relations among cabinet members became the center of attention because they had a direct effect on the government's ability to reach agreement on central policy issues. Indeed, the extent and intensity of squabbles within the government increased significantly during the 1984–1988 tenure of the first national unity government. Ariel Sharon openly challenged Shimon Peres's leadership and policies during the 1984–1986 period. When Yitzhak Moda'i pursued a similar course, he was forced by Peres to resign from the finance ministry. The Shamir-Peres relationship deteriorated after Shamir took over the office of prime minister in 1986. The frequently acrimonious tenor of these debates should not obscure the fact that they were a natural by-product of the increase in executive authority. Because the stakes at this level were much higher, it followed that conflicts would be exacerbated.

The national unity government dealt with these divisions by a process of internal reorganization. A triumvirate consisting of Shimon Peres, Yitzhak Shamir (alternately prime minister or foreign minister), and Yitzhak Rabin (defense minister) established a system of joint rule.[19] The cabinet operated through a division of labor which allowed each minister a large degree of autonomy in his or her sphere and guaranteed a minimum amount of intervention on the part of other cabinet members. This mechanism facilitated the daily operation of the government, but reduced the collective responsibility of its members for their combined actions. These arrangements also augmented the power of Rabin, who as minister of defense assumed almost full authority over external security and the administration of the occupied territories, leaving Shamir and Peres to argue over the formulation of longer-term Israeli policy directions (the one area which could not be neatly divided among the members of the cabinet). This modus vivendi adversely affected the ability to launch foreign policy initiatives which deviated from the rigid guidelines laid down in the coalition agreements.

In this setting, the importance attached to leadership styles and preferences was magnified. During the first two years of the national unity government, Peres attempted to cultivate the image of manager and conciliator as a counterpoint to the more strident rhetorical notes struck by his Likud predecessors.[20] Peres's demeanor unquestionably had an impact on the climate of political life in the country and on the way Israel was viewed abroad. But although Peres was successful in instilling a modicum of calm in the political arena, his substantive impact was limited. As prime minister, he was able to maintain some harmony in the coalition; he did so, however, not only by appealing to the broadest common denominator on vital issues but also by sacrificing the possibility of breaking new ground in favor of conciliation within the governing circle. Peres set a new political tone; he did not simultaneously implement innovative departures in policy directions.

Yitzhak Shamir, in contrast, projected a more detached style of leadership. As the second prime minister of the national unity government, he sought to capitalize on the stability created by the Peres administration by granting cabinet members a large measure of freedom and minimizing his intervention in the internal affairs of individual ministries. Shamir has been neither ideologically nor personally prone to promoting alterations in the status quo, and his prime ministership has been characterized by hesitation and delay rather than by creativity or initiative.

Structurally, therefore, the national unity government had considerable leeway in formulating and executing foreign policy in comparison with its partisan antecedents. It was also less accountable to what in actuality was a small and splintered opposition. The distance between the cabinet and other political institutions had grown. At the same time, the workings of the government underscored the many problems associated with the internalization of opposites in a ruling coalition. As the rules of the political game were reconsidered, it became apparent that the national unity construct which theoretically offered new opportunities for policy reorientation in fact also increased prospects for policy inactivity. The increased independence of the cabinet came together with a palpable reduction in its authority and in its power to carry out its own directives.

It is this anomaly, which encompasses the paradox of the quest for the mainstream in a divided society, that became the hallmark of the first national unity government. The fragility of this construct was a result of its heterogeneous makeup, its durability a sign of the scope of the pragmatic interests it served. Foreign policymaking in these conditions was both highly centralized and purposely ambiguous.

Many of these features were magnified in the wake of the Palestinian uprising which began in December 1987, just nine months before the end of the first national unity government's term of office. The cabinet, deeply divided on how to handle the intifada, contented itself with proclaiming in January 1988 that Israel would take any steps necessary to quell the resistance. Responsibility for planning and implementing official strategy was delegated to the ministry of defense, whose actions became a substitute for rigorous policy design and execution. The first national unity government proved incapable of decisively meeting the most serious challenge to the twenty-one-year Israeli occupation of the West Bank and the Gaza Strip, especially in an election year during which political tensions ran high.

The 1988 polls were held under the shadow of the uprising, although their outcome could not fully reflect the impact of these events on the Israeli polity.[21] The electoral strength of Likud and Labor continued to deteriorate, as religious and ultrareligious parties experienced an upsurge, the far-right parties fragmented (barely maintaining their 1984 representation), and the parties to the left of Labor increased the number of their seats in the Knesset. The election results, without excluding the possibility of a narrow Likud-led coalition, favored the creation of a second national unity government.

The new unity formation, however, differed from its predecessor in several important respects. First, the Likud held a one-seat majority in the Knesset, shifting the balance of power in the new government away from full parity between the two major parties. Second, as a result, no provisions were made for the rotation of the prime ministership.

Third, Likud took over the foreign ministry, giving it control of the two pivotal positions in the high-level policymaking process. Rabin retained the defense portfolio, but Shimon Peres (who became minister of finance) was marginalized in the process. And finally, the second national unity government was even larger than the first, suggesting that internal frictions would intensify. Thus, although the 1988 elections confirmed the necessity (if not the viability) of the national unity construct, it appeared that the decisionmaking difficulties encountered during the first national unity government would be exacerbated during the tenure of its successor. Indeed, the second national unity government broke up in March 1990 in the wake of the appearance of unbridgeable differences between Labor and Likud over the peace process.

Israel's political institutions, particularly those charged with designing and implementing policies in the area of peace and security, were substantially transformed during the 1980s. As the electoral strength of the two major alignments diminished, the shift to broad governing coalitions actually reduced the cabinet's capacity to forge a unified position on key policy issues. The recurring political deadlock at the polls and the absence of government agreement indicated that decisionmaking structures could no longer provide direction as long as institutional arrangements blurred the distinction between the national interest and partisan concerns.

Constituencies

Changes in the political environment necessarily affect the role of social groups in shaping foreign policy. The end of Labor domination in 1977 was accompanied by social fluctuations, shifts in the composition of the political leadership, an increase in the intrusion of specific group claims into the political arena, and a palpable reduction in societal influence on high policy decisions. In the highly charged and extremely politicized atmosphere of Israel, the reordering of political alignments and the alteration of decisionmaking mechanisms mirror changes in the extent of societal cohesion and have a special significance for the comprehension of the impact of social groups on political processes and trends.

Israeli society has been characterized by an overlapping network of ethnic, religious, geographic, class, and ideological cleavages, compounded by national distinctions between Arab and Jewish citizens of the state.[22] Jewish society nevertheless retained a high degree of unity until the 1970s, when the domestic national consensus began to break down. Processes of polarization in the first part of the 1980s and subsequent fragmentation in the second half of the decade narrowed the scope of social interactions and had an adverse effect on the ability of social groups to affect government policy. At the same time, political leaders were less prone to abandon past policy positions for fear of alienating their progressively diffuse constituencies. Thus, although by the close of the decade, virtually every conceivable position on the Arab-Israeli conflict possessed some social backing, the capacity to mobilize these forces had diminished.

The first division in Israeli society is based on ethnicity. Ashkenazi Jews, the descendants of the original pioneers and the designers of the country's social and political institutions, are a minority of the Jewish population. They have been outstripped numerically by the Sephardim, who constitute over 55 percent of the Jewish inhabitants of Israel. Although each major ethnic group is composed of highly diverse elements, the broad differences between Sephardim and Ashkenazim—expressed in divergent cultural values and historical experiences as well as education, occupational attainment, family structure, patterns of residence, demographic characteristics, socioeconomic status, and even manners of speech and behavior—became more pronounced in the late 1960s and early 1970s.

Awareness of ethnic discrepancies grew in the period immediately following the 1973 war as young Sephardi politicians, especially in the economically stagnating development towns and the poorer neighborhoods of the major cities, mobilized their constituencies against the reigning Labor establishment. David Levy, Meir Shitrit, Moshe Katzav, David Magen, and other young and educated local politicians were central to the Likud victory in 1977.[23] Concerned with issues of socioeconomic development and more traditional in religious orientation, this new leadership group rallied around the nationalist rhetoric of Menachem Begin in the hope of rectifying deep-seated social inequities. Their support maintained the Likud in power for seven years, and their interests helped to redefine the political agenda during this period.

The second major cleavage in Israeli society, based on socioeconomic distinctions, largely overlaps ethnic divisions. As Israel evolved into an industrialized country heavily dependent on its technological skills, the differences between lower and higher income groups grew and were expressed in marked disparities in occupational status and life-styles. By the mid-1970s the Labor socialist alignment, in one of the more striking anomalies of Israeli politics, was closely identified with elitism and establishment privilege. This label persisted despite efforts to incorporate new personnel into the Labor hierarchy and a belated renewal of Labor concern with social questions. A home-grown populism fueled by ethnic considerations and spurred by political parties dominated voting patterns toward the end of the decade. The Likud benefitted from (and undoubtedly exploited) the political awakening of this class component.[24]

The third division in Israeli society is geographic. The kibbutzim, moshavot, and some of the moshavim have been associated with the concept of a Labor aristocracy. But quantitatively their electoral impact, if not their political influence, was gradually outstripped by that of the thirty-three development towns populated mostly by lower-income residents of Sephardi extraction. In the large urban areas, the distinctions between veteran residential quarters and the newer and poorer neighborhoods (the Israeli euphemism for urban ghettos) became more salient during the course of the 1970s and were translated into an electoral backlash against Labor.[25]

The fourth major grouping in Israeli society revolves around degrees of religious observance. The division between secular and religious groups in Israel has always impinged on social relations because at stake are the interpretation and substantiation of various notions of the Jewishness of the state. Religious-secular schisms were exacerbated in the 1970s as an influx of Orthodox immigrants inflated the ranks of the already rapidly growing religious community (whose birthrates are the highest among the Jewish population in the country and whose adherents grew with a rise in the phenomenon of born-again Jews).[26] The centrality of religious parties for coalition maintenance further contributed to the salience of these distinctions. Special concessions were granted to the rabbinical establishment (which consolidated its power over matters of conversion and personal law) and increased allocations were made to Orthodox institutions.[27] The assertiveness of the Orthodox inevitably evoked a strident backlash from secularists unwilling to succumb to the dictates of halachic law, thus laying the foundation for growing friction around these issues in the 1980s.

A fifth cleavage is ideological, which in Israel carries social connotations as well. The initial ideological supremacy of Labor-Zionism was gradually whittled away not only by the territorial realities of post-1967 Israel but also by its inability to supply adequate answers to the socioeconomic concerns of a vast portion of the population. The rise of the Likud in 1977 seemed to signal the victory of the geographically focused and historically rooted xenophobic statism of revisionist Zionism over the people-centered universalistic and humanitarian tradition of the proponents of mainstream Zionism.[28] This success was, however, both superficial and ephemeral. Because it could not take into account the multiplicity of divergent social concerns and was therefore unable to forge a new consensus, Herut ideology in the early 1980s had to vie with strong religious, ultranationalist, dovish, liberal-democratic, pragmatic, and socialist streams in the country. As long as the guiding symbols were not monopolized by any one group, these struggles have provided conflicting pivots for social aggregation and alternative foci for societal interaction. Thus, social cleavages among Jews in Israel, unlike the Jewish-Arab divide, have retained a fluid quality. Individual Israelis have been subjected to a variety of cross-cutting pressures, rendering the political impact of social distinctions a function of particular political constellations and circumstances.

Social agglomerations have traditionally defined the limits of acceptable government action. They have furnished an amorphous and difficult to delineate constraint on foreign policymaking. But this influence has at best been indirect. The effect of pressures emanating from diverse social groups has varied with the degree that specific ruling coalitions have had to depend on the goodwill of particular portions of the population and with the extent to which specific identities reinforced each other at various junctures in the country's political history. The precariousness of the social foundations of a government has served as an excellent barometer of its willingness to take particular demands into account.

The inauguration of the first Likud administration in 1977 coincided with the skillful drawing together of Sephardi, lower-income, traditional, populist, and nationalist elements in an electoral alliance opposed to continued Ashkenazi, middle-class, Labor-Zionist, and secular political supremacy. By accentuating the overlapping nature of certain social cleavages and molding the previously dispossessed into a formidable political force, Menachem Begin contributed significantly not only to the politicization of Israeli society but also to the use of state office to reward political backers. In the late 1970s the government skewed allocations to meet the demands of disadvantaged groups and to pacify religious interests central to the maintenance of the ruling coalition. It was also receptive to pressure from the largest extraparliamentary movement on the right, Gush Emunim, whose campaign for support for Jewish settlement in the occupied territories was met with enthusiastic official backing. Limits, however, were placed on the willingness of the government to accommodate the concerns of its social constituencies. When the interests of the high policy elite diverged from those of critical social groups in its own political camp—as on the vital question of the Gush Emunim campaign to annex the West Bank and Gaza—their demands were simply not met.

Government actions during the 1977–1981 period inevitably evoked a backlash among Ashkenazi, white-collar workers of a more liberal persuasion, who banded together to protect their previous gains and to oppose the social manipulation practiced by the Likud in office. Peace Now gained strength as the mouthpiece of moderate forces seeking to halt the settlement drive and to continue the peace momentum. By the early 1980s two grand social coalitions had emerged, which diverged from each other politically, ideologically, and programmatically.

The dichotomous form of social interaction at the beginning of the decade enfeebled the political influence of intervening organizations that in the past served as a funnel for broad interests. Academics and intellectuals monitored government activities, and business owners and industrialists coalesced into a unified interest group. The Histadrut, Israel's mammoth trade union, repeatedly clashed with the government and with recalcitrant rank-and-file workers. The civil servants, teachers, students, professional associations, and voluntary organizations possessed their own separate agendas that they transmitted with marked regularity to the attention of the public and the cabinet. Even diaspora Jews periodically entered the political fray, especially on issues of divorce and conversion.[29] But except for the defense establishment, whose concerns defy party lines and social divisions and whose strength grew at the turn of the decade,[30] none of these groups had an enduring direct effect on policy decisions, particularly in the sphere of foreign policy.[31]

The 1981 elections were purposely conducted as an open confrontation between the two major social agglomerations, with ethnicity serving as a key mechanism for galvanizing Likud and Labor support. The electoral contest highlighted the extent to which basic divisions overlapped at this juncture and could therefore be manipulated to serve party interests. The high number of votes received by each of the major parties underscored the enormity of the sociopolitical divide that existed in the country at this time. The outcome of the ballot confirmed the polarization that had set in after the ratification of the Egyptian-Israeli peace accords.

The second Likud administration's narrow political base presaged extensive government handouts to those particularistic interests that propped up the ruling coalition. Disbursements to development towns grew, as did government allocations to settler groups, particularly Gush Emunim. Businesspeople and entrepreneurs benefitted from economic liberalization, generous loans, export incentives, and an artificially overvalued currency. The defense establishment, too, enjoyed a period of increased allotments to research and development projects. Orthodox and ultra-Orthodox institutions were granted substantial sums as part of the coalition agreements, enabling them to expand their network of independent schools and yeshivas. Between 1981 and 1984 these groups were strengthened at the expense of others (most notably the trade unions, professionals, the veteran kibbutzim, and secular bodies).

The party arena and particular ministries were consequently infiltrated by specific sectional interests.[32] In these circumstances not only was the distinction between the public good and the concerns of particular groups blurred, but the political viability of the two major social constellations diminished. During this period a third, amorphous, social agglomeration encompassing groups concerned with pragmatic domestic matters began to emerge, thus reducing the centrality of the ideologically distinct and politically reinforcing bipolar social forces that had dominated the political scene after the Likud takeover in 1977.

The diversification of social groups active in the political arena was increasingly evident in the wake of the Lebanon invasion, which was marked by an intensification of intracommunal strife and by especially vituperative exchanges between opponents and proponents of government policy. The acrimonious nature and strident tones associated with social interactions at this juncture could not obscure the fact that social organizations wielded very little influence in policymaking circles and that even those groups associated with the administration acted more as organized support groups than as independent sources of pressure on decisionmaking elites. In these circumstances, with frustration running high and economic conditions deteriorating, many segments of the population maintained a studied indifference, thus further circumscribing their influence on foreign and security affairs.

The Lebanon war induced a breakdown of the major social agglomerations and had a substantial impact on the disposition of political forces in the country. Indeed, the 1984 elections underlined the absence of voting cohesion among major social constellations. Fully one-third of Sephardi voters supported Labor, and others abandoned the Likud in favor of the right-wing parties or Shas. The Tehiya depended on Ashkenazi voters as much as on the support of religious nationalists. The religious vote itself was split among four different parties, signaling the emergence of important divisions within the Orthodox camp. The kibbutzim continued to provide the backbone of Labor, but they also supported the urban, middle-class intellectual CRM on the left and the Tehiya on the right. First-time voters divided their votes between the ultranationalist parties and radical groups on the left. Electoral trends pointed to cracks in bloc voting, reaffirming the fluidity of social coalitions.

The structure of the national unity government, encompassing a large portion of the Israeli population, ostensibly gave the new government greater scope to maneuver than most of its predecessors while relieving policymakers of the obligation to court any particular group of interests. As a result, the ruling coalition was both less accessible to specific interests and less amenable to political pressures originating outside the formal political sphere. Although it could comfortably claim that it was speaking for a mainstream, however ill-defined, its members in fact used their office to reward their backers and to expand their support bases.

Inevitably, the situation had important repercussions not only on social actions and their policy ramifications but also on the definition of the boundaries of societal consensus.

First, the national unity government further constricted the already ambiguous influence of political movements on foreign affairs. During the 1984–1987 period, Peace Now, whose leadership laid claim to close ties with upper-echelon Labor leaders, lost much of its visibility. The protest tactics used when the Likud was in office were not deemed appropriate in light of Labor advocacy of many of the movement's views, and alternative methods of influencing policy were not readily available. Gush Emunim retained a greater consistency but was also hampered in its access to policymakers as well as in its overall influence. It did not, however, directly challenge the national unity government for fear of alienating its supporters in the Likud, especially in Herut.

Second, the minimalization of the role of political movements was accompanied by greater diversification of spheres of social action. New civic groups concerned with such varied topics as social tolerance, urban beautification, combating racism, and environmental issues were created. Increased activism developed around civil rights, with the Association for Civil Rights in Israel stepping up the pace of its litigation and consolidating a strong record of involvement in cases involving abuses of fundamental human rights. The establishment of the Israel Women's Network in 1984, the revival of the National Council on the Status of Women, and the creation of a more active women's lobby underlined the propensity to engage in specific, inward-oriented forms of political action.

Third, different sources of friction emerged. Ethnic tensions were substantially moderated as lower-income and Sephardi leaders were incorporated into the establishment. Preoccupation with domestic issues attenuated ideological clashes. Simultaneously, conflict along religious lines intensified. Growing distinctions between ultra-Orthodox, Orthodox, traditional, secular, and antireligious groups led to open clashes on questions of religious observance and to a rise in religiously motivated violence. Religious cleavages constituted a most serious challenge to the pluralist principles of the Israeli polity and divided the society along lines that did not neatly overlap political or ideological orientations.

Finally, under the national unity government, extremist groups surfaced well beyond the control of government. The most vociferous of these fringe groups was Meir Kahane's Kach movement; until curtailed by Knesset legislation, it openly provoked Arab citizens and called for drastic measures for the Judaization of the greater land of Israel.[33] The most violent of these formations was the Jewish underground, a well organized and armed clandestine spin-off of Gush Emunim, which carried out several lethal attacks on Palestinian leaders and educational institutions.[34] Islamic fundamentalism, which spread in Israel, the West Bank, and Gaza, provided a radical counterpoint to Jewish messianic militancy. These phenomena, an expression of dissatisfaction with political immobility and with the absence of regularized channels to affect policy options, continued throughout the tenure of the first national unity government. Official efforts to control fundamentalist activists did not stem the proliferation of these sentiments in Jewish and Arab quarters.

Social activity during the first national unity government was characterized by its lack of coherence and by its incidental impact on formal policy perspectives. Society may have become more politicized, but its actual political resonance contracted considerably because new social alliances did not take shape at this juncture. The leaders of the unity coalition were not in a position to define the limits of acceptable social action, but they could attempt to galvanize fluid social constellations. Thus Labor was less tolerant of Jewish extremism, while Likud, concerned with the possible loss of segments of its traditional constituency, was indulgent of ultranationalist groups. In a similar vein, Labor specifically courted Jews of North African extraction after Prime Minister Peres's visit to Morocco; Herut went to great lengths to appeal to middle-class voters.

Both parties welcomed the diversification and internalization of foci of group action because these preoccupations deflected attention away from peace and security issues. If in the past social identification and political orientations overlapped, in the disparate social scene of the late 1980s, ethnic, religious, class, or geographic affiliations proved to be poor indicators of ideological dispositions. Members of the national unity government used these diffuse social currents to justify whatever policies they sought to promote. This coalition saw an attenuation of social reins on government policy without a concomitant clarification of party policies or orientations.

These patterns were further magnified after the beginning of the Palestinian uprising in December 1987. Although over ninety different peace and protest movements were established in the first nine months of the intifada alone, their activities were poorly coordinated and their immediate political influence infinitesimal. Both Peace Now and Gush Emunim experienced a revival but were subjected to serious internal schisms. In the absence of overreaching social coalitions with distinctive political positions and clear access to decisionmakers, societal responses remained fragmented and unfocused.

The 1988 elections confirmed the lack of a clear correlation between social cleavages and policy orientations. The electoral losses suffered by the two major alignments and the rise in the number of parties represented in the Knesset reflected the extent of social dispersion in the country. Any semblance of societal cohesion had given way to a vast diversity of views lacking any coherent social organization. The broad base of the national unity government had blunted the power of social groups without offering a formula for their reorganization. The social support bases were undermined in the process.

Forms of social interaction during the 1980s differed dramatically from trends evident on the narrower political scene. As political structures appeared to undergo a process of consolidation, social concerns became more diffuse, with particularly problematic relations developing around purely domestic matters. This diversity and volatility were in all probability more an outcome than a cause of the lack of progress on the foreign policy front. But because social fragmentation highlighted issues of internal governability, any government could point to domestic recalcitrance as an excuse for procrastination on the Arab-Israeli conflict. At the same time, the national unity governments were also in a position to take independent action precisely because concerted societal constraints were weak and politically disoriented and domestic constituencies advocating departures from past patterns were in place. If at the outset of the 1980s social polarization impeded movement on the foreign policy front, by the end of the decade centrifugal tendencies prevented the coalescence of any unified foreign policy constituency.

Ideology and Interests

The mitigation of social influences on foreign policy designs does not imply the attenuation of the role of ideology or of specific substantive interests in external affairs. Foreign policy directly reflects shifting ideological concerns, perceptions, and priorities. The 1980s coincided with the emergence of multiple contradictions in the basic precepts of Israeli society, which were translated into growing discrepancies in attitudes toward security, territories, Arabs, and peace. By the end of the decade, foreign policy moves were inconsistent and hesitant because although some agreement could be reached on immediate measures and tactical steps, existing concepts and terms of discourse did not permit a reformulation of national objectives in light of the profound changes that had taken place in the region.[35]

Zionist ideology is the linchpin of the definition of Israeli national objectives and the fundamental prism of Israel's interaction in the global arena. In its many forms it coheres around the notion of Israel as the concrete political articulation of the liberation movement of the Jewish people. Zionism is predicated on the assumption of an integral connection between the Jewish people, the state of Israel, and the land.[36] Like many new states of the postwar era, Israel has its roots in messianic ideals. Unlike some of those countries, it has remained a visionary-democratic state whose carefully elaborated symbols seek to mirror specific goals.[37]

The definition of Zionism has never been an abstract endeavor for Israelis; it possesses an immediacy and vitality often difficult for foreign observers to comprehend. The internal debate over the essentials of Zionism took on two main forms prior to the 1980s. Labor-Zionists evinced a marked preference for a forward-looking and outward-oriented formulation of the Zionist credo. The notion of the solidarity of the Jewish people as expressed in a selective statism was given preeminence over territorial considerations. And emphasis was placed on the dignity of labor and the importance accorded to projecting a constructive Israeli presence in the international arena. Revisionist-Zionists stressed the connection between sovereignty, nationhood, military prowess, and self-reliance in a hostile environment. They accentuated parochial Jewish concerns over universal elements in the Zionist ethos and underlined the territorial integrity of the state as the concrete manifestation of Jewish historical rights.

Relations with other countries were seen by both camps as necessary for Israel's survival and for the welfare of Jewish communities elsewhere. But revisionists tended to assess foreign contacts by their contribution to the physical persistence of the state. Labor-Zionists perceived foreign relations as a confirmation of Israel's standing in the international arena— as tangible evidence of the political coming of age of the Jewish people. Thus, not only the nature but also the extent of Israel's external ties became an integral part of the country's internal political debate.

The 1967 war and the occupation of the territories, by forcing a reevaluation of the relationship between the human, geographic, and political components of the Zionist worldview, magnified the differences between these approaches and underscored some of their internal contradictions. The Likud clung to a territorial, survivalist, inward-looking interpretation of Zionist goals and began to explore the concrete implications of this worldview for the realization of its dream of a greater land of Israel. Labor continued to stress a concern with the fabric of Israeli society and its democratic underpinnings and entertained the possibility of the exchange of territories for peace. But the force of the Labor-Zionist vision was undermined as some of its proponents decried the occupation while others sought to justify it on security grounds.[38]

Both major approaches to Zionism had in common a concern for the survival, security, and Jewishness of the state of Israel. They varied, however, not only in their stances toward specific issues but also in the delineation of means and objectives. As one observer has suggested, the various strains of Zionist ideology have differing notions of doom.[39]

Thus, both on the level of abstraction and on the level of basic issues, Israeli society has been deeply divided in its image of itself and its future.

The definition of national objectives and particular concerns at any given point has derived from a wide variety of factors ranging from the psychological and the historical to the economic, religious, demographic, and immediate. Foreign policy over the years has been very much a reflection of these heterogeneous domestic issues and predilections. Nevertheless, basic precepts underlying external attitudes have varied only slightly. Each government since the creation of the state has espoused the notion that the hostile regional environment imperils the continued existence of the state and gives Israel no real alternative to fortifying itself against military threats. Each government has consequently acknowledged the country's dependence on foreign military and economic aid.[40] Policymakers have therefore constantly sought to balance their suspicion of global enmity against the need for external support. This situation, coupled with disagreement over the foreign policy ramifications of specific topical concerns, has meant that domestic conflicts over Israel's national goals and immediate needs have carried over, with marked regularity, to the sphere of foreign policy.

These difficulties have been particularly evident in relations with the United States. Israeli leaders since the late 1950s have tied Israel's future to U.S. backing. Calling on a commonality of interests, on joint democratic concerns, on moral obligations, on the need to ensure a Western presence in the Middle East, and on the interests of the U.S. Jewish community, Israel's political leadership has nurtured a multiplicity of links with the United States. At the same time, however, Israelis have been at odds with one another and with their U.S counterparts on the degree of intrusion dependence entails. The contradiction between the growing reliance on U.S. support and the ongoing quest for autonomy in the international arena collapses in its confines the many substantive questions confronting Israeli policymakers.[41]

The Israeli-Egyptian peace negotiations launched a decade of ideological ambiguity, territorial entrenchment, domestic introspection, and foreign policy indeterminacy. The internal Israeli debate over the Camp David accords laid bare major ambiguities in the two dominant approaches to Zionism. Revisionists differed over territorial concessions, the sincerity of Egyptian overtures, and the repercussions of the growing dependence on the United States. Labor-Zionists, who welcomed the peace treaty, were divided on the meaning of Menachem Begin's skillful separation of the issue of peace from the continued Israeli occupation of the West Bank and Gaza and on the direction of negotiations. Both ultranationalist and religious militants on the right and advocates of full withdrawal on the left began to carve out their distinctive places on the Israeli ideological spectrum.[42]

These ideological differences were expressed in the intensification of debates over the autonomy talks, the acceleration of the pace of Israeli settlement in the territories, the normalization of relations with Egypt, and the final withdrawal from Sinai.[43] Disagreements over the basic issues of peace, security, and foreign policy underwent a process of domestication, substantially limiting Israeli openness to outside initiatives on these issues. This trend was further accentuated as priorities on the national agenda were reordered. By reducing the urgency associated with the grand issues of the Arab-Israeli conflict and by effectively delaying the need to contend with some of the more difficult aspects of the conflict, the rapprochement with Egypt sanctioned a new concern with domestic issues, particularly with economic liberalization and social welfare. After the initial flurry of activity surrounding the Egyptian talks, the first Likud administration was clearly not disposed to any further overtures on the foreign policy front.

The tenure of the second Likud administration was marked by continuing ideological cleavages, an ongoing preoccupation with purely domestic matters, a rising security consciousness, and a decided resistance to outside efforts to maintain a peace momentum. Ideological arguments revolved initially around two major issues, the first of which related to the settlement drive in the occupied territories. Through systematic land expropriations and the redirection of development funds to projects across the Green Line (the pre-1967 borders), ninety Jewish settlements were established during the Likud's tenure in office, significantly altering the nature and the extent of the Israeli presence in the West Bank. The controversial settlement policy created new facts on the ground which led to a diversification of the range of groups with a stake in the continuation of the occupation and a growing reluctance to contemplate the relinquishment of the territories.[44]

Changes in the structure of the Israeli occupation also had a direct bearing on Israeli attitudes toward Arabs in general and Palestinians in particular. The Palestine Liberation Organization (PLO) was presented as an ongoing security threat. West Bank personalities sympathetic to the PLO were removed from office, and efforts were made to nurture a more pliable alternative leadership.[45] Anti-Arab sentiments articulated initially by the radical right were not officially denounced, thus enabling their proliferation to other segments of the population. Inevitably, intercommunal relations deteriorated as the debate within Israel escalated.[46]

These processes furnished the backdrop for the central event of the first part of the decade, the Israeli invasion of Lebanon. The motives, planning, execution, and results of the 1982 war undermined the broad consensus that had existed on issues of national security.[47] Queries were raised not only about decisionmaking procedures, military effectiveness, political judgment, and strategic conceptualization but also about the accountability of leaders and the morality of offensive undertakings of this sort.[48] Moveover, Israeli actions evoked widespread international condemnation. The political leadership, feeling itself threatened from within and from abroad, stubbornly refused to consider President Reagan's effort to renew the peace process in September 1982 and resisted additional external efforts to mediate the Lebanese impasse.

By mid-1983, however, the government was scarcely in a position to defend an operation which cost over 600 Israeli lives and more than $5 billion,[49] especially after massacres in the Sabra and Shatila Palestinian refugee camps in Beirut, the publication of the findings of the Kahan commission, and Begin's resignation. Impatience, fatigue, fear, and emotional drain combined to create a popular demand to withdraw from Lebanon as soon as possible.

The domestic debate over Lebanon coincided with a growing dissatisfaction with the management of the economy. Although the Likud years were accompanied by a rapid rise in the standard of living of many Israelis, the economy became trapped in a balance-of-payments problem of staggering proportions. Government expenditure bore little relationship to productivity, credit was too easily available, and prestige projects, many of a military nature, were launched with little attention to their economic viability.[50] By the fall of 1983, with inflation running at 200 percent a year, discontent over the Shamir government's handling of the economy peaked. Unable to plan budgets from day to day (let alone for the midterm), individuals yearned for a measure of predictability and security. It became apparent that the specter of national bankruptcy was not so remote as the country's leaders would have liked to believe. A concern with economic recovery and efficiency climbed to the top of national priorities.[51]

The tumultuous years of the second Likud administration underlined the extent to which events set in motion in order to further particular ideological objectives developed a dynamic of their own which could not easily be controlled. The country was in disarray and the capabilities of the official apparatus had reached a nadir. On the eve of the 1984 elections, the government had lost its ability to set priorities, rally public support, and impose domestic order, let alone come to terms with more long-term foreign policy issues.

The consolidation of the national unity government imposed some order on the delineation of national and hence of foreign policy priorities. Upon its assumption of office, the Peres-Shamir cabinet designed a three-tiered approach to the definition of national objectives. The first tier consisted of immediate issues of broad domestic concern and focused primarily on the twin questions of economic rehabilitation and withdrawal from Lebanon. The second level of governmental concern related to questions of security. The national unity government set out to review and redesign the system of administration in the occupied territories, to renew the faltering peace process, and to regularize the premises underlying Israel's relations with its foreign allies—particularly the United States. More fundamental questions regarding the disposition of the territories, Israel's relations with its neighbors, and the future form of the country were relegated to a third tier which the national unity government, by agreeing not to withdraw from the territories, not to accept a Palestinian state, and not to enter discussions with the PLO, excluded from the domain of policy change. This approach was to continue throughout the remainder of the four-year tenure of the government.

The thrust of the policy orientation of the national unity government from its inception was hence decidedly pragmatic. Attention was focused on dealing with solvable issues of high domestic visibility, and constraints were placed on official moves in the more difficult spheres associated with the Arab-Israeli conflict. Palpably absent throughout this period was a constructive strategy on these more intractable issues. The experience of the Peres-Shamir dyarchy confirmed this penchant for instrumental consensus and avoidance of fundamental ideological decisions.

The primary target of activity during the first few months of the new government was unquestionably the economic sphere. A wage-price freeze was imposed while plans were drawn up for the implementation of more comprehensive reforms. Within two years a new Israeli shekel had been introduced, the exchange rate had been stabilized, and inflation had dropped dramatically for the first time in over a decade. The uncertainty that had marked daily life was replaced by a more predictable and realistic economic climate. Economic issues and concerns continued to dominate domestic policymaking during the first three years of the national unity government.

The Lebanese conundrum constituted the second main focus of early policy measures. Prime Minister Peres and Defense Minister Rabin moved expeditiously, after the Israeli-Lebanese accords of May 17, 1984, were abrogated, to withdraw Israeli forces unilaterally to a security belt in the south. The operation was completed ahead of schedule, barely nine months after the induction of the new government. The efficiency with which the withdrawal was carried out was testimony to the high degree of agreement within the cabinet on this issue. It was also a reflection of a common determination to remove this question from the domestic agenda. In retrospect, the main interest of the government at this juncture was to externalize the Lebanon problem; in this respect its approach was undeniably effective.

The centrality of domestic issues was maintained throughout most of the tenure of the first unity government. Religious strife, the report of the committee established to investigate the collapse of bank stocks, several well-publicized murder trials, and a series of strikes continued to rivet attention on internal questions. At the same time, debates over racism and democracy occupied many sessions of the Knesset. The exposure of a security services cover-up added fodder to the national scandal-a-week diet. This prolonged affair, coupled with outbursts of violence against Israelis within and beyond the Green Line, domesticated the issue of terrorism and transformed it into a major internal political topic.

The course of internal policy had a twofold effect: On the one hand, uncomfortable questions—such as Lebanon—were withdrawn from the realm of internal debate; on the other hand, efforts were made to place political violence at the forefront of domestic issues, thereby redefining the focus of security concerns. This situation generated a mixture of extremism and apathy. Radical groups took advantage of the new emphasis on the security threat from within to propagate racist ideas and to form vigilante groups of their own. Most Israelis withdrew from direct involvement with major ideological issues, displaying a marked disinterest in matters that required them to go beyond mundane concerns to confront the consequences of continued Israeli rule in the occupied territories.[52] The propensity to internalize the enemy constricted the cabinet's ability to maneuver on crucial long-range issues since these matters had become further politicized. From the perspective of the government, however, these developments had the advantage of deflecting attention away from other sensitive spheres of foreign policy.

Indeed, by the mid-1980s Israel was not in a position to adopt a conscious policy of inaction in the external arena. Such a decision would cut the country off entirely from the international community, render it totally dependent on the United States, and imply that its leaders were willing to forfeit the possibility of affecting the outcome of the Arab-Israeli conflict. The image of a strong Israel standing on its own in splendid isolation, though continuing to possess some currency in the country, had little grounding in the mood of the society or the predilections of the leadership of the national unity government from its inception.

At the same time, there was no indication that Israel would accede to the demand for a full withdrawal from the territories acquired in 1967 or that it would support the creation of a Palestinian state.[53] Although such a move might go a long way to resolving the Palestinian question at the center of the Arab-Israeli conflict, help to overcome

Israel's exclusion from the mainstream of global politics, considerably augment its international standing, and herald a new phase in regional politics, too many barriers to such a policy existed: Public opinion was heavily set against a Palestinian state, distrust of the PLO was rampant, and security concerns could not be erased overnight. Although Israel did have a constituency that upheld this course with vigor, few government leaders were willing to declare their commitment to such a goal at this juncture.

Thus, it appeared that Israel's foreign policy would fluctuate between stylistic adjustments and minor procedural and structural initiatives. The shift in the modalities of Israel's foreign contacts became apparent almost immediately after Peres's arrival at the prime minister's office. Together with Foreign Minister Shamir and David Kimche, director general of the Ministry for Foreign Affairs, Peres launched a campaign to increase the number of Israel's foreign partners. This outreach was directed first to Africa, where some gains had been registered before 1984 with the restoration of relations with Zaire and Liberia. During the next three years, diplomatic relations were renewed with Cameroon, Cote d'Ivoire, and Togo.[54] Similarly, overtures were made toward China and India, and commercial contacts with Japan improved.[55] Special attention was paid to Eastern Europe, where links were established first with Hungary, Poland, and Bulgaria and then more directly with the Soviet Union. Attempts were made to enhance Israel's standing in Western Europe, as initially Peres and then Shamir courted François Mitterrand and Margaret Thatcher in order to lay the foundation for a different political relationship with the members of the European Community than had prevailed after the Venice declaration of 1978. And channels of communication were opened to Arab leaders, most notably King Hassan II of Morocco, King Hussein of Jordan, and President Hosni Mubarak of Egypt.

Relations with the United States were of special concern. Both Peres and Shamir visited Washington repeatedly, and between 1984 and late 1987 Israel negotiated a record-high aid package, a free trade agreement, and a mutual security pact with the United States. Israel was one of the few countries that actively sought to take part in Ronald Reagan's Star Wars research and unreservedly backed the U.S. position on arms control and the battle against international terrorism.

Thus, the network of Israel's ties with the United States expanded (despite the controversies that developed around the Pollard affair, the conviction of Jonathan and Ann Pollard on the charge of spying for Israel, and Irangate in 1986) precisely as Israel's global fortunes shifted. This improvement may be attributed primarily to the beginnings of the Soviet-U.S. rapprochement after Mikhail Gorbachev's rise to power,

changes in foci of international concern, and shifts in the geopolitics of
the Middle East in the wake of the ongoing conflict in Lebanon and
the termination of the Iran-Iraq war. In all probability, the ill-defined
and lax policy of the second Reagan administration vis-à-vis Israel after
the Lebanese invasion and the national unity government's less strident
and abrasive style also played a role.

It is within this context that Israeli overtures in the peace process
must be understood. In fall 1985, after preliminary contacts with Jordan,
Peres announced an Israeli peace initiative at the United Nations General
Assembly. His proposal included a call for an international peace conference (a deviation from Israel's past insistence on direct bilateral
negotiations) and a willingness to meet with Palestinian representatives.
This gesture was intended to inject some momentum into the peace
process; it also reflected a desire to mold the course of peace talks.
What was absent in these proposals, however, was an indication of the
substance of Israeli positions or an elaboration of the range of acceptable
solutions. Peres was particularly ambiguous about the composition of
the Palestinian delegation in the suggested negotiations. His plan,
therefore, simultaneously underscored the change in Israel's international
style and the government's reluctance to introduce substantial innovations
in the contents of Israeli approaches.

The reaction to the Peres initiative, which was in one sense the
Israeli response to the short-lived Hussein-Arafat accords of February
1985, highlighted the centrality of the Palestinian question. Israel's
repeated refusal to negotiate with the PLO on the one hand and the
PLO's rejection of the Jordanian demand to acknowledge UN resolutions
242 and 338 on the other hand further underlined the degree to which
issues of mutual recognition had become a serious obstacle to progress.
Despite numerous efforts to revive the peace process at this point, the
pattern of substantive deadlock continued. By the time of the rotation
of the prime ministership between Peres and Shamir in 1986, Peres had
put himself on record as favoring a new momentum; he had not, however,
designed ways to give content to this quest.

In this respect the Palestinian issue came to loom larger, not only
on the domestic and international fronts but also as a determinant of
the government's policy on the West Bank and in the Gaza Strip. The
administration of the territories during the Labor prime ministership
operated on the assumption that outright annexation was neither feasible
nor desirable and that some devolution of authority would be necessary.[56]
The idea of functional autonomy was reintroduced, based on the notion
of the separation between sovereignty over people and sovereignty over
territories and centered on the nurturing of a cooperative leadership in
the occupied territories.

At first, Israel accepted Jordanian proposals to appoint three mayors on the West Bank who were unlikely to arouse opposition in Palestinian nationalist circles. The experiment broke down with the assassination of West Bank moderate Aziz Shehadeh and then of the newly appointed mayor of Nablus, Za'afer el-Masri. Consequently, by mid-1986 the components of an Israeli-Jordanian condominium on the West Bank (to the exclusion of the PLO) were put in place, signaling yet another attempt to bypass the formal institutions of the Palestinian movement in the day-to-day administration of the areas beyond the Green Line. These moves included the appointment of pro-Jordanian mayors, the creation of an Arab banking institution on the West Bank, and the beginnings of a division of jurisdiction between Israel and Jordan in the area.

Thus, by the end of 1986 the national unity government had set in motion a flurry of international and regional activity. It had succeeded in extending Israel's credit abroad because its style was more measured and its attitudes were seemingly more flexible than those of its immediate predecessors. It had skillfully separated the issue of foreign policy and the peace process from immediate questions of security and the administration of the territories. Nevertheless, in the process the equivocal nature of the Israeli position became more apparent. Although a modus vivendi had been achieved with Lebanon and Jordan, relations with Egypt deteriorated following the killing of seven Israeli tourists at Ras Bourka in October 1985. The September 1986 agreement to refer the outstanding dispute over Taba to international arbitration and the return of the Egyptian ambassador (withdrawn during the Lebanon war) to Tel Aviv only partially alleviated the strains in Israeli-Egyptian interactions.[57] Moreover, as informal dialogues with Arabs and particularly with Palestinians (including members of the PLO) increased in quantity and frequency, the Knesset outlawed discussions with members of Palestinian liberation groups. The lack of clarity on the Palestinian issue became more salient both domestically and internationally precisely because it had been so studiously skirted by policymakers. In the absence of a willingness to confront some of the more basic dilemmas of the contemporary Zionist predicament, the pragmatic aura associated with the national unity government under Shimon Peres yielded a stalemate of not insignificant consequence.

Many of these inconsistencies were carried over and exacerbated during the Shamir incumbency. The continuation of Yitzhak Rabin as minister of defense assured that the policy guidelines for the administration of the territories elaborated by Peres would persist under his successor. Shamir, however, permitted the expansion of existing settlements, condoned disputes between settlers and residents over access to resources, supported the employment of strong-arm measures against Palestinian nationalists, and drew a particularly sharp distinction between these issues and foreign policy. Consequently, on the international front Shamir nurtured the new contacts established when he was foreign minister while consistently refusing to take any steps to advance the peace process. The differences between Peres and Shamir came to a head in spring 1987 following the London meeting between Peres and Hussein. Peres's subsequent attempt to gain government approval for an international conference as laid out in the London agreements was stonewalled by the Likud, whose leaders insisted on the resurrection of the Camp David framework.[58] The debate over procedural matters delayed any movement on the peace front and pointedly prevented serious discussion on the substantive elements of the process.

Global disinterest, Arab neglect (as evinced in the resolutions of the Arab summit held in Amman in spring 1987), PLO inaction, and the weight of the Israeli occupation combined to fuel the Palestinian uprising of late 1987. The intifada constituted a fundamental challenge to the status quo. It compelled Israelis to reassess an entire series of questions that had been ignored or repressed for well over a decade.

As the Arab-Israeli conflict assumed the form of a mass intercommunal confrontation, the parameters of the ideological debate within Israel expanded. Calls were issued for the deportation of Arabs (euphemistically called "transfer" in Hebrew) on the one hand and for the creation of a Palestinian state on the other hand. Israeli public opinion exhibited a marked fluidity and uncertainty as the psychological dimensions of the confrontation between Palestinians and Jews rose to the surface. Mutual fear, suspicion, and mistrust grew, and in some powerful quarters belief in the possibility of a peaceful resolution diminished. Signs of polarization, a hardening of positions, and moderation emerged simultaneously as it became increasingly apparent that the structure of the conflict had been irreversibly altered and that existing approaches could not be sustained.[59]

The first national unity government under Shamir, however, was incapable of adjusting its policies to meet these changing realities. While the security forces were galvanized under Rabin to put down the uprising, the cabinet continued to resist external efforts to mediate the conflict. Shamir steadfastly refused to consider the initiative of Secretary of State George Shultz to commence negotiations under international auspices.[60] And when King Hussein renounced all claims to the West Bank, in effect foreclosing the Jordanian option nurtured by the Labor party, any pretense of an understanding in government circles on foreign policy directions was abandoned on the eve of the 1988 elections.

The substance of the Israeli political agenda in the 1980s, which began and ended with an emphasis on issues of peace and security, was dominated by a concentration on immediate domestic concerns. This instrumental strain, introduced by the Likud administration and elaborated by the first national unity government, endowed the course of Israeli policy with a dual aura of pragmatism and impermanence. To be sure, the assertiveness and divisiveness of Likud policies in the early part of the decade gave way to a more realistic problem-solving approach at mid-decade, when Shimon Peres imposed a modicum of order in the handling of national affairs. The price of this stabilization, however, was a purposeful indecisiveness on central questions that entailed the formulation of future-oriented strategies.

By concentrating on the present, Israeli leaders permitted specific activities in a variety of spheres to serve as a substitute for reasoned policy design and implementation. The notion that time worked in Israel's favor nurtured the fallacy that it was possible to avoid coming to terms with the consequences of specific actions and that confrontation with fundamental issues could be delayed indefinitely. The emphasis on preservation precluded innovation and vision. Yitzhak Shamir's prime ministership in the latter part of the 1980s exemplified the extent to which this orientation stymied creativity even in the face of drastically altered realities on the ground.

Manifestations of these trends were also visible in the nature of Israel's external interactions. The emergence of Israel from the global isolation it experienced in the 1970s was not accompanied either by a greater acceptance of Israeli policies by the international community or by an enhancement of Israel's autonomy abroad. The Israeli involvement in Central America, southern Africa, and the Gulf aroused considerable criticism, as did Israel's continued occupation of the West Bank and Gaza. At the same time, consistent denunciations of Israeli actions did not impede the expansion of Israel's external contacts.

The relationship with the United States demonstrated these patterns. Throughout the 1980s Israel's reliance on the United States grew despite repeated attempts to assert Israel's independence on the foreign policy front. At the beginning of the 1980s the prospect of U.S. intervention evoked a backlash in Israeli policymaking circles. Gradually, however, Washington was drawn into the internal Israeli debate. By mid-decade specific policy measures (such as the decision to terminate the Lavi project, a plan to construct an Israeli-designed fighter plane, or the imposition of selective sanctions on South Africa) were justified as responses to U.S. requests.[61] And in the latter part of the 1980s increased U.S. involvement, often at odds with Israeli government guidelines, was absorbed without significant adverse commentary.

The Palestinian uprising drove home the message that Israel had reached the point where mild adjustments no longer sufficed as a means of coming to terms with fundamental ideological questions. Although the Labor-Likud coalition almost intentionally sought to remove these issues from the national agenda, its conduct fueled the Palestinian insurrection. The economic, political, global, and moral price of continued Israeli occupation had major implications for the future of the Zionist enterprise. The survival of the state of Israel, its democratic complexion, its Jewish character, its demographic composition, its underlying values, and its moral fabric could no longer be separated from the territorial issue.

With the early 1990s, as in the political and social spheres, so too in the substantive domain, the basic impetus for transformation in the definition of national objectives has been provided, though the core of these changes remains undefined. Recent Israeli policies have pointedly exposed the essence of the issues that the country must confront and have consequently revealed hesitations and fostered equivocation. A thorough rethinking—predicated on the need to grapple directly with the Palestinian question and Israel's standing in the Middle East in the wake of the 1990–1991 Gulf crisis—has begun to take place. The outcome of this domestic reassessment depends on the policy choices and the political course charted by the country's leaders at this critical juncture.

The Foreign Policy Process: Dynamics and Trends

The foreign policy orientations of Israel and its responses to external actions and initiatives are directly related to domestic social and political currents. Although conditions in the international arena and attitudes toward Israel delineate the range of choices available to policymakers, these factors do not dictate Israeli choices, which are filtered through a complex set of internal considerations. In the years between the signing of the Egyptian-Israeli peace accords and the commencement of the Palestinian uprising, the country experienced substantial changes in political organization, social interaction, and substantive preoccupations, all of which had a direct influence on the nature of Israeli activities abroad.

The dynamics of events during this period reflected the effects of changes in the major components of politics and modes of political interchange. Depending on the perspective adopted, the picture that emerged was one either of extremism and obduracy or, alternately, of greater apathy and paralysis. Views tended to fluctuate between the perception of stalemate and the suggestion of momentum, between polarization and fluidity, between deadlock and movement. These quite diverse observations, with their dramatically different implications, obscured the key feature of this decade: the proliferation of uncertainty, contradiction, and confusion.

The absence of consensus was accentuated and formalized during the tenure of the first national unity government. The broad coalition construct signified an acceptance of the lack of societal cohesion and ideological coherence. In this setting, disagreements, tensions, and ongoing disputes were allowed to proliferate as diversity became the norm. This pattern had a lulling effect which fostered a tendency to deal with the specific and the immediate at the expense of a more profound reexamination of fundamental values and goals. Because the shifts in the political climate lacked clear direction and purpose, the perpetuation of old concepts inhibited the translation of new modalities into precise policy terms.

The amorphous course of Israeli policy during these years was reinforced by developments on the external front. The global configuration in the first three years of the national unity government did not constitute a direct threat to Israel or require immediate policy responses. The continuation of regional strife in Central America, southern Africa, the Fertile Crescent, and parts of Asia, coupled with the preoccupation with superpower relations, initially reduced the centrality of Israel-related topics on the global agenda. The lack of precision on these questions in Washington and European capitals relieved immediate pressures on the government. And the Iran-Iraq war, together with the continuing crisis in Lebanon, diluted concerted Arab action. The external environment was relatively conducive to the nonbinding explorations of options for renewing the peace process.

Within this framework, Israel's bilateral relations with selected partners continued to inform policy options. The decision of the U.S. government to uphold the declared Israeli position on negotiations with the PLO provided a very real disincentive for Israel to reevaluate this topic. In the same vein, the predictability of U.S. economic and military assistance during the mid-1980s may have contributed to Israeli inaction.

Regional constellations also played a role in the lack of policy precision at this time. The Hussein-Mubarak rapprochement set the stage for the expansion of Israel's channels of communication in the region. The destruction of the PLO infrastructure in Lebanon and the subsequent dispersion of its leadership fostered a fragmentation in the Palestinian liberation movement which relieved direct pressure from Israel. Similarly, the Hussein-Arafat understanding, though focusing attention on issues of mutual recognition, nevertheless allowed Israel to proceed with independent steps on the West Bank. The emergence of Syria, Israel's main military antagonist, at the center of major disagreements in the Arab world further reduced the urgency for drastic policy changes.

The rhythm of politics established in the second half of the decade was shattered by the outbreak of widespread resistance to Israeli rule and by profound changes in the organization and perception of Palestinian society.[62] The insurrection in the West Bank and the Gaza Strip and its persistence despite the employment of increasingly forceful Israeli measures set in motion a series of domestic, regional, and international changes which irreversibly altered the context of the Arab-Israeli conflict. Whether Israeli leaders will continue to react to these new conditions in the piecemeal and equivocal manner molded in the past or will be able to shape a more comprehensive approach to the multiplicity of issues on the national agenda remains open to question.

As in the past, future policy directions will be guided by the interaction of domestic and external variables. The events of 1988 wrought changes in the international environment which narrowed the range of options available to Israeli decisionmakers and reduced their room for maneuverability in the global environment. The uprising eliminated the maintenance of the status quo as a viable policy course, and Hussein's disengagement from the West Bank not only foreclosed the Jordanian-Palestinian confederal option in the near future but also paved the way for the declaration of Palestinian statehood on November 15, 1988. The resolutions of the Palestine National Council in Algiers (which also included a formal commitment to a two-state solution), together with widespread disapproval of Israeli repression in the occupied territories, combined to enhance the PLO's standing in the international community. The convening of the special session of the United Nations General Assembly in Geneva in December underscored the deterioration in Israel's international position. Yasser Arafat's renunciation of terror and his reiteration of the PLO's acceptance of UN resolutions 242 and 338 prompted the opening of the U.S.-Palestinian dialogue which indicated the first major shift in U.S. policy on the conflict in over a decade.[63] And the new character of Soviet-U.S. relations suggested the likelihood of greater superpower coordination in the region.

The Israeli political system reacted slowly to the reorientation of the external environment. During 1988 continued efforts to suppress the Palestinian uprising and the preparations for the November elections prevented the elaboration of any detailed Israeli plan. The results of the elections complicated the prospects for a major departure from past approaches. The cumbersome national unity construct, with all its drawbacks, was retained in a considerably weakened form. The electorate had signaled its alienation from both major parties but did not indicate a preference for any clear-cut alternative. Domestic considerations—most notably a growing concern with economic recession, unemployment, Soviet immigration, and the deterioration of social services—resurfaced. The top leadership of the country was retained in office as prospects for the incorporation of new personalities dimmed.[64] And new tensions developed in Israel's relations with Jewish communities abroad.

As a result, by the end of the first year of the intifada, very little actual progress was registered either in the management of the conflict or in the resumption of the peace process.[65] Moreover, a different set of asymmetries had emerged which redefined the parameters of the policy context. To be sure, the asymmetry of force continued; but in the face of the superiority of the Israeli military, the residents of the West Bank and Gaza exhibited remarkable persistence and creativity. An asymmetry of resolve was also in evidence: The uprising galvanized Palestinian commitment to a negotiated resolution to the conflict while it underlined Israeli ambivalence. An asymmetry of politics became apparent, with the Palestinian community evolving coordinating institutions while the Israeli body politic remained at cross-purposes. And a profound asymmetry of perception developed depending on the degree of emphasis placed either on improved prospects for a political settlement as indicated by shifts in the international arena or on the grim realities of resistance and repression with the enormous human price the confrontation exacted and the growing mistrust it fomented.

By the beginning of 1989 rising domestic and external pressures made it abundantly clear that the government could no longer avoid designing a policy to deal with the new situation. Its task, however, was complicated by its inability to agree on ultimate goals. Within the conventional range of options, adherence to the status quo and the Jordanian option were impossible and annexation was undesirable. This left autonomy, a Palestinian state, or some combination of the two as the most obvious choices, without eliminating the possibility of examining other alternatives, such as a unilateral withdrawal from Gaza or a "Jordan is Palestine" option.[66] Because the only point of convergence among the coalition partners centered on the necessity of achieving some devolution of authority in the occupied territories, it was impossible to formulate a plan that went beyond arrangements for a transition period. In these circumstances the only course of action open to the government was to suggest a method for the de-escalation of the crisis without committing itself to a vision for its resolution.

The Shamir-Rabin plan, first presented in Washington and subsequently approved by the Israeli cabinet in the spring of 1989, sought to reduce pressure on Israel, induce some political movement, and delay any serious discussion of the final disposition of the territories. The core of the proposals, which reaffirmed Israel's objection to negotiations with the PLO and to the creation of a Palestinian state, centered on the holding of elections in the West Bank and Gaza in order to launch the autonomy plan and to determine the composition of a negotiating team for future talks. The main attraction of the Shamir-Rabin program was that it broke the impasse that had existed since the beginning of the uprising and allowed for multiple interpretations of procedures, modalities, and preferred outcomes. The main disadvantage of the initiative was that it failed to chart a substantive course or offer a clear strategy for its realization. In many respects, therefore, the government proposals exemplified the limitations of the system that had conceived them.

The domestic and international debate over the Shamir plan continued throughout 1989 as the government rejected numerous proposals to set its own initiative in motion. At the same time, divisions within Israel grew, Palestinian frustrations increased, and violence escalated. The government employed more sophisticated techniques to quell the intifada, and Palestinian extremists responded in kind. As the second year of the uprising drew to a close, the leaders of the national unity government were at loggerheads as the rivalry between Labor and Likud ministers was compounded by splits within each of the major parties. The country was still unprepared to grapple with the territorial issue, and the decisionmaking apparatus was immobilized. In effect, the capacities of the prevailing political structures had been stretched to their limit. Israeli policymakers could not confine themselves indefinitely to a holding exercise, they were unable to suggest specific ways to pursue their own declared policies, and they were incapable of making and implementing difficult choices on any of the fundamental issues confronting the country. It was difficult to foresee constructive movement in the peace process without significant changes in the domestic political realm. The collapse of the second national unity government in early spring 1990 confirmed the impossibility of maintaining existing arrangements.

Some observers have suggested that such a reordering must commence at the level of ideology and attitudes.[67] They believe that without a thoroughgoing process of reeducation focusing on the elimination of mistrust and on confidence building, no government can carry out an innovative policy course. Although the importance of attitude change cannot be underestimated, other observers have proposed that change must commence at the societal level. They view the fragmentation of Israeli society as the main impediment to concerted action on the foreign policy front and have concentrated their energies on building up a broad, peace-oriented constituency within the country.[68] Most analysts, however, have linked changes in ideology and social organization to changes at the political level. They have raised doubts about the possibility of reorienting or unifying the diverse strands of Israeli political culture without bringing about basic changes in the political conditions that have allowed these opinions and constellations to flourish. In this view, a negotiated political solution to the ongoing conflict is a precondition for real change in the Israeli body politic.

The first step toward the realization of such a goal involved the disbanding of the national unity government structure. The stability of the unity format did not augment government efficiency or increase implementation capacities, nor did the division of power within the government enhance decisionmaking capabilities. From the perspective of both the major partners of the ruling coalition, the dissipation of electoral support and the rise in intraparty discord began to outweigh the utilitarian advantages accruing from proximity to the state apparatus. Although the breakup of the national unity government may have exacerbated uncertainty in the short term, it may compel the major political parties to define their positions more precisely and present voters with a clearer choice at the polls. Such a move may also revive the opposition and conceivably furnish the conditions for the emergence or assertion of a more forceful leadership role in policy formulation and execution.

The possibilities for domestic political change will continue to be affected by shifts in the regional and global environment, especially in the aftermath of the Iraqi invasion of Kuwait, as well as by the policies of the PLO, Arab countries, the superpowers, and the international community. But as long as Israel controls the West Bank and Gaza, Israeli politics and political orientations will continue to have a dominant influence on the outcome of the conflict. The Palestinian uprising and the processes it unleashed have underlined the fact that Israel must loosen its hold on the territories, not only to regularize its standing in the Middle East but also to ensure its own integrity. The capacity of Israeli society to come to terms with the anomalies of its condition and the ability of the political system to guide the reformulation of national objectives require the empowerment of political will and not just of military might.

Israel is presently at a critical crossroads. It faces the twin challenges of overcoming uncertainty and redefining its national goals. The future course of Arab-Israeli relations depends on how it approaches these tasks.

Notes

Thanks are due to the Harry S. Truman Institute for the Advancement of Peace at the Hebrew University of Jerusalem and to Radcliffe College for providing the facilities that made the preparation and revision of this chapter possible. The editors of this book, Judith Kipper and Harold Saunders, deserve special appreciation for their thoughtful comments on earlier drafts.

1. The emphasis here is on consensus in decisionmaking quarters, not in society at large. Narrow coalitions, however unrepresentative, have often been in a position to take more vigorous positions than the national unity governments, precisely because differences between coalition partners were contained. On the reactive character of Israeli foreign policy, see Avi Schlaim and Avner Yaniv, "Domestic Politics and Foreign Policy in Israel," *International Organization,* vol. 56, no. 2 (1981), p. 242 and passim.

2. These phases are explored in Naomi Chazan, "Domestic Developments in Israel," in William B. Quandt, ed., *The Middle East: Ten Years After Camp David* (Washington, D.C.: Brookings Institution, 1988), pp. 150–186.

3. Baruch Kimmerling has suggested that three separate political cultures existed in Israel at the close of 1989: a militaristic-survivalist political culture supported by large segments of Labor and the Likud, a conflict-oriented culture propounded by the parties of the extreme right, and a peace culture advocated by the parties to the left of Labor. See his "The Effects of Protracted Conflict on Israeli Society" (Jerusalem, draft manuscript, 1989).

4. See Baruch Kimmerling, "Making Conflict a Routine: Cumulative Effects of the Arab-Jewish Conflict upon Israeli Society," *Journal of Strategic Studies,* vol. 6, no. 3 (1983), esp. p. 38.

5. For general background, see Don Peretz, *The Government and Politics of Israel* (Boulder, Colo.: Westview Press, 1979).

6. Michael Brecher, *The Foreign Policy System of Israel: Setting, Images, Process* (London: Oxford University Press, 1972), p. 346. See also Bernard Reich, "Israel's Foreign Policy and the 1977 Parliamentary Elections," in Howard R. Penniman, ed., *Israel at the Polls: The Knesset Elections of 1977* (Washington, D.C.: American Enterprise Institute, 1979), pp. 255–282.

7. For the impact of these divisions on the Egyptian-Israeli negotiations, see Dan Jacobson, "Intraparty Dissensus and Interparty Conflict Resolution: A Laboratory Experiment in the Context of the Middle East Conflict," *Journal of Conflict Resolution,* vol. 25 (1981), pp. 471–494.

8. William B. Quandt, *Camp David: Peacemaking and Politics* (Washington, D.C.: Brookings Institution, 1986).

9. Eleven of the nineteen negative votes and two abstentions came from within the ranks of the coalition, including such figures as Yitzhak Shamir, Moshe Arens, Ariel Sharon, and Geula Cohen.

10. Shlomo Aronson, "Israel's Leaders, Domestic Order and Foreign Policy," *Jerusalem Journal of International Relations,* vol. 6, no. 4 (1982–1983), pp. 1–29.

11. Shai Feldman and Heda Rechnitz-Kijner, *Deception, Consensus and War: Israel in Lebanon,* paper 27 (Tel Aviv University, Jaffee Center for Strategic Studies, 1984).

12. For a detailed account of the war, see Ze'ev Schiff and Ehud Ya'ari, *Israel's Lebanon War,* ed. and trans. Ina Friedman (New York: Simon and Schuster, 1984).

13. For background, see Ned Temko, *To Win or to Die: A Personal Portrait of Menachem Begin* (New York: William Morrow, 1987).

14. Emanuel Gutmann, "Begin's Israel: The End of an Era?" *International Journal,* vol. 38, no. 4 (1983), pp. 690–699.

15. See Gershom Schocken, "Israel in Election Year 1984," *Foreign Affairs,* vol. 63 (1983), p. 84 and passim.

16. See Asher Arian and Michal Shamir, eds., *The Elections in Israel— 1984* (Tel Aviv: Ramot, 1986).

17. Yossi Beilin, the newly appointed cabinet secretary, and Nimrod Novik, Shimon Peres's political adviser, were instrumental in the formation of this group.

18. Yael Yishai, *Interest Groups in Israel* (Tel Aviv: Am Oved, 1987), in Hebrew.

19. This point is highlighted in Chazan, "Domestic Developments in Israel," p. 172.

20. The leadership styles of Shamir and Peres were analyzed skillfully by Thomas Friedman in a series of articles in the *New York Times,* October 1986.

21. Detailed analyses of the 1988 elections have not yet been published. See, for example, Avraham Diskin, "The 1988 Elections in Israel" (Jerusalem, draft manuscript, 1989).

22. Judith Shuval, "The Structure and Dilemmas of Israeli Pluralism," in Baruch Kimmerling, ed., *The Israeli State and Society: Boundaries and Frontiers* (Albany: State University of New York Press, 1989), pp. 216–237.

23. Lee E. Dutter, "The Political Relevance of Ethnicity Among Israeli Jews," *Plural Societies,* vol. 14, nos. 1–2 (1983), p. 18 and passim.

24. Asher Arian, "The Electorate: Israel 1977," in Penniman, *Israel at the Polls,* pp. 59–89.

25. Efraim Ben-Zadok and Giora Goldberg, "A Sociopolitical Change in the Israeli Development Towns: An Analysis of Voting Patterns of Oriental Jews," *Plural Societies,* vol. 14, nos 1–2 (1983), pp. 49–65.

26. For an excellent study of this phenomenon, see Janet Aviad, *Return to Judaism: Religious Renewal in Israel* (Chicago: University of Chicago Press, 1982).

27. Eliezer Don-Yehiya, "Religious Leaders in the Political Arena: The Case of Israel," *Middle Eastern Studies,* vol. 20, no. 2 (1984), pp. 154–171.

28. On the loss of Labor hegemony, see Myron J. Aronoff, "The Decline of the Israeli Labor Party: Causes and Significance," in Penniman, *Israel at the Polls,* pp. 115–145.

29. Baruch Kimmerling, "Between 'Alexandria-on-the-Hudson' and Zion," in Kimmerling, *The Israeli State and Society,* pp. 237–264.

30. Alex Mintz, "The Military-Industrial Complex: The Israeli Case," *Journal of Strategic Studies*, vol. 6, no. 3 (1983), pp. 103–127.

31. Brecher, *Foreign Policy System of Israel*, pp. 547–548.

32. Asher Arian, "Interest Groups in Israel" (paper presented at the annual meeting of the American Political Science Association, Atlanta, Georgia, August 1989), p. 1.

33. Yair Kotler in *Heil Kahane* (New York: Adama Books, 1986) provides background on Kahane and his movement.

34. Ehud Sprinzak, "From Messianic Pioneering to Vigilante Terrorism: The Case of the Gush Emunim Underground," *Journal of Strategic Studies*, vol. 10, no. 4 (1987), p. 200 and passim.

35. On the inability to entertain paradigm changes, see Zvi Lanir, "Academic Research and National Misconception," *Jerusalem Quarterly*, vol. 32 (1984), pp. 36–47.

36. Arthur Hertzberg, ed., *The Zionist Idea* (New York: Atheneum, 1975); and Shlomo Avineri, *The Making of Modern Zionism: The Intellectual Origins of the Jewish State* (New York: Basic Books, 1981).

37. Charles S. Liebman and Eliezer Don-Yehiya, "The Dilemma of Reconciling Traditional Culture and Political Needs: Civil Religion in Israel," *Comparative Politics*, vol. 16 (1983), pp. 53–66.

38. For an example of this ambiguity, see Shlomo Avineri, "Ideology and Israel's Foreign Policy," *Jerusalem Quarterly*, vol. 37 (1986), pp. 3–13.

39. Yehoshafat Harkabi has made this point in several of his works. See his *Fateful Decisions* (Tel Aviv: Am Oved, 1987), in Hebrew; *The Bar Kochba Syndrome: Risk and Realism in International Politics* (New York: Rossel Books, 1983); and "A Policy for the Moment of Truth" (Washington, D.C.: Foundation for Middle East Peace, 1988).

40. Brecher, *Foreign Policy System of Israel*, pp. 555–556.

41. For an overview, see Stephen L. Spiegel, *The Other Arab-Israel Conflict* (Chicago: University of Chicago Press, 1986).

42. Shlomo Avineri, "Beyond Camp David," *Foreign Policy*, no. 46 (Spring 1982), pp. 22–23.

43. For details, see Gadi Wolsfeld, *The Politics of Provocation: Participation and Protest in Israel* (Albany: State University of New York Press, 1988).

44. Meron Benvenisti, *The West Bank Data Project: A Survey of Israel's Policies* (Washington, D.C.: American Enterprise Institute, 1984).

45. Emile Sahliye, *In Search of Leadership: West Bank Politics Since 1967* (Washington, D.C.: Brookings Institution, 1988).

46. Moshe Ma'oz, "Israeli Positions Regarding the Palestinian Question," *Vierteljahresberichte*, no. 98 (1985), pp. 21–28.

47. Dan Horowitz, "Israel's War in Lebanon: New Patterns of Strategic Thinking and Civilian-Military Relations," *Journal of Strategic Studies*, vol. 6, no. 3 (1983), pp. 83–102.

48. Many of these criticisms are systematically stated in a pamphlet published by Peace Now, "The War in Lebanon" (Jerusalem, 1983 and 1984).

49. Haim Barkai, "Reflections on the Economic Cost of the Lebanon War," *Jerusalem Quarterly*, vol. 37 (1986), pp. 95–106.

50. Gerald M. Steinberg, "Large-scale National Projects as Political Symbols: The Case of Israel," *Comparative Politics*, vol. 19 (1987), pp. 331–346.

51. Avi Gottlieb and Ephraim Yuchtman-Yaar, "Materialism, Postmaterialism, and Public Views on Socioeconomic Policy: The Case of Israel," *Comparative Political Studies*, vol. 16, no. 3 (1983), pp. 307–336.

52. David Grossman, *The Yellow Wind*, trans. Haim Watzman (New York: Farrar, Straus and Giroux, 1988).

53. For an intriguing exploration of this issue, see Mark A. Heller, *A Palestinian State: The Implications for Israel* (Cambridge, Mass.: Harvard University Press, 1983).

54. See Arye Oded, *Africa and the Middle East Conflict* (Boulder, Colo.: Lynne Rienner Publishers, 1987); and Naomi Chazan, "Israel and Africa in the 1980s: The Dilemmas of Complexity and Ambiguity," in Olajide Aluko, ed., *Africa and the Great Powers in the 1980s* (Washington, D.C.: University Press of America, 1987), pp. 201–235.

55. Yossi Melman, "Israeli Chinese Relations and Their Future Prospects," *Asian Survey*, vol. 17, no. 4 (1987), pp. 395–407. Also see Ben Ami Shillony, "Japan and Israel," *Middle East Review*, vol. 18, no. 2 (1985), pp. 17–24.

56. This approach was validated by the forceful rejection by the Knesset of a resolution to annex the West Bank in early 1986.

57. For a detailed analysis, see Shimon Shamir, "Israeli Views of Egypt and the Peace Process: The Duality of Vision," in Quandt, *The Middle East: Ten Years After Camp David*, pp. 187–216.

58. The text of the Peres-Hussein agreement (the London Document) of April 11, 1987, is reproduced in Quandt, *The Middle East: Ten Years After Camp David*, pp. 475–476.

59. Asher Arian and Raphael Ventura, "Public Opinion in Israel and the Intifada: Changes in Security Attitudes 1987–1988" (Tel Aviv: Jaffee Center for Strategic Studies, memorandum no. 28, August 1989).

60. "The Shultz Initiative, March 4, 1988," in Quandt, *The Middle East: Ten Years After Camp David*, pp. 488–489.

61. For details on shifts in Israel's policy toward South Africa, see Naomi Chazan, "Israeli Perspectives on the Israel–South African Relationship" (London: Institute of Jewish Affairs, Research Report 9–10, 1987).

62. Jim Lederman, "Dateline West Bank: Interpreting the Intifada," *Foreign Policy*, no. 172 (1988), pp. 230–246.

63. Leonard Binder, "The Changing American Role in the Middle East," *Current History*, vol. 88, no. 535 (1989), pp. 65–68, 96–97.

64. Perhaps the one exception is Aryeh Der'i, the young Shas leader who became minister of interior in the new government.

65. This point is made skillfully by Aaron David Miller, "Palestinians and the Intifada: One Year Later," *Current History*, vol. 88, no. 535 (1989), p. 73.

66. These options are discussed in detail in The Jaffee Center for Strategic Studies, *The West Bank and Gaza: Israel's Options for Peace* (Tel Aviv: Report of a JCSS Study Group, 1989). Also see the JCSS 1989 summary and proposal contained in "Israel, The West Bank and Gaza: Toward a Solution," which

advocates an interim autonomy plan leading to the creation of a Palestinian state.

67. See Mark A. Heller, "Israeli Politics and the Arab-Israel Peace Process," *Washington Quarterly,* vol. 10, no. 2 (1987), p. 129.

68. See Mordechai Baron, "The Impact of the Intifada on Israeli Society and the Prospects of Peace" (paper presented at the Twenty-second United Nations Seminar on the Question of Palestine, New York, June 1989).

6
The Changing Role of Congress in U.S. Middle East Policy

William Green Miller

The New Role of Congress in National Security Affairs

The role of Congress in national security affairs has changed dramatically since the end of World War II. From a position of generally unquestioning support of executive-branch initiatives, Congress has become an assertive, sometimes contentious partner in the making of national security policy. This change in the balance between the roles of the president and the Congress accelerated in the aftermath of the failure of Vietnam, the weakening of the presidency because of the Watergate scandals, the continuing debate over how strategic arms agreements with the Soviet Union should be negiotated, the search for meaningful procedural safeguards to protect an open constitutional system against possible abuses by secret intelligence agencies, and a host of other policymaking and procedural issues. Many of the concerns continue to be institutional questions of constitutional balance, of how to achieve more effective oversight, and of how to strike the proper balance between the legislative and executive branches, but not all the concerns are procedural. Not least of these other substantive issues is Middle East policy.

Shared Responsibility Between the Legislative and Executive Branches for the Making of Foreign Policy

An uneasy compromise has been struck between the legislative and executive branches on the making of foreign and defense policy. The present balance is characterized by an acceptance of the view that the Constitution calls for shared responsibilities in the making of policy; the necessity for continual and effective congressional oversight and the monitoring of the means used to carry out policies decided upon; and a continuing search for more practical ways to review and, if necessary, to reconsider policy decisions once they are made. Clearly, the president and the executive branch as a whole had far less policy flexibility in the decade of the 1980s than in the immediate post–World War II period. Not only must policymaking be shared with the Congress, but congressional attitudes must be taken into account in planning for any new directions. This post-Vietnam legislative attitude is best exemplified in the twists and turns of the short unhappy history of the War Powers Act, the creation of permanent intelligence oversight committees in the House and Senate, and the continuing policy controversy over fundamental defense and foreign policy issues, which include how to maintain and, in the light of radically changed circumstances, restructure the most vital of security alliances such as NATO, how best to approach the changes in the Soviet Union and Eastern Europe, and how best to balance U.S. interests in the Middle East.

An Opening Up of the Policymaking Process

Since the late 1960s, there has been, in effect, an opening up of the policymaking process. The new legislative/executive power relationships not only have widened the circle of policymakers to include a substantial number in the Congress, but an even wider circle of legislators and their staffs have been made privy to sensitive information regarded as necessary to make policy judgments in defense and foreign policy issues. One effect of the struggle between the legislative and executive branches over the enactment of a series of statutes aimed at definition of the proper constitutional balance between the branches has been the requirement to share with the designated relevant committees of Congress whatever information is produced by the intelligence agencies for the White House and the State and Defense departments. There are, for example, no categories of intelligence information, no matter how sensitive, that have not been shared with the intelligence oversight committees of the Congress. In addition, the standing committees of the Congress on foreign relations and defense are now fully informed of intelligence reports and analyses of policy concern.

Another example of the change that has occurred in the policy process since World War II is the continuing policy conflicts in the Congress over the deployment of new weaponry. It would have been almost unthinkable in 1947 when the National Security Act was passed creating the Department of Defense, the National Security Council, and the Central Intelligence Agency that the Congress would be so deeply involved in weapons decisions, but from the beginning of the ABM debate in 1968, the development and deployment of weapons systems— particularly if deployments affect arms control possibilities—have been closely examined and often challenged in the Congress. In 1947, foreign policy and defense deployments were thought by an overwhelming majority to be the proper province of experts: diplomats, military planners, and intelligence analysts. Members of Congress whose concerns and experience were turned inward to domestic concerns seldom if ever challenged the wisdom of military experts. That era is clearly over.

The Impact of Television, Jet Travel, and More Extensive Media Coverage of the Middle East

The remarkable ability of the media to give in-depth coverage of wars, national disasters, political changes, and cultural events in the most distant corners of the world brought the beginnings of a sense of global interdependence to vast national television audiences. Jet aircraft, which made it possible to span continents and oceans in a few hours in ease and comfort, carried growing numbers of leaders of govermental departments and agencies and of private-sector commercial and banking organizations, not to mention armies of leisured tourists. The impact of the worldwide spread of the telephone, television, and rapid jet travel cannot be minimized; these expedients have reduced time required for communication from weeks and days to hours and minutes, and their extent and immediacy have contributed more than any other factor toward the creation of a sophisticated awareness and to a growing involvement in international affairs. The realities of life in Beirut, Cairo, Riyadh, Jerusalem, Damascus, Abu Dhabi, or Tehran have been directly experienced by diverse and large enough groups of influential leaders and ordinary citizens to such a degree that it is now possible and widely acceptable for the U.S. citizenry to begin to deal with policy alternatives in terms that go beyond simplistic frameworks.

The Changed Nature of Diplomacy in the Middle East

Just as the base of knowledge about the world generally, and the Middle East in particular, has expanded to include a broad spectrum of political, economic, and cultural interests as a result of the communications boom and the growing interdependence of nations, so too have diplomacy and the way governments deal with each other been transformed. The change in the nature and practice of diplomacy following World War II is a key factor bearing on the nature of U.S. policy in the Middle East.

As the United States began to exercise its new role of superpower, the size, scope of activity, and even the physical appearance of its diplomatic establishments reflected that new status. The diplomacy of prewar days—elegant embassies geared to a formal diplomatic life centered about exchanges of information with other diplomatic missions and an emphasis on close relationships with the host foreign office and the elite ruling groups—was superseded, if not entirely replaced, by a new kind of active diplomacy. In countries considered important to U.S. interests, the size of embassies increased ten times, in some cases hundreds of times, and the complement of traditional career Foreign Service diplomats was dwarfed by the legions staffing the expanded activity. U.S. Agency for International Development (USAID) economic assistance missions, U.S. Information Agency (USIA) cultural missions, commercial attachés, Central Intelligence Agency (CIA) stations, military assistance groups, Peace Corps groups, agricultural advisers, U.S. Treasury attachés, drug enforcement agents, Federal Aviation Authority experts—these were only some of the U.S. government agencies and groups attached to embassies that grew in size and number as the postwar period progressed.

Foreign affairs was no longer the sole province of Foreign Service diplomats. The energies of an assertive superpower were formally reflected in these new highly active organizations. One consequence of their vitality and extensive presence and influence was that these new organizations often held different points of view about what U.S. policy should be and fought for those interests and views in the policymaking councils of the executive branch.

The orderly expression of all of this overseas activity, which sometimes operated at cross-purposes, was termed in the Eisenhower administration the "country team." In theory, each country team worked in a hierarchical chain of command under the direction of the ambassador. But the quality of ambassadors varied, and the dominant figure expressing U.S. interests may have in fact been the commanding general of the military assistance group, the CIA station chief, or perhaps the USAID director, depending on the particular country involved or the ability of the ambassador.

This burgeoning of overseas embassy activity in every conceivable area of political, economic, and cultural interest reflected the dynamisms of the national security bureaucracies in Washington. The interplay between the perspectives of the Departments of State and Defense and the intelligence agencies, the political requirements of the White House, and a range of domestic pressures created the conditions conducive to a constant policy struggle. In the past twenty years, various and changing mechanisms were developed at every level of authority in attempts to sort out the shifting differences of view between the military, the State Department, USAID, and the many other involved agencies. At the highest levels, the National Security Council functioned reasonably well to determine the broad outlines of the complex of foreign policies, defense strategies, and aid programs to create the amalgam now commonly called national security policy.

Policy Changes Reflect the Dynamic Politics of the Middle East

Although there have been policy constants in the post–World War II period, there have been many fundamental changes of policy. Some of the alliance and treaty alignments drawn up in the immediate postwar period have survived—NATO, for example—but most of the world has altered dramatically. Because of the major shifts taking place in the Soviet Union, even NATO and the Warsaw Pact have undergone radical change. Indeed, most of the world's power relationships have evolved into new alignments and arrangements, with new leaders holding perspectives very different from those of national leaders in World War II.

Egypt is only one example of radically different changes of leadership. King Farouk marked the end of the old regime, and the successive presidencies of Nassar, Sadat, and now Mubarak reflect the dynamic changes in the nature of Egyptian domestic policies and international relations, including the country's relative position in the Middle East and the world. It was unthinkable when Nassar came to power to believe that a Sinai agreement would be possible or that the Egyptians or Israel under Menachem Begin would become party to anything like the Camp David process. Sadat's late 1977 journey to Jerusalem seems miraculous when looked at from the bitter, dark circumstances of Suez in 1956.

Changed Government and Popular Perspectives

Generational change has not been unique to the Middle East. It has been paralleled in the United States among the leaders within the national security bureaucracy and in Congress, as well as in the character and experience of seven presidents and ten secretaries of state. The significance of radical shifts of governmental points of view and subsequent policy changes cannot be minimized. One way to analyze the reasons for the changes in points of view in successive generations of postwar leadership is to examine the differences in the quality and emphasis of university education, the great impact of the flood of young travelers abroad, the involvement of young Americans throughout the world through organizations such as the Peace Corps, the effect of new immigration to the United States, and perhaps most significant the impact of the electronic revolution.

As low-cost travel and television news have opened up the world for Americans, foreign policy and defense issues have ceased to be considered the arcane province of experts; rather, foreign policy issues such as Central America, emergency food assistance to Ethiopia, the uprising in Gaza or the West Bank, the sale of arms to Saudi Arabia, or the conduct of war in the Gulf have become everyday matters. Citizens express opinions about these issues just as freely as they do about domestic problems like budget deficits, interest rates, inflation, or agricultural subsidies. Examining U.S. public opinion about Middle East policies from this perspective reveals profound changes in relative awareness and assertiveness about events and long-term policies in the Middle East in recent years.

One early example of this change is contained in an important survey of leadership groups, including the Congress, and the broad spectrum of public opinion. *American Public Opinion and U.S. Foreign Policy 1983*, which was undertaken for the Chicago Council on Foreign Relations by the Gallup organization and issued in the spring of that year, reported these findings on the Middle East:

> Public concern over Saudi Arabia was especially striking. Presumably because of that country's abundant oil reserves, Saudi Arabia was perceived as one of the top countries in terms of vital interest to the United States. Clearly, the Middle East is now seen as an area of major U.S. interest in the world, along with our neighbors and traditional allies.
>
> The 1982 results indicate some slippage in public favorability toward Israel and a significant drop in favorability toward Prime Minister Menachem Begin. The explanation lies in a widespread negative assessment of Israeli policies, particularly among the leaders. A majority of the public and two-thirds of the leaders disapproved of Israel's recent actions in Lebanon. President Reagan's Middle East peace plan, which was rejected by the Israeli government, is favored two to one by the American public, as is formation of a separate and independent Palestinian state. A strong majority of the public feels that the U.S. should require that all weapons sent to Israel should be used for defensive purposes only. About one-third of the public and one-quarter of the leaders want to see U.S. military aid and arms sales to Israel decreased or stopped altogether.
>
> On the other hand, Americans continue to show a strong margin of sympathy for Israel over the Arabs. And despite recent events in Lebanon,

PLO leader Yasser Arafat ranks far below Menachem Begin in personal popularity. The longterm sympathy trends in the Middle East show that the 1982 events in Lebanon did have an effect on American public opinion. Sympathy for the Arab cause is now somewhat higher than it was before June 1982. On the other hand, sympathy for Israel, which had gone up in early 1982, returned to a relatively high level toward the end of the year. Overall, public opinion now shows more sympathy for both sides than has been the case in the past.[1]

The Middle East is less and less identified in the public mind in stereotypes of sandy deserts, bedouins on camels, oil wells, and Israel. In the more than four decades since the end of World War II, tangible knowledge about the Middle East has been brought to Americans by television and the press, and the powerful imprint of the steady reportage of events there, including the war with Iraq, has had cumulative effect. Three waves of revolutions in the Middle East have left their mark on the American consciousness. The breakup of the colonial empire (the British and French mandates) and the collapse of successor regimes in the immediate postwar period were followed by dynamic surges of nationalist movements such as Egyptian pan-Arabism, Syrian and Iraqi Baathism, and the new socialist republics of Algeria and Libya and by the creation in the 1970s of new city-state sheikdoms in the Gulf. In recent years the establishment by revolution of an Islamic regime in Iran led by the Shia clergy is a recent expression of nationalism. These new revolutionary societies coexist somewhat useasily alongside kingdoms led by the lineal descendants of tribal chiefs. Constantly bubbling mixtures of political experiment, great extremes of economic wealth and poverty, breathtakingly rapid urbanization, tremendous rates of economic growth and social change, not to mention the rise and fall of charismatic leaders, repeated bloody wars and revolutions, U.S. embassies held hostage and in other cases destroyed—all these events have been brought into the living rooms of all Americans by television and the media.

Congressional Awareness
Parallels Public Awareness

This deepening public awareness of the turmoil and problems of the Middle East has helped to foster the necessity of legislators to broaden their knowledge about the complexities and problems of the area. If the number, extent, detail, and frequency of hearings are tracked over the postwar period, the number of committees involved and the variety of subjects covered certainly underline the growing belief on the part of most Americans that the Middle East is an area of vital importance to the United States. The phenomenon of increasing numbers of congressional delegations traveling on official business to every part of the globe for orientation or to observe the activities of U.S. diplomatic, military, or economic efforts on the spot also reflects the new focus. There is no question that extensive travel has enabled members of Congress to gain firsthand knowledge about the world's problems. This frequency of travel is true not only of relatively nearby Europe, with its obvious attractions and NATO alliance–Warsaw Pact policy focus, but also to areas more remote from the United States, such as the Soviet Union or the Middle East, despite the difficulties and occasional dangers involved.

The chairmen and senior members of the Senate Foreign Relations and House Foreign Affairs committees and the leadership of other major committees have attained their positions after serving many terms in office. These legislative leaders have had more direct experience with the major foreign policy and security issues facing the United States and more direct contact with the leaders of other nations than has any White House leadership. The repeated travel to areas of concern has deepened the experience of key legislators who have to make judgments about military and economic assistance and the positioning and use of U.S. military forces. This extensive legislative experience and firsthand observations gained over decades of service have given them a position of independence, a sense of confidence and authority, and a sophistication of viewpoint not evident in the earlier period.

Key Congressional Committees

The Senate Foreign Relations Committee and the House Foreign Affairs Committee are the most important committees governing foreign policy issues affecting the Middle East. Although these committees generally authorize foreign assistance programs, the Armed Services committees of both houses also play a major role in determining policy affecting the military aspects of the programs. Many other committees share authority in the making of policies on the Middle East and appropriating funds to carry them out. The main committees are Appropriations, Finance, and Intelligence of both houses. But from time to time, because of the way that committee jurisdictions have been apportioned, other standing committees (or on occasion subcommittees) can play a crucial role in policy issues affecting the Middle East. Indeed, in the Senate, where rulings about the relevancy of amendments tend to be extremely flexible, amendments can be proposed for attachment to most pending bills. It is very difficult to block a test on a strongly held policy view about the Middle East.

An examination of the membership of the relevant committees or subcommittees reveals that groups of congressmen and senators who share a common viewpoint not only try to find places on key committees but also attempt to attain and maintain a majority bloc. But because at least eight standing committees and a much larger number of subcommittees play important roles in the making of policy concerning the Middle East, it is now difficult, if not impossible, for one point of view to prevail, even that of the administration, without going through extensive hearings and test votes, if there are substantial differences of view in the Senate and House.

The Role of Lobbies in Influencing Congressional Attitudes Toward the Middle East

This is not to say that lobbies, both domestic and those that function as registered agents of a foreign power do not continue to play an important role in influencing and shaping opinion and policy in the Congress on the Middle East. The American Israel Public Affairs Committee (AIPAC), B'nai B'rith, the United Jewish Appeal (UJA), and other Jewish groups are certain to have their views expressed in forceful terms on any issue affecting Israel or the Middle East generally. These lobbies have great capacity to shape the legislative agenda and to promote in both houses resolutions and other forms of legislative action for pro-Israeli positions that will receive majority support. Each member of Congress is certain to receive regular visits from prominent rabbis and laypersons from his or her district and state. These Washington lobbies and their well-coordinated national networks have been active in every election campaign, and their support is sought by most candidates from both parties.

It is not surprising that out of the nearly three million Americans of Arab ethnic origin, there are a number of substantial communities in the United States of Americans of Arab descent. Detroit, for example, has a significant population of over 250,000 people who look to the Middle East as their place of origin, and many other U.S. cities have substantial Arab minority populations. There are a number of pro-Arab counterparts to the well-established Jewish lobbies, such as the American-Arab Antidiscrimination Committee, which parallels the work of B'nai B'rith, and the National Association of Arab-Americans; these groups work to promote legislative positions favorable to Arab causes. A number of independent religious and charitable groups that focus on the Middle East, such as the American Friends of the Middle East, also have some influence. Their pattern of approach and activity are similar to those of the Jewish lobbies, but their tenure, number, and reach are in no way comparable.

In recent years there has been considerable controversy in the U.S. Jewish community about the direction of policies in Israel and its actions elsewhere in the Middle East. The splits are not unlike the differences of viewpoints in Israel between the main socialist Labor and the conservative Likud coalitions as well as the groups on the left, including the Communists and the dovish Peace Now group, and religious fringe groups on the furthest right, including the militant followers of Rabbi Meir Kahane. The Congress has members that are sympathetic to the views of almost the full spectrum of Israeli politics, a mixture reflecting the richness of the brew of democratic politics in Israel.

The Influence of the Israeli Embassy and Other Middle Eastern Embassies on the Congress

The Israeli embassy has long been regarded as one of the most effective diplomatic missions in Washington. Its officers have close ties with U.S. Jewish groups and as a result of their long tours of duty in the United States have come to know many U.S. leaders from all walks of life. One particular focus of attention quite understandably is the Congress, and embassy contacts on Capitol Hill with members and their staffs are extensive and effectively nurtured.

The embassies of other Middle Eastern nations have been generally less effective on the Hill, with some notable exceptions. There was the remarkable success of Egypt's distinguished former ambassador, Ashraf Ghorbal, in changing congressional attitudes toward Egypt; he also helped open the way to direct Egyptian-Israeli talks. In the period before the Iranian revolution, few ambassadors had such access to the White House, the State Department, or the Hill as did Iranian Ambassador Ardeshir Zahedi. The ambassador of Saudi Arabia, Prince Bandar bin Sultan bin Abdulaziz Al Saud, has demonstrated the ability to gain congressional support for the sale of arms to Saudi Arabia in the face of concerted Israeli opposition. He played a continuing role in the mid-1980s in facilitating negotiations attempting to reach a temporary settlement in Lebanon and was a key figure in forging the U.S.-Saudi solidarity in taking action against the Iraqi seizure of Kuwait.

The Importance of Visits by Middle East Leaders to the United States

Taking their cue from the frequent trips to Washington of Israeli prime ministers, Egypt's Anwar Sadat and Jordan's King Hussein were well aware of how important regular visits to the United States are as a means of taking their case directly to the administration, Congress, and the U.S. public. The heads of state of other nations in the Middle East have come far less frequently, but the annual opening sessions of the United Nations General Assembly each fall in New York offer the opportunity to visit Washington to meet with the leaders and key committees of the Congress and executive-branch officials, including the president on occasion. These visits and the invitations to come to the Middle East that are inevitably extended have served to expose Congress to different perspectives. These visits are often timed to take place when aid or arms sales packages are under consideration. There is a clear recognition that it is vitally important to meet directly with the key members of the House and the Senate. This recognition has created a far more open situation on Middle Eastern questions than was the case in pre-1973 oil embargo times.

Fundamental U.S. Policy Toward Israel

It has been a fundamental foreign policy principle of the United States since Israel's creation to view the Israeli state as an ally and to give Israel the economic and, since the 1960s, the military assistance required to ensure its survival and to give Israel every chance to prosper as a "bastion of democracy" in the Middle East. Strong and continuing support of this policy in the Congress is not surprising given the many strong ties that exist between the Israeli and U.S. peoples. There has been some emigration from the United States to Israel, particularly in recent years; family ties bridge the differences in nationality. The revered former prime minister of Israel, Golda Meir, lived for many years in Minneapolis, and Hubert Humphrey was among her many lifelong friends who were fervent supporters of Israel. Rabbi Kahane was born in Brooklyn, and Israeli Defense Minister Moshe Arens spent many years as a student and teacher in the United States.

There is no question that support of Israel remains and will remain a basic tenet of U.S. foreign policy in the Middle East. This is not to say, however, that the United States accepts and supports all of the positions held by the Israeli government. The U.S. Jewish community expressed considerable opposition to Begin's Lebanon and West Bank settlement policies and has been increasingly uneasy over the policies of Yitzhak Shamir's government in repressing the Palestinian uprising.

No Congress and no administration is likely to take policy positions greatly at variance with the views held by the U.S. Jewish community as a whole, but as that community and Israel become increasingly divided over the Palestinian issue, they may find more need to adopt independent positions. Breakthroughs leading to peaceful settlements of disputes in the area are always possible, as the Camp David agreements so dramatically showed. Although there was opposition to the Camp David process initially, the opportunity created by Anwar Sadat's courageous and dramatic journey to Jerusalem removed what seemed impossible obstacles. But the present power stalemate between the Likud and Labor parties reflects profound policy differences that now exist among Israelis. Many of these differences are ethnic in origin and reflect very different political, economic, and cultural values among the diverse groups that make up the Israeli nation. The Labor/Likud stalemate in Israel extends to foreign policy and defense attitudes. There is no clear consensus in Israel on how to proceed with the West Bank, how to resolve the problem of Lebanon, how to deal with Syria, what relationships there should be with Jordan or the Soviet Union, how to handle the immigration of Soviet Jews, the intifada uprising, and the evolving Palestinian movement—all of the major Arab-Israeli questions are at issue and have a range of possible answers in the present Israeli context. This uncertainty in Israel about future policies has resulted in a status quo stance and clearly has its reflection in the U.S. Congress.

In addition, other events in the Middle East have given new dimensions to the Arab-Israeli problem. When oil was cut off by the oil-producing nations in 1973, the power of oil embargoes as a weapon for Middle East nations to use in dealing with the West was clearly demonstrated. In the aftermath of the Iranian revolution, AWACS (airborne warning and communications system) aircraft were sent to the Gulf and stationed in Saudi Arabia. Subsequent sales of these aircraft to Saudi Arabia were authorized despite Israeli fears and hard-fought opposition because larger issues of regional stability in this instance seemed to policymakers in both the executive branch and in the Congress to outweigh what were seen to be narrower Israeli concerns that such sales to Saudi Arabia might significantly alter the margin of Israeli military capabilities against combined Arab forces in another round of Arab-Israeli wars. These will remain important factors in the minds of members of Congress as they begin to think about how to address a post–Iraq war Middle East peace conference.

The fundamentalist revolution in Iran, the threat such a revolution posed to the newly created Gulf states, the role of Syria as a key power in the continuing Lebanon crisis, the aftermath of the Iran-Iraq war, the return of Egypt into the family of Arab nations, and the Palestinian uprising are all factors that weigh heavily in the framing of U.S. policies toward the Middle East. These policies are now undergoing radical review. At the same time, the future of NATO is being examined in a new light now that the Soviet Union is undergoing dramatic internal changes. The view is heard that because of perestroika, glasnost, and democratization, perhaps there is no longer a need to support NATO as the West has done over the past forty years.

The call to look at U.S.-Soviet relations or NATO with fresh eyes does not mean that U.S. support for NATO will change, but it does signal recognition that the nature of the East-West competition has changed in fundamental respects, particularly in light of Mikhail Gorbachev's more conciliatory approaches, and that there must be political, economic, and military adjustments to reflect those changes. In the same vein, the questions raised in the Congress, in the press, and in the universities about the nature of the relationship between the United States and Israel does not mean that fundamental support for Israel's security and well-being has changed. What it does mean is that there is an awareness of the changes taking place in Israeli society, politics, economy, defense, and foreign policy. The questioning, criticism, and debate that have arisen about the basic tenets and details of the U.S.-Israeli relationship reflect in large measure the internal debate and differences of view in Israel itself.

In addition, the war with Iraq has created powerful pressures to settle the Arab-Israeli dispute. The recent alliance between the United States and the Soviet Union has produced a new impetus to negotiate return of the West Bank and the Golan Heights. It is likely, too, that arms sales to all parties in the region will be severely limited as a result of the disastrous wars of the last decade.

A Growing Understanding of Other Regional Concerns in the Middle East

Over the last twenty years the Arab-Israeli conflict has been gradually placed by the Congress within larger regional contexts. One important reason for the broadening and sophistication of foreign policy views has been the change in the pattern of Soviet influence in the Middle East. The ebbs and flows of Soviet influence in the area have been seen by a number of influential congressional leaders as evidence of the importance of regional political movements independent of Soviet efforts of domination. Further, the Soviet Union is not in a confrontation with the United States over the Middle East. On the contrary, there are increasing areas of policy agreement concerning the Arab-Israeli conflict, the importance of combating terrorism and maintaining stability through regional agreements, and the use of UN peacekeeping. At the present time Soviet influence in Egypt is minimal. On the other hand, tensions between the United States and Jordan have grown because of the Iraq war and the pro-Iraq stand of the Palestinians. As alliances change, as revolutions erupt, as opponents shift sides, as tactical accommodations are made in the Middle East, so too does the once firm understanding of who is an ally in the East-West equation become murky and uncertain, particularly with the United States and the Soviet Union coming closer together on basic beliefs that maintaining peace in the Middle East is a first order of priority.

An example of present policy complication is the difficult issue of terrorism. Several U.S. embassies have suffered attack, there has been considerable loss of life, and hostages have been taken. Normal diplomatic activities have been placed in jeopardy by the deliberate tactics of militant political groups that use violence as a means to carry out their political objectives and to dramatize and publicize their views. The Abu Nidal group, Libyan-supported groups, the Islamic Jihad, and extremist groups on the fringe of the Palestine Liberation Organization are a few examples of terrorist groups that have attacked the established governments and selected foreign embassies in the area. But one group's terrorist is another group's freedom fighter. It is recalled by many in Congress that the freedom fighters in the last years of the Palestinian mandate before the creation of Israel were viewed by many British and U.S. observers as terrorists. Many of those freedom fighters who were then seen by opponents as terrorists are now condemning as terrorism the violent activities taking place in the West Bank, Gaza, Lebanon, Iran, Egypt, and throughout the Middle East. The continuing debate in the Congress over how to deal with violent terrorism in the Middle East and with international terrorism generally reflects, in some measure, the clash of value systems, ideas, and legitimacies of the contending forces of the Middle East.

The confusion of wars of liberation with defensive wars to protect the homeland has also blurred clear distinctions of who is an aggressor and who has been unjustly attacked. The effort to protect borders from shelling and terrorist attack becomes complicated and less clearly defensive when viewed from the perspective of occupied Lebanon, the shelling of Beirut, and the massacres of Shatila and Sabra.

As more and more congressional members and private citizens visit the Middle East, they have become conscious of the tragedy of peoples who have suffered greatly. They see repeated evidence of the plight of the two peoples in the Arab-Israeli conflict with a long history who have experienced diaspora and who both claim religious and legal right to the same land. There is a recognition that the intertwined human tragedies of Israelis and Palestinians have no easy solutions. The desire of successive administrations and Congress to help achieve a peaceful solution satisfactory to all parties has grown in recent years and will continue. The bloodshed and human suffering caused by six major wars between Israel and Arab states and groups and by the present Palestinian uprising have resulted in a series of sustained efforts at the United Nations and by the United States acting singly and in concert with other nations to bring about a settlement. Camp David, the Reagan plan, the summit statements made at Fez by the assembled Arab states (positions stated repeatedly since then) of a willingness to accept a peaceful settlement with Israel, a whole host of United Nations missions— all these reflected, and the war with Iraq over Kuwait has reinforced, the need to achieve an overall peace settlement that will include some reasonable national and territorial legitimacy for the Palestinians as well as a full acceptance by the Arabs of national legitimacy for the Israelis.

In the late 1960s, at a time of strained relations between the United States and Egypt, a prominent U.S. Jewish legislator, Senator Jacob Javits, joined with Senator John Sherman Cooper in a visit to Cairo. This visit by two prominent members of the Foreign Relations Committee was made in order to see whether peaceful steps satisfactory to both Israel and the Arab states could be taken in the Middle East. The visit was arranged by Ashraf Ghorbal, who later became one of the most successful ambassadors in Washington and did much to strengthen U.S.-Egyptian-Israeli relations. Other visits by larger congressional delegations followed and are now commonplace. This kind of extensive travel throughout the area has clearly fostered the possibilities of creative thought and the opening up of new policy alternatives.

Congressional Delegations and U.S. Embassies in the Middle East

One of the most distinguished U.S. diplomats of recent years, who served as ambassador in Cairo at the time of Sadat's presidency and the Camp David process, Hermann Eilts, has observed in testimony before Congress that the many congressional delegations that visited Egypt during his tenure played a crucial role in bettering relationships between Egypt, the United States, and Israel. Eilts recalled how Sadat would take time out from his other duties whenever any members of Congress came to Egypt, making every effort to explain the Egyptian point of view and encouraging and assisting these visitors to learn as much as they could about Egypt and the Middle East. Eilts acknowledged these visits were hard work because they altered embassy routines, but in Eilts's view they provided a kind of diplomatic opportunity that would reap great future benefits. Eilts further observed that Sadat was encouraged to visit the United States repeatedly and that he took advantage of those opportunities, meeting with as many congressional committees and individual legislators and television, press, university, and influential business groups as possible in order to explain his points of view and to better understand U.S. perspectives about the Middle East. Eilts noted that Sadat understood the impact, value, and effects of his direct personal diplomacy. All of the states in the Middle East have come to understand the necessity of this kind of diplomacy in their dealings with the United States.

The Role of Congress in U.S. Middle East Policy in the Coming Decade

Both the House and the Senate have been under control of the Democratic party since 1986. President Bush now faces (just as President Reagan faced before him) far more difficulties in getting congressional acquiescence for foreign policy initiatives anywhere in the world, not to mention the Middle East. The pace, content, and result of hearings, inquiries, and votes on Middle East proposals are all much less amenable to a president's wishes if his party does not also control the Senate and the House.

Of far greater significance was the dramatic though temporary drop in popular confidence in President Reagan's ability to lead in foreign policy or national security matters. The Iran-contra affair, which precipitated President Reagan's fall from the towering heights of popular esteem, persisted for much of 1987. The Reagan plan, the Marine disaster in Beirut, and the Iran-contra affair were all regarded by congressional leaders as foreign policy failures. Yet it was not until the details of the Iran-contra affair began to emerge that fundamental contradictions and the lack of any clear policy for the Middle East became evident to the Congress and the public. Vehement public rhetoric and overt diplomatic pressures for a tough approach toward terrorists, no ransom for hostages, and the application of punitive measures against those nations that urged different approaches were all policies undermined when the secret arms-for-hostages deals with Iran, directed by the National Security Council and brokered by Israel, were revealed.

Most congressional leaders were of the view that whatever merit there might have been in the idea that over the long term a working relationship with the Iranian government is in the U.S. interest, the arms-for-hostages transactions, the use of the Israelis as intermediaries, and the overall means used were ill-advised and could only serve to prevent a long-term policy from ever succeeding. The difference between the public policy position of the Reagan administration and its actual practice served to cast doubt on its overall ability to conduct an effective foreign policy in the Middle East. President George Bush and Secretary of State James Baker have approached Middle East policy with a new sense of reality and pragmatism and, as the Iraq-Kuwait war showed, worked very closely with the Congress on the war and began to work together on peaceful solutions to the continuing tragedies of the Middle East.

Of growing importance is the greater prominence and effect that Mikhail Gorbachev's less militant and more conciliatory foreign policies are having throughout the world but particularly in the Middle East. In official rhetoric, personnel changes, and policy initiatives such as the withdrawal from Afghanistan, trade agreements with Iran, and the opening of greater diplomatic channels with Arab states, Gorbachev has made it clear the Soviet Union intends to play a new assertive role in the Middle East. This new role of the Soviet Union and the constructive diplomacy it has exercised in the UN Security Council as a key member of the alliance against Iraq pose a challenge of far greater complexity to long-term U.S. policy interests in the Middle East than has been the case in the past several decades. The response to these Soviet initiatives requires a fresh examination of U.S. policies and goals for the Middle East. Present efforts by the Bush administration have taken into account to some extent the challenge of Gorbachev's new directions.

Against the background of powerful dynamic movements in the Middle East, it is clear that for the next several years the region will be a policy arena of change and turmoil, with great importance to the U.S. national interest that will require the Congress to play a central role. In fall 1984, shortly after the reelection of Ronald Reagan, members of the House and Senate were confronted by the front pages of national newspapers and periodicals, underlined by continuing nightly television news segments, that carried detailed stories of new alignments, the splitting off of the Syrian-dominated elements in the PLO, proposed U.S. arms sales to Arab nations, and the likely increase in military and economic assistance to Israel, perhaps amounting to over $3 billion annually. There were also stories on OPEC and stable oil prices, Libyan assassination plots, other forms of state-sponsored terrorism, the status of clerical rule in Ayatollah Khomeini's Iran, the war between Iran and Iraq, and further efforts by Iran to negotiate a withdrawal of forces from Lebanon. These issues, reflecting just one moment in a long series of very difficult problems that faced Congress in the 1980s, are of a pattern that can be expected for the coming decade.

The role of the United States in the Middle East has been and is now crucial. Despite the failure of the Reagan plan, despite the collapse of U.S. efforts to bring about a settlement in Lebanon, and despite the

Iran-contra affair, the United States, as leader of the UN coalition against Iraq, is looked to for leadership, and its power and influence are still believed by all nations in the Middle East to be of the greatest importance. The George Shultz initiative of 1988 signaling the beginnings of PLO-U.S. dialogue was the first step of a new policy reflecting new realities.

The U.S. foreign policy process has gradually become more open in the years since Vietnam, with many more forces and groups at work, and issues in the Middle East, such as the Iraq-Kuwait war, have become central to the lives of U.S. citizens. Thus the possibilities for responding to new opportunities for peace between the Israelis and the Arabs are greater than they were in the pre-Vietnam era, when many happenings in the Middle East were only faintly recognized and, except for issues relating to aid to Israel, were thought by congressmen to be too remote and complex. Very few issues in the Middle East, even aid to Israel, are now seen by Congress as simple; rather, the interrelationships and the complexities of how any particular course of action will affect other interests in the region and larger East-West concerns will weigh heavily in any future congressional considerations.

When the issue of economic assistance for Israel came before the Congress in 1984, many groups in Congress pointed out that domestic inflation had been fueled in large measure by the heavy burden of Israel's defense needs and by its invasion and continued occupation of Lebanon. The House Foreign Affairs Committee and the Senate Foreign Relations Committee will have to consider repeated requests by Israel for support even as they consider requests from a number of Arab states close to the United States, most notably Egypt, Jordan, and Saudi Arabia. These frequent arms requests have always created great problems for U.S. policymakers in both the executive branch and in the House and Senate. It is clear to all concerned that for the coming decade at least, any extensive future arms transfers or any close U.S. military partnership with Jordan, Egypt, Saudi Arabia, or the smaller Gulf states will obviously affect the Arab-Israeli military balance. In the light of the Iraq-Kuwait war, there is great uncertainty in the United States about any future provision of arms to either Israel or the Arab states. Further, the aggressive ideological assertiveness of the Islamic regime in Iran and the occupation of Kuwait by Iraq and the subsequent war on Iraq by the United States and its allies have created new diplomatic and defense requirements that will complicate further an already complex equation of forces. The Congress will continue to be deeply involved in these policy matters.

Congress is well aware of the continuing dilemma facing all Arab states: They must support the Palestinian cause, but a constant problem is precisely how and which groupings within the evolving Palestinian movement are supported because the conservative Arab states fear the reactions of their Arab neighbors almost as much as they fear Israel. There is an understanding that the Arab states also recognize the impact that a constantly escalating Arab-Israeli arms race will have on efforts to develop their societies. After so many wars between Israel and the Arabs, the uprising in the West Bank and Gaza, the terrible tragedy of factional war in Lebanon, and the Iraq-Kuwait war, there is a widespread fear of the consequences of going to war yet again.

The effort to negotiate a Lebanese settlement confined to Lebanon and Israel to the exclusion of Syria proved to be a disastrous if not impossible policy direction. The Soviets under Gorbachev made it clear then and have said plainly since the Iraq-Kuwait war began that they intend to play a role in the Middle East and must be considered a key factor in any settlements. Wherever the United States turns in its relations with the Middle East, reverberations are immediately transmitted that make it impossible to deal with an issue in isolation. All of the major questions are so intertwined that any policy steps must consider all of the local, regional, and East-West ramifications and possibilities.

The growing complexity and intractability of policy issues in the Middle East, particularly because of the Iraq-Kuwait war, ironically now require an open and considered policy review, with Congress as a major participant. Despite the forceful lobbying efforts of interested groups, the question of aid to Israel, which ten years ago would have had an automatic result, now will require the relevant committees of Congress to carefully consider, usually with extensive hearings and contentious debate, the provision of aid to Egypt and lesser amounts to Jordan and arms sales to the Gulf states. In recent years the aid levels to Egypt and Israel have been roughly similar. Further, in an era of enormous deficits, adverse balance of payments, and great pressures to cut federal budgets, the expansion of foreign assistance programs is going to be extremely hard to find support for in the Congress.

To many in the Congress, it seemed evident that in the first half of the 1980s, the Arab states were positioning themselves to begin to settle their conflict with Israel. The Saudi peace proposal and the Fez conference, the willingness of all Arab states except Libya and Syria to accept Egypt back into the Arab League, realignments in the PLO, and repeated, sometimes unambiguous, statements by its chairman, Yasser Arafat, of a willingness to accept a two-state solution and to recognize Israel all suggested that the process toward a settlement of the Palestinian problem has begun. All of these earlier moves were capped by the PLO declarations of 1988 that it accepted the reality of the Israeli state and was prepared to negotiate a two-state solution to the problem.

The view that Israel must do more to help the peace process can be illustrated by a hearing on the situation on the West Bank held on

May 26, 1982, by the Subcommittee on Europe and the Middle East of the Committee on Foreign Affairs of the House of Representatives, during which Chairman Lee Hamilton observed:

> The United States engaged in intensive diplomacy with Israel and Egypt. The fruits of that venture at Camp David culminated in the treaty of peace between Israel and Egypt which is a milestone on the road toward a comprehensive settlement in the Middle East.
>
> Unfortunately, the envisaged second and integral part of the Camp David process, negotiations to create an interim period of full automony for the Palestinians of the occupied West Bank and Gaza, had not borne results. Regrettably, Jordan and the Palestinians of the West Bank and Gaza have avoided the Camp David process and have focused more on what Israel can do to help the peace process than on what they can do to advance the peace process and promote mutual recognition. Israel has undertaken a series of policies on the West Bank and Gaza which have had the consequence of making the prospects for a negotiated compromise on the West Bank considerably more difficult.[2]

As these and other hearings in the House and Senate indicated, Congress was engaged in a process of thorough consideration of these pressing and difficult issues.

Since the PLO declarations of 1988, there has been growing evidence of a readiness on the Arab side to negotiate with Israel, but it may be very difficult, absent a breakthrough, to overcome the policy immobility that seems to have gripped Israel—under both its uneasy coalition government and the successor Shamir government. Israel is deeply divided and its economic problems are again becoming more severe because of the rising influx of immigrants from the Soviet Union and the costs of the Iraq war. The heightened sense of possible future conflicts in the Arab world only adds to the uncertainty.

Congressional leaders who have been involved in the Middle East policy process are increasingly of the view that unless there are negotiations in the next few years leading to a peace settlement, and if present inflexible patterns continue, Israel will have no choice but to continue to increase its defense effort, with the United States footing a substantial portion of the bill. The kind of delicate balance that had to be struck whenever each cycle of the Arab-Israeli arms race requires another round in arms sales and grants to the Arabs and the Israelis only reinforces the present view of congressional leaders that because of the Iraq war, it makes even more sense to press for a peaceful solution. The kinds of difficulties encountered in the past in the AWACS sale to Saudi Arabia, the adverse reaction by Israeli lobbying groups to Stinger missile sales to Jordan, the dangerously strained relations between Jordan and the United States, and the repercussions of the Iran-contra affair and the far-reaching role of Israel in the matter only underline the complexities faced by U.S. policymakers concerned with the Middle East.

Many members of Congress have pointed out that the United States will be called upon in the coming decade not only to provide more arms and economic aid to support Israel but also to meet a complex variety of problems elsewhere in the Middle East. The United States will have to continue its support for Egypt and to help Saudi Arabia and the Gulf states to protect their interests in new ways in the wake of the Gulf crisis. It will face the situations in Iran that began to appear after Khomeini died and the Iran-Iraq war ended as well as continued civil war in Afghanistan following Soviet troop withdrawal and new civil strife in Iraq following the Iraq-Kuwait crisis. Members of Congress are well aware in the aftermath of the Iraq-Kuwait crisis and war that they will be called upon to vote for and to fund far-reaching new Middle East policies.

As difficult as these new problems will be, it is clear that overarching all of the Middle East policy considerations that will be put before Congress in the aftermath of the Iraq war is the growing belief that despite the present stalemated immobility, continuing the efforts begun at Camp David to obtain a comprehensive Arab-Israeli peace remains the best way to prevent a major war from breaking out between Israel and Syria. Beginning the process of building a stable and workable relationship with both Iran and Iraq is crucial if future turmoil in the Gulf and the possible loss of oil supplies to the West are to be prevented.

There are some who contend that although the realities and the difficulties of the central issues in the Middle East are reasonably well understood in the Congress and are reinforced daily in the media, the pressures of lobbies and obligations of political debts will prevent any thorough consideration of the full dimensions of problems in the Middle East. But the new realities created by the Palestinian uprising, by the opening of dialogue with the PLO, and, most significantly, by the Iraq war and the new peaceful Soviet initiatives in the Middle East will result in repeated hearings by at least eight committees and a larger number of subcommittees and two select committees seeking advice about the best policy to pursue. Travel to the area by congressional delegations of diverse party and regional makeup and frequent visits to the United States by Middle East leaders of all perspectives will not only continue but are likely to increase. This state of affairs gives strength to the view that Congress will confront with much more objectivity than in the past the crucial issues of vital overriding significance to U.S. security and the peace of the world. Members of Congress will necessarily have to face the knotty but crucial issues of the Middle East with a greater openness and pragmatism than they have ever before brought to the subject. Policies toward the Middle East will be no less controversial, but the costs of the Iraq war, the new peaceful constructive role of the Soviet Union in the UN Security Council, and the growing awareness of the dire consequences of a continued failure to resolve the Palestinian issue will demand a far more deliberate and objective balancing of competing domestic and international policy interests.

Notes

1. John E. Rielly, ed., *American Public Opinion and U.S. Foreign Policy 1983*, Chicago Council on Foreign Relations, 1983, p. 5.

2. Hearing on the Situation on the West Bank, Subcommittee on Europe and the Middle East, Committee on Foreign Affairs, House of Representatives, May 26, 1982, p. 1.

PART THREE

Military Force

7
The Uses and Abuses of Military Power in the Middle East

Anthony H. Cordesman

It is far easier to discuss the abuses of military force in the Middle East than it is to discuss the uses. Even the briefest summary of military trends since 1973 produces a long litany of miscalculation and enduring conflicts:

- A massive regional arms race has helped destabilize the area without giving any regional power either a stable deterrence or the most effective military forces.
- The Camp David agreement and the peace treaty between Egypt and Israel ended the war between those states, but neither the follow-on negotiations nor the Reagan peace initiative led to expanded peace talks that include Jordan and Syria, to any improvement in the condition of the Arabs in Gaza or on the West Bank, to prevention of a civil disobedience campaign there, or to major reductions in Israeli and Egyptian defense spending.
- Israel's 1982 invasion of Lebanon turned into a de facto defeat for Israel without becoming a victory for Syria or bringing peace or stability to Lebanon. Lebanon remains a "trap" for Israel, Syria, and the Lebanese.
- Israel and Syria remain locked in a high-technology arms race that neither state can afford. This arms race does not directly threaten Israel in the near future, but the long-term social and economic strains of Israeli defense spending and funding the immigration of Soviet Jews may well threaten Israel's ability to maintain its military edge. Further, Iraq's Scud attacks on Israel in 1991 and the alignment of the PLO and Jordan with Iraq created new Israeli fears of attacks by a mix of Arab states.

- Jordan remains threatened by Syria and Israel, but cannot obtain modern arms or effective support from the West or from the Soviet Union. It cannot move toward effective peace initiatives because of continued opposition by the Palestine Liberation Organization (PLO). Jordan's current military weakness is being compounded by reductions in aid from the other Arab states and in Jordan's revenues from foreign workers and by the hostile reaction of the Gulf states to Jordan's support of Iraq in the 1990–1991 Gulf crisis.
- The Iran-Iraq war transformed an Iraqi attempt to dominate the Gulf into a war of attrition between the Gulf's most populated states. This struggle, in one way or another, involved Bahrain, Kuwait, and Saudi Arabia in low-level conflicts with Iran and expanded to increase both Soviet and U.S. involvement.
- Although the Iran-Iraq war ended in a cease-fire in 1988, it both left Iraq deeply in debt and fueled Saddam Hussein's ambitions to the point where he seized Kuwait in August 1990. The result was a war between Iraq and a U.S.-led coalition that seemed certain to lead to further new problems and instabilities in the Gulf.
- Kuwaiti and Saudi aid helped purchase a "peace" between the Yemens and between South Yemen and Oman, but the unity of North and South Yemen remains highly unstable, and a low-level border war exists between Yemen and Saudi Arabia. There is only a limited prospect of long-term stability.
- The complex struggle in the Horn of Africa has involved continued rivalry between all of the Horn states and internal instability and civil war in the Sudan, Ethiopia, and Somalia.
- Libyan ambitions continue to increase the instability in the weaker states in the region and to exacerbate the arms race throughout the area.
- Morocco remains locked in an arms race with the Polisario and, indirectly, with Algeria that may continue for years.

The Middle East is filled with self-inflicted wounds, many of which have become structurally embedded in the societies and politics of the region. In spite of constant regional complaints about the superpowers and outside interference, the ultimate source of most regional struggles is local ambition, hatreds, struggles for political and economic power, and ideology.

The end result is almost constant abuse of military power in the most pragmatic sense of the term. Military adventure and civil struggles are sustained without any clear grand strategic objective or "end game."

Short-term tactical advantage is confused with long-term victory, and the purchase of arms is confused with the purchase of political power and military effectiveness.

It does not require much vision to see that tomorrow's political and military historians will be brutal in judging today's military trends and uses of military force. Their judgment toward the Arab world may be that its present leaders wasted a priceless historic opportunity—a vast and ephemeral burst of oil wealth—partly on arms. What could have been a generation of development has ended in increased foreign debt, half-modernized and unsustainable economies, and high-priced military "junkyards."

Historians' judgment regarding Israel may be that it copied the Crusaders in failing to exploit its opportunities to live with the peoples of the region and in seeking impossible levels of security—to a point where it alienated the foreign support it depended on, became isolated from every moderate force in the region, and finally found its own "field of thorns."

The challenge to U.S. policy is to avoid an equally critical judgment. The war between the U.S.-led United Nations coalition and Iraq showed that the United States had little hope of avoiding continuing regional entanglements. However, it can avoid becoming enmeshed in regional conflicts of limited strategic priority, avoid wasting resources and influence it can ill afford to spend, and avoid letting domestic politics shape its tactics and actions when it should be able to encourage regional stability and enhance its own security.

If the United States is to avoid this judgment, it must find ways to use its military resources to preserve its true strategic interests in the Middle East at a reasonable cost and must avoid becoming involved in the self-inflicted conflicts of the region. The United States must limit its military commitments to levels which match the strategic importance of each area and nation in the Middle East and must then find ways to use arms transfers, military aid, military alliances, and its own military forces to reinforce its political and economic efforts to bring strategic stability to the area.

The Need for Realism in U.S. Use of Force and Strategic Commitments

The starting point in meeting this challenge and in laying the groundwork for the effective use of military force is to set honest priorities for U.S. strategic interests. Rhetoric aside, the Middle East has only two features which are of vital strategic importance to the United States and the West: oil and lines of communication.

Oil is the more important of these two interests, but its importance must be kept in perspective and affects only part of the Middle East. The West has other sources of oil, and there is little immediate prospect of world demand creating an oil shortage as long as key exporting nations continue to export. Many Middle Eastern oil states have declining reserves or limited production capability. Algeria, Egypt, Libya, Oman, and Qatar are not major oil powers in today's world.

In fact, all of the key oil-exporting states in the Middle East are concentrated in one comparatively compact region in the Gulf. These include Saudi Arabia (with reserves well in excess of 165 billion barrels), Kuwait (93 billion), Iran (55 billion), and Iraq (40–90 billion). These four states have more than 50 percent of the free world's proven oil reserves.[1]

Iraq's invasion of Kuwait in 1990 showed that radical control of any of the smaller Gulf states can threaten Western oil supplies. At the same time, it showed that the smaller Gulf states can be significant strategic assets.[2] Oman, for example, has major importance because of its strategic location and control of the passages through the Strait of Hormuz and its willingness to provide the United States with contingency facilities. Bahrain, Qatar, and the individual sheikdoms of the UAE have shown they can be equally important in helping to defend the southern Gulf and Gulf waters. Although there are sources of oil outside the Gulf, major pipelines now reach the Red Sea, and the tanker routes in the Red Sea can be bypassed by sailing around the Cape of Good Hope, the defense of the southern Gulf is not easily divisible. The United States has a strategic interest in the security of all the conservative and moderate southern Gulf states, as well as in maintaining the independence of Iraq and Iran and establishing friendly relations with their governments to the extent their internal politics will permit.

Most of the states in the Levant, eastern Mediterranean, and North Africa, however, have far more limited strategic importance to the United States. Turkey is a useful fulcrum in limiting Soviet, Iraqi, and Iranian military expansion and in providing the United States with potential access to the Gulf. Egypt has strategic importance because of its pivotal position adjoining Africa and the Arabian Peninsula, its ability to provide military forces to aid other moderate Arab states, and its air routes and the Suez Canal.

Israel's strategic importance is more indirect, but is still significant. While it presents problems for the United States in dealing with the Arab world, its military strength and power projection capabilities pose a constant threat to any radical or aggressive Arab state and act as a powerful damper on the ambitions of Iraq, Syria, and Libya. Israel often serves U.S. strategic interests best as a silent threat to radical leaders, but no one can deny that it often serves as a major strategic asset.

In contrast, Jordan, Lebanon, and Syria have substantially less strategic importance than Turkey, Egypt, and the Gulf states. Each nation can advance or threaten broader U.S. interests in the Middle East because of its impact on the Gulf, because of the broader political implications of the Arab-Israeli conflict, and because of Soviet ability to exploit regional tensions. All of these states, however, have one thing in common: None is currently a major, much less a vital, U.S. strategic interest.

Syria and Lebanon are of particularly limited strategic value. Jordan, in contrast, has the potential to be an important moderate shield to Saudi Arabia and the Red Sea. Israel has the military potential to be of major value to the United States in defending the eastern Mediterranean. Syria and Lebanon, however, are important only because of the threat that either might become a Soviet proxy or satellite in the near future.

The Arab states of North Africa are literally of peripheral strategic value. They could pose an important threat to the West if they became active Soviet bases, but Morocco is the only state whose geography makes it critical to the defense of the Mediterranean. Algeria and Libya are oil exporters, but not the kind of exporters whose exports have a major impact on world oil markets or who can afford to restrict production for any length of time. Tunisia is politically important as a moderate state, but has marginal strategic importance at best.

More broadly, U.S. strategic interests do not compel the United States to race the USSR to become entangled in every military quagmire that arises in the Middle East. The United States has no need to make major military commitments or involvements in areas where the worst that can happen is that the Soviet Union or some aggressive local power will become bogged down in local struggles and where every limited victory will ultimately raise the cost of pursuing ambitions which lack enduring credibility or purpose. The region's social, border, and revolutionary conflicts are unlikely to end with this century, and in most cases the United States can afford to wait them out while relying on its political and economic influence to contain temporary threats or damage.

The Use of Force and the Limits to U.S. Power

The challenge the United States faces is to shape its strategic relations around these realities instead of its historical and political ties to the Levant. The issue is not one of choosing between Israel and its Arab neighbors—it is one of ensuring Israel's security while recognizing that the primary U.S. strategic interests lie in the Gulf and not along the coast of the eastern Mediterranean.

The United States can scarcely abandon Israel, but the conflict with Iraq showed that the United States must solidify its military relationships with the critical Gulf oil states, seeking to sustain these ties on a long-term basis and in the face of further regional conflicts. The United States need not make revolutionary changes in its security policy, but rather must assert a new balance which better reflects U.S. interests.

The Impact of Other Global Commitments

This balancing act would not be easy at the best of times, but the need for the United States to reassess its strategic priorities in the Middle East is compounded by broader global pressures that most Middle East experts tend to ignore. The United States faces not only a major budget crisis that is likely to force it to cut its power projection forces by nearly a third by the late 1990s but also challenges to its strategic interests and military power in other regions of the world.

Although Middle East analysts can afford some myopia about the importance of their region, the United States obviously has other major national security concerns. It must establish a new national security relationship with the Soviet Union, in which it seeks to maximize the potential benefits of glasnost while preserving its own security. It must redefine the structure of its security posture in Europe and find ways to preserve the security of NATO while moving ahead with arms reductions. It must deal with the changing role of Japan and South Korea, with changes in the relations between the Soviet Union and the People's Republic of China (PRC), and with the broad basing and strategic-posture problems created by the instability of the Philippines.

The United States must try to meet this growing global challenge in an environment in which the cost of its existing forces already places severe strains on its defense budget and budget deficit—at a time when the United States and Western Europe are making major cuts in real defense spending, and Europe is also reducing its power projection forces. It must still meet major military commitments in Asia and do so in spite of the facts that it may lose its bases in the Philippines and that Japan has shown it will not play a military role beyond its own self-defense.

After the war with Iraq, the United States faced major problems in maintaining a military presence in the Gulf. The United States cannot afford expensive (or even inexpensive) diversions in the Middle East in a future holding so many commitments for U.S. military forces and resources. The United States cannot afford to project any more military power over 12,000 kilometers by air from its East Coast or 20,600 kilometers by sea from its West Coast than it must.[3] It cannot afford to commit military forces or carelessly assign strategic value to Middle Eastern nations that do not really merit such a U.S. commitment.

In short, future U.S. uses of military force must be shaped by a far more realistic approach to defining strategic interests than was needed when the United States had considerably more power projection strength relative to hostile third world nations.

The Limitations on U.S. Regional Military Capabilities

Much will depend on just how serious the coming U.S. budget cuts are and how much force the United States can leave in the region after the 1991 Gulf war. Although the United States has improved its strategic lift capabilities since 1973, it will face important limitations on the military power it can project into the Middle East, particularly into the Gulf. It also will need close ties to friendly Gulf states. Although the U.S. naval presence in the Gulf unquestionably contributed to the end of the Iran-Iraq war and to ensuring the security of the West's supplies of oil, it was also clear that such presence could never have been effective without the quiet support of Bahrain, Kuwait, and Saudi Arabia. The same was true of the U.S. buildup to drive Iraq out of Kuwait. Both events showed that the United States can play a powerful role if it has the support of regional states, but it cannot act alone. It cannot deploy naval forces into areas like the Gulf or eastern Mediterranean in more than low-level conflicts without local staging points and air support. It cannot deploy troops or aircraft into areas with thousands of tanks and hundreds of high-performance jets without allies.

As the buildup in the Gulf showed in 1990 and 1991, deploying U.S. land forces presents special difficulties. In spite of continuing efforts to improve U.S. contingency capabilities outside of NATO, and in spite of ongoing improvements in unit firepower, support, and readiness, the U.S. forces allocated to USCENTCOM for contingency planning purposes are normally limited to maximum land force deployments of about 7 division equivalents (5 Army and 2 Marine Corps). Even this level of strength takes two to three months to deploy fully, and the resulting force would still be comparatively lightly equipped with armor and heavy weapons. Further, the United States might well be limited in practice to only two or three divisions because of logistic and support problems.

Supply and support capabilities improved in the years before the United States deployed to oppose Iraq. U.S. units acquired more combat helicopters, improved light armored vehicles, and other weapons. Seventeen chartered prepositioning cargo ships anchored at Diego Garcia were replaced by early 1987 with 13 far more capable, specially designed maritime prepositioning cargo ships (MPS). These ships hold enough equipment and stocks to support three Marine Amphibious Brigades (a 48,000-troop force) for 30 days and proved to be extremely useful when the United States had to deploy suddenly to defend Saudi Arabia after August 2, 1990.

The United States also expanded its strategic lift. It raised its total of fast sealift ships from 4 to 8 by mid-1986, and these ships proved they could reach the Gulf in less than two weeks if they transit through the Suez Canal, versus 24–27 days for ordinary cargo vessels.[4] The United States sharply increased its airlift capacity between 1984 and 1989. It added in-flight refueling capability to its C-141s and expanded each aircraft by 23 feet to increase its cargo-carrying capacity by 30 percent. It modified all 77 of its C-5s by 1987 to increase their life and reliability. It acquired a total of 60 KC-10 tankers and 50 new C-5Bs by 1989 and plans to begin the new C-17 in 1992.[5]

These shifts in readiness and capability played a critical role in the period between Iraq's invasion of Kuwait in August 1990 and the beginning of the war between the U.S.-led allies and Iraq in January 1991. U.S. land forces built up to 200,000 troops in October and to over 500,000 in January. By the time the war started, the U.S. Army had eight divisions in the theater and the Marine Corps had two Marine Expeditionary Forces and elements of a third, with a combined total of over 2,000 main battle tanks.

The bulk of the U.S. land forces, however, took at least three months to reach the Gulf, and nearly one-third of the armored forces the U.S. deployed did not reach the Gulf until the month before the war began—more than four months after the Iraqi invasion. For nearly one critical week after Iraq seized Kuwait, the only force between Iraq and control of the Saudi oilfields was a single brigade.

It is clear that unless the United States continues to deploy land forces or prepositions most of the armor and heavy land force equipment it needs in the Gulf, it will be unable to deploy significant armored strength to the region in less than 30 to 60 days. Further, cutbacks in plans to modernize U.S. strategic air lift will leave the United States well over 20 million ton-miles per day short of its goal of 66 million. Unless current force plans change, the United States will have significantly less strategic lift in the mid-1990s than it had in 1990, when it deployed to check Iraqi aggression.

There are other reasons for prepositioning or maintaining some form of U.S. land force deployments in or near the Gulf after the war with Iraq. The land forces the United States will be able to project rapidly into the Middle East without such measures will be relatively lightly equipped with heavy weapons. Unless the United States has 30–45 days of warning, it might only have time to deploy elements of one Marine Expeditionary Brigade (11,000 to 16,000 troops and fewer than 60 tanks) or the 82nd Airborne Division (16,000 troops and limited armor).

The time to deploy a Marine Expeditionary Brigade (MEB) would depend on the location of a conflict, but deploying the mobility-intensive 7th MEB from its base at Twenty-nine Palms in California to the Gulf and rendezvousing with equipment on prepositioned ships at Diego Garcia would take at least 7 to 11 days. The 82nd Airborne would take 5 to 14 days to airlift to the Gulf and could compete for airlift resources with the buildup of U.S. Air Force units. The heavier 101st Airborne Division would take at least two weeks to move by air if the 82nd Airborne was deployed first and 30–35 days to move by sea. Once either unit arrives in the theater, another 7–15 days will be needed to deploy it and make it combat-ready.

The only unit with heavy armor now on the USCENTCOM force list is the 24th Mechanized Division with 216 tanks. All of the other Army and Marine Corps units allocated to USCENTCOM have only a maximum of 150 tanks per unit. Without prepositioning or predeployment, however, a "heavy" unit like the 24th Division will take at least 30 days to move by sea, assuming that the 101st Airborne was not competing for sealift. Although the United States may yet buy enough fast sealift to cut this transit time to 12–17 days in the 1990s, it would still take 25–30 days to deploy completely the 24th Mechanized Division in the Gulf as a fully effective combat force.[6]

Under almost all scenarios, the United States will need friendly forward deployment and support facilities and the support of friendly land forces. The land forces the United States can deploy have a professionalism most regional forces lack, superior command and control capabilities, and key elements like advanced attack helicopters that could be of great benefit to a combined force. At the same time, friendly forces could make up for what the United States lacks in numbers, heavy armor and overall firepower, and rapidly deployable support capability.

The situation in terms of seapower is currently more favorable. The United States still has overwhelming superiority in the Mediterranean, Red Sea, and Indian Ocean. The United States can now sustain two to three full carrier groups anywhere in the region for six months or more. Each carrier can carry more than 90 aircraft, and the A-6 and

F-18 attack fighters have ranges of up to 1,100 to 2,700 miles, depending on payload and refueling.

The U.S. carrier groups are, however, vulnerable to attacks by land-based attack aircraft, bombers, missiles, and submarines and increasingly to air- and sea-launched antiship missiles. Nations like Syria, Libya, Iraq, and Iran have already acquired large numbers of such missiles as the Exocet, Silkworm, Harpoon, and Soviet-made systems. U.S. carrier aircraft also face threats from regional air forces that are increasingly being equipped with aircraft like the Mirage F-1, SU-24, SU-27, MiG-29, and TU-22 and from long-range land- and air-based Soviet-made cruise missiles. This is steadily increasing the need for friendly bases that can be used to stage U.S. carrier aircraft, allow carrier task forces to "stand off" farther from potential threats, and provide repair and emergency land facilities.

Further, U.S. task forces may include only 10 active carrier battle groups by the mid-1990s, although 15 carrier and 3 battleship battle groups were once planned for this period. Coupled to the potential loss of bases in the Philippines, this will probably sharply reduce both the speed and size of the naval forces the United States can deploy to the Gulf and the Middle East.

The U.S. Air Force units available to USCENTCOM can now deploy more land-based combat aircraft than friendly air bases can normally accommodate. Before the United States deployed to defend Saudi Arabia, the forces allocated to USCENTCOM had increased from roughly 7 wings (504 aircraft) in the mid-1980s to 10 wings (720 aircraft).[7] The United States deployed some 1,800 aircraft to the Gulf in 1991, including more than 1,300 combat aircraft from the Air Force, Marine Corps, and Navy.

The United States does, however, plan to cut its tactical air wings by roughly a third by the mid-1990s. Coupled to similar plans to cut the U.S. Air Force tanker force and delays and cancellations in key new tactical combat aircraft like the ATA and ATF, the U.S. Air Force will have substantially less capability.

The Air Force will also remain dependent on friendly air bases. Land-based U.S. tactical air units must operate from bases no more than 400–600 miles from their objective and must have shelters, air base defense, C³I (command, control, communications, and intelligence) and air control and warning capabilities, existing stocks of fuel and munitions, and a host of support facilities. The U.S. Air Force no longer is operating against unsophisticated air defenses that allow U.S. air units to deploy to exposed bases and operate on a "bare bones" basis.

The United States faces other problems. Only U.S. carrier forces, Marine Corps forces, and a limited number of special forces are designed for "forced entry" (occupying areas where a friendly state does not make bases available or permit U.S. landings or air movements to occur unopposed). Even the Marine Corps is limited to amphibious and air assault forces of no more than 17,000 troops.

Although the United States acted decisively to reverse Iraq's invasion of Kuwait, the legacy of U.S. involvement in Vietnam and of the withdrawal of U.S. military forces from Lebanon placed political constraints on U.S. use of force. Neither the Congress nor the U.S. public is ready to see the United States sustain serious casualties in politically complex and morally ambiguous low-level conflicts. The public and congressional debates over every clash between the U.S. and Iranian navies in 1987 and 1988, and the use of force against Iraq, showed that U.S. use of military force must take full account of these constraints if it is to be successful. They may often be more important than limitations on the number of forces available or U.S. rapid deployment capabilities. This means that the United States can normally only use large amounts of force when it has access to regional facilities and can obtain support from host countries.

All of these constraints reinforce the incentives to the United States to create military ties to key regional states that would allow such states to bear the primary burden of deterrence and defense against low-level threats and that would allow the United States to use regional military facilities if it did have to commit forces. Similar incentives exist to create a mix of U.S. and local forces and local facilities that will allow the United States to emphasize air and naval power rather than ground forces. The use of air and naval power generally involves far lower casualties, allows the United States to deploy forces rapidly from "over the horizon" and take maximum advantage of its superior technology, and provides the assets friendly regional states most lack. It also minimizes the political risks and involvements inevitable in deploying U.S. Army or Marine Corps forces into the middle of a different culture and largely alien politics.

Dependence on Regional Contingency Facilities

The United States has built a wide range of regional basing and contingency arrangements for operations in the Middle East since the fall of the Shah of Iran in 1979. Although these major contingency facilities cover a geographic sweep from the Azores to Diego Garcia, the island of Diego Garcia in the central Indian Ocean is the only base the United States can use without depending on friendly regional states and without consideration of local issues. Diego Garcia, however, is 5,500 kilometers from the end of the Gulf, almost as far as Dublin, Ireland.

The Logic of Arms

This need to link U.S. strategy and the use of U.S. military forces to ties with carefully selected friendly states is reinforced by the military trends in the West and the Middle East. In spite of a decade of fairly intensive effort, the United States has made only limited progress in improving NATO out-of-area capabilities and in persuading its NATO allies to increase their forces in the Gulf area as compensation for U.S. commitments. Belgium, Britain, France, Italy, and the Netherlands did deploy forces to the Gulf in 1987 and 1988, and all five states and Canada deployed forces to liberate Kuwait in 1991, but these deployments were only temporary. Only Britain and France normally deploy forces in the region, and these forces are small. Britain maintains a small (2–4) ship squadron in the Indian Ocean, but faces the near certainty of further cuts in its power projection forces and out-of-area capabilities. It already has phased all of its major fleet carriers out of its force structure. France has a significant base in Djibouti, still has a light carrier it can deploy to the region from the Atlantic, and maintains 6–9 ships in the Indian Ocean. However, France cannot operate modern aircraft from its carriers. Like Britain, it faces major budget pressures and may well have to make significant cuts in its naval modernization plans for the mid and late 1990s.

At the same time, the United States faces an environment in which the sheer volume of arms going to the Middle East is being reinforced by the acquisition of far more sophisticated military technology. Coupled to the severe strains the United States faces on its military resources, these transfers are gradually changing the strategic map of the Middle East. They are creating more and more local forces with heavy armor and the strength to threaten the land units the United States can project into the region, more forces with modern attack aircraft and interceptors, and more forces with antiship missiles that can attack U.S. ships.

The Volume of Arms and the Risk of Proliferation

The current pattern of arms transfers to states in North Africa, the Levant, Arabia, and the Gulf provides a grim picture of the competition to sell arms to the region and of the rate of transfer of modern arms. To put these figures in perspective, the region had already bought 11,450 main battle tanks during the 1972–1976 period, a total roughly equal to NATO's present tank strength in the Central Region of Europe. It bought 10,092 more tanks during the period 1977–1984, and another 3,338 were sold between 1984 and 1986. It is hardly surprising, therefore, that such sales represent more than 70 percent of all the tanks sold to the third world during the last five years. Further, most of the tanks sold since 1980 roughly matched in quality the tanks held by NATO and Warsaw Pact forces, although many lacked fully equivalent fire control systems and aids.

The transfer of modern supersonic jet combat aircraft has been somewhat slower, but still totaled over 4,600 aircraft between 1972 and 1981. Another 1,178 jet fighters were sold between 1982 and 1984, and 788 were sold between 1984 and 1988. These sales produced a total roughly equal to the total active inventory of jet combat aircraft in the Central Region of NATO. Tanks and jet aircraft are not, however, the worst cases. The region bought about two times as many light armored vehicles (APCs and AFVs) as all NATO states during the period 1972–1981, four times as much artillery, and three times more surface-to-air missiles.[8]

These figures represent an incredible absorption of modern arms, and it is a process from which the United States cannot stand aside. Although it may be able to obtain some degree of international cooperation in embargoing or reducing the flow of arms to the most aggressive states in the region, the United States must compete with the Soviet Union and other states to retain its influence in the Middle East and must strengthen its friends and their ability to deter and conduct low-level wars without U.S. assistance. It must seek to create regional forces with sufficient stockpiles and interoperability to ease U.S. capability to deploy and sustain higher levels of combat in those contingencies when U.S. forces will be required. It must maintain the flow of arms to help maintain the prestige and international security of key regions and governments and to ensure the support of key military elites.

These arms transfers represent a monumental waste of resources that all of the nations involved could far better devote to economic development. No one can deny the theoretical desirability of regional restraint or efforts at arms control by the major sellers. However, no one is likely to argue that the flow of arms will stop before there have been more wars. It will be decades before the complex mix of revolution, power, and regional hatreds in the Middle East creates a more stable balance of political and military interests than exists today.

In the interim, the United States must respond to the arms transfers of others and try to shape regional security and stability by tailoring its own arms transfers to meet its strategic objectives. The United States must also treat each country differently and in most cases must work with other Western states to achieve its strategic objectives even as it competes in making sales.

U.S. arms exports no longer dominate transfers to friendly or pro-Western states. Western Europe sells more arms to the Gulf and North Africa than the United States, and NATO's true out-of-area contribution to the defense of the Gulf consists of arms sales rather than military forces.

One of the major weaknesses in U.S. and European policy is, in fact, the West's inability to achieve a collective approach to arms sales that acts to build effective regional deterrents. The dollar competition in Gulf arms sales is mirrored in the sale of large numbers of aircraft, ships, surface-to-air missiles, sensors, and C^3I systems that have limited interoperability, lack standardization, and are difficult to integrate into effective air defense or maritime surveillance systems. There is little practical chance that the West can end its competition with itself, but it might seek agreement on methods that will produce far more military effectiveness and deterrent value.

At the same time, the United States must try to confine its search for arms sales relations and contingency arrangements to match its strategic priorities. It cannot maintain military relations with regional states and avoid entanglements in regional quarrels and issues, but it can minimize the side effects of such relations by structuring its military relations as carefully as possible.

Finally, the United States must make every possible effort to halt the proliferation of chemical, biological, and nuclear weapons—and long-range missiles and strike aircraft—to the region. Iran's and Iraq's use of chemical weapons during the Iran-Iraq war, Iraq's Scud strikes on Israeli and Saudi cities in 1991, and the threat of chemical and biological warfare that became all too real during the war to liberate Kuwait are tangible illustrations of the problems involved. At the same time, Egypt, Israel, Libya, and Syria have all been actively involved in efforts to acquire weapons of mass destruction.

Although it may be too late to halt proliferation in the region, it is a threat to every state and population in the Middle East as well as to U.S. forces. Any effort that reduces this risk must be given high priority by U.S. policymakers.

The Impact of Regional Military Forces

Three countries have special importance to U.S. efforts to link U.S. strategic interests and contingency needs to the development and capability of regional military forces. These three nations are Saudi Arabia, Egypt, and Israel. Each already has significant military forces, each has sufficient resources to play a major regional role, and each is in a key strategic location.

At the same time, the United States must use its arms sales and military aid to strengthen other friendly states, which include the smaller southern Gulf states, Morocco, and possibly Jordan. This will require a pattern of arms sales tailored to each nation's mix of military forces, military technology, location, and military competence.

Saudi Arabia will be particularly important. None of the southern Gulf states can generate the same number of forces per dollar as the other Middle Eastern states. Although Saudi Arabia is emerging as a regional military power by Gulf standards, the southern Gulf states will remain heavily dependent on USCENTCOM forces or some other source of military forces in any major contingency involving a northern Gulf state, a threat in the Red Sea, or any Soviet military threat. At the same time, it is clear from the buildup of allied forces to check Iraq in 1990 and 1991 that Egypt is the only friendly Arab state with the strength significantly to reinforce Gulf and Red Sea stability.

The issue of force quality is more complex. Today, the United States can count on a virtual monopoly in advanced battle management capabilities and on a decisive advantage in intelligence, combat sensors, and electronic warfare. Friendly pro-Western states have also been able to count on access to superior weapons, battle management technology, and support and training. However, the Falklands conflict, the Iran-Iraq war, Israel's June 1982 invasion of Lebanon, and the Soviet invasion of Afghanistan acted to trigger a major shift in the level of technology being transferred to both friendly and unfriendly Middle Eastern states.

It may be premature to draw any such conclusion, but force trends by early 1991 seem to indicate that the arms race in the Middle East has entered a new phase, with the past emphasis on force quantity giving way to a new emphasis on technology and force quality. The uncertainty, in any case, is not whether the nations in the region will insist on—and get—the first-line technology available in the West and the Soviet Union, but whether they will seek to buy both force quality and force quantity.

The United States will almost certainly still retain a major edge in military electronics, advanced battle management and sensor systems, and many other important aspects of tactical technology. It will not, however, retain its present edge in aircraft or weapons quality. Given the advantage regional forces will have in basing, the United States may also face net parity in weapons systems effectiveness in some areas of the Middle East in 1991 and beyond and will then have to rely on human factors like training, organization, and superior support capability.

These pressures may well mean that the U.S. use of the battleship *New Jersey* in 1983 may literally be the last time the United States will seriously try to influence the situation in the Middle East simply by using unilateral gunboat diplomacy. The Western experience in the Gulf since 1987 has shown that the United States and Europe must work closely with regional states. The steady rise in the size and sophistication of threat forces will also act as a further set of pressures on the United States to use its military strength in combination with regional states, to emphasize arms transfers instead of the use of U.S. forces, and to avoid adventures in high-risk, low-level wars.

Partnership with the Southern Gulf States

Given this background, U.S. strategy must give priority to stabilizing the military situation in the Gulf. The Gulf is where the oil is, and the oil is the reason for a U.S. strategic commitment in the region. The United States is generally well positioned to achieve this goal, but it also faces a number of important regional problems.

The most important of these problems has been the difficulties the United States has had in balancing its strategic interests in the Gulf with its ties to Israel. The United States does not need to choose between the Gulf and Israel. Saudi Arabia, other friendly southern Gulf states, and Egypt are not likely to emerge from the war to liberate Kuwait by putting significant pressure on the United States to cut its ties to Israel. Each regime understands that it has no real prospect of forcing such a choice. At the same time, each regime will have to shape its military and political ties to the United States on the basis of two other aspects of U.S. policy. The first is the presence or absence of a visible U.S. commitment to the Arab-Israeli peace process, and the second is the ability of the United States to act as a reliable supplier of arms.

The challenge of creating a viable Arab-Israeli peace process is beyond the scope of this analysis, but the issue of being a reliable arms supplier is not—and is perhaps the most understated and underemphasized aspect of U.S. policy in the Gulf. No Gulf state finds U.S. diplomats to be as popular as U.S. fighter planes. Access to first-line Western military technology has not only become the key factor shaping Gulf military procurements, it has become the continuing litmus test of whether the southern Gulf states can cooperate informally with the United States in building a meaningful Gulf Cooperation Council (GCC) air defense system and can get U.S. aid in building the deterrent forces the southern Gulf states seek.

It is a litmus test that the United States has often failed—and that requires more understanding of U.S. strategic priorities on the part of Israel. The Reagan administration was unable to reach internal agreement on how to sell first-line U.S. fighter planes to several southern Gulf states, and Saudi Arabia had to be told that the main reason the administration could not offer fighters like the F-16, F-15, or F-18 was that it could not obtain congressional approval of such sales because of the political power of Israel and its supporters.

The end result was that Saudi Arabia and most other Gulf Cooperation Council states shifted to the purchase of French fighters and European technology. This approach generally gave them a far greater technical capacity to threaten Israel than they could have acquired had they bought weapons with the technical and operational constraints the United States would have enforced. More important, the failure of U.S. arms transfer policy almost led to the near collapse of quiet U.S. efforts to obtain agreement on the kind of integrated air and maritime defenses that are essential to creating an effective regional deterrent and providing the standardization, interoperability, and facilities necessary to support efficient U.S. over-the-horizon deployments in a major military contingency.

The United States must not repeat this mistake in the future. It must not offer the GCC states a blank check in terms of arms sales or rush in advanced technologies that might seriously threaten Israel, but it must reinforce its ties to its major military pivot in the Gulf: the Saudi Air Force. Important as U.S. economic ties to the Gulf and contingency bases in Oman and Bahrain may be, U.S. military ties to the Saudi Air Force are critical. Aside from the strategic benefits both nations draw from the relationship, there are tangible benefits to both U.S. and Saudi military forces. Saudi Arabia needs U.S. arms sales, advice, and technology. The United States needs a Saudi basing structure that gives it extensive de facto contingency bases in the southern Gulf with surplus shelters and extensive facilities and munitions to draw on. U.S. sales of the F-15 fighter and the E-3A AWACS (airborne warning and communications system) aircraft, which now underpin Saudi Arabia's military position, allowed the Saudi Air Force to shoot down Iranian aircraft in July 1984 when they penetrated Saudi airspace and allowed a Saudi fighter pilot to score the first double kill against Iraqi fighters in 1991. These ties also make U.S. technology the potential core of a broader air and maritime defense system in the southern Gulf.

During the late 1980s, the United States forced Saudi Arabia to turn to Britain and Europe for its future purchases of modern combat aircraft. The Saudis sought additional F-15 aircraft and the multiple ejection racks to use their existing F-15s as attack fighters when the Iran-Iraq war first began to threaten Iraq's survival in 1982. They were told for more than four years that such a purchase could not obtain congressional approval. President Reagan then personally promised King Fahd that he would seek congressional approval of such sales in early

1986, only to break his promise when this seemed likely to affect the November 1986 elections and Republican control of the Senate.

All during this time, European nations offered two major competing aircraft: the Mirage 2000 and the Tornado. It is scarcely surprising, therefore, that Saudi patience finally ran out. The Saudis bought the Tornado from Britain. Ironically, the Saudis ended up with over 130 Tornado attack and air defense fighters with far more advanced attack and air combat capabilities than they would have gotten in the configuration of the F-15 that Saudi Arabia sought from the United States.

The irony of this arms sale controversy was that the success of Israel and its supporters in reducing U.S. arms sales to Saudi Arabia both increased the theoretical Saudi threat to Israel and weakened U.S. influence in getting Saudi support of a peace settlement. It undermined U.S. ties to a critical strategic asset, while it tended to make Israel a strategic liability because of its interference with U.S. plans and strategy. This situation was only marginally better when the United States did agree to sell Kuwait the F-18 in 1988. The sale came only after a pointlessly embarrassing U.S. political debate over Kuwait as a threat to Israel, which further damaged U.S. relations with the region.

The importance of U.S. arms sales to the Gulf states in terms of political and military prestige may be hard for people in the United States to understand, particularly in view of the sacrifices the United States has had to make in liberating Kuwait. Nevertheless, such sales are the tangible focus of U.S. military policy in the Gulf. The United States, after all, has already sold the Saudis more than $15 billion worth of fighter aircraft, E-3A AWACS, land-based air defenses, and C^3I battle management systems. The United States has also been the nation that convinced the Saudis that a mix of air and maritime defense can substitute for Saudi Arabia's lack of ground forces and deter action by Iran or Iraq. It has convinced Saudi Arabia that the Saudi dependence on U.S. air and C^3I technology can make U.S. reinforcements both politically and militarily convincing.

This problem in aircraft sales to the Gulf has been reinforced by similar problems in selling other systems. The United States has had to deny the sale of Stinger missiles to Bahrain, Kuwait, Qatar, and Saudi Arabia. There have been debates over the sales of artillery and armor.

It is one thing to debate the sale of large numbers of the most advanced U.S. weapons to the southern Gulf states, and no one can ignore the potential risks of transferring systems like the Patriot or unmodified F-15E attack fighters. It is another to debate routine or carefully constrained arms transfers, to ignore the benefits to Israel of close ties between the United States and southern Gulf states, and to neglect the fact that most high-technology U.S. arms transfers mean dependence on U.S. technical support for any sustained combat.

Accordingly, this aspect of U.S. policy needs to be given the importance it deserves. Specifically, the United States and Israel need to find a modus vivendi that will allow the United States to conduct major arms sales without making every major sale to the Gulf into a domestic political battle. It needs to stop treating the issue of Gulf defense as a sideshow, or form of "oil offset," and give it high priority in any U.S. use of arms.

The United States needs to build on the alliance it has forged in the Gulf to strengthen its longstanding military ties to Saudi Arabia, Oman, and Bahrain and its new ties to the UAE, Qatar, and Kuwait. The map of the Gulf dictates the vulnerability of Kuwait, but this vulnerability does not need to be nearly as acute as it was when Iraq invaded. The F-18 sale to Kuwait in 1987 was only a slow beginning. The U.S. offer of more Improved Hawks, new radars (including the balloon-carried TPS-63), and rapid deployment of the key elements of a modern C^3I system in 1987 would have strengthened Kuwait if the United States could have handled this aspect of its politico-military relations with Kuwait without becoming involved in a debate with Israel.

Similar progress might have been made in providing the UAE with Project Lambda—the C^3I system it needs for effective air defense coverage. This project remained on the books for years, and the key barrier was political. So was the UAE's selection of the Mirage over the F-20 and F-16A. Yet the Iran-Iraq war, Operation Earnest Will (the 1987–1988 U.S. naval operation in the Gulf) and the war to liberate Kuwait clearly demonstrated the importance of linking the air and maritime defenses of Gulf states like the UAE and Saudi Arabia. During the period 1984–1988, for example, Iran was able to take advantage of the fact that the Saudi system could not cover the southeastern coast of the Gulf and repeatedly struck at tankers east of Qatar precisely because the UAE lacked any effective ability to respond. The end result was that the United States was forced to intervene under far more negative conditions than would otherwise have been the case.

The United States also needs to give proper attention to improving its cooperation with France and Britain to achieve true interoperability in the air and maritime defense links of the southern Gulf states. Having helped create the chaotic force mix mentioned earlier, the United States must now seek to create order out of the result. It cannot hope to dominate the overall pattern of arms sales to the southern Gulf states, even if it changes its current policies. The United States must work to make all Western arms sales to the southern Gulf as effective as possible. The best way it can use military force in the Gulf, with the least risk of involvement with Iran or Iraq, is through arms sales and military assistance. The United States has nothing to gain from direct military entanglements in the region if it can possibly avoid them.

Dealing with Iran and Iraq

The United States must try to improve its relations with both a revolutionary Iran and a postwar Iraq. It must, however, have no illusions. It may be decades before Iran fully emerges from its revolution into a stable and predictable regime that can live with its neighbors and the West. In the interim, it may fluctuate between moderation and extremism and between hostility and indifference.

Iran has not yet rebuilt its forces to anything like the level of relative capability they had under the Shah, but it still has some 500,000 men in uniform, 100 operational combat aircraft, 1,300 armored weapons, and 700 major artillery pieces. If this is a half-formed military force, with little power projection capability, its future potential cannot be dismissed.

Iraq's future is as unpredictable as the long-range political and strategic consequences of the war to liberate Kuwait. Iraq entered the war with chemical and biological weapons, long-range missiles, an active nuclear weapons program, 1 million men in uniform, 806 combat aircraft, and 5,600 main battle tanks. It emerged from the war much weaker. Any postwar regime is unlikely soon to be a stable friend of the United States or the southern Gulf states. One of its aims will be to rebuild considerable military strength.

Given this background, the United States has no real hope of finding a "pillar" in either northern Gulf state and little to gain from playing one state off against the other. The United States also has little to gain from arming either state as a buffer against the Soviet Union or otherwise trying to manipulate their future political alignments. Iran and Iraq should be left to their own political and economic course.

What the United States may be able to do is to build on the arms embargo it first set up against Iran (1983–1988) and then against Iraq (1990–1991) and work with other Western nations, the Soviet Union, and the PRC to halt or limit severely the flow of arms to both Iran and Iraq. The civilian populations of both countries, the other Gulf states, and all oil-importing nations will all benefit if another Iranian-Iraqi arms race can be avoided.

The United States, however, cannot let its hopes for an embargo and arms control or its efforts to strengthen the southern Gulf states lead it to slack off its efforts to improve and modernize USCENTCOM. The United States could still come into new conflicts with Iran or Iraq in the Gulf and must demonstrate that it retains enough strength and capability to deal with any sudden future aggression against the southern Gulf states. The United States also must maintain a strong deterrent against any renewal of Soviet interest in regional adventures.

Every improvement in strategic and theater lift, in USCENTCOM prepositioning of equipment, in the equipment of USCENTCOM combat forces, and in the regional contingency bases will reinforce this deterrence, particularly if U.S. combat forces must withdraw from the Gulf after the war to liberate Kuwait and remain over the horizon. The best way of avoiding any use of USCENTCOM is to give it the priority it needs to steadily improve its credibility and effectiveness.

The Game in the Yemens, the Horn, and the Red Sea

The trade routes through the Suez Canal and the Red Sea and the security of Oman's and Saudi Arabia's southeastern borders rank next to Gulf oil in terms of U.S. strategic interests in the Middle East. These areas are far more important to the United States than the Levant and all of North Africa except Egypt and Morocco. At the same time, the security of the area is largely dependent on other regional states and not on U.S. military aid or forces.

The United States can do little to influence the complex political struggle in the Yemens except try to encourage the more moderate element in the now "unified" government of North and South Yemen. The United States is clearly allied with Saudi Arabia and has never been a major military supplier to either state. It has never sold arms to South Yemen, and in recent years, the United States supplied only 11 percent of North Yemen's arms, whereas 43 percent came from the Soviet Union, 12 percent from other Soviet bloc states, 4 percent from Europe, and 31 percent from other sources—principally Saudi Arabia.[9] The most the United States can do is keep a foothold in Yemen and hope for yet another reversal in that nation's troubled politics. As to South Yemen's border war with Saudi Arabia, the United States may have to provide military support to Oman and Saudi Arabia, but it has no current reason to plan to use its own forces.

The ongoing civil strife in Ethiopia and Somalia is more complex. Until the nature of change in the Ethiopian regime becomes clearer, there is little point in any form of U.S. military involvement in any aspect of Ethiopia's civil wars. It is far too soon to know what the new regime in Somalia will be, but the end of the cold war leaves little reason for continued U.S. military involvement. The United States must seek to keep Somalia strong enough to survive, as it has done in the past. However, Somalia is not a U.S. game, regardless of the past negotiation of contingency bases.

The United States can regularly deploy naval forces to the Red Sea and show its commitment to the defense of its interests in the region. The U.S. minesweeping effort in the region in August and September 1984 was a good example of the kind of U.S. presence required, but so are exercises in Egypt and port calls in Saudi Arabia and Djibouti. The United States should also continue to encourage the French presence in Djibouti and the Red Sea. It is France, not Britain, that has the largest European presence in the Red Sea and the Gulf, and the French presence in Djibouti is a tangible symbol of Western strength and an important regional deterrent to any adventures by Ethiopia and South Yemen.

As for the Sudan, the primary thrust of U.S. policy must be to encourage moderation, economic reform, and some form of peace settlement between the government and the rebels in the south. The key U.S. role in the Sudan is political and economic, not military, and even then will be peripheral to the efforts of moderate Arab states. Libya is a token threat, but the fact remains that the main threat to the Sudan is internal, not external. Some U.S. military aid may be justified—if it can ever be tied to a reasonable balance between backing the government in the north and encouraging its willingness to negotiate with the south. U.S. arms totaled 34 percent of the Sudan's arms imports during the period 1984–1988. Roughly 8 percent have come from France, 8 percent from the PRC, 3 percent from the United Kingdom, and 46 percent from the rest of the world. If the United States cuts off its aid on a sustained basis, it may simply drive the Sudan toward Libya. At the same time, caution is necessary. Although there is a growing chance that the Sudan may degenerate into full-scale civil war or come under a more hostile regime, there is little the United States can do through any direct use of arms.

Partnership with Egypt

Egypt draws its strategic importance from several factors. Although it is a comparatively small oil producer, its production of about 1 million barrels per day is still equal to that of a North Sea producer like Norway. It acts as a moderate force in both the Red Sea and North Africa. Egypt is the primary supporter of the Sudan and the primary check to any expansion of Libyan influence. It controls the Suez Canal, and its SUMED pipeline allows the shipment of limited volumes of oil even if the canal should be closed. Egypt provides the United States with key staging bases near Cairo and can provide it with Red Sea facilities at Ras Banas or air bases in the Sinai. As it showed in the war to liberate Kuwait, Egypt is a strong and faithful ally and can project a substantial amount of power into the Gulf.

Giving Egypt the military and economic aid it needs to maintain a moderate and democratic government and to maintain its peace with Israel is also the key to securing the U.S. position in the Levant in a way that virtually eliminates the need for any major U.S. military intervention in defense of Israel. No immediately foreseeable combination of hard-line Arab states can threaten Israel as long as Egypt remains at peace, and no amount of arms transfers to a nation like Syria can build up Syrian forces to a point where a broader superpower intervention in the Arab-Israeli conflict seems likely to be necessary. This is of more than passing importance because direct U.S. military support of Israel in any major war would come only after Israel's own defenses failed, and U.S. reinforcements might then come too late to avoid a serious defeat.

At the same time, strong U.S. ties to Egypt maintain the starting point for renewing the peace process and moving toward a broader solution of the Arab-Israeli conflict. They help indirectly to secure Jordan and the new oil ports Saudi Arabia is building on its northwestern Red Sea coast. Something like 4–6 million barrels of oil can now be shipped through the upper end of the Red Sea and Suez Canal. Combined with the restoration of Iraq's ability to ship over 1.7 million barrels a day through Turkey, this will greatly reduce the vulnerability of Gulf oil shipments to Iranian pressure or other naval and air threats.

If Egypt should complete the final phase of the Suez Canal expansion, this would allow transit by all but the very largest supertankers and create a Red Sea "hinge" that would be a far more effective defense of the West's access to oil than any investment in power projection capability could be. Oil is, after all, the strategic key to the Gulf and the Middle East. It does not matter whether this oil export capability is protected by the use of arms or through passive defenses such as strategic pipelines, rapid facility repair kits, strategic reserves, or any other means. In fact, passive defense is generally less provocative and more likely to prevent local regional tensions from having a broad effect on the world's oil supplies.

The key to preserving close U.S. relations with Egypt is aid and arms sales. In recent years, the United States has spent about $2 billion annually in grant aid on Egypt, or over 20 percent of its total foreign aid program. This aid is well spent. It is unquestionably cheaper than any compensating expenditure on U.S. forces and cheaper than efforts to compensate Israel for loss of the security it now draws from Camp

David. It ensures a far better mix of political and military security than the United States could otherwise hope to obtain.

Restructuring U.S. Military Ties to Israel

Israel is both the third pivot of U.S. strategic interests in the Middle East and a major problem for U.S. strategic planning. The United States is virtually Israel's only source of external military, political, and economic support. U.S. aid to Israel has now totaled in excess of $30 billion and seems likely to remain at roughly $3 billion annually during the period from FY 1991 to FY 1995. The United States must provide Israel with the key weapons and military technology it needs to maintain its military edge over Syria and any likely combination of confrontation states and pay the cost of preserving Israel's peace with Egypt.

Israel's strength is a powerful deterrent to any radical aggressive Arab state, and Israel represents a critical U.S. moral commitment, both in terms of supporting a small and vulnerable democracy and because of Western guilt for the Nazi holocaust. Nevertheless, some of the current strains on U.S. military power in the Middle East have been the product of U.S. ties to Israel and of the Arab-Israeli conflict.

These problems have been compounded in past years by internal political shifts in Israel that have produced hard-line Likud governments committed to the annexation of the Golan Heights and West Bank, to military adventures in Lebanon, and to opposing the strengthening of U.S. ties to key moderate Arab states like Jordan and Saudi Arabia. Prime Minister Begin and his second Likud government helped block any progress toward peace, although the PLO's failure at that time to recognize Israel's right to exist and to emerge as a responsible negotiating partner must be given equal blame. These factors also helped drag the United States and Lebanon into the mire of Israel's first major strategic defeat: its June 1982 invasion of Lebanon.

Since that time, Israel's government has slowed its absorption of Arab territory and showed far more understanding of both U.S. strategic needs in the Gulf and the benefits Israel can gain from close U.S. relations with moderate Arab states. Israeli leaders have not, however, been able to agree on an effective approach to peace that can deal with the PLO or the Palestinian uprising in Gaza and on the West Bank.

The United States and Israel must work together to create the kind of relationship that will not interfere with U.S. strategic ties to the Gulf and efforts to build the forces of the Gulf Cooperation Council into a meaningful deterrent. They must work together with the common understanding that both Israel's long-term regional interests and the broad strategic position of the United States in the Middle East depend on creating a peace process that would at least attempt to move toward peace, protect the rights of the Arabs living in the occupied territories, and ensure Israel's security.

The United States must also put its military relations with Israel on a more stable and enduring basis. Such a shift in U.S. policy should have the following elements.

Establishing Israel as a Mediterranean Ally

Many of the problems in U.S.-Israeli relations stem from Israel's awareness that much of the U.S. political rhetoric about the strategic importance of Israel is the product of U.S. domestic politics and not of Israel's actual military position. Whatever Israel's leaders may say publicly, they realize Israel cannot firmly count on self-interest to underpin U.S. military relations with Israel.

The United States needs to create a strategic relationship with Israel that will make it into a true strategic asset, but do so in a way that will not be seen as threatening by the Arab states. This means the United States cannot use Israel to help it secure access to Gulf oil. Israeli forces cannot play a role in the Arab world in the foreseeable future. They would alienate far more Arabs than any military contribution could be worth, and even the most impressive short-range victory would be offset by the long-run political and strategic price tag associated with such a use of Israeli forces. The United States faces the same price tag if it prepositions equipment or munitions in Israel or uses Israel as a base. The United States might well cause more casualties by using Israel as a medical base than it could save because of the probable heightening of hostile Arab resistance.

This situation would be different, however, if the United States supported Israel in becoming a Mediterranean power. The United States now has only about 60 percent of the force strength NATO's Supreme Allied Command in Europe is seeking in the eastern Mediterranean and must cut its own forces sharply in the future. The United States faces grave uncertainties about the strategic position of Greece, and although the Cold War may be over, the United States would greatly benefit from a medium-sized naval and air power in the area and from a contingency base for eastern Mediterranean operations.[10] Israel can provide an ideal mix of technology, geography, and force numbers. Egypt's role lies elsewhere, and Turkey and Italy cannot expand their role to cover the region.

With the exception of Syria and Libya—which the United States can and must discount in this instance—Arab states will not object to this kind of strategic relationship, particularly if they see it as a means of reassuring Israel, of giving it the security it needs to move toward a broader military peace, and of moving Israel away from further adventures in the Arab world.

Providing a Stable Long-Term Military Aid Plan

The United States can also help to secure Israel and its position in the Arab world by negotiating the kind of long-term military aid program that will be large enough to remove any Israeli incentive to take local risks or adventures. Much of the problem in U.S. military aid to Israel has been that it has never been of sufficient size or duration to meet Israel's needs and has never had a clear strategic purpose.

A long-term military aid plan that emphasizes the creation of the proper level of Israeli military capability, rather than simply the transfer of funds, would also be far more effective. For example, the United States could work with Israel to ensure that it retained its present edge in air defense. Funding the transfer of the Arrow antiballistic missile system, the transfer of more Patriot surface-to-air missiles, advanced radar sensors and battle management systems, specially configured AWACS, advanced air-to-air missiles like the AMRAAM and Aim-9L, and support of coproduction of the F-16C or Arrow ATBM can almost certainly offset any foreseeable level of technology transfers to hostile Arab states.

Such a clear plan for future arms transfers could provide Israel the security it needs to reduce its resistance to the sale of first-line weapons to nations like Egypt, Jordan, and Saudi Arabia. The United States could then sell the export versions of the F-15, F-16, F-18, the M-1 tank, the Improved Hawk, Stinger, and "controversial" systems while relying on tactical technology, rather than weapons numbers and quality, to give Israel a defensive edge.

The United States can also help secure Israel by working with it to create the new mixtures of weapons and technology that will allow it to secure its borders against major Arab offensives without having to rely on defense in depth and the retention of Arab territory. This approach should involve some carefully negotiated constraints on Israel's use of such U.S. weapons and technology and should include a clear link to a peace process. This, however, should be acceptable to Israel if it can count on adequate long-term levels of aid.

The technologies the United States has evolved as part of its Air Land Battle 2000, ET (emerging technology), and "Deep Strike" conventional capabilities for NATO offer much of the solution to giving Israel such a defense. These technologies include sensors and targeting aids that can rapidly locate any armor massing on Israel's northern border; runway cratering and air base suppression weapons that can help break up any Arab air offensive; and submunitions that can make Israeli fighters and multiple rocket launchers far more lethal against a major armored advance. Although the choice of any given mix of such weapons requires careful planning, it is fairly obvious that any major new conventional technologies designed to deal with Soviet mass and depth will be far more effective against a force like Syria, particularly because the competition in electronic warfare is likely to remain far less sophisticated than that from the Soviet Union.

Creating the Military Infrastructure for Peace

The United States also needs to work closely with Israel on the development of improved warning, surveillance, and low-level conflict technology of the kind that will allow Israel to withdraw from territory like the southern part of Lebanon and from as much of the West Bank as possible. One of the major errors in U.S. policy has been to seek political solutions before seeking a stable military solution. The alternative is to work with Israel now to help define secure borders in a way that will allow Israel to return as much territory as possible and to grant its Arab population maximum freedom throughout Israel. This may be principally a political decision, but it is also one that can be strongly affected by modern technology.

Israel could, for example, benefit from "smart" sensors in key border areas, a specially configured AWACS or balloon-carried set of radars with high land contrast capability, with special weapons munitions packages that could deal with sudden deployments of armor, with improved sensor packages for its remotely piloted vehicles, with a specially designed and dedicated satellite that would remove Israel's need to occupy high ground, and a wide range of similar technologies. There will always be "facts on the ground" from a military viewpoint, but U.S. aid and military technology can adjust and alter these facts to serve the cause of peace.

The Nuclear Dimension

Finally, the United States will need to work carefully with Israel to avoid an overt Israeli shift to dependence on nuclear deterrence while ensuring that no radical Arab state can use nuclear, chemical, or biological proliferation to create a unilateral threat to Israel. The immediate risk of added nuclear proliferation is limited, but even the moderate Arab states are likely to expand their efforts to acquire chemical, biological, and even nuclear weapons if Israel openly deploys a nuclear armed missile and fighter force.

U.S. Pressure on Israel

It is temping to add to the preceding list the need for the United States to make new efforts to get Israel to agree to a more flexible peace process, but this involves issues that go far beyond U.S. use of force in the Middle East. What is vital to protect U.S. strategic interests is to persuade Israel to minimize any low-level uses of military force and to obtain a clear quid pro quo from the Israeli government and its supporters regarding U.S. arms transfers to moderate Arab states.

U.S. Arms Transfers and the Problem of Jordan

Jordan has become a special problem for U.S. policy. Its ties to Iraq during the war to liberate Kuwait scarcely serve as much of an incentive for strong U.S. aid. Nevertheless, Jordan has strategic importance to the United States for at least three reasons. First, a moderate Jordan further reduces the risk of any need for U.S. involvement in an Arab-Israeli conflict. Second, Jordan can play an important role in securing Saudi Arabia's western border and potential oil shipments through Aqaba. Third, Jordan has potential ability to support friendly Gulf regimes in low-level conflicts or internal political emergencies.

The situation in Jordan has, however, become critical. Past U.S. inability to provide Jordan with moderate amounts of modern arms drove it into making major arms purchases from the Soviet Union, left Jordan increasingly vulnerable to Syria, made it increasingly less credible as a partner in guaranteeing any demilitarized Palestinian entity on the West Bank, and led it into dependence on Iraq.

Once again, arms transfers had a vital political importance that U.S. diplomacy was disinclined to recognize. If Jordan is to rebuild its ties to the United States, it will need a modern force structure with aircraft such as the F-16; it will need U.S. aid in developing a modern air C^3I and battle management system; and it will need effective mobile surface-to-air missiles like the Improved Hawk. It will not need these in numbers that directly threaten Israel's security.

Jordan now has only 35 fully modern aircraft in its air force. These, the Mirage F-1C/E, lack a full modern avionics suite, are difficult to maintain, and have only limited superiority to Jordan's 75 F-5E/Fs. This air power compares with some 553–655 combat aircraft in Israel, including 47 F-15s and 139 F-16s and F-16C/Ds. Israel also has 95 Kfirs, 112 F-4E/Hs, and 121 A-4H/Ns. All of Jordan's 14 Improved Hawk units are mounted on fixed sites and are so vulnerable as to be largely ineffective in war.[11]

The sale of modern U.S. fighters, mobile Hawk defenses, C^{3}I systems, and shorter-range air defense systems that Jordan has sought from the United States would not, therefore, have tilted the balance half as much as the sale of French Mirage 2000s and British Tornados that Jordan has tried to buy from Europe. This is particularly true because Israel has acquired Patriots and will buy even more advanced U.S. fighters and AWACS technology. The sales could act as a powerful deterrent to a Syria that now has over 4,000 medium tanks (to Jordan's 1,130) and 558 combat aircraft (to Jordan's 104).[12]

The proper mix of U.S. military ties and arms transfers to Jordan is far more likely to help avoid the use of military force than encourage it. It is also likely to help preserve a moderate Jordan under Hashemite rule that is unlikely to risk any new conflicts or adventures. Jordan's future lies in peace negotiations and economic development. A Jordan that is forced to turn to Arab radicals for arms or that becomes the captive of Islamic or Palestinian radicals will inevitably be more of a threat and less interested in peace. If Jordan ceases to be Hashemite, there is little conceivable prospect that any other regime will be as likely to seek peace or share a common strategic interest with the United States.

The Lebanese Morass

In 1983 the United States described Lebanon as a vital strategic interest and had some 35 warships, including the battleship *New Jersey* and two carriers with 180 aircraft, offshore. Onshore were 1,500 Marines and 83 Army personnel assigned to advisory roles and small fire units. U.S. forces had already taken roughly 50 percent of the combat fatalities Israel had suffered during its successful advance on Beirut.

It is now all too clear that Lebanon is not a vital U.S. strategic interest, and works by Jonathan Randall and Ze'ev Schiff have explained in detail many of the problems that led to the U.S. failure to understand the situation in Lebanon.[13] The most important lessons, however, had nothing to do with the conventional lessons of politics and war fighting. They involve three basic problems in U.S. strategy:

• First, the United States committed forces out of sentiment rather than out of the hard logic that should govern any use of arms. Lebanon was not a major U.S. strategic interest and did not merit the extensive use of U.S. forces.

• Second, the United States became involved in taking the side of two contradictory factions—the Maronites and Israelis. It failed to pursue its own national interests. As a result, it confused moralism with morality and compounded the Israeli and Maronite mistakes that have helped turn Lebanon into a strategic morass.

• Third, the United States became involved in a kind of low-level war with no clear enemy and with no clear reason to believe that the U.S. public would support the commitment of U.S. forces if anything went wrong or the war became prolonged. The Reagan administration failed to remember the limits Vietnam placed on any U.S. use of force, its inability to sustain casualties in unpopular conflicts, and the political difficulty of fighting low-level wars in populated areas. These are difficulties that no foreseeable change in U.S. tactics, technology, or force strength can change.

War is never simply an extension of politics by other means. It invariably involves far higher risks than politics, and it rapidly takes on a dynamic of its own and creates new political realities that are dominated by the conditions of the conflict, not by the conditions that led to it. Lebanon was a mistake precisely because the United States should have stopped at politics; it was a sideshow that did not justify the use of U.S. forces.

The United States needs to remember this. Lebanon is only one regional killing ground, and it will inevitably be followed by similarly bloody sideshows in the Levant, Red Sea, and North Africa. The United States must be prepared to ignore problems that do not affect its vital strategic interests. It must let others use force and take the consequences, and it must confine its role in such conflicts to a political and economic one. It may well have to provide arms and military advice, but it cannot confuse this with a need to protect every friendly regime or government from its own actions.

Syria and the Military Balance

The Lebanese problem inevitably raises the issue of Syria, and it is interesting to note that Syria is now experiencing its fourth trip into the Lebanese morass with virtually the same problems it experienced during its first journey. Syria is also a special case in that it is the only Soviet-equipped and -supplied military power in the Middle East that still can pose a serious threat to U.S. interests or to key friendly states in the Middle East.

Syria has acquired significant first-line Soviet and European military technology. Roughly 950 of its 4,000 tanks are T-72s; another 1,000 are T-62s. It has 2,250 modern Soviet BMP fighting vehicles and a full brigade of new Soviet SS-21 surface-to-surface missile launchers. Syria now has over 2,100 major artillery weapons, including the M-1943 and M-1973 Soviet self-propelled tube artillery weapons and new modifications of the BM-21 multiple rocket launcher. It has improved versions of the Soviet Sagger and Spigot and French-made Milan and HOT third-generation antitank guided missiles. Syria has had major problems in funding new equipment, spare parts, and readiness since 1987, but Syrian military training and organization have improved sharply since the June 1982 fighting.

Syria's air defense system also has built up rapidly since then. It is still vulnerable and lacks first-line Soviet radars, electronic warfare aids, and C³I assets, but it is now far better organized and trained and has Soviet cadres in several key battle management functions. Although Syria's SA-5 surface-to-air missile launchers are more for show than for threat, it is also acquiring improved SA-6s, SA-8s, SA-9s, and SA-13s. There are now some 60,000 troops and 91 major surface-to-air missile batteries in Syrian forces.

Syrian air forces now include more than 100 combat helicopters equipped with antitank guided weapons and 558 combat aircraft. These include 80 MiG-23MFs, 172 MiG-21PF/MFs, 30 MiG29s, 22 Su-24s, 35 Su-20s, 30 MiG-25Es, 6 MiG-25Rs, and 60 MiG-23BNs. These aircraft are not fully equipped with the avionics and radars standard on Soviet aircraft, but Syria is also gradually beginning to acquire modern Soviet air-to-air missiles like the AA-7, AA-8, and AA-10. The lack of such missiles was a critical deficiency in the June 1982 fighting.[14]

Nevertheless, Syria still poses only a comparatively limited threat to U.S. strategic interests. Syria was never a Soviet satellite or major Soviet base. It backed the United States against Iraq in the war to liberate Kuwait and even indicated it would not oppose Israel if it responded to Iraq's Scud attacks. Syria has always played an uncertain and highly nationalistic role, but it has also shown a willingness to cut mutually advantageous deals with Israel and the United States that can scarcely please the Soviet Union.

Syria also has little near-term hope of translating its growing military strength into any leverage over Israel. It will continue to lack the economic resources and personnel skill levels to match its equipment and technology for at least another half decade, and unless it can persuade the Soviet Union or Europe to change radically the level of technology it will transfer to Syria, the United States can sustain Israel's technical edge for the foreseeable future. This, at worst, makes Syria a local rather than regional threat and one that is likely to remain peripheral to U.S. strategic interests. It also leaves Syria as Israel's military problem rather than a U.S. one. The United States must certainly provide Israel and Jordan with military aid, but has no present reason to contemplate the commitment of U.S. forces.

North Africa: Ignoring Libya While Strengthening Ties to Tunisia and Morocco

North Africa is not literally part of the Middle East, but any use of U.S. force in the region cannot be decoupled from a consideration of Libya or from U.S. ties to Tunisia and Morocco. Libya, however, has no prospect of transforming its large arms imports and weapons inventories into a major threat as long as the United States continues to support Egypt, as long as France continues to play a major role in Africa, and as long as the United States can build solid military relations with the other key Arab states. Like Iran, Libya is a serious threat only when it can exploit U.S. tensions with key Arab states or exploit their internal conflicts.

The United States does not, therefore, need to contemplate more than further demonstrative uses of force. It may again have to demonstrate its resolve and repeat its air strikes on Libya or its clashes with the Libyan air force. The United States may have to speed arms shipments to neighboring states or deploy token forces like the AWACS, but it can generally afford to treat Libya with what might be termed "malign neglect." Qaddafi is sufficiently shaky—and the probability of his being replaced by a more pro-Soviet regime is sufficiently slight—that the United States has to be more careful of giving him added status or making him into a martyr than concerned about his various military and political adventures.

As for the rest of North Africa, it is important to note that Soviet arms transfers to Algeria have done little or nothing to create any threat from that country. Further, there are no immediate prospects the United States will have to use more than token amounts of force in defense of either Morocco or Tunisia. The major threats to both Morocco and Tunisia are, in any case, domestic and political. Even Morocco's war with the Polisario is of token strategic interest to the United States. It is important that King Hassan should not fall, but the future of the Spanish Sahara is one of the most unimportant issues affecting U.S. security.

The United States and the Abuse of Military Force

There is no "golden thread" that connects all of the complex military factors in the Middle East that affect U.S. policy. Any U.S. use of military force must ultimately be shaped by the politics and military position of individual nations, the resource and political constraints that limit any active U.S. use of force, and the growing need to focus U.S. strategic commitments and to link any use of U.S. forces to the bases and forces of friendly states.

In practice, however, this means that the United States must strengthen its relations with Egypt and Saudi Arabia. It means that the United States must build stronger ties to the rest of the Gulf Cooperation Council states and try to rebuild its ties to Jordan. It means the United States must redefine its U.S. military ties to Israel to give them meaning in the defense of the Mediterranean, to decouple them from the defense of the Gulf, and to help resolve the Arab-Israeli conflict.

There is one other thread, however, that deserves special mention. The Soviet Union still has major military forces it can deploy in the Middle East and the Gulf. The forces the Soviet Union can use to threaten the West's oil supplies include 9 land divisions in the forward area: 1 tank, 1 airborne, and 7 motorized rifle. One Soviet tank division has roughly the total tank strength that USCENTCOM could deploy within 21 days. The Soviet Union has two more airborne divisions ready for immediate deployment (the 107th in Turkestan and the 104th in the Transcaucasus military districts).

There are nearly 30 divisions deployed in the southern Soviet Union above Afghanistan, with 6,400 tanks, 6,500 artillery weapons, and 190 FROG and Scud missile launchers. The Soviet Union could rapidly deploy two to three Tactical Air Armies with 400–600 fighter aircraft to its border area. It already bases advanced Su-25, Su-24, MiG-23, and MiG-27 fighters and Mi-24 attack helicopters in the region. The Soviet surface navy is still not a serious competitor to its U.S. counterpart, but its submarines and naval bombers pose a threat and it has extensive airlift.

The Soviet Union has 55 AN-22s (equivalent to the C-5A) and 150 Il-76s (equivalent to the C-141) and will soon deploy the An-40, the world's largest military air transport aircraft. The Soviet Union tested large-scale air movements from the Black Sea area and Tashkent to Ethiopia and South Yemen as early as 1978. It has formerly used naval facilities at Aden and Socotra in South Yemen and is improving the naval facilities at Dahlak, Masawa, and Asab in Ethiopia. It faces major problems in power projection to the southern Gulf, but it has an obvious geographic advantage in any conflict affecting Iraq, Iran, Turkey, or Pakistan. It also is transferring massive amounts of arms to client states.

Those capabilities cannot be totally ignored, although there is little present sign that the Soviet Union will use these forces unless it can be assured of a political context in which it acts in unison with the United States or under conditions where some client state would invite it into the region without a direct confrontation with the United States.

The Soviet Union has structured most of these forces for defense and seems unlikely to repeat its experience in Afghanistan by launching an equally unpopular war anywhere else. The United States faces many problems in using military force in the Middle East, but these problems no longer are dominated by the Soviet buildup of regional military forces, by technology transfer, or by the threat posed by Soviet military strength.

The primary problems the United States faces are the lack of a continuing Arab-Israeli peace process, past difficulties in establishing firm ties to key friendly Arab states, its inability to act as a reliable arms supplier, and its failure to create a military relationship with Israel that is shaped and managed in a way that serves the long-term interests of either country. These problems are particularly important because the radical states in the region must rely on exploiting the self-inflicted weaknesses and contradictions in the U.S. strategic position rather than on their own strengths. Thus, the use or abuse of U.S. military force in the Middle East depends on the quality of U.S. policy and strategy; it is not dictated by outside forces. The greatest problem the United States faces is not its potential enemies but itself and its friends.

Notes

1. See Anthony H. Cordesman, *The Gulf and the Search for Strategic Stability* (Boulder, Colo.: Westview Press, 1984), pp. 20–25; and Cordesman, *The Gulf and the West* (Boulder, Colo.: Westview Press, 1988), pp. 15–29.

2. One semantic problem in U.S. relations with Middle Eastern states is that "ally" literally means a state with which the United States has a formal treaty, whereas "friend" can mean virtually anything. Few states in the region wish to announce publicly the full degree of their cooperation with the United States, and neither it nor its de facto allies have any political or military incentive to create formal treaties.

3. The minimum air transport distance to any key Middle Eastern nation except Morocco is 12,800 kilometers (7,000 nautical miles). The distance by sea by the Cape of Good Hope route is 22,000 kilometers (12,000 nautical miles).

4. More than 31 days by the Cape route.

5. The United States now has 62 operational C-5As, 218 C-141s, 38 KC-10s, 216 C-130s, 67 long-range CRAF cargo aircraft, and 227 long-range CRAF passenger aircraft.

6. These estimates are based on discussions with USCENTCOM and on the FY 1987 USCENTCOM background brief.

7. See Raphael Iungerich, "U.S. Rapid Deployment Forces," *Armed Forces Journal*, October 1984, pp. 89–193; Department of Defense, *Annual Posture Statement, FY 1987*, Washington, D.C., pp. 212 and 229–246; Office of the Joint Chiefs of Staff, *Military Posture, FY 1987*, Washington, D.C., pp. 66–70; and

Secretary of Defense Frank C. Carlucci, *Annual Report to the Congress, FY 1990*, Washington, D.C., pp. 169–175.

8. These figures are estimated using data from the U.S. State Department, *Conventional Arms Transfers in the Third World*, Special Report no. 102, August 1982, page 2; the work of Richard F. Grimmet of the Congressional Research Service and his annual series on the *Trends in Conventional Arms Transfers to the Third World by Major Supplier;* and various annual editions of U.S. Arms Control and Disarmament Agency (ACDA), *World Military Expenditures and Arms Transfers*.

9. ACDA, *World Military Expenditures and Arms Transfers, 1989*, Washington, D.C., 1990.

10. Based on *SACLANT Summary Force Briefing*, SACLANT Headquarters, Norfolk, Virginia, 1988.

11. IISS, *Military Balance, 1990–1991*, IISS, London, 1990. See the section on the Middle East.

12. For further analysis of these issues, see Anthony H. Cordesman, *Jordan and the Middle East Balance* (Washington, D.C.: Middle East Institute, 1983 and 1985).

13. See Jonathan C. Randal, *Going All the Way* (New York: Viking Press, 1983); and Ze'ev Schiff and Ehud Ya-ari, *Israel's Lebanon War* (New York: Simon and Schuster, 1984).

14. IISS, *Military Balance, 1990–1991*, IISS, London, 1990. See the sections on the Middle East.

8
The Syrian Doctrine
of Strategic Parity

Ahmed S. Khalidi and Hussein Agha

The basic thrust of Syria's policy during the last two decades has been to develop a coherent strategy that could serve to contain what it believes to be Israel's hegemonic designs in the area and to retrieve Syrian and Arab lands lost in the 1967 war. Underlying these views is also an apparently strong conviction that the struggle with Israel is no mere political or territorial dispute but rather a clash of destinies affecting the fate and future of the Middle East.

Syrian strategy can thus be seen to combine some rational cost-benefit calculus as to the instrumentality of force with a broader, more ideological grounding. This blend often appears to propel Syrian policies in one direction and then the other, and occasionally in both directions at once. At the same time, the Syrian approach has been characterized by as much flexibility as dogma. The Syrian-Israeli relationship in Lebanon since the mid-1970s affords one example of Syrian readiness to reach a de facto accommodation with Israel—and vice versa—even though the potential for a confrontation between the two sides in this arena has never been entirely absent. The scrupulousness with which Syria adheres to the cease-fire agreements on the Golan Heights is another example of Syrian caution and circumspection when dealing with Israel.

Partly as a result of deliberate policy and partly as a reflection of Syria's blend of realism and dogmatism, its precise motives and objectives often remain obscure. This makes it difficult to ascertain the exact course of Syrian grand strategy and leaves the door open for varied interpretations of its overall design. The readiness to resort to force, however, appears to retain a prominent position as an instrument of policy, as demonstrated practically against Israel in 1973 and in Lebanon since. As opposed to the views of other Arab actors (e.g., Jordan, Egypt, and to a large extent the PLO), the Arab "military option" appears alive or at least revivable from the Syrian point of view. This is seen as a necessary element for defense against Israeli aggrandizement and as a function of Syria's perceived role as a regional superpower, including its ability to participate in any diplomatic process leading to an equitable Arab-Israeli settlement.

Yet Syria has also shown a clear awareness of the constraints facing military action against Israel. It has repeatedly counseled against the precipitate use of force (e.g., on the part of guerrilla groups) and has often stated its refusal to be dragged into a confrontation with Israel in circumstances inappropriate from its point of view. (Such a position lay at the heart of its refusal to broaden the conflict with Israel in 1982 and most notably Iraq's attempt to turn the Gulf war into an Arab-Israeli confrontation involving Syria in 1991.) This approach, however, has also been bound up with the view that force, whether active or passive, is the final arbiter of the conflict with Israel and the ultimate guarantor of any settlement in the area. From this perspective, Syria has not openly subscribed to the view that there is a credible alternative to military strength when dealing with Israel.

Arab politico-strategic doctrine has long recognized an imbalance of power in the region arising from a combination of Israel's military and technological superiority and its alliance with the United States. A number of routes toward redressing this imbalance have been attempted.

• First, in the 1950s and 1960s, Nasserite and other pan-Arab movements (such as the Baath party) called for integral Arab political unity as a precondition of any successful confrontation with Israel. According to this view, the creation of a supranational Arab entity would allow for the full mobilization of Arab moral and material resources and would help to transform quantitative Arab superiority into a qualitative one.

• Second, the difficulties facing integral unity, highlighted by the failure of the Egyptian-Syrian union of 1958–1961 and the defeat of 1967, gave impetus to the notion of revolutionary transformation and armed struggle. This view, which reflected the growth of the Palestinian national movement and interacted with it, assumed that only a fundamental restructuring of Arab society could pose a credible strategic challenge to Israel and its allies.

• Third, by the mid-1970s a new school of thought had emerged. While proposing no substantial change in the existing Arab order, it sought to correct the strategic imbalance by exploring the possibilities of functional cooperation between coexisting regimes. In the military sphere, functional coordination reached a new effectiveness in the Syrian-Egyptian campaign of 1973. Politically, this school proposed programs of action based on inter-Arab détente and the lowest common denominator, such as the Fez peace plan of 1982.

• Fourth, a convergent but separate school of thought, which can best be seen in President Sadat's policy toward Israel after 1973, sought to decouple Israel from the United States by politico-diplomatic means. This school argued that if Israel's alliance with the United States was a major factor behind the strategic imbalance in the area, the most effective way to correct the imbalance would be for Arab states to embrace the United States as well and align the Arab side with its policies. This would increase the chances of the United States distancing itself from Israel and paying more heed to Arab interests in the conflict.

• Fifth, a new school based on Islamic revivalism and activism has emerged. Still in its initial phases, the overall direction of this trend remains uncertain, but it may well develop a clearer strategic line alongside the evolution of its tactical and operational methods. Inspired by Iran but not necessarily in direct alliance with it, this school argues that the strategic imbalance with Israel can be corrected only through a "return" to Islamic (as opposed to secular, national, or pan-Arab) modes of action. This approach entails a process of cultural, political, and military confrontation with Israel and the Western powers that support it as well as with the Arab parties that reject a return to Islamic values or that stand in its way.

Syria's position among the major Arab parties is distinctive in that almost all the attempts to correct the strategic imbalance with Israel have been reflected in its public posture or political practice over the years. Integral Arab unity, for instance, remains the cornerstone of Baath party ideology, even though Syrian policies have moved away from an activist line in this respect. In 1966 Syria officially espoused "revolutionary armed struggle" as the basis of its strategy, seeing this element as necessary to ultimate negation of Israel's technical and technological superiority. Syria reaffirmed this doctrine periodically up to the 1973 war, when it participated in the only real example of functional Arab military cooperation since 1948. Politically, Syria has in the past pursued functional cooperation with Jordan bilaterally, while attempting to stiffen the terms for a resolution of the conflict within the context of collective Arab politico-diplomatic action. Although officially secular in outlook, Syria maintains significant contacts with the Islamic revivalist school through its relationship with Iran and through the role it plays in Lebanon, including its support for anti-Israeli resistance activities since 1982. Perhaps the school of thought least representative of Syria's approach is that associated with President Sadat's attempt to decouple the United States from Israel. There appears to be, however, a growing Syrian awareness of the need to establish better relations with the United States, an awareness that has been sharpened by the new relationship between the two countries evolving out of the Gulf crisis and subsequent war.

Development of the Doctrine of Strategic Parity

As yet Syrian politico-strategic doctrine is still based on the call for strategic parity with Israel. Although elements from the different Arab schools of thought can be traced in this doctrine, it represents a distinctive and separate view of this problem. Its formal theoretical framework, however, remains ambiguous because there is no official public text elaborating its meaning and content. From available sources it appears that the Syrian doctrine of parity can be understood in a number of different senses.[1]

First, strategic parity implies that given the current situation in the Middle East and the limited prospects for functional military cooperation with any major Arab party (specifically Egypt but including Jordan and Iraq), in the near future Syria, acting largely on its own, should build up its military strength and potential until the gap with Israel has been breached or at least neutralized. This would entail the general expansion of Syrian armed force, with particular stress on reducing Israel's lead in those areas where it has demonstrated its superiority, for example, air-to-air and air-to-ground operations and the use of advanced, modern command, control, communication, and intelligence (C^3I) techniques. A substantial narrowing of the gap between Israel and Syria in such key areas might then allow for a limited Syrian military initiative, with the object of achieving some positive politico-military or territorial gains that could be used to improve the Syrian-Arab position in any subsequent talks between the two sides. Such initiatives could include a surprise attack along the Golan Heights aimed at the eviction of Israeli forces from selected positions, a low-level war of attrition against Israeli forces in the Golan Heights or Lebanon, or escalation of Syrian support for guerrilla operations in south Lebanon or across the Israeli border. Most important for the Syrians would be the ability to withstand possible Israeli counteractions such that any initial gains would not be totally reversed in the process. In this scenario the Syrians need not aspire to a clear-cut victory themselves but merely to the ability to deny this prospect to Israel.

Second, another reading of strategic parity is that it requires the buildup of Syrian military power to a credible deterrent posture. Here the stress may not be so much on developing the means for a Syrian military initiative but rather on raising the cost of any Israeli military action against Syria. One important aspect of this deterrent capability would be the acquisition of delivery systems and warheads that can strike deep into Israeli territory and that could be targeted accurately against key military or civilian installations; examples of tactical ground-to-ground missiles include the SS-21s currently in Syrian service. Delivery systems of this sort would somewhat offset Israel's ability to project its force deep into the Syrian-Arab hinterland and would cause Israel to think twice before embarking on any major military confrontation with Syria. Added to this would be the expansion of Syrian defenses along the Golan Heights so that any Israeli attempt at a direct breakthrough on the ground would be extremely costly.

Of much concern to Syria (and other major Arab actors) is the issue of Israel's nuclear capacity. Within this context Syria has apparently sought to reinforce its strategic deterrent through the acquisition of chemical warheads that can be teamed with its ballistic missile force. Chemical warheads are likely to be perceived by Syria as the most effective and readily obtainable means by which Israel's nuclear superiority can be partially redressed if not neutralized. The combination of accurate ballistic missiles (the SS-21s in particular) and chemical warheads could give Syria the option of a credible countervalue targeting strategy as well as the ability to attack Israeli military targets as part of any first strike or retaliatory blow.

Such a deterrent capability could allow for a Syrian strategic posture based more on the threat of force than actual recourse to it. Depending on its ability to cause comparatively high civilian or military casualties, Syria might feel secure enough from Israeli attack to enter into negotiations from a position of relative strength.

Third, parity can also be understood in a broader sense. Indeed, the doctrine of strategic parity grew directly out of the political and strategic developments of the past decade, in particular the Egyptian-Israeli peace treaty and the general move toward a political resolution to the Arab-Israeli conflict. During this period Syria has consistently held that no just and durable settlement with Israel is possible given Israel's military preponderance and overall superiority. From this perspective, rectification of the imbalance requires a sustained effort at political and social change and the mobilization of all available Arab resources to match Israel's societal and technological advantages and overcome them. Syria, which would play a pivotal role in this process, would also seek to bring other Arab parties within a mutually acceptable framework for cooperation. With strategic parity in this sense attained, the Arab military option would appear more credible, immeasurably improving the Arab negotiating position in any peace talks with Israel.

These different interpretations of strategic parity are not mutually exclusive but may be seen as interlocking or alternating phases within a singular course of action, with an occasional Syrian shift of emphasis from one to another depending on the internal and external conditions obtaining. The first two interpretations perhaps reflect the Syrians' belief in their ability to go it alone in their pursuit of parity with Israel, if necessary. In this context a deterrent posture clearly does not negate the prospects for a military initiative, although such an initiative need not form an integral part of Syrian deterrence. The third interpretation suggests that parity cannot be fully attained without substantial change in the Arab environment including a reactivated southern front and perhaps a revived eastern front, incorporating Jordan and Iraq as well as Syria. This notion may have been substantially altered by the turn of events during the Gulf crisis and could well be seen as essentially obsolete given the new realities in the Middle East. Going it alone may thus be a worst-case or fallback position pending the development of wider military and political cooperation with other Arab parties or even more integral forms of association. In the absence of the optimal means toward a strategic parity with Israel, the Syrians may be forced to accept the less desirable conditions attached to going it alone.

The Constituents of Strategic Parity

Regardless of the precise Syrian scenario for attaining parity, Syrian action toward correcting the strategic imbalance with Israel comprises the following elements: an arms buildup, an alliance with the Soviets, the exploitation of Lebanon, various domestic factors, and a more unified Arab strategy.

An Arms Buildup and the Expansion of Syrian Military Power

The Syrian armed forces have undergone rapid and extensive growth over the past few years.[2] Since the Lebanon war of 1982, Syrian forces have expanded as follows:

- an 80 percent increase in the regular armed forces, from about 240,000 to approximately 400,000
- a 50 percent increase in the number of armored and mechanized divisions, from 6 to 9
- a 35 percent increase in the number of main battle tanks (MBTs), from 3,200 to about 4,200

- a 200 percent increase in the number of tactical ballistic missile launchers, from 33 to about 100
- a 50 percent increase in the number of surface-to-air batteries, from 100 to approximately 150
- a 45 percent increase in the number of combat aircraft, from 440 to about 650
- a 150 percent increase in the number of attack helicopters, from 40 to about 100
- a 40 percent increase in the number of missile attack craft, from 20 to 28
- an absolute increase in the number of submarines, from 0 to 3

These quantitative increases in Syrian military strength and arms acquisition have been matched by parallel increases in the quality of weapons received. New weapons systems that have entered service with the Syrian armed forces since 1982 include the following:

- SS-21 tactical ballistic missiles (range of 120 kilometers, circle error of probability of 50 meters) and Sepal shore-to-shore (or shore-to-sea) missiles (range of 300 kilometers)
- a new range of surface-to-air missiles (SAMs) comprising the SAM-5, -11, -13, and -14 as well as improved versions of the SAM-6 and SAM-8 missiles in service with the Syrians in 1982
- T-80, T-72M, and T-74 main battle tanks, which along with older variants of the T-72 now constitute at least 30–40 percent of Syrian armored strength
- BM-27 220-millimeter multiple rocket launchers, which represent a significant addition to Syrian mobile artillery forces
- MiG-29 counterair fighters, which have recently entered service in squadron strength with the Syrian air force, along with full-up versions of the MiG-23 (known as the MiG-23MF/Flogger-G) as opposed to the downgraded export versions previously in service
- AA-7 Acrid and AA-8 Aphid air-to-air missiles, representing an important improvement in Syrian air combat capabilities over the AA-2 Atoll previously in service
- new tactical C^3I and electronic warfare systems, including DR-30 and UR-1 remotely piloted drones (RPVs) and Mi-17 Elint (electronic intelligence) helicopters
- chemical warfare delivery systems, possibly including chemical warheads for tactical ballistic missiles

TABLE 8.1   Ratio of Syrian Forces (n) to Israeli Forces (1.00), 1982 and 1989

	*1982*n	*1989*n
Armed Forces		
Regulars	1.85	3.00
Reserves	1.35	0.90
Total	1.50	1.55
Armored and mechanized divisions	0.55	0.75
Tanks	0.80	1.00
Artillery and mortars	2.30	2.30
High-quality combat aircraft	0.50	0.50
SAM batteries	4.00	5.00
SSM launchers	2.30	2.00
Missile boats	0.80	0.90

Sources: The Middle East in Military Balance, ed. Mark Heller, Jerusalem Post/Westview Press, Boulder, Colorado, Tel Aviv University Jaffe Center for Strategic Studies, annual editions 1984–1988; *The Military Balance,* International Institute for Strategic Studies, London, annual editions 1984–1988; *An-Nashra al-Istrajjiyah* (Strategic Review) vols. 6–10 (1985–1989), London; and *Istratijya,* no. 34, December 1984, and no. 35, January 1985, Beirut.

This quantitative improvement in Syrian armed strength must, however, be measured against any similar quantitative improvements on the Israeli side. A comparison of Syrian-Israeli force ratios in 1982 and 1989 in some key sectors appears in Table 8.1. The result of Syria's arms buildup since 1982 can be evaluated with respect to the quantitative balance between the two sides.

First, Syrian regular forces now outnumber Israeli regulars about 3 to 1. This has been achieved by drawing down Syrian reserves so that the total armed forces available to both sides have not changed substantially since 1982. Syria, however, is now nominally in a better position to move more quickly and with greater mass against the relatively small Israeli standing forces that rely heavily on a period of grace or early warning of between twenty-four and seventy-two hours to attain full mobilization. Syria's advantage in this respect has been increased by the expansion in the number of armored and mechanized divisions available, even though the Israeli High Command can still field 25 percent more such formations after full mobilization (twelve divisions to Syria's nine). Increasing the number of regular Syrian formations also improves Syria's defensive posture insofar as it necessitates a greater degree of Israeli mobilization before any offensive or preemptive action and thus decreases the prospect for an Israeli surprise attack.

Second, Syria has succeeded in either preventing a deterioration of the quantitative balance or improving its position vis-à-vis Israel in almost every major category of armed strength since 1982. Its tank

TABLE 8.2   Syria's Response to Military Shortcomings, 1982–1989

Area	Nature of Gap	Remedy
Air-to-air combat	Lack of high-performance fighters and modern air-to-air missiles (AAMs)	Acquisition of new generation of MiG-29s and AAMs
Surface-to-air combat	Lack of integrated and effective systems	Much-expanded SAM system with better radar and electronic countermeasures (ECMs)
Ground combat	Limited number of modern main battle tanks (MBTs)	Large number of T-72 and T-74 MBTs brought into front-line service
CC³I	Lack of AWACS or equivalent, limited tactical CC³I, inadequate ECMs	Acquisition of specific anti-AWACS system (SAM-5), acquisition of tactical CC³I (RPVs), improved ECM, possible AWACs acquisition
Strategic deterrence	Limited ability to strike enemy depth, limited counterforce capability	Acquisition of SS-21 tactical SSMs with high degree of accuracy and possible chemical warheads for credible counterforce and countervalue strikes; other new SSMs brought into service

Source: Compiled from authors' estimates.

forces are now numerically equivalent to those of Israel, and it has maintained its longstanding lead in artillery, SAM defenses, and SSM launchers. The one vital category in which no substantial progress has been made is high-quality combat aircraft; force ratios remain much the same as in 1982.

The qualitative difference in Syrian and Israeli weaponry seems to suggest that some specific shortcomings highlighted by the 1982 war have been seriously addressed by the Syrians (see Table 8.2). All of these improvements in the quantity and quality of the weapons systems currently available to the Syrian armed forces and their potential impact on the strategic balance with Israel should, however, be examined in the light of Israeli superiority in technology and in weaponry.

Israeli Technical and Technological Superiority. Although difficult to measure accurately, Israeli technical and technological superiority is still manifest in such key areas as aerial operations, where all evidence suggests that the Israeli Air Force (IAF) would dominate the sky in any new confrontation. (For example, there is not one substantiated instance of an Israeli aircraft being brought down in air-to-air combat with Syrians since 1973, the last dogfight between the two air forces taking place at the end of 1985.) Israel's technological superiority is also clearly evident in the capability of its arms industry to produce a very wide range of sophisticated weapons systems, with particular emphasis on high-technology products in electronics, command and control, and missile technology.

Syria's attempts at breaching the qualitative gap are hampered by the relative narrowness of its technological base and its shortage of qualified personnel. Israeli sources report constant Syrian maintenance and serviceability problems and difficulties in keeping pace with the increased rate of arms acquisitions. According to one source, up to 30 percent of Syria's 4,200 tanks may be held in storage or as static antitank guns alongside an indeterminate number of combat aircraft.[3] Despite wide-scale mobilization of available personnel, the demands of high-technology systems (especially in fields like C[3]I) are likely to pose a constant obstacle to qualitative parity with Israel.

Israel's Lead in Training, Command, and Operational Techniques. Israel's leadership in these areas arises from the technical-technological gap between the two parties but also reflects sociopolitical factors. Recently the Syrians have made a sustained effort to improve the performance of their officer material and field formations through a program of extensive training, including offensive combined-arms exercises. Israeli sources, however, continue to question the realism and effectiveness of such training as compared with the training techniques adopted by the Israeli army itself; there apparently is a substantial gap between the realism and flexibility of training in Western-style armies and the less realistic and more doctrinaire training adopted by Soviet-style armies.

Lack of effective training interacts with such basic societal problems as generally low-grade professional standards for noncommissioned officers and junior officers and the lack of experience and suitable candidates for higher military office. This in turn is a symptom of the overlap between military and politico-communitarian issues, where party and communal loyalties can take precedence over sheer professional skills. All of these factors together contribute to inhibiting the development of effective operational abilities and techniques sufficient to narrow the gap with the generally proficient performance of the Israeli Defense Forces (IDF) in this respect. It may be worth noting, however, that some Israeli sources believe that the relative performance of Israeli ground forces has degenerated in some vital aspects, such as tank-to-tank combat, and that Syrian capabilities in such specialized areas as special forces or commando operations have improved.[4]

Israel's Lead in the Quality of Weapons. Israel maintains an important edge in the quality of weapons available to its armed forces at almost all levels. The issue of Israel's qualitative lead in weaponry can be further broken down into several components.

First is the superiority of Israeli- and Western-made weaponry, which on the whole is superior to the Soviet systems in service with Syria. Although Syria has made some effort to diversify its sources of arms, it still relies on the Soviet Union for 90 to 95 percent of all its equipment. Syria has obtained some specialized electronic systems as well as an effective combination of attack helicopters and antitank missiles from the West (the Gazelle and HOT), but their effort on the overall balance is marginal.[5] Because Israeli weapons systems are tailor-made for the operational requirements of the IDF, either in cooperation with the U.S. suppliers or as a result of Israel's own research and development efforts, Syria suffers a further disadvantage. By way of contrast, Syrian forces generally have to make do with what the Soviet Union produces for its own particular needs, which may differ in important respects from those of Syria.

Second is the availability of effective countermeasures to Israeli systems. In some cases Syria cannot narrow the qualitative gap with Israel simply because the necessary equivalent or countermeasure is not produced by the Soviets. Thus, Israeli superiority in aerial C^3I in 1982 drew heavily upon the effective utilization of E-2C Hawkeye mini-AWACS aircraft by the Israeli Air Force, an aircraft with no exact equivalent in the Soviet inventory despite the existence of relatively primitive Soviet AWACS aircraft such as the TU-126. Syria was thus forced to rely on a different category of countermeasure in the form of long-range SAM-5 missiles, which may be effective in interdicting the Hawkeye but gives the Syrians no AWACS capability of their own. Even where effective equivalents or countermeasures are available, Syria cannot always rely on Soviet readiness to provide the requisite items. In many cases the Soviet Union has offered downgraded export models of certain front-line equipment, which do not always reach the standards of opposing Western and Israeli equipment (the export model MiG-23/Flogger-E as compared with the F-16, for example). The provision of export models of basic weapons systems to Syria in part reflects Soviet concern about security and loss of techological secrets to the West, but also signals a more general Soviet reluctance to encourage Syrian military adventures or to provide Syria with the means to escalate the conflict.

Syrian reliance on the Soviet Union as the sole source of virtually all advanced weaponry is an important constraint on the direction of the Syrian military buildup. In addition to the Soviet Union's reluctance to proffering its latest technology, Syria remains largely bound by the overall state of the Soviet technological cycle. Given the technological gap between the Soviets and the West—including Israel—and despite some major qualitative improvements in Soviet military technology in recent years, Syria often finds itself at the tail end of one technological cycle at a time when Israel is at the cutting edge of the next. The MiG-29, for example, only recently entered Syrian service after its rough equivalents—the F-15 and the F-16—had been in service with Israel for over a decade and almost in tandem with Israeli efforts to secure the next generation of combat aircraft—the Agile Falcon, the advanced tactical fighter (ATF), and the like. Thus, the qualitative gap in weaponry may be temporarily narrowed at the junction between the end of one generation of equipment and the beginning of another, but this gap is likely to widen again as the pace of the coming technological cycle accelerates. The revolutionary changes in conventional weaponry on the way in fields like microprocessing, fiber optics, millimeter wave guidance, composite materials, and artificial intelligence will probably affect the military balance in particularly significant ways. In all such fields the West currently holds the lead, with Israel playing an active part. But even assuming a Soviet ability to narrow the current technological gap substantially, the local imbalance in weaponry is likely to remain in Israel's favor barring any basic shift in Syrian policy toward the West or full-scale Syrian access to advanced Soviet (or Western) technology.

The ultimate viability of Syria's strategic deterrent posture may also be open to question. There is as yet no direct means of defense against ballistic missile attack, but the Israelis are currently giving high priority to their antitactical ballistic missile program. This centers on the Hetz/Arrow missile being developed jointly with the United States as part of Israel's participation in the Strategic Defense Initiative. The Hetz/Arrow, designed to intercept and destroy incoming ballistic missiles at the earliest possible point after launch, is scheduled to enter operational service in Israel around 1992 or 1993. Although it is unlikely that this missile in itself would be capable of totally neutralizing the threat of Syrian missiles armed with chemical warheads, the credibility of this threat could be significantly reduced. The recently demonstrated effectiveness of U.S.-built Patriot antimissile missiles against Iraqi SSM attacks must have caused the Syrian High Command to reassess the ability and efficiency of a missile-based deterrent.

In the short to medium term, Syria may thus find itself in a position whereby its strategic deterrent has been devalued, while the overall technological gap with Israel widens once again. This may presage increased instability in the Israeli-Syrian military balance and reduce the prospects for attaining strategic parity as currently conceived.

The Alliance with the Soviet Union

The Israeli-U.S. relationship forms one vital aspect of the strategic imbalance in the area from a Syrian-Arab point of view. Syria's achievement of parity with Israel depends partly on its formation of an alliance with the Soviet Union to offset the Israeli-U.S. partnership.

A strong Syrian-Soviet relationship has been one of the more permanent features of regional politics since the mid-1950s. In 1986 the U.S. Department of Defense described Syria as the largest Soviet arms client in the third world, having contracted for a total of $19 billion worth of arms, including an estimated $2–3 billion since 1982. Syria is also a major recipient of Soviet economic aid, having obtained over $1 billion in credits from the Soviet Union between 1982 and 1985, according to the Defense Department.[6] The Soviet Union has long seen Syrian nationalist and pan-Arab tendencies as a valuable element in obstructing a wider Western presence in the area, a role that may have increased in significance for the Soviets as most other Arab regimes have become better disposed toward the West in recent years. Syria's geostrategic position astride Lebanon, Jordan, and Israel also guarantees its position as a major regional actor, thus highlighting Soviet interest in Syria as a means of access to the core Middle Eastern arena.

Besides the Soviet Union's role as a source of military and economic aid, the ultimate significance of Soviet-Syrian relations for Syria resides in the perceived deterrent value of these relations in the conflict with Israel. That role has been evident on a number of occasions since 1967 and may have been formalized to some degree in the Soviet-Syrian Treaty of Friendship and Cooperation signed in 1980, although this remains uncertain. Nonetheless, Soviet relations with Syria are widely held to impose some ceiling on Israel's freedom of action, even though the actual limits have neither been challenged nor well defined.

Despite a broad band of common Soviet-Syrian interests, the relationship between the two parties is unlikely to become a comprehensive strategic alliance that fully replicates Israeli relations with the United States. Five structural factors inhibit the Soviet-Syrian relationship in this respect.

First, there is no real harmony or ideological or political empathy between Syria and the Soviet Union. At root, Syrian nationalism and pan-Arabism are antagonistic toward communism and vice versa. Although it is true that the Soviet Union has drifted away from a more doctrinaire position in dealing with the Middle East in particular and the third world in general, the foundation of its relationship with countries like Syria remains substantially different from the ideological and politcal symbiosis at the basis of Israeli-U.S. relations. This special relationship is reflected not only in the way that the United States directly ascribes Western-democratic values to Israel but also in the gradual integration of Israel within the U.S. global strategic system, a process that has no counterpart on the Soviet-Syrian side. Some in the United States no longer see Israel as merely a regional ally capable of "holding" the Middle East on its behalf but rather as an active partner capable of promoting U.S.-Western interests worldwide. Israel's role in this partnership extends from participation in the Strategic Defense Initiative to help in dealing with Iran. In contrast, Syria can do little in support of Soviet global interests, priding itself, on the contrary, on its independence of political will and its unwillingness to act as a proxy or agent for any outside party.

Second, underlying the politico-ideological affinity between Israel and the United States is the powerful influence of a common cultural and religious heritage. Over and above the perception of Israel as a Western-style democracy are the strong historical links between the two countries that manifest themselves in societal values, prevailing norms and attitudes, and overall aspirations. An extensive network of institutional and individual ties and a process of constant interaction at every level reinforce these links.

Nothing like this exists between Syria and the Soviet Union, which have few historical links and virtually no common cultural bonds. One dominant factor—Islam—plays, if anything, a negative role in the potential development of Syrian-Soviet ties. Furthermore, although Syria may find the Soviet Union more commendable than the United States in regional policy and world outlook, the Soviet Union seems to have little to offer in broad cultural benefits that can compete with the West or satisfy particular Syrian needs and interests. In short, the Soviet model in its political, organizational, and cultural dimensions is not one that Syria generally aspires to replicate or emulate.

Third, the high degree of economic integration between the United States and Israel has no parallel in the Syrian-Soviet relationship. The unique aspects of the U.S.-Israeli economic relationship include (1) Israel's preeminent position as a recipient of U.S. foreign aid, with U.S. commitments to Israel currently running at over 20 percent of all external economic and military aid; (2) the U.S.-Israeli free trade agreement signed in 1985, which allows preferential Israeli access to the domestic U.S. market at a time of growing protectionism in the United States; (3) the extension of most-favored-nation status to Israel with respect to the import of U.S. technology and the export of Israeli military goods and services (the recently reaffirmed memorandum of understanding grants Israel the same rights and privileges as NATO countries in this respect and has opened up the prospects for wide-scale cooperation in joint ventures that could provide the Israeli economy with billions of dollars worth of contracts in the next few years); and (4) the allocation of all U.S. military and economic aid to Israel since 1983 on a grants-only basis, thus substantially reducing Israel's debt burden. In addition, the United States has reduced the interest payable on preexisting loans and has guaranteed that aid will not drop below the minimum needed to service this debt in any circumstances.

Israel's free trade agreements with the European Economic Community (EEC) and its extensive economic and financial links with all the major Western powers (including expanding relations with Japan) clearly place it in a more complex and advanced position than the equivalent relationship of Syria and the Soviet Union. For example, total Soviet bloc economic aid to Syria between 1954 and 1985 is estimated at around $3 billion, compared with around $12 billion in economic aid to Israel from the United States alone during this period.[7] This aid may increase Israeli dependency on the United States, but it also points to the significant strength of U.S.-Israeli ties in comparison with those between Syria and the Soviet Union.

Fourth, there is in the Soviet Union no equivalent to the highly organized and politically active Jewish lobby in the United States. The impact of the Jewish lobby on the U.S. electoral process and its ability to influence U.S. public opinion form an integral part of the U.S.-Israeli political process, and it is largely accepted as such by both countries. The Jewish lobby serves to maintain and safeguard basic Israeli interests in a manner that cannot be replicated by the Syrians (or any other Arab party) in their relationship with either superpower. Although the Jewish lobby may not be capable of dictating U.S. policies toward Israel and the Arab-Israeli conflict, it has shown itself to be efficacious in promoting Israeli interests and in confronting those policies that Israel strongly opposes, particularly with regard to arms sales to the Arabs. With no similar lobby acting on their behalf, Syrian-Arab interests have no such safety net, notwithstanding the possible reemergence of a pro–third world lobby within the Soviet military-political establishment.

Fifth, there is a degree of stability in the U.S.-Israeli strategic relationship that is absent from Syrian-Soviet relations. One vital factor affecting the U.S. alliance with Israel is the belief in both countries that political changes within either will not fundamentally affect the orientation of their respective policies toward the other. A change of government in Israel is thus unlikely to cause any radical shift in Israeli relations with the United States in particular and the West generally; neither is it likely that any administration will renege on the basic commitments of the United States toward Israel (along the lines, say, of the shift in Israeli-French relations after 1967).

The experience of the Soviet Union with a whole bloc of Arab countries—Egypt, Iraq, Algeria, Libya, Sudan, and North Yemen— between the mid-1950s and the mid-1970s is likely to have discouraged the Soviet Union from the belief that similarly stable relations can be forged with the Arab side. From the Soviet point of view, even long-standing friendly Arab parties remain subject to sudden or unforeseen internal or external developments that can cause a major realignment of their foreign policy toward the West. (It is perhaps noteworthy that the past two decades have seen no example of a substantial move in the opposite direction.) Although the Soviet-Syrian partnership stretches back to 1955 and is one of the apparently more stable relationships in the area, the Soviet Union is still likely to be wary about attempting a more comprehensive strategic alliance with Syria because of the uncertainties involved. By the early 1990s this wariness was reflected in reduced arms sales to Syria (and other Middle East clients generally) as well as in a more open attitude toward the West regarding arms control in the Middle East.

In addition to such factors affecting Syrian-Soviet relations, recent trends in Soviet foreign policy suggest that these relations may come under increasing pressure from a number of different directions. Despite Soviet willingness to talk to the United States about regional matters and some measure of agreement between the superpowers concerning the desirability of reaching a settlement in the Arab-Israeli conflict, this conflict is probably not a high-priority item on the current Soviet foreign policy agenda. It is possible that the Soviet Union no longer sees the Arab-Israeli arena as one with potentially substantial rewards. Soviet activism in the area in the 1950s, 1960s, and 1970s has not yielded commensurate politico-strategic gains, and there is not much to suggest that this will change in the foreseeable future. In the absence of any seriously disruptive developments such as an all-out Syrian-Israeli war, the Soviet Union's incentive to act on the Arab-Israeli front does not seem great. This is likely to accentuate the asymmetry between Soviet-Syrian relations on the one hand and U.S.-Israeli relations on the other, especially because the United States appears ever ready to act on Israel's behalf. For example, the Shultz initiative in 1988 appeared to Syria, as it did to other Arab parties, primarily as a U.S. attempt to rescue Israel from the consequences of the Palestinian uprising in the occupied territories.

The Soviet Union seems to have come to the conclusion that a more forward and open policy toward Israel is necessary for improving its bilateral relations with the United States as well as its prospects as a valid interlocutor in the Arab-Israeli peace process. Although Syria may be ready to recognize the ultimate need for the Soviet Union to reestablish diplomatic ties with Israel as part of any settlement, it is possible that the current pace and direction of Israeli-Soviet normalization are not to Syria's liking, particularly because there do not appear to have been any significant Israeli concessions to the Soviet-Arab side in compensation.

Soviet policy in the area has consciously sought to broaden the base of Arab-Soviet ties in the past few years. The Soviets have made progress in improving relations with a number of conservative and pro-Western Arab states and in supplying arms to Jordan and Kuwait, while establishing full diplomatic relations for the first time with Oman and the United Arab Emirates. Such a policy may not directly conflict with Syrian interests, but a Soviet shift away from exclusive reliance on ties with the radical Arab states is not necessarily encouraging from the Syrian point of view.

Developments in the Gulf may also have affected the Soviet Union's near-term regional priorities. Soviet interest in preventing a permanent expansion of U.S. military power in the Gulf must be of a high order even though hostilities in the Gulf have ceased. Although the Gulf may not have replaced the Arab-Israeli conflict as the major focus of Soviet concern in the area, the Soviets could view the situation there as less stable than that on the Arab-Israeli front, recent events in the occupied territories notwithstanding. Soviet policy toward the Gulf, as well as the desire to improve relations with both Iran and the Arab states in the Gulf (including Iraq), could thus impinge on Soviet-Syrian relations and on the Soviets' willingness or ability to engage themselves fully in the Arab-Israeli conflict.

Syria's developing relations with the United States may also have a negative impact on Soviet-Syrian ties. Constant Syrian-U.S. contacts do not appear to have brought about a significant narrowing of the differences between the two countries, despite a new U.S. awareness of the importance of Syria's regional role and its political influence in the area. Nonetheless, recent U.S.-Syrian cooperation in Lebanon and the Gulf has highlighted areas of mutual interest between the two countries and the possibility that both could act in support of these interests irrespective of close Soviet-Syrian ties.

It would be misleading to assume some sort of equivalence between improved Syrian-U.S. relations on the one hand and better Israeli-Soviet relations on the other. Improved Syrian-U.S. relations are likely to come at the expense of the Soviet Union and to indicate a diminution of Soviet influence in Syria, whereas the same does not hold with regard to the United States in the case of better Israeli-Soviet ties. In addition, the United States has long sought a normalization of Israel's relations with the Soviets and has insisted on a change in Soviet policy toward

Israel both as a precondition for Soviet participation in the Middle East peace process and as a requirement for better relations with the United States itself. No such considerations affect the Soviet attitude toward better Syrian-U.S. ties.

The Soviet Union's longstanding experience as Syria's largest arms supplier and major external ally must have emphasized the limitations of this type of relationship as well as its advantages for the Soviets. Soviet influence on Syrian decisionmaking often appears minimal (such as in Syria's policy toward Lebanon and the Palestine Liberation Organization), and there must be some question in the minds of Soviet policymakers about the value of returns to the Soviet Union on its vast investment in the Syrian force buildup over the past years.

The Soviets are likely to be concerned that Syria could precipitate a conflict with Israel, forcing them to make difficult politico-strategic choices in defense of the Syrian regime or hinterland. As against supporting possible Syrian "adventurism," however, the Soviets are probably convinced that a secure Syrian deterrent posture helps curb Israeli military adventurism and maintain some stability in the Arab-Israeli military equation. In this context the Soviet Union has to draw a very fine line between providing Syria with those components of military strength that are sufficiently credible as a deterrent against Israel but at the same time are unlikely to give Syria the self-assurance to embark on a wide-scale military initiative of its own. Although it is difficult to ascertain the exact terms of Syrian-Soviet negotiations over arms supplies, Israeli sources report that the Soviets in recent years refused to provide Syria with additional and more advanced ground-to-ground missiles such as the SS-23, which could reinforce Syria's ability to undertake a counterforce or first strike.[8]

It could be argued that the Soviets have a certain ambivalence toward the Syrian notion of strategic parity, particularly if that notion is interpreted as allowing Syria to develop offensive options, with the Soviet Union providing an ultimate ceiling on Israeli counteraction. The Soviet Union has also declared its growing concern as to the spread of ballistic missiles in the area, and it may be increasingly reluctant to satisfy any future demands by Syria (or other local clients) in this respect. The Soviets may not be hostile to the concept of "parity" as such, however, if that means strengthening Syria's ability to restrict Israeli freedom of action and raising the cost of any Israeli military move against Syria.

In general, the Soviets have consistently counseled their Arab allies with caution about the dangers of initiating a conflict with Israel. This partly reflects Soviet concern over entanglement in escalating regional hostility leading to a possible confrontation with the United States, especially given the degree of U.S. commitment to Israel. Equally, however, the Soviets have had little real belief in the credibility of the Arab military option and in its utility as an instrument for achieving realistic political objectives. The emergent "new thinking" in Soviet foreign policy toward the Arab-Israeli conflict and local conflicts in the third world is likely to reemphasize these traditional trends, with perhaps even greater scope than in the past for Syrian-Soviet differences over the purpose of the Syrian arms buildup and its efficacy.

The Role of the Lebanese Arena

The Lebanese arena plays a vital role in Syria's attempt at achieving strategic parity with Israel. In general, Lebanon provides Syria with a number of advantages to be exploited as well as a number of vulnerabilities to be neutralized.

Conventional Warfare. The Biqaa valley forms a direct conduit from the Lebanese-Israeli border into the Syrian hinterland via the Hermel area of north Lebanon and on to the major north Syrian towns of Homs and Hama. Equally, the central Biqaa affords the possibility for a flanking attack against Damascus from the west down the Beirut-Damascus highway. Lebanon thus represents a major potential axis for any Israeli attack and a source of vital concern to Syrian national security. The importance of Lebanon as an alternative attack route into Syria has increased in recent years as the sheer density of Syrian defenses along the Golan and the limited room for maneuver on this front have made it more and more difficult for Israel to develop credible offensive options.

Defense of the southern Biqaa short of the Beirut-Damascus highway is thus a central element in Syrian military planning and of crucial importance to the notion of strategic parity with Israel. Neutralization of the Israeli threat in this sector has been attempted by a combination of measures, including the extension of Syrian SAM defenses along the Lebanese-Syrian border covering much of south and central Lebanon as well as the preparation of forward fortifications in the Lake Qarun area. Conversely, Syria could exploit the southern Lebanese front to its advantage in any active campaign against Israel. From its current prepared positions in southern and central Biqaa, it could launch an assault on northern Israel with relatively short warning. Such an assault could be either in support of a Syrian offensive on the Golan front or a limited maneuver in its own right. Syrian artillery in south Lebanon could interdict Israeli troop movements into the Golan as well as shell major Israeli installations and military targets in the Galilee. Syrian SAM positions in Lebanon could interdict Israeli air activities over parts of the Golan and Syrian territory to the west. Activating the south Lebanon front could also be part of a feint designed to draw Israeli attention away from the Golan, as a preliminary to a major Syrian offensive there.

As opposed to these apparent advantages, however, Syria faces a number of distinct strategic disadvantages in the Lebanese arena. First, the Syrian High Command must, of necessity, split its forces between two different fronts with limited access between them, across relatively vulnerable lines of communications. In any major conflict with Israel, lateral movement of Syrian troops would be increasingly difficult as the war escalated and the full effect of Israeli air power against Syrian lines of communications began to take effect. Second, Israel still maintains strict politico-geographic and military "red lines" with regard to Syrian troop movements in central and south Lebanon. Crossing these lines may trigger an Israeli response regardless of Syria's real intentions. Although Syria currently deploys one-and-a-half to two divisions in Lebanon at any one time—mostly concentrated in central and northern Lebanon—these troops are generally deployed defensively and are largely held in readiness to meet internal Lebanese developments. As such, their ability to pose a real military threat to Israel is limited. Any substantial reinforcement of these troops or significant change in their disposition could constitute a casus belli from the Israeli point of view. Third, Syrian action against Israel from Lebanese territory is bound to elict a strong and probably disproportionate Israeli response. Moreover, Syria may well have to contend with wide-scale harassment from local pro-Israeli factions or other Lebanese groups who may regard a Syrian-Israeli conflagration as an opportune moment to better their position at Syria's expense.

On balance, the Lebanese arena does not appear to give Syria any outstanding advantage in conventional warfare against Israel and as such may be more a burden than an asset in Syria's attempt to attain strategic parity, especially in light of the ever-growing Syrian involvement in the internal Lebanese crisis. The limited prospects for Syrian offensive action may be more than counterbalanced by the vital demands of preventing an Israeli breakthrough into the Syrian hinterland either as a preemptive or as a retaliatory move.

Nevertheless, two elements regarding a conventional war may recommend themselves to Syria: the use of Lebanon as a pressure point against Israel and the possible engagement of Israel in a limited conflict.

First, Lebanon remains a potential pressure point against Israel. Israel must divert resources and effort to confront the Syrian presence in Lebanon even when this presence is not directly aimed at Israel. Although the degree to which this adds to the overall Israeli defense burden or weakens Israel's posture on other fronts such as the Golan is likely limited, Israel may not be free to let down its guard against Syrian intentions and capabilities in Lebanon.

Second, and more important perhaps, Lebanon affords the possibility of engaging Israel in a limited conflict. Although any Syrian-Israeli confrontation could escalate into a full-scale war involving both Syrian and Israeli territory, the availability of Lebanon as a possible battlefield could limit the escalatory process and confine the geographic area of operations. In one sense Syria and Israel can "fight it out" in Lebanon with fewer risks than would accompany full-scale attacks on each other's national soil. This, it should be added, could be to both sides' advantage and may well be to Israel's benefit in certain circumstances (for example, the Soviet defensive umbrella over Syria is not thought to extend to the Syrian military presence in Lebanon). Some Syrian conventional war scenarios, however, could be based on exploiting Lebanon in the hope of preventing or limiting any spillover into Syrian territory proper.

Indirect or Covert Conflict. Both Israel and Syria have used Lebanon for pursuing indirect means of warfare and other covert modes of action against each other. The possibility of indirect warfare against Israel from Lebanon holds several advantages for Syria. First, Syria can act by proxy by supporting the anti-Israeli activities of local Lebanese or Palestinian groups. The exact role played by Syria in the highly successful guerrilla campaign to oust Israel from south Lebanon in 1982–1985 is uncertain, but Syrian logistical backup and the presence of Syrian troops in the Biqaa must have helped to sustain this campaign and bolster its effectiveness. Syria is aware of the low threshold of Israeli tolerance for such attacks, particularly with regard to Syrian sponsorship of cross-border raids into Israel proper, but the availability of proxy forces leaves some room for maneuver and plausible denial of any such Syrian role, without precluding guerrilla action to pressure Israel. In short, indirect warfare by proxy may offer Syria a viable option with relatively limited costs and calculable risks.

Second, Syria's actual or potential options for covert action help to sustain a point of "live" contact with Israel. This could be significant in keeping the issue of a possible wider Israeli-Syrian conflagration on the Middle East agenda and in providing Syria with a means by which it can assert its importance as a major regional actor. In view of the strict security regime on the Golan Heights, relinquishing Lebanon as a potential flashpoint might affect Syria's perceived role as a confrontation state, both in the inter-Arab arena and in its relations with major external actors, including the superpowers.

The role of Lebanon as a flashpoint or catalyst for regional conflict is not necessarily confined to indirect warfare between Israel and Syria and may be relevant in a conventional conflict as well. But the crisis potential of unconventional or indirect warfare often appears greater, partly because of its unpredictability and the possibility of loss of control (particularly in Lebanon) and partly because of the relative absence of established means for managing such crises. By comparison, direct state-to-state crises, even between Israel and Syria, seem to retain a greater measure of manageability. (The U.S. role as an intermediary has been of value in this respect as in the Syrian missile crises of 1981 and 1985 and the reentry of Syrian troops into Beirut in 1987.)

The effectiveness of Syrian-sponsored indirect warfare may be linked to the nature and extent of Israel's presence in Lebanon. Paradoxically, Syrian action seemed most effective when Israel's politico-military presence reached its peak in 1982–1985. Since then, various local and Palestinian groups have kept up a constant guerrilla campaign against the IDF and Israeli proxy forces in south Lebanon, but the overall effect on Israel has diminished. In fact it is arguable that it is generally the Israeli side that may now have the better opportunity to pursue indirect warfare against Syria in Lebanon. With Syria adopting the role of arbiter of the internal Lebanese conflict, the potential for disrupting this role and undermining Syria's credibility with relative economy of effort must appear quite high to the Israelis. To this end, Israel can draw on its links with a number of groups active in Lebanon and in particular its remaining foothold among the strongly anti-Syrian elements within the Maronite camp. Covert action against Syrian troops or their allies and the possibility of keeping Syria engaged in successive crises by fanning differences with other local groups afford Israel a wide margin of maneuver across the whole spectrum of indirect or covert warfare.

In addition, Israel can use Lebanon as a springboard for covert warfare against Syria itself. For Syria this constitutes one of the dangers inherent in the ongoing Lebanese crisis and a possible deterrent to Syrian involvement in similar activities against Israel. Although Israel may not necessarily need Lebanon to undertake indirect action against Syria, its links with various Lebanese proxy forces may make such action both easier and more credibly deniable.

Syrian Preoccupation with Lebanon. Besides Lebanon's role in any active Syrian campaign against Israel (direct or indirect), the Lebanese cirsis has been a constant Syrian preoccupation for the past sixteen years. This can be seen in the degree to which Syrian policymakers have been engaged in the search for a solution to the crisis and in the role played by senior figures from the politico-military establishment in dealing with the time-consuming and often fruitless negotiations that have accompanied this process, almost certainly at the expense of attending to the needs of the Syrian armed forces themselves. In addition, the cost of Syria's involvement in Lebanon has been high. No exact figures are available for total Syrian troop losses, but relatively large numbers have been killed and wounded in major battles with Palestinian, Maronite, and Lebanese factions since 1975, not to mention the estimated 1,200 killed in 1982. The financial burden of Syria's military deployment in Lebanon has also been substantial, estimated at around $1 million a day in the early 1980s.[9] In addition, some unquantifiable political and moral costs affect Syria's overall position, such as the erosion of Syrian morale as a result of garrison duties in Lebanon and the negative image projected across much of the Arab world by Syria's role in the "war of the camps" against the PLO in Lebanon in 1985–1988, and other aspects of its intervention in the Lebanese crisis.

The continuation of the Lebanese crisis may be to Israel's advantage insofar as it constitutes a drain on Syrian resources and diverts Syrian attention away from the conflict with Israel. In this context Israel needs to take little direct or indirect action besides ensuring its own security and keeping the crisis alive with minimal effort, as is necessary. Conversely, Syria is probably unlikely to turn its full attention to the question of attaining strategic parity with Israel as long as the Lebanese crisis remains a major point of concern, cost, and pressure. At one level, a stable Syrian-leaning Lebanon could help to bolster Syria's regional posture and to relieve it of much of the burden it has carried since 1975. Whether a "new" Lebanon—even one closely aligned with Syria— would be willing or able to play any significant part in the struggle against Israel except in a purely defensive and supportive role is uncertain; to this extent, such a Lebanon may not necessarily be to Israel's disadvantage.

The Domestic Factor

Two major domestic elements affect Syria's prospects for attaining strategic parity with Israel, the economy and the home front.

The Economy. The economic burden of Syria's recent defense efforts has been substantial. Syrian defense expenditure for 1986 has been put at $3.68 billion excluding arms procurement, with the total security burden estimated by one Israeli source as high as 55 percent of the national annual budget for that year. In 1984, 1985, and 1986 Syria's defense budget continued to grow, but there is some indication of a major slowdown in 1986–1987, although published figures are somewhat distorted by the discrepancy between official and unofficial inflation rates.[10]

According to a 1988 study by the International Monetary Fund (IMF), Syrian foreign exchange reserves stood at between $10 million and $62 million at the end of 1986. The IMF report observes that the Syrian economy is "beset by shortages, and burdened by a sluggish industrial sector," with mounting arrears on debt payments. According to the IMF, external medium- and long-term civilian debt stood at $2.5 billion at the end of 1986, and the short-term external liabilities of the banking system were equivalent to around $4 billion.[11]

Recently, inflation has been officially reported at around 100 percent per year as opposed to an official rate of 13.6 percent as of December 1986.[12] The Soviet Union has apparently been applying pressure to settle some of Syria's longstanding debt by repayment in bartered foodstuffs and cotton, which has led to an additional squeeze on supplies available for export. The rapid depreciation in the value of the Syrian pound, another symptom of the weakness of the economy, has been a major cause of inflation because Syria imports half its food requirements. By mid-1988, the official rate of exchange stood at 11.25 Syrian pounds to the dollar, with the black-market rate running at between 50 and 60 Syrian pounds, representing a depreciation of about 100 percent over the previous year.[13]

The importance of the Syrian economic crisis is reflected in the fact that in 1987 fourteen out of a total of thirty-six ministerial positions were related to the economy in one way or another. In late 1987 the Syrian cabinet decided to reassess the 1986–1990 five-year plan after only 55 percent of the projects undertaken had achieved their target by that date.[14] Recent attempts at economic liberalization, such as a relaxation of allocations of foreign exchange to private business for raw materials imports, are reported to have had little effect on an industrial sector still constrained by a web of bureaucratic regulations and petty impediments.

In addition to these difficulties, financial support to Syria from oil-producing Arab states is reported to have fallen as a consequence of the general decline in oil revenues over the past few years and a diversion of support to Iraq in the period before the Gulf War. Syria was promised $1.8 billion in annual aid under the terms of the Baghdad summit, but Israeli sources suggest that less than half that amount was received in 1984 and 1985 (mostly from Saudi Arabia). Libyan and Iranian contributions have helped to make up for some of this shortfall in the past, although Libya itself is facing increasing financial constraints and Iranian aid—in the form of oil—has increasingly become a bone of contention between the two countries.[15]

The net result of these economic difficulties seems to have been a reduction in the size of the standing Syrian land forces in 1986–1987 from 320,000 to 300,000 troops, with possible cuts in the purchase of new arms from the Soviet Union as well as the mothballing of certain items of equipment. Precise figures for overall Syrian force cutbacks remain unobtainable, but Israeli sources have reported the transfer of active service units to reserve status, and more recently it has been suggested that some units have been withdrawn from the Syrian active order of battle, at least for the foreseeable future. As far as can be discerned, these reductions do not appear to have touched on vital force components such as the air force or air defense units, while the navy continues its expansion program.[16]

The impact of the economic crisis on Syria's attempt to attain strategic parity seems open to interpretation. According to some Israeli accounts, Syria has all but abandoned this attempt under threat of imminent economic collapse. Other estimates, however, suggest that Syrian priorities have shifted, with the economy now taking the forefront and the attempt at parity temporarily postponed rather than given up altogether.[17]

In fact, economic reform now appears to be perceived as essential to the achievement of parity with Israel. Without such reform, internal stability could also suffer, which would strike at another vital element in the attempt at parity, that is, the home front. The new economic policy adopted in the late 1980s may receive a significant boost if new oil finds in the Deir al-Zor area prove as promising as they appear to be. Increased oil revenues as well as additional aid from the Gulf states may have helped to relieve some of the economic pressure of recent years. By late 1988 Syrian officials were claiming some measure of success in revising the economy, with an estimated growth rate of 7 or 8 percent over the previous year. Equally, new reforms in the private sector and agriculture were reportedly bearing fruit, and new financial discipline was being introduced.[18]

The actual extent of damage to Syria's war-fighting ability from the economic crisis appears marginal under all circumstances. Although the strategic gap with Israel may not have narrowed any further because of this crisis, to assume that Syria has given up its goals would be misleading. In late 1987 President Assad reaffirmed these goals when he denied any change in Syria's declared objectives. According to Assad, "Strategic parity should be achieved and there is no change or rethinking of our attitude in this regard—any country that desires a just peace in this region should view the strategic parity we are seeking as a fundamental, positive factor in achieving peace." Such statements of intent need not necessarily be accepted at face value, but there is as yet no sufficient cause to doubt their veracity.[19]

The Home Front. The Syrian home front was shaken by two consecutive shocks in the early and mid-1980s. The first was the challenge to the regime posed by Sunni-Islamic fundamentalism and the Muslim Brotherhood, and the second was a threatened "war of succession" between rival groups within the Baath party military hierarchy. Both these challenges appear to have been contained by a combination of force (such as in Hama in 1982) and delicate internal balancing (the defense companies, Saraya al-Difa', which formed a power base in the struggle between President Assad's brother Rifa't and other officers, have now been dissolved and integrated into the army's high command structure).

Generally there seems to be some consensus on the current stability of the regime. In late 1986 Israeli military intelligence estimated that President Assad was firmly in control, although there were problems with internal unrest, terrorism, and dissatisfaction with economic conditions. Israeli sources have reported that although Assad's much-discussed health problems could pose a threat to his government, "there is no evidence that anyone has accumulated enough power to challenge or threaten him as yet."[20]

Part of the attempt at consolidating the internal situation—and thus aiding the process of building parity with Israel—has been an effort to revitalize the role of the Baath party and give it greater popular credence after most party institutions have become ossified and moribund over the years. Equally, the regime maintains its policy of a broad national front with non-Baathist representation in the government (Communist, Nasserite, independent, and others).

The attitude of the home front is crucial to the attainment of parity with Israel. Widespread dissatisfaction with the social and economic burden of the defense effort could seriously hamper these chances, and the current defense slowdown may be seen partly in this light. At the same time, the drive for parity could well be a catalyst for internal socioeconomic and political reforms, which may in turn generate a measure of popular support for the regime's overall objectives, and it is perhaps in this context that the Soviet Union has apparently been urging the adoption of a Syrian version of perestroika and glasnost.

In general, however, there appears to be a high tolerance for sacrifice for the sake of Syrian national security interests. Some evidence of this tolerance emerges from the attitude toward the Syrian role in Lebanon but perhaps more important from the experience of the conflict with

Israel. According to Israeli estimates, one of the distinct advantages held by the Syrian armed forces over the IDF is their greater capacity, "stemming from the nature of the Syrian regime and society,"[21] to sustain losses of troops and combat materiel. In the 1973 war, for example, the IDF destroyed over 1,000 Syrian tanks out of an active force of about 1,300—an extremely high rate of loss by any standards. Despite such losses in tanks and tank crews, Syria persisted in the war and embarked almost immediately afterward on an effective campaign of attrition in the Golan Heights. In 1982 the Syrian air force lost up to 25 percent of its front-line strength in only three days of serious battle with the IAF but continued in its attempt to challenge Israeli air superiority against the odds.[22]

Although the ability of the Syrian armed forces to absorb heavy punishment may not necessarily apply to Syrian society as a whole, it remains one indicator by which this can be measured. Generally, the examples of Iraq, Iran, and Lebanon seem to support the notion that local societies have great resilience even when faced with the full weight of modern means of destruction. In many cases, however, this resilience may be difficult to ascertain except when the society in question is under direct assault.

The Arab Dimension

Within the context of Syria's attempt to achieve parity with Israel, Syrian-Arab policy has comprised several basic elements: dealing with Egypt, reviving the eastern front, and consolidating the Arab politico-diplomatic position.

Dealing with Egypt. After 1979 Syria sought to convince or pressure Egypt into reneging on the Camp David accords and reactivating Israel's southern front. The revival of such a two-front Arab strategy would clearly have gone a long way toward obviating Israel's current superiority given the size and potential of Egypt's armed forces (12 divisions, 2,250 tanks, 440 combat aircraft, and so on).

Syria's doctrine of strategic parity was developed partly at least in response to Egypt's defection from the conflict with Israel. Undoing the results of Camp David appeared at one stage as a vital step in the direction of a broader, more expansive version of that doctrine. This strand of Syrian policy appears now to be essentially defunct. Egypt has been able to return to the Arab fold with little or no concession to Syria's point of view. Egypt's unconditional readmission to the Arab League was officially sanctioned by Syria itself (and all other Arab countries) at the 1989 Casablanca summit. The prospects for any significant

Egyptian deviation from the peace accords with Israel thus appears extremely remote, especially in the context of the overall Arab commitment to the peace process made evident at Casablanca.

In response to such developments, Syria at present appears to be seeking good relations with Egypt more as an element of its inter-Arab policy than as an attempt to reinvigorate the Syrian-Egyptian strategic alliance against Israel. This does not mean that Syria's attitude toward Egypt no longer has any bearing on its views concerning the prerequisites of the struggle against Israel. Syria recognizes Egypt's crucial diplomatic and political role in this respect and seeks to prevent its total isolation from the peace process, as well as solidify the consolidation of the new Arab bloc that has emerged as a result of the Gulf war. From this perspective, current Syrian policy is largely based on retaining some leverage against the other Arab parties to the conflict as a means of constraining the Arab mainstream from taking decisions on the politico-diplomatic front that do not concur with Syria's goals and perceived interests.

In this sense the relationship now sought with Egypt is essentially political and not military. In the long term, however, Syria believes that its own skeptical view of the prospects for peace will be vindicated as a result of Israel's continued intransigence. This may open the door for a more advanced relationship that could serve to redress more directly the balance with Israel. However, the exact contours of such a relationship may be still unclear from the Syrian point of view and may be based more on a sense of expectation than on any precise reading of the future strategic map in the area.

Reviving the Eastern Front. The eastern front, comprising Syria, Iraq, and Jordan, has traditionally been seen as an elaboration of the two-front strategy, including Egypt. After Camp David, a strong eastern front was briefly proposed as an alternative to the two-front approach, based primarily on the integration of Syrian and Iraqi armed strength. Since then, there has been little attempt to pursue this option actively, largely because of the continuing antagonism between Syria and Iraq, aggravated by the Iran-Iraq war, Syria's alliance with Iran, and Jordan's adoption of a security concept based entirely on a self-sufficient deterrent and defensive posture with no attempt at cooperation or coordination with other Arab parties.

One ideal scenario for achieving strategic parity would have been based on the commitment of Iraq's massive military resources to the struggle against Israel after the end of the Iran-Iraq war. Even a relatively small Iraqi contingent (4–8 divisions) would have served well in bridging the gap with Israel and bolstered Syria's current divisional order of battle by anything up to 90 percent. Completing this ideal scenario from Syria's viewpoint would have been a Jordanian contribution to the Syrian war effort of one or two of its four divisions and perhaps up to 25 percent of its tank force of 1,000 main battle tanks (MBTs).[23]

As a result of the destruction of Iraq's war machine in the 1991 Gulf war, this scenario no longer appears remotely feasible, and none of these eventualities is likely to form part of current Syrian operational planning. The prospect for inducing Jordan to adopt a more active military stance appears equally remote, although Jordan's ability to prevent an Israeli flanking movement through the Yarmouk River valley and along the Dera'a axis is vital to Syria's security needs on the Golan. To this extent, any improvement in Jordan's defensive capabilities may be to Syria's advantage, even in the absence of direct military coordination between the two sides.

Syria has viewed the eastern front in two basic contexts. The first has been based on the premise that Jordan and to a lesser extent Iraq can play a minimally supportive role in case Syria comes under direct military pressure from Israel as in 1973. The second has presumed a broader basis for military coordination pending the fulfillment of certain political conditions and a large measure of strategic understanding between the different parties. The prospects for attaining the first objective remain difficult for the foreseeable future; the second appears more a hypothetical than a real possibility. In the short term at least, Syria is more likely to concentrate on securing a major role in any Arab or regional security regime that may emerge from the Gulf war. Collective security could thus be seen as providing a measure of deterrence against Israel while improving Syria's defensive and political stance in case of any serious progress toward an overall Arab-Israeli settlement.

Consolidating the Arab Politico-Diplomatic Position. The Syrian drive for strategic parity in any of its different senses is based on the assumption that a just settlement of the Arab-Israeli conflict cannot be attained under the current balance of power. It follows from this that moves toward a settlement outside the context of parity with Israel will not yield any positive result from the Arab point of view. This line of reasoning lies behind much of Syria's skepticism toward the peace process over the past years, as well as its opposition to any unilateral moves by other major Arab actors such as Jordan or the PLO toward a negotiated settlement.

Given the perceived need for strategic parity, it is clear that, in Syria's eyes, the general Arab politico-diplomatic line should remain steadfast, pending the kind of transformations in Syria's military strength or the Arab strategic environment that would make such parity possible.

Syria's close relationship with Jordan since 1986 can be seen as a reflection of this policy and as an attempt to contain as far as possible any Jordanian inclination to "go it alone" with Israel. Equally, Syria's differences with the PLO are to a large extent—but not exclusively—based on Syrian concern about a softening of the Palestinian line toward Israel, either unilaterally or in concert with Egypt or Jordan.

Syria's current position toward the peace process is marked by some ambiguities. Some interpretations of Syrian policy have assumed a correlation between Syria's readiness to talk and its insistence on pursuing parity, so that a move toward negotiation indicates a move away from attempts at parity. More likely is that Syria sees no contradiction between the two. When there is substantial movement on the diplomatic front, maintaining some ability to influence the course of negotiations from within and keeping well abreast of possible developments, as well as minimizing Syria's negative rejectionist-obstructionist image, seem prudent. This need not contradict Syria's perception that little is likely to emerge from such negotiations in the near future or that strategic parity is still a necessary goal.

The Arab dimension is of particular political and ideological importance to the pan-Arab Baathist regime in Syria. The Syrians are acutely aware, however, of the limitations of reliance on Arab support and participation even though inter-Arab concord is often seen as central to Syria's current political objectives. At heart, Syrians realize that to achieve strategic parity they might need to prepare for going it alone, even though this is the least desirable option.

Conclusion

Syria's attempt to attain strategic parity with Israel appears to have made some headway since 1982, and the overall military gap between the two countries may have narrowed in some important respects since the early 1980s. Nevertheless, the prospects for a stable Israeli-Syrian balance are uncertain.

The next few years may witness a significant change in this strategic balance, especially if Israel obtains the means to undercut the threat posed by ballistic missiles armed with chemical or other conventional or unconventional warheads. In such circumstances, Israel may feel that it is capable of launching a successful preemptive strike against Syria with a credible safety-net sufficient to blunt Syria's strategic response (e.g., attacking the Israeli heartland). Israel's confidence in this result may be further bolstered by the belief that its command of the new conventional technologies will enable it to neutralize much of Syria's military might, perhaps even undermining the packed Syrian defenses along the Golan front.

Equally, the perception that such a situation may arise could be sufficient to motivate Syria toward acting in the short term and while its comparative gains since 1982 are still relevant and effective. This near-term instability in the Syrian-Israeli balance could be further compounded by Israeli fears of such a Syrian move, and the cycle of action and counteraction could escalate out of control.

But even if Syria were to attain a measure of defensive/deterrent immunity against Israel in the near future, it is not self-evident that this would be sufficient in itself to force Israel into negotiations under conditions favorable to the Syrian point of view. Although the cost of attacking Syria may increase, the incentive to offer it any substantive concessions may not. Israel may well feel that its own deterrent would be sufficient to prevent any serious Syrian military initiative, while its punitive capacity would ensure that such an initiative would carry heavy penalties for Syria itself. In short, a purely defensive "parity" would not necessarily generate any great pressure on Israel to move closer to Syria's terms for a settlement.

It follows from this that Syria may have to develop a clearer vision of the nature and purpose of the parity it seeks. One option would be to ensure that this parity encompasses a strong coercive element with perhaps increased emphasis on unconventional (chemical and biological weapons). But how this can be brought about without triggering an Israeli preemptive attack is not altogether clear. Alternatively, Syria may adopt the view that the prime purpose of its military buildup is not so much to force Israel to the negotiating table as it is to instill confidence in Syria's own capability to resist Israeli aggrandizement. This may lead in precisely the opposite direction—a Syrian readiness to concede certain politico-territorial points within an overall policy of containing Israeli power and restricting its influence and fields of action. Although this may on the surface contradict the more extreme version of the "clash of destinies" approach, a policy of containment may ultimately seem the most rational and effective means by which "parity" can be put to use against Israel.

Notes

1. For some of the best available official expositions of the doctrine of parity and overall Syrian strategic thought, see interview with Syrian Defense Minister Lt. Gen. Mustafa Tlas with *Der Speigel*, translated as "War of Liberation: A Talk with the Syrian Defense Minister" in *The New York Review of Books*, 22/11/1984; and more recently, interview with President Assad in the Kuwaiti

daily *al-Qabas*, 24/1/1987. See also *Washington Post* interview with President Assad carried by the *International Herald Tribune*, 21/9/1987, and article carried by the Syrian government daily *Tishrin*, 18/11/1987. For an Israeli reading of the doctrine of parity, see "The Military Balance Between Syria and Israel" by Aharon Levran in *The Middle East Military Balance 1985*, ed. Mark Heller, Aharon Levran, and Zeev Eytan, Jerusalem Post/Westview Press, Boulder, Colorado, Tel Aviv University Jaffe Center for Strategic Studies, 1986, also subsequent annual editions for 1986 and 1987–1988 (hereafter referred to as *MEMB*).

2. See annual editions of *MEMB* 1984 through 1988. See also annual editions for the same period of *The Military Balance*, International Institute for Strategic Studies, London (hereafter referred to as *MB*). Other sources for Syrian arms buildup include the Arabic-language London-based fortnightly *An-Nashra al-Istrajjiyah* (Strategic Review), vols. 6–10 (1985–1989), and the Beirut monthly *Istratijya*, no. 34, December 1984, and no. 35, January 1985.

3. *MB* 1987–1988, p. 114.

4. See, for instance, Martin Van Crevald, "The War: A Questioning Look," *Jerusalem Post* (International Edition), 12/12/1982.

5. Refer to *MEMB* 1987–1988, pp. 396–404, for balance of Syrian purchases from Western and Soviet-bloc sources and for Western equipment in Syrian service.

6. U.S. Department of Defense, *Soviet Military Power*, 5th ed. 1986, U.S. Government Printing Office, Washington, D.C., p. 133.

7. Soviet and Soviet-bloc aid to Syria 1954–1981 was estimated at around $2 billion according to U.S. State Department figures given in *The Soviet Union in the Third World: Threat to World Peace?* ed. J. G. Whelan and M. J. Dixon, Pergamon-Brassey's, Oxford, 1986, p. 182; economic aid 1983–1985 was estimated as $1 billion by the U.S. Defense Department in *Soviet Military Power*. Figures for U.S. aid were derived from table of all U.S. financial aid to Israel 1951–1985 in *The Israeli Connection: Whom Israel Arms and Why*, by Benjamin Beit-Hallahmi, I. B. Tauris, London, 1988, pp. 194–195.

8. *MEMB* 1987–1988, p. 131.

9. See Richard A. Gabriel, *Operation Peace for Galilee*, Hill and Wang, New York, 1984, for an estimate of Syrian losses in the 1982 war.

10. See *MB* 1987–1988, p. 113, and *MEMB* 1987–1988, p. 199.

11. *Financial Times* (London), 10/5/1988.

12. Ibid., and *ABC Group Economic and Financial Quarterly* (London), September 1987, p. 8.

13. *Financial Times*, 10/5/88. See also *The Economist* (London), 18/6/1988, on Soviet financial and economic pressure on Syria.

14. *As-Sharq al-Awsat* (London), 26/11/1987.

15. *MEMB* 1986, p. 177, and *MEMB* 1987–1988, p. 199.

16. See *MEMB* 1987–1988, pp. 197–198.

17. See interview with Gen. Amnon Shahak, head of Israeli military intelligence, in the *Jerusalem Post* (International Edition), 11/10/86, and reading of Syrian position by G. Ben-Dror from Haifa University in *Haaretz*, 28/12/1987.

18. *Financial Times*, 10/5/1988 and 4/1/1989. See also *Middle East Economic Survey* (Cyprus), 25/4/1988, on Iranian supplies of oil to Syria.

19. *International Herald Tribune*, 21/9/1987.

20. *Jerusalem Post*, 11/10/1986, and Dan Petreanu, "Middle East Intelligence Update," in *IDF Journal*, vol. 4, no. 3, 1987, p. 8.

21. *MEMB* 1985, pp. 281–282.

22. See, for instance, "An Interview with a Senior Israeli Air Force Officer," *Flight International* (London), 16/10/1982.

23. *MEMB* 1986, pp. 86–87.

9
The Use of Military Force: An Israeli Analysis

General Avraham Tamir (Ret.)

Military planners in a state such as Israel live between worlds. On one level, we have faced a classic military threat from conventionally armed neighboring Arab states, and we have designed traditional defensive strategies to deter their attacks and to defend ourselves as necessary. On two other levels, we live in a world described at one end of a spectrum by the undefined association of states in the Middle East with the superpower alliance systems and nuclear umbrellas. At the other end of the spectrum, it is a world described by the actions of nonstate organizations and unorganized populations and by enemies with the eventual potential of acquiring nuclear weapons without any theories or experience or precedence for avoiding their use. In this survey I focus on three aspects of the issue: the general policy of using military force, limits on freedom of action in using military force, and Israel's policy in the use of military force.

General Policy of Using Military Force

No substantive change has taken place in the general policy of using military force since ancient times. The distinction between aggressor and defender still holds. The aggressor resorts to aggressive strategy in order to liquidate the other party or to force conditions upon it. When the aggressor has freedom of action to use military force, this actor's aggressive strategy may include the use of such force. The defender resorts to a defensive strategy in order to prevent the aggressor from liquidating it or forcing upon it certain conditions, and to this end the defender must use military force in order to eliminate military threats.

Both the aggressor and defender may use military force for the purpose of deterrence, attack, or defense. The aggressor may use force for deterrence to protect its gains and existence, while the defender may also seek to protect its existence against the aggressor and to prevent the aggressor from making gains. The aggressor may attack in order to change the defender's status; to defend it, the defender may attack. The aggressor may use force for defense to protect its gains; the defender uses force to prevent the aggressor from making gains.

Freedom of Action in Using Military Force

Since World War II, nuclear deterrence has brought about a total revolution in the determination of the political and military objectives of using military force. A number of lessons have been learned. As long as the United States and U.S.S.R. maintain balanced nuclear deterrence capability, one must conclude that a strategic policy which operates within limits imposed by nuclear deterrence is preferable to committing suicide with a policy which could result in a nuclear exchange. Nuclear deterrence imposes the following limits on freedom of action in the use of force:

- First, neither superpower will use *nuclear* weapons against the other superpower (or against any state which is part of the other superpower's strategic alliance) and is therefore protected by the umbrella of nuclear deterrence.
- Second, neither superpower will use *conventional* weapons against the other superpower (or against any state which is part of the other superpower's strategic alliance) and is therefore protected by the umbrella of nuclear deterrence.
- Third, neither superpower will allow any state included in its strategic alliance to use unconventional or conventional weapons to change the status of a state in the other superpower's strategic alliance.
- Fourth, both superpowers may cooperate on an ad hoc basis to prevent a local war in a region vital to both superpowers from dragging them into a military confrontation with one another, e.g., the Sinai war in 1956.

The constraints forced upon the superpowers as a result of the nuclear balance of terror have, in effect, limited the freedom of all states within each of the two strategic allinaces to use conventional and unconventional weapons against states in the other alliance. To no less extent, states outside the two alliances are prevented from attacking states within the alliances. As long as this situation remains, a considerable percentage of states around the world remain protected against external military threats. These protected states include the superpowers, the countries of the NATO and Warsaw alliances, and the states under U.S. strategic protection in the Pacific Ocean, including Japan, South Korea, Taiwan, Thailand, Australia, and New Zealand.

Yet there remains a great gap of uncertainty regarding most third world states which are not associated with the strategic alliances of either superpower. For these states, neither superpower is willing to apply nuclear deterrence or conventional military force to protect them against destruction or imposed conditions. In the continents of the third world—Africa, South and West Asia, and South and Central America—freedom of action exists for aggression designed to alter the political or territorial status of other countries. The source of this freedom of action lies in political, economic, and demographic instability.[1] These conditions create fertile ground for the growth of extremist regimes and their exploitation by the U.S.S.R. for its expansionist aims in the third world.

Soviet Strategy and the U.S. Response

Because Soviet expansion is thwarted by NATO in Europe and by China and U.S. allies in East Asia, third world states—including those in the Middle East—have become the primary targets of Soviet expansionist efforts.

The Soviet Union has two major motives for expanding its influence in the third world. First, the U.S.S.R. seeks to control, directly or indirectly, the sources of raw materials needed to turn the wheels of the industrialized economies in the free world (the "capitalist world" according to Marxist doctrine). The resulting economic instability may stimulate the proletariat to arise and "throw off its chains." This has been a traditional Soviet goal since the October 1917 revolution which transformed czarist Russia into the Soviet Union. As early as the interwar period we witnessed Soviet expansionist efforts among the colonies—now known as third world states—of imperialist nations such as Britain, France, Belgium, Holland, Portugal, and Spain.

Second, the Soviet Union seeks political footholds which will allow it to establish the necessary infrastructure for its global military strategy. This infrastructure includes factors such as bases for Soviet sea and air forces, arms depots and equipment depots for Soviet land forces, navy services, air field services, and command and control installations. Such infrastructure permits the Soviet Union to

- threaten major navigation routes on which the economy of the free world depends

- intervene militarily—either directly or through surrogates—to assist revolutionary elements fighting to bring more states into the Soviet camp
- create a conventional military capability
- cut off free world nations from navigation routes during time of war
- maintain a sea-based system for attacking submarines and supply convoys during a war with the United States
- provide nuclear submarine bases to maintain the strategic balance of terror

This global military strategy requires, as a top priority, maritime superiority over free world fleets plus strategic installations in the following areas: along the shores of the oceans (Atlantic, Pacific, and Indian); along the shores of the seas (Mediterranean, Red, and Caribbean); along the sea straits (Gibraltar, Dardanelles, Bab el Mandeb, Hormuz, the Suez Canal, the Panama Canal); in or near areas where strategic raw materials are located (such as the oil depots in the Gulf).

Since the 1960s, we have witnessed the development and production of a military arsenal in the Soviet Union which has dramatically changed Soviet strategic capabilities. Formerly, the Soviet Union pursued a land-based strategy relying upon domestically based forces directed toward neighboring states. Now, the U.S.S.R. has the capacity for a global strategy based on naval and air forces using strategic footholds along the shores of the world's oceans, seas, and straits.

The Soviet navy today has a quantitative advantage over navies of the free world in nuclear submarines, hunting submarines, cruisers and destroyers armed with missiles, and helicopter carriers. The U.S.S.R. is also making a great effort to achieve qualitative naval superiority, with cruise missiles and sophisticated nuclear submarine missiles. A major investment is also being made in a system of intercontinental transport aircraft, providing the capability to activate several airborne divisions throughout the world.

The Soviet Union today has the capacity to implement a global military strategy, with bases or naval services in the Caribbean Sea (Cuba), the Atlantic Ocean (Angola and Congo), the Mediterranean (Libya and Syria), the Red Sea and the Bab el Mandeb Straits (Ethiopia and South Yemen), the Indian Ocean (Mozambique, Madagascar, India, and Sri Lanka), and the Pacific Ocean (Vietnam).

The U.S.S.R. uses several means to achieve its objectives in third world countries. These include (1) military and economic aid to Marxist regimes, such as Angola, Ethiopia, Congo, and the People's Democratic Repubic of Yemen; (2) military aid to regimes dependent on Soviet aid for maintaining their political-strategic positions, such as Syria and Libya; (3) aid to underground groups striving to bring to power new regimes under Soviet tutelage; or (4) direct invasions, as in Afghanistan.

The Soviets have learned from experience that military aid alone is insufficient to achieve lasting strategic gains, because the recipient regime may unexpectedly switch to the U.S. camp. As in the case of Egypt, this may occur when the recipient finds it can obtain objectives it could not achieve with the U.S.S.R. As a result, the Soviets are now placing greater emphasis on setting down deep roots in third world countries to establish Marxist regimes in these states. The resulting Marxist regimes will then be subject to Soviet ideological influence, not only strategic influence (such as Cuba, Angola, Mozambique, and Ethiopia).

Since the 1970s we have witnessed a U.S. strategy taking shape which is designed to eliminate the threat of Soviet expansion in the Middle East and elsewhere in the third world. This strategy is composed of the following elements:

- resolving conflict which provides fertile ground for Soviet expansion (such as Arab-Israeli conflict)
- providing military and economic aid to protect moderate, friendly, and vulnerable regimes and those regimes which might be freed from Soviet influence, such as Afghanistan
- establishing a basis for U.S. military intervention to protect oil sources in the Gulf
- cooperating strategically with key states in the third world to thwart Soviet expansion
- deploying international forces, which include U.S. forces, to increase stability and prevent conflict, as in the Sinai
- protecting countries against Soviet intervention by providing direct or indirect security guarantees
- deploying naval forces with deterrence and intervention capability in the Indian Ocean, the Mediterranean Sea, and the Caribbean Sea

This emerging U.S. policy has led to the establishment of infrastructure in Diego Garcia, Egypt, Somalia, Kenya, and Oman. This infrastructure provides capability for U.S. intervention in the Gulf and for deterring Soviet intervention in the region.

The Soviet Union has responded with countermeasures to protect its footholds in the region. It has deepened its military involvement in states under its protection by increasing the amount of military aid it provides, signing strategic agreements with them, and guaranteeing their defense. The most salient example is the military aid and strategic guarantees given to Syria following the "Peace for Galilee" war in 1982.

As a result of these developments, some nations in the third world are coming under constraints which limit their freedom of action in using military forces. These constraints are the result of the strategic protection which the superpowers—each implementing its own strategic policy—are offering to third world states in key strategic and economic regions. This strategic protection is sufficient to make it known that threatening the existence of a protected state may bring about superpower escalation, even when the protected state is not formally included in the strategic alliance of its patron. One may assume that these considerations influence the options the United States has regarding Syria, Cuba, Mozambique, Ethiopia, Libya, and other countries under Soviet protection.

Israel's Policy in the Use of Military Force

Israel's strategy in using military force has normally been a "defensive strategy" intended to protect its existence, integrity, security, and sovereign rights. Israel has not used—and will not use—its military forces for the objective of changing the status of another country. Since the establishment of Israel on May 15, 1948, it has been struggling against the Arab regimes and terrorist organizations which immediately declared war and have been attacking Israel ever since in their effort to destroy it. Israel's strategy for defense responds to three levels of threats to its existence and sovereignty:

First is *the threat posed by Arab confrontation states* which results from their policy of aggression against Israel, their proximity to Israel's borders, and their quantitative advantage in total military forces, in regular military forces (including those deployed on their borders and in their sea and air bases), in strategic depth, in economic resources, and in human resources. Because these states control the main oil sources required by the economies of the West and Japan, they are able to influence the policy of the superpowers as well as of other states in the free world.

Second is *the threat of Soviet expansionism.* Soviet strategy is an aggressive strategy conducted primarily through indirect means such as political subversion. The threat derives from the military aid the U.S.S.R. provides Arab regimes that are developing their military might to attack Israel; from the umbrella of strategic deterrence the Soviet Union provides to Arab regimes under its protection; from the political aid the Soviet Union gives to countries which endanger Israel's existence; and from the possibility that Soviet forces might participate in a war between

Soviet protectorates and Israel. For example, in Syria, Soviet units manned surface-to-air missile batteries, and in the past Soviet interception aircraft were deployed in Egypt.

Third is *the threat from PLO terrorist organizations*. This threat derives from the bases these groups establish with the help of Arab regimes; from their relative freedom of action against Israelis and Jews in countries of the free world; from the military aid they receive from the Soviet Union, China, the Eastern bloc, and Arab states; from the political protection they receive from Arab states and other countries throughout the world; from their dependence in financial matters upon Saudi Arabia and other Arab states; from their activity among the Arab populations in the West Bank and Gaza Strip; and from their relations with other terrorist organizations.

In light of these threats, the national security of the state of Israel is based on a defensive strategy. This strategy includes the following elements: a balance of power which enables Israel to protect itself; deterrence against the confrontation states, dissuading them from pursuing the war; ensuring the ability of the IDF to achieve its objectives; and strategic cooperation with the United States to deter the Soviet Union from endangering Israel's existence.

The Balance of Power

I use the term "balance of power" broadly, to refer not only to relative military capacity (the quantity of formations, units, weapons systems, and the like) but to additional elements of national security which complement the military component, securing the defense of the state of Israel even under conditions of relative disadvantage in territorial depth, resources, and the balance of regular forces deployed to stop a surprise attack. The elements of national security include:

- The use of all of Israel's resources for its national defense. The ultimate expression of this is Israel's ability quickly to mobilize its entire population and infrastructure for use in the war effort. They can be organized both within the IDF framework and within the total framework of national defense, such as defense of the rear and mobilization of industry to feed the war effort.
- The existence of qualitative superiority over Arab armies—in force levels, equipment, organization, military doctrine, and infrastructure for research, development, and production of the means of war.
- Defense of the state of Israel, based on its existing borders. This involves, among other things, preventing the establishment of

hostile structures in the areas of Judea, Samaria, the Gaza Strip, or the Golan Heights. Such hostile structures would endanger the existence and security of the state of Israel and deprive it of the strategic depth needed to protect its population centers, its economy, and its very existence.

- Prevention of accumulation of threats which might endanger Israel's existence, including nuclear threats, violation of security arrangements established through political agreements, and deployment of Iraqi, Syrian, or Jordanian forces (including deployment of Iraqi forces in southern Syria or deployment of Syrian forces near the Israel-Lebanon border).
- The independent capacity of Israel to protect itself, even under conditions of being cut off from outside sources of supply. This capacity is based on strategic supplies and an indigenous infrastructure for development and production.
- Ability to absorb strategic bombings. This is accomplished by dispersal of population and economic centers, sheltering and civil defense, rescue and medical services, and early warning.
- Demilitarized zones of limited forces and weapons which have been established along Israel's borders (in Sinai and on the Golan Heights) as a result of political agreements.
- National consensus regarding Israeli defense policy and its objectives.

Deterrence

In light of the lessons of World War II, it is commonly observed that states or alliances which maintain the nuclear balance of terror shy away from attacking each other with either nuclear weapons or conventional forces. But can states with only conventional forces deter others from conventional warfare?

The answer, in light of the Israeli experience since the 1948 war of independence, is that it is not possible to deter Arab countries from using conventional force against Israel, but it is possible to influence, through conventional deterrence, their military goals and objectives. This was demonstrated with Egypt and Syria during the Yom Kippur War and again with Syria in the Peace for Galilee conflict. It was possible to curb the confrontation states' ambition to obtain political and territorial gains through military means, to deter them from continuing the war, and ultimately to influence them to prefer to resolve the conflict through political rather than military means. This happened with Jordan after the Six-Day War and with Egypt following the Yom Kippur War.

Deterring Arab confrontation states from continuing the war and bringing them to the negotiating table to resolve the Arab-Israeli conflict are the primary objectives of Israel's national security policy. Deterrence against continuing a war in order to impose political conditions will be achieved only when the existing regimes that wage war against Israel realize that war is futile. This realization is the result of failure thus far to force conditions upon Israel through military or terrorist pressure and an assessment and recognition that Israel can thwart such efforts in the future as well.

Ensuring the Capability of the IDF
to Achieve Its Goals

Development and strengthening of the IDF is based on a multiyear plan designed to ensure its capability. The plan consists of eight elements:

1. To thwart the war efforts of the Arab military coalition (of any number of states or military forces) in any aggressive attempt, including surprise attack, to liquidate the state of Israel, change its borders, or cause it insufferable losses and damage.
2. To shift the terror of war to enemy territory even following a surprise attack on Israel in order to exact a price which will contribute to the enemy's realization of the futility of trying to use military force to force conditions on Israel and to make the enemy more aware of the need to stop the fighting and turn to the negotiating table.
3. To accelerate the rate of military decision in war through air superiority which permits concentration of air attacks on land maneuvers—especially those relying heavily on armored and mechanized forces—as well as on airborne and seaborne forces. Special operations are designed to disrupt command, communications, and support systems in the enemy's rear. Military doctrine, organization, training, and equipment are designed to produce decisive military victories in all terrain and weather conditions.
4. To strengthen the territorial defense of the state by combining territorial defense formations, including settlements, with mobile formation for counterattack.
5. To limit the enemy's freedom of action in employing sea forces to attack Israel from the sea and cut off its navigation routes and, by contrast, to enable freedom of action to permit Israeli maritime forces to attack hostile states from the sea and to cut off their sea routes.
6. To defend Israel against air attacks by combining air defenses with absorption capability (dispersion, sheltering, rescue services, medical services).

7. To fight terror in order to prevent it from achieving military gains and causing material damages and loss. This is accomplished through a combination of territorial defense and preventive action. ·
8. To maintain readiness based on early warning and on prior planning and organization in order to stop any aggression at its outset, to prevent violations of security arrangements determined by political agreements, to destroy the basis for any attack before it is initiated, to destroy weapons systems endangering Israel's existence, and—when warranted by an emergency—to mobilize the entire reserve system.

Strategic Cooperation with the United States

Israel's defense strategy requires the independent use of the IDF as the country's military force. The main reason for this is that if Israel is dragged into a war, the time element will have a decisive effect on the ability of the IDF to stop the aggression before it destroys Israel. Dependence on foreign forces could delay Israel's action. The decision of an allied country to send forces depends on considerations unrelated to Israel's defense. Woe to a country whose national defense depends on the decisions of other states while the noose is tightening around the defender's neck!

Israel has had enough experience with international guarantees to know they are unreliable. It still remembers the guarantees given by the United States after the Sinai war in 1956 that the Tiran Straits would remain open to Israeli navigation and that a UN force would be deployed in the northern Sinai, by the straits, and in the Gaza Strip to deter Egyptian aggression. These guarantees persuaded Israel to remove its forces from these areas, but in May 1967 these guarantees were dashed by Egyptian President Gamal Abdel Nasser. After Egypt blocked the Tiran Straits, U.S. promises to reopen them to Israeli navigation with an international fleet came to naught. The situation deteriorated, resulting in the Six-Day War.

Similarly, the results of the guarantee given Israel after it conquered southern Lebanon in 1978 are still fresh in Israel's memory. Israel had occupied the area up to the Litani River in order to destroy PLO capability in that area. The PLO had been firing directly at Israeli settlements in the northern Galilee and along the border roads, causing intolerable losses in human life and property. Israel agreed to leave southern Lebanon because it believed that the United Nations Interim Force in Lebanon (UNIFIL) mandated by the UN Security Council would prevent reorganization of terrorist groups and stop terrorist infiltration across that region toward Israel. Israel soon realized that UNIFIL was stopping neither terrorist reorganization nor transit of terrorists through the area. The resulting deterioration eventually led to the Peace for Galilee war.

Israel's defense strategy alone does not have the capability of deterring the Soviet Union from endangering Israel's existence. Therefore, Israel believes that it must cooperate with the United States to achieve this goal. Israel is part of the free world—a Jewish state after one thousand years of persecution and pogroms and the holocaust. It is a state prepared to fight any foreign forces that might attack it—and as such is a key state for establishing a regional defense system.

Cooperation with the United States exists on two levels: (1) supply of weapons and equipment to Israel necessary for maintaining the balance of power which guarantees the defense of Israel against the aggression of Arab regimes dependent upon the U.S.S.R. as their primary source of weapons and (2) cooperation with the United States to deter the Soviet Union from direct or indirect involvement.

Whenever war is forced upon Israel, Israel takes into account the danger of Soviet involvement. This is especially true in situations when the U.S.S.R. might consider intervening militarily to save one of its client states from defeat. Yet Israel will not accept a situation in which the Soviet umbrella of deterrence allows an Arab aggressor to have freedom of action while paralyzing Israel's ability to counter the aggression.

Conclusion

The greatest threat to global security and the existence of third world nations will present itself if aggressive third world states acquire nuclear weapons. Regimes pursuing aggressive strategies frequently come to power in the third world and in the Middle East. Nuclear weapons in the hands of terrorist organizations would present a similar peril. If such parties acquire nuclear weapons, other staes fearing for their existence would be forced to develop their own nuclear deterrent. Proliferation of nuclear weapons in the Middle East would create a situation in which extreme regimes could become the detonators for global destruction if a regional nuclear war escalated into a nuclear exchange between the superpowers.

Can nuclear proliferation be prevented? There is no clear answer. We can only estimate the probability of the alternative developments which could result from proliferation. One possible development is that third world states would not be deterred from using nuclear weapons. If a third world state could use nuclear weapons against another state which lacked a nuclear deterrent, global chaos would result. A second alternative is that both superpowers would collaborate to deter other states from using nuclear weapons, or one superpower would unilaterally provide deterrence. A third scenario is that more states would be added to the strategic alliances of the superpowers. The new states added to the alliances would then operate under the same constraints of nuclear terror which today contrain those within the two alliances.

In light of nuclear proliferation, it is difficult to ascertain in which direction the world is headed. A country such as Israel—surrounded by enemies that still seek to destroy it, existing in a region where chronic instability has provided fertile ground for wars, terrorism, conflicts, political upheavals, and superpower rivalry—has been and will be forced to prepare to defend its existence against the most grievous threats. These perils may now sound like the figment of an overly fertile imagination, but they are indeed a serious possibility in today's world, which has already experienced previously unimaginable upheavals.

Notes

1. The factor of demographic instability applies to states with ethnic or tribal divisions, for example, Lebanon in the Middle East and Uganda in East Africa.

PART FOUR

Economic Interdependence and Leverage

10
The Politics and Limitations
of Economic Leverage

Robert D. Hormats

The drama of Middle East diplomacy in the early 1970s was intensified by the decision of Arab oil exporters to cut production and to embargo oil exports to the United States and other Western nations in order to influence the course of events. For the first time in the history of U.S. involvement in the Middle East, Arab nations had mobilized a formidable economic "weapon" of their own.

With the benefit of hindsight, we may now draw certain conclusions from that experience about national motivations in employing and reacting to the oil weapon during that period. These, in turn, can provide an insight into whether similar types of pressures might be applied in the future and what the responses might be.

In addition, other types of economic pressures—such as the withholding of financial assistance—were employed during the 1970s by the United States vis-à-vis Israel and by several Arab nations vis-à-vis their neighbors. We shall also examine these pressures to determine their costs and benefits.

The Middle East experience surrounding the 1973 war tells us a great deal about the changing nature of economic power—specifically that the effects of economic leverage in a world of complex and intertwined economic relationships among nations are by no means clear-cut issues. Economic pressures that on the surface appear likely to induce policy changes by the target nation frequently fail to attain their desired goals and on occasion lead to perverse outcomes. The complicated questions that relate to the use of economic pressures in the 1970s lead to the conclusion that a better understanding of the repercussions of politically inspired leverage as well as closer contacts between economists and those formulating foreign policy and security policy are needed to ensure a more considered, realistic approach to the subject.

The October 1973 Middle East war leads to four general conclusions about oil and financial pressures:

1. Nations generally can be counted on to resist compromising what they believe to be their fundamental political and security interests in the face of outside economic pressures.
2. Internal or external countervailing influences often make economic leverage difficult or unwise for one nation successfully to apply to another and on occasion harmful to its own interests when sustained.
3. Economic pressures frequently generate reactions that over time render them ineffective—for example, by motivating a nation that has been a target of those pressures to reduce its future vulnerability.
4. Because the economic interests of many nations are so closely intertwined, Middle Eastern governments are unlikely in the future to believe they can use oil (or other types of economic leverage) neatly and without derivative consequences to themselves, but use of such leverage can never be ruled out in this region.

The oil and financial leverage applied in the 1970s was different from the United Nations sanctions imposed on Iraq after its August 1990 invasion of Kuwait. The Arab oil embargo against the West was intended to weaken Western, particularly U.S., support for Israel; the anti-Iraq embargo begun in August 1990 was intended to make it unacceptably costly for Saddam Hussein's forces to continue to occupy Kuwait. The differences between the two actions lie in their scope and character: The breadth of the 1990 embargo against Iraq, the coverage of exports as well as imports, the extent of international support for them, and the additional emphasis resulting from deployment of large numbers of allied troops made the 1990 sanctions considerably more potent than the oil embargo in 1973-1974.

Notwithstanding these differences, many of the conclusions summarized previously regarding the experience of the 1970s also apply to the sanctions against Iraq. Saddam Hussein did not withdraw from Kuwait in the face of sanctions that had a far greater impact on his economy than did the oil embargo on the United States; he did not alter his position in the face of these measures any more than the United States altered its Middle East policy in the face of the oil embargo.

A second similarity relates to the impact of sanctions on those applying them. Higher oil prices resulting from the Arab oil embargo of the 1970s and production cutbacks set off a concerted production and conservation effort in the West that ultimately proved damaging to the countries that had imposed the embargo. The sanctions applied against Baghdad in 1990 adversely affected key U.S. allies such as Turkey, which lost oil pipeline revenues; other neighboring states such as Jordan and Syria, which suffered a collapse in trade; and those Eastern European nations that depended on oil imports from and manufactured exports to Iraq.

The application of economic leverage in the Middle East during the 1970s involved three intermingled sets of contentious and conflicted relationships: the Arabs versus Israel, the United States versus the Soviet Union, and the region's radicals versus its moderates. At some points during the period, one relationship received the most attention, but all were always in play and must be included in any policy analysis.

Why and How Oil Leverage Came to Be Used

As late as 1972, King Faisal stated that oil and politics did not mix. Saudi Arabia had only reluctantly acquiesced in the brief and ineffective 1967 oil embargo. At the time, the kingdom had neither the financial resources to sustain an embargo nor the desire to permit Egypt's President Nasser to dictate Saudi production levels or to determine its markets in order to serve his objectives.

In the years after 1967, the Western appetite for oil grew steadily. That led to dramatic increases in imports from Middle Eastern and North African producers, who in turn came to recognize their sharply increased market strength. The then-significant, but in retrospect modest, oil price increases imposed by producers well before the October 1973 war attest to their increased perception of their growing market strength, as did the move of several producing nations to take from the companies equity control of oil facilities on their territories. The market strength of producers over time emboldened those who believed that oil could be an effective political instrument.

Nasser's death in September 1971 and the succession of Anwar Sadat, with whom the Saudis were particularly close, changed the political climate. Months before the 1973 war, the Saudis had hinted that they would not increase production to meet growing Western oil needs unless the United States pressed the Israelis to return land captured from the Arabs in the 1967 war. But even this position posed a dilemma for Riyadh. On the one hand, the Saudi leaders considered themselves friends of the United States; they depended ultimately on the U.S. security umbrella, and often sought Washington's diplomatic support to moderate the Israeli position. On the other, they were being pressed by forces from within the kingdom and by friends in the Arab world to threaten oil-related measures in order to promote important Arab objectives—namely, the return of Israeli-captured land. Issuing such threats, the Saudis realized, would risk provoking a negative reaction in the United States. That could have reduced Washington's willingness to support—even to a modest degree—Arab interests and created a rift between Saudi Arabia and the United States; the latter effect might have emboldened the Soviets in the region. Saudi statements about the possible use of oil leverage were therefore presented not as threats but as strong hints, which were often conveyed by middlemen. Washington, however, failed to take them sufficiently seriously, even when they later came from the king himself.

By the time the October 1973 war broke out, the decision to employ the oil weapon in support of the Arab position had in principle already been made by the Saudis. However, the conditions and details of the application of this weapon had probably not yet been worked out, and the magnitude of the price effects of the production cuts that were to follow were probably not altogether understood.

Decisions regarding oil price increases, production cuts, and the embargo were taken separately. First, meeting in Kuwait on October 16, 1973, a number of large OPEC suppliers (for the first time unilaterally, rather than in negotiations with the major oil companies as in the past) jacked up the price of crude, by roughly 70 percent. This was primarily an economic decision, designed to take advantage of the tight oil market.

The Iranian delegation then left the meeting; several Arab delegations that were not in the original OPEC core group joined in for an essentially political discussion. This group of Arab Middle Eastern and North African producers collectively decided on a schedule of production cuts designed to apply pressure on the West. Although it was not widely understood at the time, these cuts were to have a far more devastating economic impact on oil-importing nations than either the just-agreed price increase or the embargo that was to follow. Production was to be reduced by 5 percent immediately and by a further 5 percent each month until "such time as total evacuation of Israeli forces from all Arab territory occupied during the June 1967 war is completed and the legitimate rights of the Palestinian people are restored."[1]

But the more pointed political decision was yet to be made. Despite the massive U.S. airlift of military equipment and munitions to Israel early in the war, there was no decision at the Kuwait meeting to impose an embargo. The Saudis hoped that an Arab delegation then in Washington, which included their minister of state for foreign affairs, Omar Saqqaf, would favorably influence the U.S. position and so opposed an embargo motion at Kuwait. It was agreed, however, that each country would retain the right to impose an embargo unilaterally. In any case, oil shipments were not to be cut to "any friendly state which has extended or may in the future extend effective, concrete assistance to the Arabs."[2] It was only following President Nixon's request to Congress for $2.3 billion to pay for the supplies delivered to Israel in the airlift— which convinced Riyadh that the United States was unwilling to play a moderating role vis-à-vis Israel—that the Saudis and other Arab producers embargoed the United States and, for the pro-Israel statements of its ministers, the Netherlands.

Reactions in the West differed sharply. Much of Europe and Japan— whose dependence on imported oil was especially high—tried in varying degrees by their statements and policies to demonstrate sympathy, or support, for the Arab position. The U.S. reaction was considerably different. Washington's diplomatic goal was to demonstrate (1) to Arab leaders that it had the ability to influence Israel to agree to cease hostilities and ultimately to return captured Arab territories and (2) to Israeli leaders that it could influence the Arabs, or at least those in the moderate camp, to move toward a sustainable peace with Israel. The effort started with the difficult cease-fire negotiations, in which the United States had largely supported the Israeli position, while the Soviets had done the same for Egypt. But Secretary of State Henry Kissinger wanted the United States to be not just a key player but the *central* player in the negotiating process—a process in which he wanted to completely exclude the Soviets. President Sadat gave him his opportunity when, only a few days into the war, he invited Kissinger to Cairo.

The U.S. strategy after the war was, step by step, to obtain a troop disengagement, then move the troops farther and farther apart (ending the encirclement of the Egyptian Third Army), and then encourage the warring parties to move gradually toward a more permanent settlement. In the process, the United States hoped to build the confidence of both sides in U.S. diplomacy and in each other. Kissinger believed that progress would not only diminish the danger of another war—which would have seriously polarized the Middle East and risked direct great power confrontation—but also would reduce Soviet influence in the area for years to come. Initial communications with President Sadat and King Faisal had led him to conclude that their goals were similar.

The oil embargo and production cuts were major sources of tension in already strained U.S.-Arab relations; they constituted significant points of friction between the United States and its Western allies. Oil pressures profoundly affected the atmosphere in which U.S. diplomacy was conducted. They reinforced the need for the United States to demonstrate balance in its diplomacy, to maintain a dialogue that would enable it to understand the objectives and apprehensions of both sides, and to deliver at least some of what each side wanted.

But Washington drew a clear distinction between recognizing the new circumstances created by the oil embargo and altering U.S. diplomatic strategy in significant ways simply to relieve oil supply pressure on itself or its allies. In the view of U.S. policymakers, to have departed from their fundamental diplomatic strategy in the face of the embargo would have jeopardized attainment of longer-term U.S. strategic objectives.

First, initial Arab demands that the United States persuade Israel to return to its pre-1967 borders were seen by Washington as unrealistic. And even had the demands been more modest, U.S. attempts to induce Israel to concede land for additional oil deliveries to the West would have reduced U.S. influence in Jerusalem, increased Israeli recalcitrance, and been politically unsupportable in the United States. Moreover, Israeli leaders, of course, would have flatly rejected the very notion of such a trade-off. In addition, Kissinger concluded, there would have been a great risk—if the oil-for-territory link had been established—of an escalating series of Arab demands, with new ones being put forward as old ones were fulfilled.

Second, if European and Japanese allies of the United States had been able to obtain major changes in Washington's diplomacy (as they sought to do) in return for a reduction in oil supply pressures, they could have been the target of escalating demands by producers desirous of exacting further concessions from the United States. As it was, the U.S. position that allied importuning would not alter its diplomacy, coupled with European and Japanese support for certain aspects of the Arab position and recognition in some Middle East capitals that production cuts were damaging Western economies, led to some supply relief for Europe and Japan.

Third, by succumbing to oil pressures, the United States would likely have weakened the position of Arab moderates. They, after all, had the largest portion of Arab oil reserves and were the West's largest suppliers. Had Washington been able to persuade Israel to accept certain withdrawal targets in return for some restoration of oil production (which it probably could not force Jerusalem to do in any case), the radicals might well have insisted that once the initial goals had been met, moderate producers hold out for more. However, the moderates' objective was not to embitter the United States but to involve Washington constructively in the diplomatic process in order to obtain Israeli withdrawal from captured lands and counter Soviet influence in the Middle East. So acquiescence in radical pressure to escalate the use of oil pressures would have placed those nations in a highly awkward situation.

Washington's rejection of the oil-for-territory link therefore, paradoxically, reduced the vulnerability of the moderates.

Sadat understood that lifting the embargo would improve U.S. relations with the Arab moderates. He suggested to Arab producers that the embargo be ended after he saw the Kissinger diplomatic scenario begin to unfold. However, Syria, Algeria, and Iraq blocked the Saudis and others from fully restoring production levels or normalizing exports to the United States for two months from the time Sadat initially sought this. Eventually, Egyptian-Israeli disengagement and U.S. willingness to work toward an Israeli-Syrian agreement created a political environment in which the Saudis could lift the embargo.

The Problems of Applying Oil Leverage

The complex pressures and considerations faced by the Arab nations in maintaining the embargo and pursuing their diplomatic goals can best be understood by examining the countervailing influences at play.

First, the Saudis, Kuwaitis, and other Gulf moderates initially supported Egypt and Syria by applying the oil weapon in their behalf. But once initiated in an act of Arab solidarity, the embargo became a hostage to the demands of a broader group of countries. Radical influence on its production policy had been feared by Saudi Arabia in 1967; early in 1974 these concerns proved correct.

Second, as already noted, the Arab moderates had both a political and an economic stake in their relations with the West, in particular with the United States. Large portions of their funds were deposited in Western banks, Western technology was needed to develop their economies, and U.S. arms were needed to reduce Soviet influence in the area. The oil weapon, therefore, had to be used carefully. It had to be strong enough to convince hard-liners within the kingdom and the Arab world that Saudi Arabia and other moderate producers were vigorously supporting the Arab cause. And it had to be credible enough to encourage the United States to play a balanced and active negotiating role. But the Saudis and other moderates also recognized that the oil weapon could not be used so heavy-handedly as to undermine Western economies and drive the United States closer to the Israelis. That could have reduced prospects of Israeli disengagement and improved prospects for the Soviets and their more radical Middle Eastern allies to close ranks.

The Oil Weapon Loses Its Punch

Over time the Saudis came to recognize that sharp increases in the price of oil would generate enormous incentives for investment in new energy production capacity and new conservation measures in importing countries. But this market response emerged surprisingly slowly. Indeed, after the quadrupling of oil prices in 1973–1974, a period of lower and more stable prices led to complacency among (and increased the consumption by) major importers—that is, until the price shocks that followed the fall of the Shah in 1979. In the highly politicized atmosphere of the early 1970s, however, and in light of the apparent absence, or at least slowness, of a conservation and supply response abroad, the case for price moderation was hardly an easy one for the Saudis to make—even if they understood the long-term market consequences of high prices.

However, market forces were beginning to take hold in the 1970s. In the latter part of the decade new drilling proceeded at a frenetic pace. Nonoil sources of energy, such as coal and natural gas, were being rapidly developed. Conservation became an economic imperative for households and business—and a national goal in many Western countries. New laws, regulations, and subsidies accelerated this trend. Recessions in many countries in the early 1980s deepened the drop in oil imports. And strategic reserves of oil were constituted to reduce the impact of any future embargo.

Trends that began slowly in the 1970s hit with great force in the 1980s. In member countries of the Organization for Economic Cooperation and Development (OECD), oil consumption fell from 41 million barrels a day in 1979 to less than 34 million barrels a day in 1985. Purchases shifted away from Middle Eastern suppliers; the share of OPEC oil in free world consumption fell from 60 percent in 1979 to 35 percent in 1985.

The problem for OPEC was compounded by the desperate attempt of many producers to hold market share by lowering prices. As the result of a free-for-all competition for markets, the spot price of oil fell to below $9 per barrel in the summer of 1986 from $28 per barrel in December 1985. In 1986 OPEC finally agreed on production cuts to boost the price to the $14–$18 range. This was made possible by a stopgap deal in which Saudi Arabia and Iran called a truce in their dispute over production levels. By this time the price had been paid by oil producers.

Western complacency about conservation and laxity in the development of domestic sources of energy will make Middle Eastern oil increasingly indispensable. That is a risk for the United States today. Dependence on imported oil is rising dramatically and threatens soon to exceed levels of the early 1970s. And the next time leverage is used, the protagonists might not be a moderate Saudi king as in the 1970s, but the militant mullahs of Iran or radical leaders in other nations committed to using the oil weapon with fervor.

Oil will in any case remain a political issue. With the occupation of Kuwait, Saddam Hussein came to control 19 percent of the world's oil. One of his additional aims was directly or through intimidation to exert dominant influence over Saudi oil decisions; that would have enabled him effectively to influence the price and production of 44 percent of the world's supplies and, in time, a far larger portion, including that of the other Gulf states. Iraq would have had by far the strongest voice in OPEC. Saddam Hussein said openly that he wanted to control Kuwait in order to control oil prices, which would have enabled him to pay for his war machine.

With the military defeat of Iraq in 1991, however, oil stability is far from assured. Anti-Western fundamentalism in the moderate nations of the region could subject all of the area's oil to disruption or make it vulnerable to being withheld from certain nations for political reasons.

A Retrospective: Oil Leverage Poses Risks for Both Sides

The events of the 1970s lead to certain assumptions about future policy motivations regarding the oil weapon.

First, just as the memories of the inflation of the 1930s continue strongly to motivate German economic polity to avert inflation and those of the Great Depression influence the United States to combat unemployment, so should recollections of the embargo of 1973–1974 impel policymakers in importing countries to avoid future vulnerability to the cutoff of oil or any other vital commodity. Unfortunately, U.S. memories of the embargo and price disruptions a decade ago faded rapidly. At the end of 1990, U.S. oil production was running at a level of 7.2 million barrels per day—the lowest level since 1961. The United States today produces 14 percent of the world's oil and consumes 26 percent. Although the country now uses oil far more efficiently than it did in the 1970s and early 1980s, demand grew steadily from its lows of 1982–1983, causing a substantial growth in imports and greater vulnerability to disruptions of Middle East supplies.

Although it is conventionally argued that the United States has less of an interest in Gulf oil production than do Japan and much of Western Europe because they depend on it for a larger portion of their imports than does the United States, the latter imports more oil than any other nation; were Gulf oil shipments to be interrupted to Japan and Western Europe, they would purchase more oil from countries now selling oil to the United States, resulting in higher prices and shortages in this country. The integrated character of world oil markets, coupled with the enormous and growing U.S. dependence on imported oil, makes the U.S. vulnerable to disrupted oil supplies from the Middle East and elsewhere.

Second, in the final analysis the producers paid dearly for the overly ambitious use of the oil weapon and for the lack of price restraint. Oil pressures did underscore the need for the United States to pursue a balanced negotiating strategy after the October 1973 war, but the probability was high that it would have done most of what it did for its own strategic reasons without pressure from the embargo. The economic harm of oil production cuts and sharp price increases—in the short term to consumers, in the long run to producers—however, has been enormous. Indeed, the Shah probably lost his throne in part because of the political and economic instability resulting from very rapid growth based on sharp increases in oil revenues. And the collapse of prices— the inevitable effect of rapid increases—unleashed a new set of desta- bilizing pressures in the Gulf, Nigeria, and other producing countries.

Third, a nation that changes its fundamental strategy in the face of an oil or any other type of embargo would risk strengthening the hands of those least well disposed to use it—in the case of the 1973 war the more radical producers—and undermining its own position. Oil producers now better recognize this possibility, which U.S. policymakers also must bear in mind when put in similar situations in the future. By the same token, U.S. officials who pride themselves on resisting foreign pressures should understand that U.S. attempts to apply economic pressures are unlikely to force policy changes in other countries for similar reasons; this clearly appeared to be the case when international sanctions against Iraq failed to reverse Saddam Hussein's occupation of Kuwait.

New Dimensions in Cooperation
Between Oil Importers and Exporters

As noted, growing economic linkages will likely limit the willingness or ability of oil producers to use the oil weapon in a heavy-handed way in the future. In the mid-1970s the United States and Saudi Arabia established the Joint Commission on Economic Cooperation to promote Saudi economic development and to increase the role of U.S. technology and of U.S. firms in Saudi development. It was also intended to strengthen political ties, to increase the number of Saudis who saw their interests intertwined with those of the United States, and to create a disincentive to future production cuts.

Efforts to attract petrodollars into long-term U.S. financial instruments were considered helpful in fostering financial stability at the time. The depth of the New York and European financial markets and attractive investment opportunities provided strong incentives for oil producers to make investment decisions on economic rather than political grounds. Moreover, even while oil was being politicized, financially strong exporters were in no mood to lose money on their investments by shifting their assets around and destabilizing currencies and markets, in order to achieve some nebulous political point.

The financial linkages are even more important today. As oil earnings have diminished, dividends and interest payments constitute an increasingly important portion of the revenues of a number of major oil-exporting nations. Such nations will be unlikely to disrupt the financial markets that their funds are invested in and that provide large inflows of cash.

Opportunities for trade and financial pressures of a more subtle sort in the future are, however, quite likely. Restricting imports from countries that disagree with them on major policies, lending to countries that they support, favoring products of nations in return for political favors, and providing oil on concessional terms for particular importers for political reasons are ways oil exporters can exercise influence.

The most important opportunity for the oil producers to use economic influence in the future is in the developing world and in the more industrialized Mediterranean nations. These nations are increasing the use of oil more rapidly than are the United States, northern Europe, and Japan. They also want to expand exports, and Gulf oil producers continue to constitute important markets for them.

OPEC investments and loans to developing countries are also important. On numerous occasions, the United States has asked Saudi Arabia to provide economic assistance to countries it wanted to help, particularly to those where it perceived a parallel Saudi interest. Often Saudi support has made up for the inability of the U.S. administration to obtain congressional appropriations sufficient to meet the financial needs of friendly Middle Eastern or African nations.

Economic support from moderate oil producers for governments in the third world can be an important factor in promoting stability. However, the United States will now have to make such requests only when funds are absolutely necessary, when palpable Saudi or other moderate interests are involved, and when the support will not cause friction between the donors and their less moderate neighbors.

We can also expect approaches by Middle Eastern countries for preferential U.S., European, and Japanese treatment on trade. In a highly competitive world economy, access to the enormous U.S. market for products other than oil takes on special importance to Middle Eastern nations. This is true because oil prices could remain weak for some time after the Iraq war if production in the Gulf is fully restored and producers that increased capacity and output during the war maintain outputs. And the petrochemical and related industries, built by oil producers with oil revenues—and with strong Western encouragement as a way of boosting Western exports of capital goods and absorbing large sums of petrodollars—will require new markets. The oil producers will look to the West, particularly to the United States, to boost exports. Dependence on Western markets will further restrain leverage.

Because the United States has negotiated a bilateral free trade agreement with Israel, a number of Arab nations are likely to seek similar arrangements. At the least, they will want to be assured that market access for their exports of energy-based products is not restricted.

Over the longer term, the question of market access for Middle East–manufactured products may become loosely tied up in the diplomacy of the area. The United States might be tempted to provide special market access for goods from Arab nations that pursue moderate policies. And some oil producers might be willing to adjust—albeit modestly— their foreign policies in return for special treatment for their goods in the U.S. market. Europeans will be more likely to improve trade ties with Middle Eastern nations without political preconditions. And indeed, as the European Economic Community establishes its Single Internal Market in 1992, it is likely to negotiate bilateral trade agreements with individual Middle Eastern nations. For such nations, these arrangements may well prove more important than trade ties with the United States in many product areas.

Over the longer run, should the oil market tighten and shortages develop, Middle Eastern producers may link deliveries of crude to the willingness of industrialized nations to accept large amounts of their manufactured imports. But the high degree of trade interdependence between Middle Eastern nations and industrialized countries will reduce their latitude for manipulating trade to obtain political leverage; trade agreements will likely be based more on economic than on political considerations.

Bitterness Without Benefits
in the Use of Financial Leverage

A different type of constraint limited the effectiveness of financial leverage in the Middle East. Successive administrations in Washington have on occasion attempted to withhold or delay economic assistance to Israel to influence its policies. Soon after the start of the October 1973 war, President Nixon considered withholding a portion of the $2.2 billion supplemental appropriation request to Congress. His objective was to put pressure on Jerusalem to adopt a flexible negotiating approach vis-à-vis Egypt. This notion was eventually dropped on grounds that, as Kissinger argued, it would make Israel more reluctant to cooperate in the negotiating process and would embolden Israel's Arab adversaries.

But in May 1975, frustrated by the failure of the Kissinger shuttle to reach a second Sinai disengagement agreement, the United States announced a "reassessment" of its policy toward the Middle East. During this time it considered delaying delivery of weapons to Israel and suspending negotiations for new economic and military assistance. The United States was contemplating a departure from the earlier step-by-step strategy; it was planning instead to press for a comprehensive Middle Eastern settlement that called for significant Israeli pullbacks.

Israel and its supporters understood the implications of this pressure. They believed that it would weaken Israel's negotiating position toward the Arabs. Opposing such pressure, seventy-six U.S. senators signed a May 1975 letter to President Ford stating that "withholding military equipment from Israel would be dangerous, discouraging accommodation by Israel's neighbors and encouraging a resort to force. . . . Within the next several weeks, the Congress expects to receive your foreign aid requests for fiscal year 1976. We trust that your recommendations will be responsive to Israel's urgent military and economic needs."[3] The pressure quickly ceased. In any case, the main reason for Israel's return to negotiations was its stake in a step-by-step diplomatic process.

In the different context of the debate over the West Bank, Senator Adlai E. Stevenson III of Illinois proposed withholding a relatively small portion of the roughly $2 billion administration aid request until the president had determined that Israel had ceased expansion of settlements in the West Bank. This was resisted by a large number of members of Congress on the grounds that, in the view of Senator Jacob Javits of New York, it would drive Israel "into a corner" and disrupt the Camp David peace process. Or, in the words of Senator Charles Percy of Illinois, it "might be looked upon as coercion, might get people's backs up, and might imply that a policy has a price to it."[4]

As these examples suggest, U.S. economic leverage has been used sparingly and awkwardly in U.S.-Israeli relations because of political opposition in the United States, resistance in Israel, negative strategic implications, and other factors. The "letter of seventy-six" and the criticism of the Stevenson proposal illustrate the depth of U.S. domestic opposition to such economic pressure. Israeli leaders are keenly aware of this opposition. Therefore, Israel's policy can, for the most part, be carried out with little fear of sustained economic coercion from Washington.

Most Arab governments have come to recognize Israel's formidable ability to avert or resist U.S. pressures as a reality they can do little about. In U.S. relations with Israel as well as with the Arabs, the least satisfactory approach appears to have been a threat to withhold aid in order to try to force changes in Israeli policy. Invariably U.S. domestic pressures force the U.S. government to back off. The result is bitterness in Israel that the pressure was applied in the first place, as well as an erosion of U.S. credibility in the Arab world because the administration's attempt has been undermined by Congress or by domestic political pressure.

A related argument used in the United States against economic pressure on Israel is the sharply negative Israeli reaction to it. Successive U.S. administrations have come to understand that Israel strongly resists external pressures in favor of what it considers to be its vital security interests. Whether or not the United States completely shares these judgments, it is unlikely to force Israel to compromise these interests by using economic leverage.

Other aspects of Israel's policy—for example, West Bank settlements—are related as much to Israeli domestic politics as to its security. But U.S. attempts to modify even these often produce an exaggerated reaction in Israel, which considers such pressures as damaging to its security.

Finally, in an East-West context the United States has believed at times that it had to provide unqualified economic as well as security assistance to Israel. At the start of the October 1973 war, for example, the United States thought it had to demonstrate support for Israel to counter the Soviet Union's assistance to its friends in the area. Failure to do this, in Kissinger's view, would have strengthened the Soviet position in the Middle East and encouraged other Arab states to participate more actively in the war.

Israel had to strike a balance between, on one hand, demonstrating its high vulnerability to Arab arms and thus the urgent need for large-scale military and economic aid and, on the other, showing its intention to resist U.S. leverage. By questioning the U.S. commitment to Israel, the Israeli government could force U.S. politicians to stop threatening to apply economic pressure. But if Israel questioned the U.S. commitment too much, it risked convincing its Middle East adversaries, and the Soviets, that the United States might not come to Israel's aid if they launched a major attack.

Economic pressure was also an issue in relations between other nations in the area. The Saudis had provided generous assistance to

Egypt after the 1973 war; indeed, one benefit of Egypt's turn away from the Soviets was Saudi willingness to provide large-scale economic aid. In view of this support, Sadat's failure to consult with Riyadh before announcing his trip to Jerusalem was highly irritating to the Saudis. Although it avoided a major break with Cairo at the time, the kingdom felt taken for granted. After the signing of the Egyptian-Israeli peace treaty, Saudi Arabia and other Arab nations imposed an economic embargo of Egypt.

This step came as a major blow to the United States and Israel. It resulted in increased Egyptian reliance on U.S. aid, which rose to more than $1 billion annually. In part because of U.S. assistance, however, the break with the Saudis did not deter Egypt from its Camp David strategy. Thus Egyptian reaction to economic pressure was similar to that of Israel, and frustrations in Riyadh were probably similar to those in Washington.

Economic assistance from the wealthier Arab nations after the October 1973 war also played a considerable role in other parts of the Middle East. In 1974 the Saudis provided significant support for Sudan's President Jaafer Numeiri, a strong supporter of Sadat, who had survived a coup attempt organized by Libya and was facing serious domestic economic problems. They also provided economic assistance to lure Somalia—which was becoming irritated at Soviet denial of large-scale military assistance—into a more moderate posture.

Finally, U.S. economic assistance to some Arab states was used as a positive incentive rather than an instrument of leverage. In certain cases (for example, Syria and Somalia), U.S. assistance—albeit modest— was intended to draw countries away from or to weaken their ties with the Soviets. In others (for example, Jordan), it was given because the king was a longstanding friend. And in still others (such as Egypt), it was to reinforce the peace process. Most of this assistance went for development projects, food imports, and the financing of current account deficits.

What Role Will Economic Influence Play in Future Middle East Diplomacy?

The increased number and intensity of economic ties between the West and the Middle East, and within the Middle East, make it hard, if not impossible, for one side to punish the other without also hurting itself. And one nation's attempt to apply economic pressure to another is often subject to internal countervailing influences that make the prolongation of such pressure undesirable to the nation applying it.

Recognizing these linkages, policymakers are bound to see significant ambiguities when they ask themselves whether, and how, these financial and commercial ties permit economics to be used as an instrument of political pressure in Middle East diplomacy.

In the real world, few nations are likely to relinquish the potential use of economic leverage completely. It is part of their diplomatic and strategic arsenals. The prudent course, then, is to understand how such leverage might be used and how others will react. In the Middle East an understanding of the potential for future application of economic leverage requires an analysis of the strengths, weaknesses, and motivations of nations in two contexts: one, Arab-Israeli, and the other, among Islamic nations of the area.

Actions to Affect Relations Between Israel and the Arab States

Israel over the years has sought with considerable success to prevent U.S. economic assistance from being used to influence its strategic decisions vis-à-vis its Arab neighbors. It has, with less success, sought to prevent the establishment of close economic ties between the United States and key Arab nations and has expressed fears that such ties would weaken Washington's political support for Israel.

The new reduced economic and energy power of some Middle Eastern oil producers should allay some of Israel's concerns on this score—concerns that proved largely unwarranted even at the height of Arab economic strength. Nonetheless, Israel will probably be wary of— and will resist in the U.S. Congress—closer bilateral trade ties between the United States and Egypt or Saudi Arabia. Senator J. William Fulbright of Arkansas said that Israel's concerns were rooted "in a deep-seated, perhaps not even wholly conscious fear that the association will be good for the United States—so very good indeed as to erode or undercut our all-out emotional commitment to Israel."[5] At the same time, Israel will try to intensify trade links with the United States under the recent bilateral agreement. It is also likely to voice alarm at any weakening of Western oil conservation or production efforts for fear of renewed Western vulnerability.

Paradoxically, oil is more likely to be a significant source of leverage in the future if the price of oil is weak for several years, encouraging nations to relax their production and conservation efforts. Although Middle Eastern policymakers probably do not expect oil leverage to become an effective policy tool in the near future, it might be used in the 1990s when a greater share of world needs will be provided by OPEC, especially Middle East, suppliers.

The wealthier Arab nations are likely to use their still formidable economic strength to influence other nations in the Middle East. Egypt, with many unmet economic needs and a growing population, wants to improve its economic infrastructure, increase agricultural output, and modernize its industry. Western aid, mainly from the United States, has helped in this process. But Egypt needs funds from the Arab world as well. If Egypt should become disenchanted with its relations with Israel, aid from other Islamic states that oppose the peace process could influence it to take a harder line toward Israel or the United States. The moderate Arabs, however, have a strong interest in keeping Egypt from developing a closer relationship with the more radical nations, such as Libya; they are therefore unlikely to apply economic pressures to force Egypt to take steps that would polarize the Arab world and lead to a confrontation with the United States.

Syria also continues to need outside assistance. Over the years financial support from the Arab world has been of great importance psychologically and economically. The Saudis recognize that their support for Syria carries little influence in Damascus. Unless a major breach develops, however, the Saudis probably will not unilaterally cut off financial assistance.

Saudi and Kuwaiti assistance to front-line states in the fight against Iraq was vital after August 1990. In contrast, the cutoff of support for Jordan punished it for supporting Saddam Hussein. This brings us back to the question of U.S. economic leverage on Israel and its neighbors. There have been examples, such as the U.S. scaling down of its response to Israeli requests for F-15s and F-16s and the U.S. policy "reassessment" in which Washington threatened to withhold aid. As noted earlier, however, the United States seems unlikely to be willing to apply sustained economic pressure to influence Israeli diplomacy on strategically important matters. Although U.S. financial assistance levels can be and surely will be modified for U.S. domestic budgetary reasons and to encourage sound domestic economic policy in Israel, opposition to the application of U.S. economic pressure on Israeli strategic policy remains strong in both nations. Israeli strategy generally assumes that such pressures will not be applied.

The United States will probably continue to provide economic assistance to moderate Arab states to keep them in the peace process and to help them avert pressure from radical nations of the region. Israel's supporters and others in the United States who have become skeptical of financial support for certain Arab nations have, however, become increasingly effective in curtailing such assistance. Since the mid-1970s, the United States has given much support to Egypt, linked to that country's moderate policies. Jordan also remains a recipient of

U.S. assistance, increasingly tied by Congress to Jordan's moderate policies vis-à-vis Israel, but this could change in light of Jordan's position after the invasion of Kuwait. After the 1974 disengagement agreement, the U.S. administration put forward a large assistance package for Syria, but it eroded to nothing because of resistance in Congress. Future assistance to Syria will likely depend on its position vis-à-vis Iraq in the postwar period.

In coming years, large-scale U.S. assistance to Israel is a virtual certainty. Support for Arab moderates will depend on their positions on Iraqi and Israeli issues. But in any case, large-scale U.S. aid for these countries will become hard to muster, especially in light of domestic pressures to reduce the federal budget deficit and attempts to shift a larger share of the burden to wealthier Arab and Western nations.

Economic Influences on
Moderate-Radical Relationships

The oil weapon, as noted, although primarily aimed at persuading the West to press Israel to relinquish captured territory, had other ramifications. The politics of oil caused intense frictions among the Arab states as Egypt and then Saudi Arabia came to believe that the embargo should be lifted while Syria, Algeria, and Iraq insisted that it be prolonged. In the future, the major oil-exporting countries will probably seek to use oil for diplomatic leverage in ways that give them flexibility to modify their leverage unilaterally rather than requiring them to obtain permission from nations with different goals. In the event that the domestic politics of large oil producers such as Saudi Arabia and Kuwait, once it regains its sovereignty, become more radical, however, or if Iran expands its influence in the region, the oil weapon could be used more aggressively in a broad display of solidarity that would limit the ability of each nation individually to modify its use.

Another countervailing pressure is the recognition by producers of the damage caused to their own societies by the oil price increases of the 1970s. These overheated economic developments forced the pace of change beyond the tolerance of countries such as Iran and caused a crisis of values that strengthened fundamentalism in some producing nations. From an internal point of view, many Middle Eastern nations are likely to see excessively ambitious use of oil price leverage as a potentially costly type of pressure, although some will be tempted to boost prices for economic reasons in order to make up for recent declines, which, of course, have also been disruptive.

Economic pressures within the region also have their limitations. If moderates cut their aid to other moderates excessively, because of relations with Israel, for instance, the cuts could weaken the target country and produce political instability. And moderate support for more radical nations is unlikely to influence their behavior in ways the donor would prefer.

A second deterrent to leverage is the flow of labor among nations of the region. When the Arab states at Baghdad in 1978 declared an economic boycott against Egypt, they exempted remittances by Egyptian workers abroad. They did so for good reason. Egyptian labor was important to oil producers in the region. They also depend—though less so now than in the 1970s—on Pakistanis, Iranians, Lebanese, and Palestinians. Thus, sanctions that prevent worker remittances would also deny the oil producers the benefits of inexpensive imported labor.

Assistance to the PLO or other Palestinian groups will continue to be used by governments in the Gulf to prevent Palestinians from disrupting domestic politics or economies in the region. In addition, maintaining reasonable economic relations with Iran is doubtless seen in Riyadh as a way of discouraging Tehran from employing Shiites to radicalize politics in the Gulf or teaming up with Syria or Iraq to destabilize the kingdom.

More broadly, Saddam Hussein's appeal to the "Arab in the street" with the claim that he was champion of the Arab poor will need to be countered no matter who governs Iraq. An institutionalized effort will be required to mobilize resources in order to improve development prospects in the region. Promoting economic development in Egypt will be critical; it is the most populous Arab nation, critical to stability in the Arab world and a necessary counterweight to the more radical regimes in the eastern part of the Gulf.

Saudi Arabia and Kuwait have given a significant amount of aid to poorer nations in the region, while providing jobs to hundreds of thousands of migrant workers. Yet the enormous income disparities in the area constantly remind the have-nots in the Arab world of the enormous wealth that exists in the less populated countries of the Gulf and the poverty of their own circumstances. And much of the outside aid to the area has had disappointing results. Saudi Arabia's King Fahd has already spoken of the need for a more "scientific" approach to development assistance in order to improve its quality and effectiveness. The kingdom can be expected to exercise leadership in identifying new and better means of supporting development in the area. This will be a necessary component in a more stable postwar structure.

To avert economic instability—a fertile ground for fundamentalists and those seeking to overthrow Arab moderates and Gulf monarchies—a concerted development program will be needed. The European Bank for Reconstruction and Development, which includes the USSR, the

United States, and Western and Eastern European nations, might be a good long-term model; it was founded by these countries and seeks to mobilize resources to boost growth in Eastern Europe. But in the nearer term, a broad institutional solution of this sort is unlikely to reduce rivalries in the region. Saudi and Kuwaiti leaders are likely to limit their aid only to nations that supported their interests in the period following Iraq's invasion of Kuwait. They will want to attach political conditions to aid in order to reward friends and attach economic conditions to ensure that the money is used efficiently.

Trade relations will also be a major factor in Middle East politics. The markets of the oil producers are important to less prosperous nations of the region. Over time, nations such as Libya may be the target of or may feel vulnerable to trade sanctions by Western nations. The collective result may well be greater attention to regional trade. Although the similarity of products made in the region may make these countries competitors in a number of oil-based commodities, they might become more interested in establishing an organization similar to the Association of Southeast Asian Nations to strengthen economic ties and to broaden the type of cooperation already promoted by the Gulf Cooperation Council.

Conclusions

To some degree, economic pressures will likely be a part of the ongoing effort of nations to exert influence, positive and negative, in the Middle East. But policymakers in the region who might otherwise consider employing another oil embargo, applying financial leverage, or using other economic instruments should have learned from the period of the 1970s and that following Iraq's invasion of Kuwait. They now have enough experience to understand that links among economies are intense and that the results of employing leverage are too ambiguous to commend this strategy for frequent use.

Nations frequently employ economic leverage, however, for reasons that are not completely logical—for example, to impress domestic constituencies or foreign allies. On occasion, nations employing such leverage are hurt as much as the target. Nor do targets always act in a totally rational fashion—they often resist succumbing to pressures well beyond the point that pure economic logic might lead one to conclude they would collapse. Policymakers might therefore find it useful to refresh their memories constantly about the history of sanctions and responses. That could reduce chances of future miscalculations or counterproductive actions. The possibility that oil or other types of economic influence will be applied to affect diplomatic or strategic events in the Middle

East can never be ruled out. Logical or not, in this area of the world the wisest counsel is to expect the unexpected.

In a broader sense, the 1973 experience of the Middle East raised issues that go to the very heart of the question of when and how to utilize economic leverage in the world at large. All too frequently, the United States has found that its efforts to influence the policy of another nation by denying it certain U.S. exports—for example, grain and high-technology products—failed to achieve the desired effect and actually hurt the U.S. companies that produce these goods. Although frequently impelled to project at home and abroad a "tough" posture, governments find that such measures tend to fall short of their desired objective and often have perverse effects. The economic community, which is usually not consulted in such cases, might anticipate such effects and the political and security communities might be able to make more realistic assessments of the effectiveness of sanctions if the initial decision to apply the leverage has been made in a less charged environment.

Notes

1. Middle East Economic Survey, October 19, 1973, Supp., p. iii.

2. Ibid.

3. Press release of May 22, 1975, issued by the offices of Senators Jacob Javits of New York and Birch Bayh of Indiana.

4. Both quoted in Seth Tillman, *The United States in the Middle East* (Bloomington: Indiana University Press, 1982), p. 168.

5. "Beyond the Interim Agreement," address to the annual conference of the Middle East Institute, Washington, D.C., October 3, 1975, as cited in Tillman, *The United States in The Middle East*, p. 100.

PART FIVE

The Peace Process in a Changing World

11
Notes on the U.S. Role in the Middle East

Stanley Hoffmann

The Theoretical Context

Scholars of international relations have found the world that has emerged after World War II challenging and bewildering. On the one hand, traditional concepts of state power, of power politics, of balance of power, of alliance building, and of uses of force in behalf of national interests have remained valid, both for the study of the contest between the superpowers and for that of the relations among the new actors who gained their independence after the breakup of the colonial empires. On the other hand, the universe described by "realist" theory since Thucydides differs markedly from the world of today. First, nuclear weapons have, so far, induced those who possess them both to restrain their resort to force and to seek understanding aimed at reducing the risks of war and of nuclear proliferation. Second, many of the new states, though formally independent, are so weak or heterogeneous, so deeply marked by ethnic, religious, or ideological conflicts, that they constitute a very different kind of "actor" from the states that realist theory has usually taken for granted. Third, the broad participation of the public in the politics of many states and the fact that the needs and demands of this public can often be satisfied only by the acts and decisions of foreign governments mean that international relations can no longer be seen only as a "game" in which diplomats and soldiers represent states; it is a process in which diplomats also represent interest groups or political forces, in which bureaucratic agencies conclude alliances across borders, and in which private actors such as multinational corporations or scientists can exert great influence on the world stage. Fourth, the development of a single world economy has not only transformed the agenda of world politics—economic issues are often the foremost priority of governments—but also has required that scholars pay attention both to the way in which economic interdependence tempers state competition and to the multiple, often multilateral forms international cooperation now takes.

Current theories of international relations take two quite different approaches. One is strategic (concerned predominantly, but not exclusively, with nuclear deterrence and nuclear war). It suffers from three flaws: First, it is inevitably more concerned with the grammar of violence than with its logic (I am referring to Karl von Clausewitz's famous remark that war has its own grammar but that its logic is provided by politics).[1] Second, strategic theory is almost relentlessly bipolar, a feature criticized by Hedley Bull a quarter of a century ago.[2] Third, it does not examine vigorously enough the effectiveness (or the ineffectiveness) of coercion in contemporary world politics. When can force or the threat of force be used successfully? What are the instances in which coercion simply does not work? Force can be impotent when there is a grotesque disproportion between ends and violent means (as in the use of force, say, to deal with a rise in oil prices or with a purely commercial conflict); or when there is a fuzziness about ends that makes the resort to force ineffectual, for it can succeed only if it is fitted to a specific end (for example, the posting of the U.S. Marines in Lebanon in 1982–1983); or when the ends are unreachable through external coercion (the reshaping of Lebanon, attempted both by Syria since 1976 and by Israel in 1982); or when force is defeated by a politically well-organized popular resistance or national liberation movement; or when the punishment of a troublesome but important ally could cause its collapse.

The other approach to international relations theory focuses on international economics and "regimes." It is concerned with the activities of states in the different arenas of the world economy; the role played by nonstates (such as fragments of bureaucracies or multinational corporations); and the norms and procedures of international regimes that provide both a framework for cooperation in the many areas in which a state cannot hope to achieve its objectives by itself and an alternative to economic and financial chaos when there is no hegemonic power capable of enforcing its preferred rules on other players.

This has been an exciting field of study and speculation, but it suffers from its own limitations. Although it is increasingly unfair to accuse all the theorists of the world economy of focusing on cooperation rather than on conflict, the fact is they have not yet seriously begun to analyze the relations between the arenas and phenomena they scrutinize and the vast realm that Raymond Aron called the strategic-diplomatic domain (for instance, the way in which economic statecraft can complement diplomacy and military instruments).[3] The "rise of the trading state," to use the title of Richard Rosecrance's book,[4] does not mean the fall of the state as a military actor: Most states are both, and it is the integration of the two that matters most. Moreover, the attempt by theorists to use rational choice theory in general and game theory in particular as the conceptual framework of their analyses strikes me as particularly inadequate for application to the strategic-diplomatic domain, where the only rationality one can find tends to be what Max Weber called a "rationality of ends." That is, one can make sense of the actors' moves only by first understanding their goals, whose selection by the actors cannot be grasped in the utilitarian terms of rational choice theory.

As a result, the theory of international relations is of limited help in understanding the politics of the Middle East. Theorists of international economic affairs and regimes may help us better to understand the economic strategies of the oil producers, for instance, but the way these strategies interact with the diplomatic and military games of the players remains unaccounted for. Conversely, strategic theory, precisely because it is technical and bipolar, is of very small utility.

Important insights, however, can be derived from contemporary theoretical work. The first one is stark: International relations remains a complex game played in a framework of anarchy—no central power, few compelling common values. As a result, each state's concern for security remains the most intense consideration, especially when a state is locked in a contest with another power (as was the United States during the cold war) or surrounded by hostile states (as is Israel). The self-righteousness and suspicion anarchy breeds in the actors—the conviction of each that its own intentions are good, or purely defensive, and hence its tendency to underestimate the effects of its own moves on other actors, and its frequent exaggeration of the hostility and aggressive intent of others—impose sharp limits on cooperation and on diplomatic settlements whenever important issues of security arise.

A second insight derives from research on the world political economy and from theories of decisionmaking. The relations among countries can no longer be analyzed as if they take place among rational "unitary actors," as if statesmen were merely, to use Clausewitzian language, the "personified intelligence of the state." We know now that international relations is a concept encompassing the encounters, bonds, and collisions of societies. Each state engaged in a negotiation or a contest is in fact a collection of services and agencies with different worldviews, perceptions, interests, and values; therefore, coalitions among "fragments" of state bureaucracies can eventually arise across borders. A state determined to influence another—that is, to use its power to affect the behavior of a partner or a rival—must try to move not only the policymakers with whom it deals officially but also those domestic forces from which the policymakers derive their support.

If such action turns out to be difficult because of the nature of the political system (in authoritarian or totalitarian countries), the state that tries to affect this system must at least be able to show to the policymakers how certain actions would either improve or weaken their ability to achieve their domestic goals or to retain the confidence of their subjects. This is precisely where rewards and sanctions come in: They are instruments that influence a foreign government insofar as they affect the domestic conditions in its country. There is a useful, if modest, role for nonofficial individuals in diplomatic affairs: Contacts between reasonably influential private citizens, across borders, can change perceptions, erode preconceptions, and soften hostility. A climate of opinion from which state policymakers eager to move in more cooperative directions could take heart, and which could allow them to take initiatives previously inconceivable, might thus be created little by little.

The Global Context

Understanding the role of the United States in the Middle East requires, first, understanding the nation's global role.

Despite the relative decline in U.S. economic power, the United States remains the most influential participant in the world economy for three reasons. One is the role of the dollar as the main reserve currency and unit of transactions. The second is the very size of the U.S. economy, which continues, despite Japan's challenge, to exert what François Perroux called domination effects on the financial markets and trade flows of smaller economies. The third is that only the United States, unlike Japan or the EEC, can integrate with its foreign policy a vast array of economic and strategic-diplomatic instruments.

In the years to come, the U.S. dominance is likely to persist. The main choice remains one between the liberal strategies pursued by most of the postwar administrations and the more protectionist strategies advocated by those who are worried about the influx of foreign goods. The liberal strategy often consists of forcing U.S. goods and capital through the closed doors of other countries, at the cost of allowing various sectors of the U.S. industrial economy to decline because of foreign competition on U.S. markets, and at the risk of becoming heavily indebted to foreign financers of the U.S. budget deficit. My own guess is that the liberal approach will prevail, with occasional exceptions in the form of either piecemeal protectionism or voluntary agreements to manage certain markets. In this way, the fragile but familiar tapestry of economic interdependence will be preserved, to the benefit of the

United States, insofar as the approach sharply limits the number and scope of knife slashes that other countries, eager for relative economic gains or greater political power, are likely to inflict on the tapestry. The edifying story of OPEC's rise and decline is not likely to be forgotten.

Second, Soviet-U.S. competition might remain what Arnold Wolfers called the "relationship of major tension." This is so even though the USSR is a superpower only in the military realm and despite the new, daring policy of Mikhail Gorbachev—a retreat from the emphasis on military might and an attempt at helping resolve regional conflicts. It is so because the USSR is determined, even at the cost of economic sacrifices at home, not to let itself be outdistanced militarily by the United States and because the economic and political reforms of Gorbachev, which entail some retrenchment abroad, are obviously aimed at providing in the long run a broader and more efficient foundation for Soviet strength and a regaining of influence abroad through diplomatic skill.

Moreover, the internal difficulties and uncertainties of the Soviet Union make it difficult to predict whether the cooperation between the superpowers, so marked in 1989–1990, will continue and put an end to the rivalry, or whether we might have to deal with an authoritarian regime concentrating on internal law and order but far more hostile to the West than Gorbachev between 1985 and 1990.

The Middle East Context

The very uncertainty that hangs over the world role of the United States in the strategic-diplomatic realm obliges us (or makes it possible for us) to be more prescriptive than predictive about U.S. policy in the Middle East. But the greater certainty about the role of the United States in the world economic networks allows one to predict a continuing U.S. involvement in the economies of those countries of the area that will remain threads in the webs of dependence and interdependence. The key questions are whether the United States will use its involvement (and the economic dependence of some of the key actors, such as Israel and Egypt, on U.S. assistance) to achieve political objectives, and what these objectives ought to be.

I would argue strongly against two courses of action that are in some ways quite different but that have important points in common. The first is the course that can be summed up by the term that General Alexander Haig made famous: the search for a strategic consensus. The second is diplomatic disinvolvement. The quest for strategic consensus did not begin or disappear with President Reagan's first secretary of state. It has been a recurrent inclination, characteristic of all the administrations that applied a predominantly bipolar grid to the problems of the area and believed that the main U.S. strategic interest in it was the erection of a barrier against the Soviet Union. The Baghdad pact, the Eisenhower doctrine, and the Carter doctrine of 1980 come immediately to mind.

But Kissinger's diplomacy in the Middle East was not fundamentally different. In its first phase—from 1969 to the October 1973 war—its immobility was, he tells us, the result of his determination not to "reward" the Soviets and their allies in the area and to prove instead both to Moscow and its clients that radicalism does not pay. (This strategy led him in 1972–1973 to reject both Soviet overtures and Sadat's approaches, thus making the October war inevitable.) After the October war, his step-by-step diplomacy remained marked by the quasi-exclusion of the USSR and by a strategy aimed, simultaneously and somewhat acrobatically, at providing some rewards to those Arab states that turned away from Moscow and at limiting concessions by Israel, the chief U.S. ally in the area.

The problem with that approach is, first, that it can never succeed in building an anti-Soviet front as long as the countries in the region feel more threatened by one another than by Moscow. Second, it cannot by itself help resolve the Arab-Israeli conflict and may indeed make it worse insofar as Israel appears as the principal anti-Soviet ally of the United States and acts, under that cloak, for its own purposes (as in Lebanon in 1982). Third, as long as that conflict lasts, Moscow will find a clientele, and the domestic reverberations of the conflict in the United States (that is, the hostility of many members of Congress to any moves, such as certain arms sales to Jordan or Saudi Arabia, which Israel and its U.S. supporters reject) will keep exasperating even the Arab friends of Washington. Fourth, the evolution of Soviet diplomacy in the Middle East makes the whole notion of a dominant "Soviet threat" somewhat absurd.

For these reasons many U.S. analysts and policymakers have often advocated what could be called a course of diplomatic passivity. They argue—correctly—that many of the problems of the area are strictly uncontrollable and unsolvable by the United States: domestic turbulence caused by the nature of certain Arab regimes and by the dislocations that accompany economic modernization; traditional rivalries among Arab states or between Iran and Arab states; situations of self-perpetuating strife as in Lebanon; ideological battles between fundamentalist and secular forces; and so on. How could the United States cope with such issues? Moreover, how bad is the status quo? Soviet influence is low, precisely because Moscow can, unlike Washington, provide arms, but neither economic assistance nor peace. The chief U.S. strategic asset,

Israel, is in an inexpungable position, while the chief U.S. economic partner, Saudi Arabia, is too weak to be diplomatically troublesome. Sooner or later, the Arab states will have to resign themselves to Israel and its faits accompli. In the meantime, the U.S. role should merely be to preserve the balance of power—which favors Israel—and to continue to provide economic assistance to or remain economically involved in friendly Arab states—to keep them friendly. Finally, it is said the Arab-Israeli conflict is not "ripe" for U.S. activism. Despite the insurrection of the Palestinians, despite the greater moderation of the PLO, the Israeli government and public are simply not ready to satisfy the demands of their adversaries. Indeed, the insurrection has only hardened Israel's position.

The problem with this approach is that, exactly like the policy of anti-Soviet containment, it fails to take seriously the effects of the continuing Arab-Israeli conflict. To be sure, Israel cannot be overrun. But the failure to move toward a general settlement is likely to feed and foster radicalism in the Arab world, whether it takes the form of anti-U.S. Islamic fundamentalism, Palestinian terrorist splintering, or state-sponsored terrorism manipulated by leaders hostile to the status quo. This failure also endangers the position of so-called Arab moderates, obliged to put increasing distance between Israel and themselves (Egypt) or tempted to close the breach between more intransigent Arab actors and themselves (Jordan) in order to force Israel to come closer to them.

Moreover, such a policy would intensify a regional arms race because U.S. support for Israel is likely to push Israel's Arab neighbors toward other arms suppliers, Soviet or European. The Arab-Israeli conflict is clearly not the only powder keg in the area, but it has the potential of making all the others more explosive—especially because it is likely to weaken those Arab regimes that are friendly to a passive (and therefore "objectively" pro-Israeli) United States and to harden an Israel that tries to square the circle of being a Jewish state while sitting on a vast and rebellious Arab population and of being a democracy while occupying Arab lands. Finally, U.S. passivity can only lead either to increasing unrest and repression in the occupied territories or to so brutal a crushing of the rebellion that international condemnation and the corruption of Israel's basic values would ensue.

Both these courses, therefore, are undesirable (the second one has often been followed after the failure of more activist efforts, as in 1979–1980 and in 1984–1987). A third one, suggested at times, is unrealistic: reliance, for the purpose of "stability," on "regional influentials." Iran, however, one of the so-called regional influentials, had a revolution that made it both more influential ideologically and rabidly anti-U.S., which the exhausting war with Iraq did not lessen. As for Saudi Arabia, it has never felt capable of matching its economic leverage (currently reduced) with political boldness, partly because of its internal and external vulnerability. And the most powerful influence in the area, Israel, also happens to be a major part of the problem rather than an element of the solution.

For all these reasons, I support a policy that may at first sight appear paradoxical. I agree with many of the champions of relative disinvolvement when they argue that many of the problems of the area are beyond U.S. material and psychological resources. Lebanon showed (as Vietnam already had) what happens when the United States pursues unreachable objectives with inadequate means. Neither U.S. military assets nor economic capabilities are able to control domestic developments, which are neither understood nor anticipated. The United States has an interest in protecting its Arab friends from Soviet aggression. It had an interest in helping prevent a defeat of Iraq by Iran, without, however, compromising an eventual improvement in U.S.-Iranian relations (or forgetting that the war resulted from an Iraqi attack). It continues to have an interest in the survival and security of Israel, though not in the perpetuation of conquests by it. But when it comes to the domestic turbulence of the Arab countries or to the rivalries among them, the best the United States can do for its friends is to help strengthen them by using its skills and resources toward a comprehensive and fair settlement of the Arab-Israeli conflict.

Nobody has written more cogently about the process and the substance of a settlement than Harold Saunders, whose arguments need not be repeated.[5] What remains clear is that without committed involvement of the United States, very little will happen. For a variety of reasons, the United States by itself cannot impose any solution, if only because several Arab states are anxious to involve both superpowers and other external powers as well. But the United States can play a crucial role at key points: in encouraging the Israelis to negotiate not only with Jordan but also with Syria and with the PLO, now that the PLO has renounced terrorism, accepted UN resolution 242, and recognized Israel's existence; in helping the PLO overcome its reluctance to trust Jordan with a role in negotiations over the West Bank and Gaza by endorsing the principle of Palestinian self-determination; and, paradoxically, by insisting throughout the process on both the importance of security guarantees for Israel and the necessity of not treating the Palestinians as an object left to the manipulations of Israelis, Jordanians, and Syrians. (Any settlement aimed merely at eliminating the PLO would sow the seeds of its own destruction.) The policy recommended here would have the double merit of introducing some peace and justice in an area where both have been missing and of inducing Soviet-U.S.

cooperation for superpower restraint in one of the world's most dangerous regions.

The task calls for remarkable skill and for the art of playing on the domestic underpinnings of states to which I alluded earlier. Indeed, in the case of the Palestinians, it requires that the United States try to affect the contest of factions and splinter groups that have weakened an actor that as yet only aspires to be a state. This attempt is now possible since the opening of a dialogue between the PLO and the United States. The only way in which Yasser Arafat's moderate core of the Palestine Liberation Organization can be helped to produce useful results for the Palestinian people, given its weak place in the constellation of Arab forces, is to support its participation in an entirely open-ended negotiation—hence the need for the United States to recognize the legitimacy of the demand for self-determination. Equally legitimate security fears of even those Israelis who consider the continuing oc-cupation of the West Bank and Gaza a calamity for Israel have to be addressed—hence the importance not of precluding (as U.S. diplomacy has tended to so far) the possibility of a Palestinian state but of making sure that such a state could not be a threat to Israel's security. Indeed, self-determination means that the option of a Palestinian state cannot be arbitrarily excluded, a point the king of Jordan has very well understood and publicly accepted.

The greatest obstacle to any settlement of the Palestinian issue has been the deadlock of the Israeli political system, a deadlock that has resulted in large part from the pervasiveness of the fear for survival. In theory, the United States, as the main economic and military prop of Israel, has had the means to break this deadlock by threatening to withhold assistance. But means of coercion that are potentially so destructive tend not to be usable. Moreover, the Israeli government has its own means of retaliation in the U.S. political system. Thus, Washington has been deterred from using its absolute weapons, and the Israeli "threat" of playing on the pro-Israeli forces and feelings in the United States has been far more effective than the theoretical U.S. ability to coerce Israel. For the United States to resort to its ultimate means, it needs to be in a position to show to the Israeli public and political forces that self-determination for the Palestinians is not a first step toward the destruction of Israel. Thus, two prenegotiations, in which unofficial personalities may play an important role, appear necessary: one between the United States and Arafat's PLO to define as much as possible in advance the assurances the PLO would give to Israel in exchange for self-determination, and one between the United States and the more moderate Israeli politicians to make sure they would accept and exploit a U.S. initiative for peace along the lines suggested here.

The Sadat precedent, often mentioned by Israelis, is not relevant: Sadat was chief of state; he came to Jerusalem in a position of force, knowing he would be well received and also that most Israelis did not consider the possession of the Sinai a matter of life and death. Arafat's position among his own people and in relation to Israel is completely different. Sadat was able, through his initiative, to pull the Carter administration with him and to push Israel toward peace by changing its political climate and by transforming Israeli perceptions not of "the Arabs" but of Egypt. In the case of the Palestinians, the United States (or the United States in cooperation with the Soviet Union) would have to do the pushing and the pulling.

A look back at U.S. policy shows that this course has never been tried. Jimmy Carter was struggling toward it when President Sadat went on his own spectacular but quite different course. One of the lessons of what could be called the Camp David period (November 1977–March 1979) is that it is not enough for the United States to serve as a benevolent mediator; the attempt to find a halfway point between Israel's tough negotiating stances and the Arab states can lead only to fiasco if both sides are equally firm, or to a compromise that satisfies mainly Israel if it is the Arab side that makes most of the concessions. One of the reasons the considerable U.S. economic leverage in the area has yielded so little in the strategic-diplomatic realm is that it has almost never been used to achieve comprehensive settlement. This explains both the limited results of the U.S. attempts at enlisting Arab states in joint military enterprises against Soviet expansionism and Israel's ability to manipulate U.S. policy despite its dependence on U.S. arms and money.

Events in 1990–1991 made matters much more difficult. The collapse of the U.S.-PLO dialogue, Arafat's fateful decision to lean toward Saddam Hussein in the crisis over Kuwait, and close cooperation between the United States and Israel during the Gulf war (after months of tension between the Shamir government and the Bush administration) have hardened positions on all sides. However, the principal obstacle remains a domestic one: the nature of the U.S. process of foreign policy elaboration and enforcement. But unless one is willing to accept George Kennan's gloomy verdict that a democracy such as the United States cannot have a coherent foreign policy, or to settle for the no less discouraging conclusion that its only domestically manageable external strategy must be a Manichaean one of straight cold war and containment, it is impossible to resign oneself to a prospect of paralysis.

The domestic task faced by a U.S. administration determined to move in the direction I have indicated is similar to the task it must undertake to enlist the cooperation of the Israeli body politic: It must be able to show, before it unveils its initiative, that the new path will be a reasonably safe one for Israel and that it has the support of Arab friends of the United States, particularly of those who are already on speaking terms with Israel. In addition, it will have to be able to prove that the Israeli government, or at least a major portion of the Israeli political forces, supports the initiative, so as to disarm those pro-Israeli groups in the United States that tend to be *plus royalistes que le roi.*

Two conclusions emerge. One, because the nature of the exercise far exceeds the dimensions of traditional state-to-state diplomacy, the involvement of the U.S. president will be indispensable at every step. Second, the public process will have to be anything *but* open-ended if it is to have any chance of succeeding. What took place openly between November 1977 and the Camp David meetings will have to occur behind the scenes, in a variety of forums. The challenge for U.S. statecraft, both abroad and at home, is monumental.

Notes

1. *On War* (Princeton: Princeton University Press, 1968).
2. *The Control of Nuclear Weapons* (N.Y.: Praeger, 1965).
3. *Peace and War* (N.Y.: Doubleday, 1966).
4. *The Rise of the Trading State* (N.Y.: Basic Books, 1986).
5. Harold H. Saunders, *The Other Walls: The Politics of the Arab-Israeli Peace Process* (Washington, D.C.: American Enterprise Institute, 1985); and "Reconstituting the Arab-Israeli Peace Process," in William B. Quandt, ed., *The Middle East: Ten Years After Camp David* (Washington, D.C.: Brookings Institution, 1988), pp. 413–441.

12
Lebanon: The Disparity Between Ideal Commitments and Practical Implementation

Ghassan Tuéni

This chapter does not claim, in the present context of Middle Eastern wars and revolutions, to be a comprehensive assessment of U.S. diplomacy. Its only ambition is to offer a case study of the U.S. role in the events of the mid-1980s that caused Lebanon to become a hostage to East-West confrontation. It was the Israeli invasion of Lebanon in 1982 that gave the Lebanese crisis its full international dimension. Indeed, it was the culmination of eleven dramatic years during which Lebanon had become a microcosm of all the crises, revolutions, and wars that had long divided the Middle East and imperiled international peace and security.

Assessing the impact of the 1982 Israeli invasion on present and future U.S. diplomacy is now passe—the 1991 Gulf war has changed radically the rules of the game. Furthermore, the end of the cold war was bound to alter not only U.S. behavior but also the attitudes and strategies of the various parties to the Middle East question. Additional influences, of course, will be the outcome of the Gulf war and its now-unpredictable fallout. All one can say at present is that Washington seemed, after its tragic Lebanese experiment, paralyzed by another "Vietnam Syndrome." Nervousness, bitterness, frustration, and symptoms of psychological withdrawal were displayed with determination and nurtured in arrogance—not the arrogance of power reacquired or rediscovered and then unleashed, but of power unused or misused. The U.S. intervention in the Lebanese crisis, even more than in Iran, demonstrated the uselessness of power when not at the service of a consistent, feasible, and credible policy.

It is beyond the scope of this chapter to review all the events that led to the invasion of Lebanon, to evaluate the invasion, or even to summarize the efforts deployed to bring about an acceptable and just settlement. We shall merely concentrate on four specific aspects of the U.S. role, going back to the first invasion of Lebanon in 1978, in the hope of drawing some pragmatic conclusions.

UNIFIL: Unfinished Peacekeeping

Although Washington knew that Israel sought a pretext for a major "punitive operation," it allowed the March 1978 invasion of south Lebanon to take place and intervened only when the invasion was about to go beyond its major stated objectives. Subsequently, at Lebanon's timid request, the United States proposed to the UN Security Council the formation of a UN interim peacekeeping force. As stated by the U.S. representative, the mandate of the force was to "confirm the withdrawal" of Israel beyond "the internationally recognized boundaries of Lebanon" and to "assist the Government of Lebanon in restoring its authority and regaining its sovereignty." Resolution 425 was passed unanimously by the Security Council on March 19, 1978, against a background of Arab euphoria, détente with the U.S.S.R., and confrontation with Israel.

The tragic, agonizing history of UNIFIL (United Nations Interim Force in Lebanon) is well known. Israel was allowed unhindered to establish a so-called security zone within Lebanon's internationally recognized boundaries, to govern this zone, and through it to conduct, with the help of a Lebanese mercenary army, offensive operations against both Lebanon and the UN, causing the death of many UNIFIL soldiers from nations friendly to the United States.

Never did Washington seriously try to persuade Israel to withdraw from this territory, the national identity of which, unlike occupied Palestine, was beyond dispute. And when Lebanon tried—at great cost and with understandable hesitation, despite past U.S. encouragement—to deploy its army in UNIFIL-controlled areas in the vicinity of the Israeli-occupied zones, Washington withdrew its support. Under Israeli pressure, it intervened to prevent even limited implementation of a Security Council resolution that it had itself initiated and continued to support, by approving subsequent resolutions.

Not content with using the political-military jungle of south Lebanon to prevent the deployment of Lebanese sovereignty, Israel was constantly challenging the legitimate government of Lebanon—an ally of the United States—and destabilizing the country. Its so-called open-game strategy with Syria served, in practical terms, to perpetuate the joint management of a multidimensional war that destroyed Lebanon's very structure.

The United States intervened seriously only once: to bring about a cease-fire when Syria's installation of Soviet missiles inside Lebanon gave the war a new strategic dimension. No steps were taken to prevent Syria from extending, by proxy, a Soviet umbrella over east Lebanon. Instead, Syrian deployment was limited by a "red line" drawn to the north of Israel's security zone and UNIFIL's area of operations.

Meanwhile, UNIFIL was left looking like a mere fixture on the political-military landscape. Although it maintained peace in its own area of operations, it could not even serve as an interposition force, let alone use "force in self-defense" as allowed by its terms of reference. Entrusted with a *dynamic* mission, UNIFIL was reduced to a *static* force. Never did the United States agree to support or even seriously consider Lebanon's proposal to redefine the force's mandate to make it more effective. Thus, when Israel launched its 1982 invasion, UNIFIL proved irrelevant.

The Sharon-Haig Secret Design

How General Sharon persuaded General Haig of his doctrine of reconstructing Lebanon by invading it is well known, as are the circumstances that led to Haig's later resignation as the U.S. secretary of state. In any case, the damage that resulted was disastrous and irreparable. The events that followed the 1982 invasion proved that no lesson was learned and that folly was to continue unchecked. Despite Washington's full diplomatic involvement and its proposal to create a U.S.-sponsored multinational force outside the framework of the UN, Israel was allowed to pursue its invasion. Lebanon's capital, Beirut, was destroyed and massacres of Palestinian civilians in the Sabra and Shatila camps were staged as soon as the PLO militias and the multinational force (including the U.S. Marines) departed. Israel finally occupied Beirut in blatant violation of the agreement negotiated by U.S. emissaries with the Lebanese government, Israel, and the PLO and to which the United States was committed.

Had the invasion been reversed, Israel would have been spared humiliation, defeat, and unprecedented casualties. Only catastrophes, human and political, could have resulted from Israel's appropriation of the freedom to destroy, rather than being impeached and literally forced to withdraw, immediately and unconditionally. Had the United States concurred with the international community and forced Israel to withdraw, it would have regained the confidence and trust of its allies, both in Europe and the Arab world. Diplomatic credibility could have served as an alternative to the use, and abuse, of force.

Instead, the United States placed itself outside the international consensus embodied in innumerable UN resolutions that were supported, though hestitatingly, by U.S. votes and opposed by Israel alone. By bringing the United States to this breach of consensus, which was also a breach of trust, Israel gained the United States. But the United States lost—almost irretrievably—Lebanon, its authority with the Arabs, and the confidence of some of its closest friends. Thus the United States, with its ambivalent diplomacy, jeopardized its own peace initiative.

May 17, 1983: The Impossible Agreement

The Lebanese proposed to restrict negotiations with Israel to terms of withdrawal, with appropriate security arrangements within the UN framework, on the basis of the 1949 general armistice agreement between Lebanon and Israel. Instead of accepting this proposal, Washington led the newly elected president of Lebanon to hold a quasi–peace conference. This move departed from President Reagan's stated position that withdrawal of Israeli forces from Lebanon should not be contingent on the peace treaty Israel wished to impose.

It also departed from the procedure successfully followed by Reagan's emissary, Ambassador Philip Habib. In July 1982, at the peak of the invasion, Habib had negotiated an agreement on force withdrawals and on the cessation of hostilities between warring parties (Israel, the PLO, Syria, and Lebanon) that did not even recognize each other and never met to negotiate.

The Israeli-imposed format was formal, legalistic, time-consuming, and politically costly, whereas Habib avoided all issues that were irrelevant and divisive, concentrating instead on matters that were strictly objective, limited, and implementable. He worked empirically from the particular to the general, from the specific to the comprehensive. Although he occasionally appeared to mark time, he never allowed himself or his interlocutors to become quagmired in such issues as representation, mutual recognition, commitments to seek normalization, or military cooperation between invaders and invaded.

By contrast, the tripartite negotiations that led to the May 17, 1983, accord were conducted with pomp and ceremony while "little wars" were being fueled. They threatened national and international security, ended all hope of peace, and further destroyed cities and villages. The Israeli negotiator was allowed by the United States, in the face of desperate resistance by the Lebanese, to impose the strangest innovation in international law—a full-fledged trade agreement appended to an agreement on cessation of hostilites—under the guise of "normalization."

More serious still was the self-annulment clause. An exchange of letters between the United States and Israel made Israeli withdrawal conditional upon and symmetrical with Syrian withdrawal. Syrian withdrawal, however, was neither negotiated nor negotiable—as expressly stated by Damascus. This clause should have rendered the accord superfluous before it was even signed and did cause it to be revoked after it had been approved by the Lebanese Parliament.

Indeed, when the agreement and the appended letters were about to be signed, Syria indicated its refusal to withdraw in the most unequivocal terms: by shelling the presidential palace while Secretary of State Shultz, returned from Damascus, was meeting with the Lebanese government to decide on final arrangements and a final course of action. This attitude rendered Israeli withdrawal problematic, to say the least. Furthermore, the time lost on U.S.-Israeli-Lebanese negotiations of academic issues allowed Syria to restore its military and political balance and the Soviets to stage a political comeback. Instead of organizing a symmetrical withdrawal, Israel and Syria pursued symmetrically their vicarious wars through Druzes, Maronites, and later Shiites. The War of the Mountain, which disrupted what was left of the fragile Lebanese unity, could not have occurred without the assistance the two regional powers gave to their respective client militias with each other's acquiescence.

All this happened under the noses of the freshly returned multinational force, while its commanders were engaged in Byzantine discussions on such matters as "terms of engagement," extension of the areas of operation, strategic routes, support or nonsupport of the Lebanese army, the use of force, and the limits of self-defense. When decisions were taken, they were either counterproductive or simply irrelevant.

Despite its international mandate, UNIFIL was becoming a forlorn demonstration of the axiom that a peacekeeping force can operate successfully only in a context of political and diplomatic consensus. No such context existed for the multinational force (MNF). On the contrary, this strangest of all peacekeeping forces had been operating since its inception in an environment of conflict, and it developed progressively into an instrument of confrontation. It became the tragic military expression of an equivocal diplomacy designed to enable the United States, assisted by a reluctant alliance, to solve the Lebanese question as the first step in a peace process that would exclude the Soviets.

The United States had become increasingly allergic to the UN Security Council, so it sacrificed internationality for efficacy and freedom of action. As a peacekeeping force, the MNF was committed to policy rather than consensus. Hence it should have been enabled to implement this policy. But U.S. politics made such implementation impossible. Despite a unique display of combined naval, air, and ground forces, including the almost mythical *New Jersey*, the deterrent effect of the MNF was nil. Military credibility was reduced by diplomatic hesitation and political unrealism.

The MNF and the Lebanese government—which the MNF was supposed to support—appeared to be engaged in a game of mutual delusions and illusions. The Lebanese government constantly misread the limits of the MNF's capacity to intervene in adverse circumstances even as a support force. Using the MNF as an adequate dissuasive force, ready to intervene, would have necessitated a quantitative and qualitative expansion of the various contingents, a move France, Italy, and the U.K. were not going to accept.

Furthermore, the command structure within the MNF contributed to the tragic misperceptions. It was beset by vagueness: Should decisions be made in Washington, Beirut, or in between? Was the MNF an army commanded by diplomats, by soldiers, or by politicians? Were the various national contingents supposed to act on their own or on orders issued by a multinational authority? And if the latter, at what level was coordination to be achieved?

Washington launched the MNF totally unprepared for the issues soon to be at stake: Was the MNF a *peacekeeping* or a *peace-enforcing* force? Or should it merely use military persuasion in support of diplomatic peacekeeping? And what was Washington seeking to achieve? Internal peace in Lebanon? Peace between Lebanon and Israel? Or the broader peace process, encompassing Syria and all the other participants in the Middle East conflict that were present on the Lebanese scene in one way or another?

Was this another Congo war? Another Korea? Or another Vietnam? Or was it—in imperial terms—a modern version of pax Romana, a Roman peace but without Roman legions?

These questions were still unanswered when tragedy struck. On October 23, 1983, suicide squads simultaneously destroyed the headquarters and barracks of the U.S. Marines and French troops. The death toll was almost 300, but the political casualty, equally important, was the May 17 agreement and U.S. commitment to Lebanon's peace, security, and integrity.

Four months later, on February 29, 1984, while the Marines were giving up their last positions at Beirut International Airport to Shia Amal militias and West Beirut was being taken over by the opposition forces, the U.S.S.R. vetoed a French proposal at the Security Council to replace the MNF with an enlarged UN force. The United States reluctantly agreed with the proposal, but only when it had become too late.

Terrorism: Who Is Hostage to What?

The phrase "America held hostage" acquired currency during the Iran crisis and was also applied to Lebanon. U.S. citizens were taken hostage one after another, according to a logic intelligible only to the extremists who took them. The United States was also held hostage in an institutional manner. The U.S. embassy was the target of recurrent shelling and bombing, with an intolerable number of casualties. The American University of Beirut and other institutions were placed under permanent threat of kidnapping and assassination. And the Marines, the instruments of U.S. peacemaking, were transformed into a terrorized liability.

Freeing the hostages became the principal objective in a policy of "combating terrorism," rather than achieving a political settlement in Lebanon and in the maze of Middle Eastern conflicts. Freeing the hostages came to mean freeing the Marines or, in military terminology, disengaging.

Reviewing the U.S. policy on terrorism—if such a policy exists—is far beyond the scope of this chapter. Terrorism has assumed broader international proporations since the attack on Libya, and threats against Syria and others were added to the constant undertone directed against the PLO and the Palestinians in general. The following observations, however, pertain to the topic:

- If Lebanon has actually become a "haven for international terrorism," it has done so because it was allowed to harbor regional and international conflicts that exploded the structures of society and rendered government totally inadequate as an instrument of law and order. Exacerbated internal conflicts became the ideal context for the development of vicarious acts of terror.
- U.S. policy has not addressed the causes of such terrorism—the "logic of despair" behind the suicidal acts—but merely the consequences. Reluctant to use force because of its doubtful efficacy, the United States tried to soften, coax, or pressure political interlocutors—particularly Syria and Iran—that could influence the so-called terrorists and ultimately contain them. In this framework Lebanon ceased to be an interlocutor; in the diabolic game, it became a stake (and not the one most important)— exchangeable when the need arises, and dispensable if and when necessary.
- On the assumption that Lebanon had lost its credibility, its sovereignty, and its unity as a state, political and military dialogues were conducted directly with Lebanese factions. Although the

restoration of Lebanese unity was always stressed as an ultimate objective, the end result was a confirmation of the long-held Israeli strategy favoring partition. Leaders of religious and ethnic communities were accepted as the only valid interlocutors. After allowing Israel to pursue this strategy, the United States adopted it under the pretext that factions could deliver results—and hostages—whereas the Lebanese state could not. In this way the United States contributed to a partitioning of Lebanon that it had constantly condemned. By dealing with the new realities of partition in this manner instead of supporting reunification by convergence, the United States lent encouragement to the divergent forces by according them recognition. The dynamics of disunity that had been set in motion by the internal war were thus fueled and consecrated by external strategic interests.

Were any hostages delivered by this policy? Some, yes, but at tremendous cost. And U.S. policy remained crippled by (not to say hostage to) ever-increasing dilemmas and incompatible imperatives. Above all, Lebanon itself was condemned to being hostage to the following:

- The East-West confrontation, in which Lebanon found the United States ineffective, but was reluctant to slide toward the U.S.S.R. through the Syrian connection.
- The regional players—Israel, Syria, the Palestinians, and later the Iranians—each holding either territory or factions as bits and pieces of sovereignty, but unable to hold more, and unable to make peace or to settle their differences by war.
- The indigenous warlords who, having lost their freedom through their wars, were neither free to make peace nor free to pursue the impossible victories they set out to achieve.

In Lieu of a Conclusion

No further conclusions need be drawn in this chapter, beyond those implied throughout the analysis. In summary, however, the following ideas may be worth reflecting upon if a new U.S. diplomacy is to be constructed in the near future:

1. The failure of U.S. diplomacy in Lebanon and more generally in the Middle East stems from the ever-growing gap between ends and means—the disparity between proclaimed ideals and accepted policies. The use of massive means as political expedients could only lead to tragic failures and deepen the estrangement and frustration.

2. No policy can be successful if it deals only with the apparent consequences and not with the causes of crises and conflicts. Eliminating the causes is surely beyond the reach either of diplomacy or of military action. Both diplomacy and its military instruments must be geared to international and regional strategies. In this context, sheer force has proved impotent. But dialogue can produce results only in cases where common terms of reference are established, common goals are found, and a show of force can be used for persuasion and peacemaking.

3. The United States must renounce its determination to solve problems alone. In Lebanon, the United States can neither vanquish nor exclude other parties to the disputes. Even "indirect" parties have defeated or challenged U.S. initiatives or have acquired the means to do so. Peace initiatives can be successful only in a context of consensual policy, regional when possible but international when there is a strategic dimension. Common goals can be sought, and common interests can be found even with the U.S.S.R. when peace is the ultimate objective. If the military alternative is chosen, it will be neither peacemaking nor a peace initiative but, at best, an extreme form of peace enforcement. Such strategy has proved too costly and has often been counterproductive because an enforced settlement produces new problems that require still greater use of force.

Can the Lebanon Syndrome, or Vietnam Syndrome 2, be overcome? Washington has given many signals that it will try again to intervene in Lebanon and/or to help solve the Lebanese problem, if assured of the results. Situations of extreme flux like that in Lebanon offer no guarantee of success. Low-key diplomacy may be required, a "twilight-zone" diplomacy—tolerant, flexible, and pragmatic. Success will require a realistic recognition of new forces and factors and of new problems and aspirations, particularly those emerging from the development of the crisis and the war.

U.S. diplomacy can still conciliate and serve as a catalyst if it is prepared to go all the way in investing in goodwill and understanding. In any effort of reconstruction, sociopolitical or socioeconomic, U.S. means, which can never be matched by other nations, must be used without parsimony, but with reason and in the spirit of conciliation. Whatever the cost, it will be less than the cost of even the smallest "surgical" military intervention.

Arabs have tended to wage war with Soviet weapons and assistance but to seek peace in partnership with the United States. Lebanon has been alone in turning to the United States for both war and peace. Yet Lebanon feels as frustrated as any other Arab state. War has been a universal failure. Peace should still represent a valid option for all, both the vanquished of yesterday and the victors of today.

What the Gulf war has achieved so far can only confirm us in our attitude. Let us hope that nothing irreparable should happen that will render the so-called new order in the Middle East impossible—and Lebanon's independence and sovereignty more problematic than ever.

13

A Jordanian Perspective
on the United States
in the Middle East

El Hassan bin Talal

As seen by friends of the United States in the Middle East, U.S. foreign policy results from the interplay of sometimes contradictory philosophical and political factors. In the period since World War II, the United States appears to have had great difficulty in producing a policy that integrates the traditional diplomacy of global power politics with the fact that its security often depends on the ability to involve itself with understanding and sensitivity in the political dynamics of post-colonial nations in a region such as the Middle East. Similarly, U.S. scholars have themselves recognized the difficulty U.S. citizens have had in integrating their deep historical commitment to the ideals of the U.S. Declaration of Independence with the conflict they feel between the requirements of traditional power politics and the aspirations of nations that have themselves recently emerged from colonial status. As seen through friendly eyes, the challenge facing the United States at the end of the twentieth century is to find some way to integrate these contradictory factors and to produce a clear vision of its role and purpose in the world. Nowhere have these contradictions been more apparent than in the Middle East.

The U.S. concept of diplomacy should not be viewed or evaluated exclusively within the context of power relations and politics, but must also include an understanding of the overall principles that govern the U.S. system. At one time the U.S. model of democracy and social organization, with all the ideals it embodies, was held up as a prototype for other nations to emulate. To the rest of the world, the United States was the country that had successfully broken the bonds of colonization. This prompted the emergent nations to look to the United States as a model and as a source of support in their own struggle for freedom and independence. Their belief in Wilsonian ideals dominated their concept of political reality and prevented them from understanding the implications and intricacies of international power politics.

During and after World War I, U.S. diplomacy embarked upon a moral crusade based on the fundamental principles of democracy and equality as first manifested in the Declaration of Independence: "We hold these Truths to be self-evident, that all Men are created equal, that they are endowed by their Creator with certain unalienable Rights, that among these are Life, Liberty, and the Pursuit of Happiness." This was understood as a comprehensive statement, instantly doing away with racial, ethnic, national, and religious differences. President Woodrow Wilson, demonstrating his concern for "all the rights and liberties of small nations," took these principles one step further. He devised a formula that would apply to the world at large: the right of all peoples to self-determination. His belief that war resulted from greed, power politics, and nationalism and his assumption that the nations of the world needed an international forum for rational discussion prompted him to call for the establishment of the League of Nations. Thus, Wilson conceived a plan for settling world disputes and created a new form of world diplomacy whose hallmark was the term "open covenants openly arrived at," which he introduced into the lexicon of international politics. Wilsonian diplomacy signified that making the world safe for democracy and the attainment of self-determination meant not only making the world safe for freedom but also ensuring the viability of the U.S. system.

In the first decades of the twentieth century, democracy and national self-determination were conceived as the main ingredients for peace and order. The philosophy of international relations at that time seemed coherent and straightforward, as did the choice of diplomatic methods and procedures. Such procedures are as vital as the clarity and coherence of the policy they are intended to promote. An unfortunate flaw of the democratic system is that it tends to assume that the burden of this clarity of vision in diplomacy falls not on the democracy itself but upon the other concerned states. This, at least, was probably true of the United States in the pre–World War II era, when U.S. democracy was not a major factor in the international policies of the Middle East. Before World War I, U.S. interest in the area was largely confined to·the educational and religious fields, until during the interwar years commercial interests began to gain importance and the State Department assumed the role of a broker, reconciling the differences arising between the entrepreneur and the missionary lobby.

Several factors account for the enlarged U.S. role in the Middle East in the wake of World War II. Chief among these were the U.S.

concept of Soviet expansionism, the increasing strategic importance of the region, the establishment of the state of Israel, and energy resources. These factors combined caused the United States to abandon its earlier policy of isolationism and to expand greatly its role in foreign affairs. With the promulgation of the Truman doctrine, a policy of "containment" of the growing international role of the Soviets was adopted, leading to greater U.S. involvement in Middle East politics. This new involvement, in turn, required a more subtle and effective diplomatic role for the United States. New devices and techniques had to be formulated and new channels found in conformity with its interests and its new role of superpower, particularly in the wake of the waning British dominance in the area. The most difficult task confronting U.S. diplomacy at that time was that of persuading the rising nations that its newly acquired political role and its rivalry with the U.S.S.R. had become matters of prime importance. U.S. diplomacy had to contend with the dilemma of reconciling basic U.S. interests with traditional ideals and thinking. The burden of "clarity of vision" in diplomacy now fell squarely upon the United States and not merely upon the other states concerned.

The rise of the U.S.S.R. as both a nuclear and a strategic rival power entailed, in most cases, globalization of regional conflicts. The advancing process of East-West polarization contained the danger of direct confrontation between the two global powers. It was this, according to Winston Churchill, that caused the "balance of power" in Europe to be replaced by a "balance of terror." Within such a context the United States began to think of the third world as a "soft area of power vacuums" to be filled by one of the superpowers. With such a newly acquired political perspective, U.S. diplomacy had to face the challenges of both the conflict diplomacy of the cold war and the traditional diplomatic methods of dealing with the countries of the third world. It was for this reason that during the Eisenhower administration the United States reverted to "coalition diplomacy." This failed in its wider application, because it did not address the real issues in the Middle East and was perceived by the former colonial nations as a new form of imperialism. Its insensitivity to the region's history created further complications.

Current U.S. diplomacy, suffering at times from lack of clarity, coherence, and resolution, is a function of the U.S. doctrines on strategy and conflict as adopted by the White House and the State Department: the debate between the globalist and the regionalist schools of thought. The globalists view the Middle East and its problems as a manifestation of the cold war and the struggle for power between Washington and Moscow, while the regionalists emphasize that regional problems should be approached as such, each on its own merit independent of the global competition between East and West.

Preoccupied with the wider scope of strategic balance, globalists are often insensitive to regional issues. John Foster Dulles's style expressed in his withdrawal of the offer to sell arms to Egypt and to finance the contruction of the Aswan Dam was, in the words of Mahmoud Riad, "arbitrary and abusive." More recently, Henry Kissinger and Alexander Haig provided good examples of advocates and practitioners of the globalist school of thought, both in theory and in practice. Their approach to the Middle East conflict was devoid of interest in an understanding of the core issue—the Palestine problem—or the real concerns and sensibilities of the area. Their prime interest was to assess the status of the parties involved by classifying them into "friendly" or "hostile" partners of the United States or the U.S.S.R.

In the wake of the October 1973 war and the Arab oil embargo, the Middle East became a focus of U.S. diplomatic attention. Kissinger, prompted by his belief that limited agreements could be achieved by compromising on some measures and by dealing with one Arab country at a time, embarked on his step-by-step diplomacy. As it turned out, he once again displayed his insensitivity to the area: His major concern was not to address the fundamental questions or to provide solutions to them, rather it was to dilute and defuse difficult situations. The beginnings of crisis management were his "shuttle diplomacy," in the course of which he traveled to and from the Middle East no fewer than ten times and carried out all negotiations himself. The tactic brought about disengagement agreements with both Syria and Egypt, but it did not seriously attempt to produce anything concrete on the Jordanian-Israeli side, nor did it address the heart of the Middle East conflict— the Palestinian issue.

Kissinger's diplomacy did not succeed in providing a comprehensive settlement, not because he lacked the tactical skills or the necessary articulation for negotiations and mediation, but simply because he did not "speak the language" of the Middle East. He ignored the crux of the conflict: the Arab consensus of 1974, designating the PLO "as the sole legitimate representative of the Palestinian people." Although Kissinger's impact on U.S. diplomacy is undeniable, his political vision of this area was indeed impaired by his indifference toward the Palestinian problem. Although indirect diplomatic contact did take place between the United States and the PLO, Kissinger issued a policy statement on the PLO that remained official U.S. policy until late 1988. The United States "will not recognize or negotiate with the Palestine Liberation Organization so long as the Palestine Liberation Organization does not recognize Israel's right to exist and does not accept Security Council

Resolutions 242 and 338." Why such a policy was made in the first place and why it continued so long baffled the peoples of the Middle East, who inevitably recalled how in the case of Vietnam the United States was negotiating with the Viet Cong while simultaneously fighting them in the field—which was not the case between the United States and the PLO.

The advent of the Carter presidency promised a new approach and a different form of diplomacy from that of his predecessor. The legacy of the globalist school was not, however, to be discarded by the incoming administration. During the first year of President Carter's term, several indicators rekindled hopes for a comprehensive settlement, and the approach entailed a new style of diplomacy that would allow for a Soviet role and a positive contribution by all the parties concerned in the conflict, including the Palestinians. These indicators ranged from Carter's involvement with human rights issues, to sympathetic and respectful gestures toward the Palestinians, to the more specific statements concerning a homeland for the Palestinians and advocating their legitimate rights.[1]

Within such a context, it was felt that the Carter administration was striving for a Wilsonian approach, entailing rational discussion among the contesting nations. Such a form of diplomacy was envisaged in the reconvening of a Geneva Middle East peace conference. All hopes for the Geneva conference were thwarted, however, and Carter shifted from the diplomacy of the Geneva conference to that of Camp David, signifying a reversion to piecemeal solutions and to Kissinger's step-by-step diplomacy.

The horizon of such diplomacy is limited: It does not allow for a comprehensive vision of all the factors and players concerned or of the multiple regional and global interests. Morover, because it is literally a one-person diplomatic function, it also leaves little room for superpower partnership. The Lebanese problem has given ample proof of the shortcomings of such a diplomacy and the inability of the United States to produce results in this way, even with the support of various diplomatic missions and despite the show of U.S. force. Furthermore, the belief that diplomacy and power must always go hand in hand is questionable. The past decade shows that unless the United States deals with the political dynamics of the region, its diplomacy will face continual challenges in the Middle East.

The advent of the United States as leader of the free world after World War II, along with the intensification of superpower rivalry, forced the United States to resort to operational means to strengthen and enhance its diplomatic moves. President Truman's introduction of the policy of containment, reinforced by the provisions of the Eisenhower doctrine, necessitated supportive means to enable U.S. diplomacy to maneuver and pursue its struggle with the U.S.S.R. for the minds of people. Rivalry between the two power camps was not confined to the European arena alone but encompassed the entire world. The attention of both superpowers was focused primarily upon the nonaligned nations.

Their direct involvement, however, was a function of world power politics rather than a result of an analysis of the objective local situations. The quest for the containment of Soviet expansion in the Middle East led the United States to seek the collaboration of all the states in the region irrespective of their relationships with each other. Moreover, to their own detriment, U.S. policymakers were (and still are) likely to gloss over the significance of the Arab-Israeli dispute in determining the international alignment of the Arab states. They did not seem to realize the Soviets attained a position of power and influence not only by virtue of their acquired superpower status but also through skillful manipulation of the dynamics of the Arab-Israeli conflict. Comprehension of the deep sense of national injury and humiliation felt by the Arabs enabled the Soviet Union to obtain its position as a power to be reckoned with in the region.

Thus, today in many parts of the Arab world, the U.S.S.R. is looked upon as a friend—indeed, an ally—whereas the United States is regarded as an antagonist. Nonetheless, U.S. policymakers, without taking Arab sensibilities into account or adopting an approach that would make suitable provision for a just and lasting settlement of the Palestinian question, expected (and continue to expect) the Arab states to join Israel and the United States in checking the expansion of Soviet power and influence in the region.

To achieve the desired end, the United States felt it merely had to adopt a policy of aid, both financial and military. Such aid was naturally welcomed by developing nations and indeed was at times vital to them; Jordan in its turn benefited from such assistance. Jordan welcomed U.S. aid and sought a qualitative relationship with the United States despite frequent vilification campaigns by other states in the region. At times, Jordan has been dubbed an ally of "Western imperialism," a position that suggests laxity toward Israel. Nonetheless, Jordan has managed to sustain its friendship with the United States while persisting in its pursuit of a centrist position, a stand that has been under constant attack by extremists in both the Arab world and Israel.

The United States had no compunction about using the promise of aid to exert pressure, especially when its diplomatic efforts seemed likely to fall short of achieving the desired result. After Camp David, for example, the United States did not hestitate to put pressure on Jordan to join the negotiations. Jordan suddenly found itself threatened with a suspension of aid should it fail to comply. Such tactics are in marked contrast with U.S. dealings with Israel. In the early 1970s, for example, the U.S. administration debated not whether to suspend military aid to Israel but whether to give it incentives toward peacemaking or to reward it for ceding the occupied territories. The latter approach focused on whether Israel should be supplied with sufficient armaments to give it a feeling of security, regardless of the extent to which it cooperated with the United States. This "arms for flexibility" approach (commonly known as a "hardware for software" approach), unfortunately still followed, was resorted to after the failure of the plan of Secretary of State William Rogers in late 1969.

Notably, the U.S.-Israeli strategic cooperation agreement of November 1983 allocated further military grants to Israel and also included a number of provisions that virtually made it a U.S. ally, with access not only to weapons but also to advanced intelligence and military technology. By contrast, President Reagan had to justify to the United Jewish Appeal the request for a proposed arms sale of Stinger missiles to Jordan and Saudi Arabia, a sale he eventually had to withdraw in the face of overwhelming congressional resistance. President Reagan's justification of the proposed sale derived from Jordan's legitimate needs in its "defense requirements against Syria and Iran." The whole affair indicated a willingness of the United States to sacrifice its friends as well as some of its basic principles and to jeopardize national interest to appease the Zionist lobby, but it also revealed a lack of political sensitivity toward Jordan's position in inter-Arab politics. The double standards and the partiality of the United States in dealing with its Arab friends and Israel played into the hands of the more radical elements, while the identification of Arab moderates as tacit friends and allies of Israel inevitably aggravated inter-Arab rivalries.

In a review of U.S. diplomatic efforts in the Middle East, the most immediate and striking feature is its lack of success not only in resolving the area's basic problems but also in defusing them effectively. The Rogers peace plan of 1969–1970 failed to achieve any tangible result, and for three years U.S. policy suffered a standstill in the area.

In the wake of the October 1973 war and the ensuing Arab oil embargo, the Middle East once again became the focus of U.S. diplomatic efforts. It would seem that U.S. diplomacy, rather than being oriented toward the long term, is activated only during a major crisis or immediately thereafter. Moreover, in retrospect, U.S. policy appears expressly designed to lull Arab sensibilities into a false sense of hope. Cynical Arab hindsight conjectures that U.S. diplomatic efforts, visits, and shuttle diplomacy were no more than attempts to anesthetize rather than cure the situation. The periodic flurries of activity appear deliberately designed to give the illusion of progress, though in fact nothing but Kissinger's personal contacts occurred, suggesting movement but ultimately going nowhere. Likewise, other U.S. channels of communication in the form of messages, personal visits of high officials and emissaries, and mediation have achieved no results. Although the United States maintained its policy of nonrecognition of the PLO, it encouraged Saudi Arabia to play a major role in the Lebanese crisis. Through the successful mediation of Saudi Arabian and United Nations officials in Lebanon, Philip Habib, U.S. presidential special envoy to the Middle East, concluded a cease-fire agreement between the PLO and Israel, signed on July 24, 1981. That agreement held firm for almost a year, until Israel invaded Lebanon in the summer of 1982, probably with prior U.S. knowledge.

The hesitancy, even lack of consistency, in U.S. diplomacy, finds another illustration in the U.S. view of the PLO. Why the United States continued its policy of noncontact with the PLO so long needs explanation. It is an open secret that as early as the Nixon administration, the United States had indirect contacts with the PLO, contacts that intensified during the Carter administration, raising expectations that a meaningful relationship between the United States and the PLO would develop.[2]

Such a relationship did not finally develop, and U.S.-PLO contacts remained covert almost to the end of the Reagan administration. Secretary of State Alexander Haig, committed to the globalist school of thought, conceived of Israel as a strategic asset and of the PLO as a threat to U.S. interests. His two concerns were the Soviet threat to the Middle East and the continued flow of oil to the West. Although Haig's obsession with oil security and his concept of the Soviet threat were understandable, they finally had the negative consequence of placing the Middle East crisis in the context of superpower rivalry. From an Arab regional perspective, such a development had the effect of a freeze, which threatened the moderates of the area. Since 1967, Arab moderates have struggled against Israeli attempts at polarizing the Middle East conflict between the two superpowers. Unfortunately, Haig's strategic consensus theory suited Israeli plans because they were plans designed to maintain the status quo.

Coming as they did in the wake of the Israeli invasion of Lebanon, the resignation of Alexander Haig and the appointment of George Shultz as the new secretary of state, followed by the Reagan peace plan of September 1, 1982, indicated renewal in the momentum toward peace in the area. U.S. diplomatic efforts concentrated essentially on Lebanon, allowing the Lebanese crisis to overshadow the Arab-Israeli conflict. The burden of the diplomatic effort to launch the Reagan plan into the right orbit fell on Jordan. Jordan was to secure a Palestinian mandate before the process of negotiation based on the plan began.

Israel's reaction to the Reagan initiative was immediate and decisive, with Prime Minister Begin's instant rejection of it as a "lifeless stillborn." Notwithstanding, Jordan launched a seven-month dialogue with the PLO that stalled on April 10, 1983. In retrospect, part of the blame for the failure of the Jordanian-Palestinian dialogue must be laid on a lack of confidence in the initiative. Although President Reagan spoke of the "immediate adoption of a settlement freeze by Israel," the optimistic mood, as it turned out, was not translated into action, and Israel, after the "safe and orderly" withdrawal of PLO military forces from Beirut, allowed the massacres at the Sabra and Shatila refugee camps to take place.

Even the initial diplomatic success of the May 17, 1983, agreement, which Secretary of State Shultz managed to secure between Israel and Lebanon, has proved impractical. Here again, U.S. diplomacy was not credible. It failed to take into consideration not only the dynamics of the Lebanese domestic scene but also those of the region, and the agreement, which addressed itself strictly to the side effects rather than the heart of the problem, collapsed.

As for a settlement freeze, the United States refrained from exerting any diplomatic pressure whatsoever on Israel to adopt such a policy. Shortly after the declaration of the plan, Michael Dekel, Israeli deputy minister of agriculture in charge of settlements, stated: "In opposition to the political thesis of Reagan, we answer with the erection of political facts in the area." At this point, according to the *New York Times* of November 12, 1982, President Reagan, when asked whether he would consider sanctions against Israeli settlement policy, answered that it would not be "good diplomacy."

Furthermore, the United States declined to use its influence with Israel to persuade it to allow representatives of West Bank residents, who were members of the Palestinian National Council, a parliamentary forum, to attend a proposed meeting of that council in December 1984. The West Bank members formed a substantial moderate block within the Palestinian National Council that could have strengthened the peace process.

Neither in the initial stages of its promulgation nor later was the Reagan plan accompanied by positive diplomatic efforts. It was observed in the region that no cabinet-level member of the administration was working on the difficulties that the plan encountered at the time; both George Shultz and Caspar Weinberger were wholly involved with the budget. Such an attitude froze the plan rather than reinforced its intention of placing a freeze on Israeli settlements in the occupied territories.

Disarray in the Arab world was indisputably a factor in the confused efforts following the initiative. Moderates saw it as a first step toward a peace settlement based on United Nations resolution 242, while radicals rejected it out of hand. Many, however, dismissed the initiative as simply another palliative, designed to forestall a comprehensive settlement rather than to serve as a step toward resolution of the conflict. That the United States did not pursue its own initiative with vigor gave a certain amount of credibility to that view. The inconsistency of the U.S. approach allowed a symbiosis to emerge as a result of the all-important interaction between Israeli and Arab extremist attitudes. Opposed and unrelated as they may appear to be, there is little doubt that the territorial claims of expansionist Israelis fed and fueled the rejectionist posture of radical Arabs, as both battled for the maximalist demands.

Although the United Nations in many ways represents the Wilsonian concept of world diplomacy—a forum of rational discussion—U.S. practices there have not managed to approximate Wilson's moral standard or the "moral imperative" to which President Reagan alluded in his peace proposals.

The political and moral support given to Israel in the arena has not only frustrated Arab moderates and the peace process but has also given credence to both Israeli and Arab extremists. Arab as well as other foreign observers have genuinely come to question the seriousness and, indeed, the credibility of the United States in the whole process. Although to create confidence in his initiative the president once called for a freeze on Israeli settlements, the U.S. characterization of the establishment of Israeli settlements as "illegal" soon changed to being simply an "obstacle" to the peace process. Subsequently the peace effort eroded still further for lack of decisive action on the part of the administration. In fact, the U.S. veto of a resolution against the establishment of Israeli settlements in the West Bank was a veritable study in retrenchment. The extent of support from the United States for its own declared principle was limited to a vote in November 1978 for a Security Council declaration, not a resolution, deploring Israeli measures that have altered the demographic composition or geographic nature of the West Bank. In 1980, when its United Nations delegate voted for a resolution against Israeli settlements in the West Bank, it was claimed that the vote had been a mistake.

As one tool in foreign policy, diplomacy must operate within the limits of that policy. It is U.S. policy to maintain the state of Israel—a policy that need not be questioned here either as it affects U.S. or Arab interests or indeed as it furthers justice and world peace. To what extent and to what extreme that policy is to be carried out are, however, reasonable questions. In the 1980s U.S. diplomacy spared little in its efforts to protect Israel from the political and moral isolation of world opinion. Even when the extremist Likud, with its avowed expansionist designs and actions, assumed power in Israel, U.S. diplomacy and policy changed little. Despite mild condemnations of Israel, no real change in attitude or strategy occurred. Once again there was an illusion of activity, yet it remained simply an illusion; Israel is still where it wants to be and no real progress has been made. On the contrary, with each succeeding year or administration, U.S. support for Israel, diplomatic or otherwise, seems to have grown.

The Arab states have to contend with a peculiar set of relationships, not only between Israel and the United States but also between U.S. Zionists and Israel. This intricate web is rendered more complex by the two-tiered relationship that the United States seems to have established with Israel. The unique pattern is governed by the concept of Israel as a small embattled state, sharing many of the goals and values of the United States, while as a regional power, it simultaneously performs the role of a surrogate of the United States in its global strategy, linked, however tenuously, with the Western defense system. Viewed in this light, there is a desperate need for the United States to decide which Israel it expects the Arabs to deal with. Israeli-U.S. interaction at all levels—economic, industrial, social, political, and military—has established an organic link between the two states that the United States must reduce to avoid the identification of its policy with that of Israel.

Congress in general and the Senate in particular have been more forthright than the presidency in their support of Zionist demands. As in recent years the efforts of the Zionist lobby have succeeded in influencing a growing number of members, the support for Israel has grown stronger, often to the detriment of U.S. interests in the area. The expanding role of Congress in the field of foreign relations has at times handicapped, if not hamstrung, the president's efforts. For example, congressional resistance to the administration's promise of arms sales to Saudi Arabia and Jordan was so strong that it forced the administration to modify or cancel the deal.

Efforts within Congress to relocate the U.S. embassy in Israel from Tel Aviv to Jerusalem is another example of congressional power within the field of foreign affairs. True, the administration has resisted this pressure, but the spectacle, unjust as it is, presents a confused picture to the outside world and inspires further anger and frustration in the Arabs.

The issue of Jerusalem is of concern not merely to the Arab states but to the entire Islamic world. The city's special significance for the three monotheistic religions prompted the United States to endorse the United Nations proposal of 1947, which under part three provided a special *regime corpus separatum* for the City of Jerusalem. Since then, in his 1982 peace plan, President Reagan called for an undivided Jerusalem whose ultimate status would be subject to negotiations. If the United States relocated its embassy, this would have signified U.S. endorsement of Jerusalem as the capital of Israel. The U.S. executive would have been held accountable for causing not only embarrassment to U.S. diplomacy but also a major setback to any U.S. role in both the Arab and the Islamic countries, as well as flagrant violation of international law and practice.

In addition to the struggle between Congress and the administration, which obstructs effective diplomacy in the Middle East, the administration seems to suffer from interoffice conflicts. These clashes have at times been the result of basic differences in policy orientation, as between Secretary of State William Rogers, the regionalist, and Henry Kissinger, the globalist. It was partly because of these differences that the Rogers peace plan failed in 1970. Former U.S. diplomats in the area, mistakenly in Jordan's view, attributed the collapse of the plan simply to the fact that it was Rogers's plan and not Kissinger's. Finally, the U.S. electorate, which forms a substantial political power, constitutes another domestic constraint. Because the country is in a perpetual state of election and preelection, the concerned electorate consists of three percent of the population and includes the Jewish community, which is organized and coordinated by the American-Israel Public Affairs Committee (AIPAC).[3] Accordingly, candidates are usually preoccupied with pleasing that particular electorate and living up to its expectations. Although a number of members of Congress have been sympathetic to the Palestinian cause, few have been strong enough to resist AIPAC efforts.

Jordan remains committed to a just and durable peace in the Middle East, but after the failure of George Shultz's peace mission in winter 1988 (which offered too little, too late to make an impact), Jordan embarked on an exhaustive reassessment of its role in the peace process and of its relation with the PLO and the occupied territories. Despite a general recognition of the long chain of historical, cultural, economic, and political links that bind the people of the two banks of the Jordan, the nation decided to sever administrative and legal links with the occupied West Bank in July 1988. The underlying reasons for this measure were varied. Having contended with the ambiguity of U.S. policy, the political immobility that characterized the approach of the national unity government in Israel to peacemaking, and the vacilation of the PLO, Jordan embarked on a bold course to break the deadlock. The immediate effect of the July 1988 decision was that Jordan would no longer be regarded as an interlocutor by the United States, a surrogate of the PLO by Israel, and a hindrance by the PLO.

The July measures removed all doubts that Jordan harbored territorial ambitions in the occupied territories. They emphasized that historical association between Jordan and the West Bank did not preclude the Palestinian people and their sole legitimate representative, the PLO, from assuming full responsibilities to determine their destiny. The PLO would undertake the duty of deciding the future course of action in the search for a peaceful and equitable settlement of the Palestine question. In doing so, the PLO would take account of the hopes and aspirations of all its constituents, especially those in the occupied territories, who have been calling for the adoption of more practical policies to break the prevailing impasse. In short, the PLO has to focus on the territorial dimension of the Palestinians' legitimate right to nationhood.

The Jordanian disengagement from the occupied territories has caused some apprehension among Palestinian communities in Jordan, in the occupied territories, and in the diaspora. Their alarm is a consequence of the move intended to highlight the significance of Palestinian national identity and the commitment to safeguard the integrity of the occupied territories. The important but emotive issue of nationality would be settled within the framework to exercise the right to national self-determination by the Palestinian people. This was made clear in a constitutional stipulation in 1951 when the union of the two banks of the Jordan was achieved. Both Jordanians and Palestinians made a commitment that the union of their two countries would in no way prejudice the outcome of a final settlement of the Palestinian question. The principle has been the foundation of Jordan's policy and has guided all its action in the long search for a just and lasting peace in the region. It was signified in the Jordanian recognition of the PLO as "the sole legitimate representative of the Palestine people" and reinforced by the July measures.

This notwithstanding, Jordan's measures have proved timely and fortuitous. It has led to a serious and radical revision of familiar positions and outmoded policy approaches by the PLO, the United States, and Israel. I feel certain that without the July measures that placed the PLO at center stage, the deliberations of the PNC meeting in Algiers in November 1988 would not have been possible. This was followed by the address of the PLO chairman to the United Nations General Assembly on December 13 and his subsequent pronouncements at a press conference the following day. In many ways these moves have radically altered the parameters of peacemaking diplomacy in the Middle East.

Jordan's concern has not been confined to bilateral talks with the PLO but has encompassed the general Arab consensus. The disarray that has plagued inter-Arab relations is detrimental not only to Arab national interests but also to the peace process. The separate peace that Egypt concluded in 1979 should not be repeated. It would plunge the

Arab world into renewed fratricidal feuds and conflicts and almost inevitably trigger a fresh wave of extremist politics.

Jordan embarked on a fresh start to rebuild Arab political consensus. The moves aimed at inter-Arab coordination and cooperation required both Arab and international support as political moderation became increasingly rare and difficult to sustain. The moderate states felt the need to stand together as a bulwark against extremist radical tendencies. In pursuit of these objectives, the Jordanian-Palestinian accord of February 11, 1985, was concluded to push the peace process forward. In a bid to readmit Egypt to the Arab fold, diplomatic relations with Egypt were restored. The reconciliation between Egypt and the Palestine Liberation Organization received Jordanian encouragement and endorsement. Close consultations between the parties are continuing to keep the peace process open and viable. The ultimate objective of these efforts was the formulation of a united Arab platform so that all the parties concerned could move forward in unison toward an overall settlement terminating the Arab-Israeli conflict once and for all. The risks entailed in its continuation are incalculable. It has already brought the region and the world close to the nuclear abyss, and the danger of nuclear conflagration igniting in the area is always present.

It has to be recognized that the Middle East is neither immune to nor isolated from the threat of a nuclear conflagration. Nuclear weapons are already in the region. The United States maintains a nuclear presence in Turkey and aboard nuclear-armed submarines in and around regional waters. More significantly, Israel has both a sizable nuclear capability and is known to deploy nuclear missiles. Its nuclear program has benefited from the direct and indirect support of nuclear and near-nuclear powers, including South Africa. Moreover, the development and proliferation of mass destructive weapons are as hazardous to everyone's future and the region's security as are nuclear weapons, perhaps more so because they are more readily accessible and can be more easily produced.

The possibilities of regional conflict and miscalculations leading to a U.S.-U.S.S.R. confrontation or of terrorist operations triggering a nuclear war make the Arab-Israeli dispute probably the most serious flash point by a small country in response to a perceived threat to its national security. Whatever the reason, it is unlikely that an outbreak could be contained within regional limits. The people of the Middle East should not be condemned to live in constant fear of a nuclear winter.

The quest for a just and lasting settlement of the Palestinian question is crucial to the stability of the region and to the security of the world. There must be a determined and sustained effort to find new ways to push the peace process forward, to explore fresh avenues, and to experiment with novel procedures to check the deterioration of regional politics into chaos and anarchy.

A credible U.S. policy in the Middle East requires a clear moral imperative as an underpinning to effective diplomacy. Neither the ephemeral pricing of oil nor the prevailing concern with the problems of international terrorism should blind us to the fundamental problems of the region. For too long U.S. policymakers have sought short-cuts to the problem, without defining its content or delineating its diverse and divergent aspects. Mere statements of foreign policy objectives are no substitute for coherent and comprehensive diplomacy. The aim should not be the imposition of a settlement but the use of influence to induce constructive results. The objective must be to ease tension so that normal peaceful means of conflict resolution can be pursued.

The United States in particular must resist domestic pressure that may adversely influence the direction of foreign policy. Measures for a more activist approach to peacemaking are required to propel the protagonists in the region, the machinery of policymaking, and the U.S. public as well as U.S. institutions into moves that can support and nourish recent developments.

It is incumbent upon all diplomats who know the area to advise Washington to stop stereotyping the Middle East and to devise even-handed U.S. policy that takes to heart U.S. national interests instead of domestic political considerations only. Such a policy will best serve U.S. interests in the Middle East. A courageous president can marshal public opinion and channel it in the right direction, as President Eisenhower did following the tripartite invasion of Egypt in 1956.

Jordan's perception of the future is based on complete implementation of the provisions of international law and respect for the dignity of people. The guiding principle of its peacemaking endeavors is the recognition of the sovereignty, independence, and territorial integrity of all states in the region. These principles are embodied in United Nations resolutions 242 and 338, which remain the broad framework for peace in the Middle East. The implementation of the United Nations resolutions would lay the solid foundations on which peace, mutual confidence, and collaboration could be built. No one state or ethnic religious community should, or can, establish its hegemony over all the others.

Jordan envisions itself, the West Bank, and Gaza as a *terra media*, a middle ground, that could combine the huge purchasing power of the oil-producing countries of the Arabian Peninsula in the hinterland with the skilled workers and technological skills available in the northern region. The aim is the transformation of this middle ground into the productive as well as experimental workshop of the Middle East.

This notion conforms with Jordan's centrist approach in the conduct of public affairs, which totally rejects the politics of extreme. The region is beset by populist, religion-based fanaticism, which is likely to leave its imprint on the politics of the region for a long time. Social diversity has assumed an ever-increasing importance among the contending populist movements, with their divergent aims. The denial of legitimate rights to the Palestinians has been compounded by the absence of authoritative institutions to safeguard their interest under Israeli occupation. The politics of despair and suppression could engender a new dimension of social conflict and communal polarization, possibly leading to the Balkanization of all states in the region, including Israel.

Time is of the essence. U.S. diplomacy has to take cognizance of the latent threat to the security and stability of the region. The centrist approach has to be fostered and protected before fanaticism overwhelms the whole area. The United States has to evolve diplomacy consonant with the interests of all states in the region and with those of its allies in Europe and the Far East. There is a desperate need for diplomatic effort based on policies that can break the longstanding deadlock in regional disputes and serve the interests of the United States.

It is evident that world security can only be ensured in the long run by regional stability. The importance of bilateral relations is no substitute for regional cooperation and collaboration. The geopolitical reality of the Middle East and the economic and cultural interdependence resulting from Jordan's long historical interaction with the West should contribute to mutual understanding and cooperation. It is imperative that the superpowers recognize that peace in this troubled region is the only insurance against instability and the continuous fanning of the flames of war.

Friends of the United States in the Middle East—and my country and I are among them—wish the United States well in meeting the urgent challenge to find integration among the contradictory tendencies in the making of its foreign policy. Many friends of the United States share the aspirations articulated in the U.S. Declaration of Independence and in the Wilsonian commitment to self-determination of peoples. Many of us believe that the strength of the United States as a world leader in the future will depend not only on its traditional military and economic power but also on its vision of how to make a reality of its ideal as one century moves toward another. Some of my fellow citizens have complained bitterly to friends from the United States, "You do not stand for what you stand for." This is a statement in frustration of the hope that the United States will find a way to marry traditional power with the political sensitivity to human rights and aspirations that lie at the core of its own commitments.

Aftermath of the 1990–1991 Gulf Crisis

The question in the wake of the Gulf crisis of 1990–1991 is, How can we work together to change? How can we achieve progress toward enduring peace? Progress toward peace in the region will require an active and determined approach by the United States. In any approach to the Middle East agenda involving Gulf security, regional economic development for all nations, and the resolution of the Arab-Israeli as well as the Palestinian-Israeli conflicts, there is a certain area of overlap. Jordan lies at the center of this overlap.

The United States today occupies a distinct position in the world clearly manifested in the management of the Gulf crisis. This has heightened peoples' expectations, especially in the Middle East, that the United States will effectively resolve regional conflicts. Many of its friends expect it to deal with other conflicts within the same international context as it did in the Gulf crisis. If the credibility of the United States has been affected in certain constituencies, then the challenge is how to strengthen this credibility. All who can contribute should do so because this is an essential prerequisite for moving toward peace. We are told that the popularity of the United States is, for example, at a low point in the Palestinian occupied territories. We in Jordan faced similar situations in the past. We should strengthen our credibilities together and not at each other's expense.

Jordan is ready to do all that it can to build confidence between all concerned. We have to work with our people in doing so. The moral integrity of our democratic process must be safeguarded because it provides the most solid foundation for durable peace. This was shown in practice in the recent Gulf crisis when our democracy preserved our internal stability. Needless to say, mutual trust between states can have an effective value only if it is anchored in credibility between governments and their respective constituencies.

The issue of small states within the context of regional security should receive the attention it deserves. What is required is to move toward collective security that meets the individual needs of small states in the region. The military defense of a small country (Israel) and the liberation of another country (Kuwait) should ultimately evolve into a new phase of strengthening small countries and beleaguered peoples to help them stand up for themselves within a viable regional security structure. In this new phase, decisive military action needs to be superseded by an equally decisive effort in the economic field to enable small countries to prosper and reinforce stability and peace.

In talking about constituencies, mention ought also to be made of the emotions engendered by the destruction caused to Iraq during the war. The suffering of the Iraqi people is felt by Arabs everywhere. In fact, the Gulf crisis has had a third-world dimension that also needs to be healed. Financial compensation to those affected countries is necessary but not sufficient to remedy all those side effects. A way must be found for the reconstruction of Iraq to commence without delay. The well-being and survival of eighteen million fellow Arabs is at stake.

In August 1941, aboard the *Augusta* off the coast of Newfoundland, Prime Minister Winston Churchill and President Franklin Roosevelt signed the Atlantic Charter. As everyone knows, the cold war tragically intervened and frustrated their hopes for a free, peaceful, and secure world. In November 1990 the leaders of thirty-four nations finally laid the cold war to rest and signed the "Charter of Paris for a New Europe" at the summit of the Conference on Security and Cooperation in Europe (CSCE). The secretary-general of the United Nations, Javier Perez de Cuellar, reminded world leaders at the Paris summit that peace and justice are indivisible. He stressed the reality of linkages between Europe and other regions of the globe where current conflicts "have their origin in actions and circumstances going back to the colonial era." He added that "the North will continue to be seated on a base of clay as long as the South does not enjoy a minimum of well-being." These words could hardly ring more true than in the case of the Middle East.

Perhaps a first bold step toward new thinking in our region is the need to rethink security. The questions of war and peace are inseparable from the questions of demography, environment, and ideology. Extensive linkages exist between security—or rather insecurity—and the degradation of people, the environment, and cultural identity. The abuse of human and political rights, ecocide, and the loss of cultural identity are all too readily apparent in the Middle East. Creating a broadly defined security concept means tackling the root causes of conflict.

Furthermore, rethinking the meaning of security requires that a number of postulates be questioned and reexamined. Not only the military but also the political and economic route maps must be carefully surveyed to identify an appropriate new path through the existing regional maze.

Many of the roadblocks on our journey are transnational in their essence. Emphasizing the political and economic dimensions of security can help provide a remedial expansion of the tools available to deal with those transnational issues. Authoritarian regimes and an apparent neglect of festering problems have contributed to the emergence of what has been termed the "politics of despair." This political economy of despair has led the entire region to an extremely precarious and insecure situation.

Democratization, freedom of expression, human rights, and the accountability of rulers provide a route toward an alternative political economy of peace and progress. I believe this is the best alternative route toward what I have termed the three Rs: *rehabilitation, reconstruction,* and *reconciliation.*

Before moving into further details, I should stress again that these long-festering conflicts must be tackled by the world community with the same determination and on the same basis as in the case of the recent Gulf crisis. Otherwise how can rehabilitation, reconstruction, and reconciliation succeed if the current situation in Lebanon, for example, continues? How can we sustain credibility and work together if the political rights and the rights of self-determination continue to be denied to the Palestinians?

A number of proposals have been made for a Helsinki-type approach for the Middle East. My purpose here is not to go into their details, but only to observe that all these proposals for a Conference on Security and Cooperation in the Middle East (CSCME) emphasize that their aim is neither to contradict particular schemes for regional security nor to divert attention from solving long-standing conflicts. They rather represent an attempt to provide a framework and an environment conducive to diplomatic or political initiatives for dealing with specific problems.

It is within the framework of such an approach that I believe we can identify common ground for the three Rs. A number of common problems confront regional adversaries in the Middle East. Energy, arms, and external debts are challenges facing not only Jordan but other countries like Turkey, Egypt, and Israel. This energy-arms-debt triangle also links the Middle East to the states involved in the Helsinki process. This group of states is the main consumer of Middle East energy, its main supplier of armaments, and its major creditor (with a few exceptions such as China, Japan, and Brazil).

The moral weight of the Helsinki process can in this way be brought to bear on the Middle East. Such paradoxical side effects as the transfer of armaments from Europe to the Middle East in the wake of the treaty on Conventional Forces in Europe (CFE) must be effectively tackled. Otherwise how can the integrity of the whole process in the Middle East be safeguarded? As far as energy is concerned, the purpose is not to refer subjectively to "cheap oil" or "expensive oil." Rather, it is to evolve an alternative to the highly politicized confrontation between sellers and buyers. "Energy" is conspicuously absent from the 1992 objectives in Europe. The charter of Paris has implicitly recognized this serious gap in welcoming "practical steps to create optimal conditions for the economic and rational development of energy resources, with due regard for environmental consideration." In fact, the Netherlands proposed at the Paris summit a "European Energy Charter" to evolve a cooperative framework that assures stable supplies, stimulates Central and East European production, and safeguards the environment. It only makes sense that the Middle East (the Gulf as well as the Maghreb) should be included in such a framework. Apart from the dependence of Europe on oil from the Gulf, there will be a steadily increasing level of importation of gas from the Maghreb producers to Italy and soon Spain, Portugal, and possibly France and Germany. On the debt issue, it is worth noting that all the nonoil-producing countries in the Middle East suffer from major external debt problems, which are linked in no small way to the issue of armaments. Unlike in Eastern Europe, so far no concept of regional economic stabilization has emerged for the Middle East. Debt-ridden countries depend on handouts and subsidies coupled with IMF structural adjustments and austerity programs. This approach has increased tensions between the haves and have-nots in the region and has provided a fertile socioeconomic environment for radicalism.

A cornerstone of a new debt strategy is arms control. The successful implementation of arms control and arms reduction will release substantial funds previously wasted on armaments. Countries abiding by such a process will qualify for the systematic and measured reduction of existing debts (most of which were accumulated through arms purchases in the first place). A cursory look at most indebted nations in the Middle East reveals that most, if not all, would no longer need continuous subsidies if the existing debt overhang is removed (this includes Turkey, Israel, and Iraq). The key issue, however, is not the write-off of debts in a vacuum. It should be part of an arms control and reduction package coupled with appropriate economic adjustment policy (stabilization and structural adjustments).

To assist in this process, a regional debt-sinking fund can be set up by the oil-rich countries in the area to share the burden in the debt-reduction process. The application of the arms control process to the oil countries themselves will help release significant resources from their defense budgets. The second pillar of the proposed debt-reduction strategy is a regional socioeconomic package. A regional development fund should be established to provide investment capital for those countries implementing stabilization and adjustment programs. National and regional infrastructural programs should be integrated to the extent possible. Regional sectoral plans for water, energy, transport, and telecommunications should be evolved. These can become the leading sectors in the economic revitalization of the postwar Middle East. Water, energy, and transport can be viewed as the "steel and coal" of a new Middle East community including the non-Arab states of the region. A study by the World Bank has shown that in the past, only 5 percent of the financial surplus of the oil-rich countries was invested in the region. There is a need to develop new investment criteria and a new basis for calculating rates of return, to help channel part of the remaining 95 percent into the region.

To avoid disaster for itself and the world, the Middle East urgently needs a remedial expansion of the tools available to promote interdependence both within the region and with nations outside the region. A utilitarian "worked-out rights" approach has to replace the ethical "intrinsic rights" approach before a meaningful cooperative strategy can emerge. What is needed is to institutionalize new regional thinking about development based on mutual gains and interests (both economic and social). Appropriate cost-benefit criteria at the regional level have to be thought through and applied to sectoral projects such as water, energy, and transportation. Welfare economics has extensive tools relating to social cost-benefit analysis that can be extended to an intraregional context. To use economic jargon, what is needed is to identify "externalities" (i.e., external socioeconomic benefits to the region from particular investments) and to "internalize" their effects by transforming the incidental benefit into a product for which a price is charged. This can apply not only to water, energy, and transportation but also to education and worker migration. A number of multilateral agencies (such as the World Bank) can easily provide the technical expertise needed to develop new investment criteria for the region. Creative investment plans can, on the basis of such new investment criteria, transform the existing regional zero-sum game into a scenario of mutual games and move us together toward rehabilitation, reconstruction, and reconciliation. Democracy, security, and prosperity provide the most solid foundation for a new stable Middle East.[4]

Notes

1. "There has to be a homeland provided for the Palestinian refugees who have suffered for so many years." President Jimmy Carter, response to a question at a town meeting, Clinton, Mass., March 16, 1977, in "The Search for Peace in the Middle East: Documents and Statements, 1967–1979" (Washington, D.C.: Government Printing Office, 1979, prepared by Library of Congress, Congressional Research Service), p. 311.

The U.S.-Soviet declaration of October 1977 stipulated for the "resolution of the Palestine question . . . ensuring the legitimate rights of the Palestinian people." "The Search for Peace in the Middle East," p. 159. The United States before 1977 had acknowledged the legitimate *interests* and not rights of the Palestinians; this was the first time that it applied this term to the Palestinians.

Carter's diplomatic handshake at a United Nations reception in his honor with the PLO observer at the United Nations differed markedly from the previous administration's attitude when the U.S. ambassador remained seated during the standing ovation given to PLO leader Yasser Arafat, again at the United Nations.

2. Carter's overture was mentioned earlier. Brzezinski, at a ceremony marking the twenty-fifth anniversary of Algerian independence, initiated a handshake with Yasser Arafat, head of the PLO. Different forms of contact took place during the Carter administration. These included the intermediaries who also met with Arafat and the international mediators who sought to amend United Nations resolution 242: Bruno Kreisky of Austria, Willy Brandt as president of Socialist International in 1976, and President Tito of Yugoslavia.

3. For more on the subject, see Paul N. McCloskey, Jr., "Public Opinion and U.S. Policy in the Arab World," in *The Challenge to U.S. Diplomacy in the Arab Gulf States* (Washington, D.C.: American-Arab Affairs Council, proceedings of a conference held in St. Louis, Missouri, September 22–23, 1983, under the sponsorship of the American-Arab Affairs Council, St. Louis University, and the World Affairs Council of St. Louis).

4. These thoughts were expressed under the title "Looking Beyond the Gulf War: Reconciliation and Reconstruction" at a conference in response to the 1991 Gulf war. This March 23, 1991, meeting in San Francisco was sponsored by the Tamalpais Institute.

14
A Broader Peace Process for the Middle East

Harold H. Saunders

After the October 1973 war, participants in the effort to move the Arab-Israeli conflict toward resolution came to call that work "the peace process." In the wake of the 1991 Gulf war, the continuing challenge is to crystallize a conceptual framework for a broader peace process that embraces the whole Middle East. The postwar agenda includes a wide range of interacting issues that stretch across the entire area. Those who must deal with these issues will deprive themselves of powerful instruments for moving toward a genuine peace if they do not equip themselves with concepts large enough to encompass that regional agenda.

Some participants in the Arab-Israeli peace process came to see it not just as a series of negotiations but as a negotiating process embedded in a larger political process. That focus on the political process—coupled with U.S. performance—sometimes generated suspicion of U.S. intent among Arab colleagues. They felt the United States concentrated on political maneuvers at the expense of dealing with basic issues. U.S. participants, in contrast, believed that broadening the approach to include the political as well as the negotiating arena was essential in moving from conflictual to more constructive relationships. We must begin focusing on what a larger peace process would involve.

The first purpose of this chapter is to explain why some U.S. participants came to see the Arab-Israeli peace process as a political process—not just as negotiation. Their conviction was rooted initially in Middle Eastern experience, but in the early 1990s they see that view reinforced by global developments. This chapter rests on the premise that placing the peace process in the context of dramatic global change strengthens the argument for the broader political approach.

The second purpose of the chapter is to begin, much more briefly, laying a foundation for a larger conception of the peace process following the Gulf war. That conception will include reconstituting the Arab-Israeli peace process but will have to go beyond it to deal with a much broader range of regional issues. I do not suggest that all issues must be formally linked; I do suggest that because many issues are intertwined in people's minds as evidence of the state of relationships, progress in one area can create an environment that makes progress in others more possible. The hope is that reflecting on what the Arab-Israeli peace process was when it worked may provide insight as we face the even more complex task of designing a peace process for a broader area and a larger agenda.

As chapters in this book suggest, familiar concepts of international relations do not always explain what we see in an area such as the Middle East, and familiar instruments of statecraft do not reliably produce the results we expect of them. The same is increasingly true on the global stage. When familiar ways stop working well, it is sensible to explore new ways. In a sense, the peace process is a product of that exploration. It is all the more powerful a concept because it finds affirmation in global experience.

I have written this concluding chapter as an interpretative essay. It reflects the odyssey of one public servant interested in peace—as a human being placing himself in the world, as a U.S. citizen representing his nation's interests, and as a person concerned for peoples in conflict in the Middle East as around the world. I write personally because the time has come for us as whole human beings—not only as practitioners of compartmentalized research methodologies—to integrate our insights into a fresh and comprehensive understanding of how nations relate in a rapidly changing world. The challenge has never been greater than after a major war between a Middle East country and a U.S.-led coalition.

In part, this is a chapter about perceptions. Perceptions make a difference because how we perceive the world begins to determine how we act in it. Chapter 1 describes the people of the world standing on the bridge between two paradigms—two ways of understanding how the world works. This chapter grounds those changing perceptions of how the world works in the experience of one region. It reflects the interplay between my deep immersion in U.S. policymaking toward the Middle East and my broader reflections about the U.S. role in a rapidly changing world. Similarly, the authors in this book—each from the perspective of her or his own experience—have revealed the tensions between familiar ways of perceiving and mounting evidence of change all around them.

This chapter—as is the purpose of this book—invites you to join me in trying to broaden our insight by placing experience in the Middle East in a global perspective. It invites you to think in a larger context as a way of enlarging understanding of how to initiate and guide change in this one region. It invites you to consider that changes in the larger setting of relationships among nations may suggest what the peace process could be.

Because this is a chapter about the evolution of perceptions, it begins by posing the challenge the Arab-Israeli peace process poses to all of us: how to change the Arab-Israeli political environment so as to make peaceful relationships possible. It then suggests that our response to that challenge—broadening our concept of peacemaking—at least instinctively reflects opportunities offered by experience both in a changing Middle East and in a changing world. Ventured next is a characterization of two ways of looking at how nations relate for the purpose of sharpening our understanding of what is involved in choosing elements of the two approaches that are likely to help move from conflict to peace. The chapter concludes with thoughts about the peace process in this global perspective, especially as we broaden the concept to include the whole Middle East.

The Arab-Israeli Peace Process in a Political Perspective

"A Framework for Peace in the Middle East Agreed at Camp David" was signed before a watching world in the East Room of the White House on Sunday evening, September 17, 1978. A few weeks later, President Jimmy Carter sent me to Jordan, Saudi Arabia, the West Bank, and Israel to try to broaden support, especially among the Arabs, for the negotiations proposed in those accords.

In Jordan, I spent many hours explaining the proposed process to King Hussein and his advisers. We argued that the accords—although not committing Israel to the final settlement the Arabs demanded—reflected changes in Israel's position that needed to be made concrete. Consolidation of the proposed transitional arrangements through negotiated changes on the ground would itself, we felt, change the political environment enough to open the door to negotiation on the final status of the West Bank and Gaza.

At the end of one session with a longtime Jordanian colleague, he said to me: "We Jordanians are a desert people. We do not leave one oasis until we know where the next one is. Therefore, there is no place in our culture or our vocabulary for your idea of an open-ended negotiating process." He was not the only one to speak this way. Many to whom I spoke doubted that the process would work without a more concrete commitment to the outcome. Later when I took an earlier version of this chapter to Arab and Israeli centers in early 1986, the consistent Arab objection was that the United States used the open-ended process as a way of avoiding fundamental issues—Israeli with-drawal and the Palestinians' right to an act of self-determination.

In May 1985, that same Jordanian colleague came to Washington with King Hussein for talks with President Ronald Reagan and Secretary of State George Shultz. He came to one of the Washington research institutes for a small lunch with members of the policy community. Beginning his informal remarks by recalling what he had told me in 1978, he went on to describe a four-step process that King Hussein was presenting to President Reagan and Secretary Shultz. It began with informal talks between a U.S. official and a group of Jordanians and "nondeclared PLO Palestinians" that would lead to PLO acceptance of UN Security Council resolution 242 and then to a PLO-U.S. dialogue; it ended in an international conference, including direct talks within an Israeli-Jordanian-Palestinian working group.

Just as in the process I had described in 1978, the scenario included no guarantees on the outcome. It was based on hope—or expectation—that an informal meeting would give the United States a forum for showing its commitment to producing a negotiation that would take seriously legitimate interests and rights of the Palestinians. It also assumed that the PLO could then respond by stating formally its readiness to make peace with Israel in a formulation that would lead to a PLO-U.S. dialogue and provide a broadened foundation for an international con-ference. It pictured several stations on the way to a peace and offered steps to change the political environment so as to make subsequent steps possible, but it could not assure that even the second step would follow the first. As events later unfolded, this time it was the United States that was reluctant to move without greater assurance about where the first step would lead.

When my colleague finished and discussion began, I said to him: "Since 1978, you have learned a great deal about designing a political process, and I have learned a great deal about the oasis." We had learned the importance of a dual agenda. First, we need to be as clear as possible in the early stages of conflict resolution about the oasis—our vision of the relationship we want to create. Second, at the same time, we must give every bit as much attention to practical steps—the political process—to build political support for that vision and to begin moving toward it.

This story captures for me the importance of focusing on politics as well as negotiation in the peace process. It highlights the challenge posed in the peace process—the persistent tension in that process that I have called its version of "squaring the circle." The tension is between two often conflicting needs: (1) the understandable desire of leaders for assurance that negotiation can produce a fair deal they can justify to constituents and (2) the difficulty of introducing such certainty at the outset without negotiating critical issues before negotiation actually begins. Resolving that tension is often more possible in politics than in negotiation.

In negotiation, the classic device has been to try to agree in advance on fundamental principles to guide the negotiation—for example, exchanging occupied territory for peace or mutual Israeli-Palestinian recognition of each people's right of self-determination and its appropriate political expression in an area defined by secure and recognized boundaries. As often as not, the more explicit one gets in defining these principles, the more one arouses political opposition in one constituency that causes one party to refuse even to come to the negotiating room.

A process that concentrates almost exclusively on negotiation risks two dangers. One is becoming so absorbed in the tactics and procedures of getting negotiation started that we give an impression of ignoring the ultimate purpose—creating a new relationship. The other risk is demanding a clear picture of the destination of negotiation without shaping political debate to change perceptions in important constituencies and to build support for that picture and for the course we want to follow. Both tasks are critical. We must be as clear and honest as we can be about where we are going, and we must also be meticulous in plotting a practical course for getting there.

As I look back on our experience in the 1970s, I draw this conclusion: Until leaders had acted politically to change the political environment, the negotiators did not have a chance. It was in the political process, not in the antechambers of the negotiating room, that leaders found instruments of change. Negotiation often became a vehicle for stimulating debate and crystallizing public judgment in favor of change, but change was initiated in the political arena.

One reason was that decisions of this magnitude could not be made only by a few dominant leaders. Dealing with Israeli democracy or working in Washington, the capital of a complex republican political system, may have made U.S. negotiators more aware of this than others. But we concluded that even in widely different political systems, leaders had to be concerned with the political processes and constituencies that impel or constrain them in setting policy directions. Even when fully representative government does not exist, leaders of complex governments living in a world of modern communication—with some exceptions for particular periods of time—are affected by domestic centers of influence such as a party or the military or by other states that affect their well-being.

The story of my exchanges with my Jordanian friend captures for me an experience on both sides of learning new ways of bringing about change in relationships among nations. He had thought about the need for political steps to change perceptions so as to make possible tomorrow what was not possible yesterday; I had learned that to change perceptions, one must find not just technical solutions but solutions that would symbolize a serious response to the fundamental fears and hopes that often underlie political barriers blocking the way to changed relationships. Working from this political perspective, I want to reflect more fully on our experience in the peace process itself before placing it in a global context.

Reflections on the Peace Process, 1967–1990

Any essay on the Arab-Israeli conflict must be subjective in some degree. This one develops the theme of tension between focusing at times on a comprehensive settlement and at other times on resolving manageable pieces of the problem and describes efforts combining the two approaches to build political support for negotiating peace. This is not a history of the peace process—simply reflections from this perspective.

From the June 1967 war and the November passage of UN Security Council resolution 242 down into 1971, the primary focus was on developing terms of reference for negotiation of a "package deal"—a series of agreements that would address every facet of the conflict from borders and recognition to refugees and peace. The implementing vehicle was a familiar diplomatic exercise: an emissary of the UN secretary-general moving back and forth among the parties trying to develop a statement of positions that could launch negotiation on a comprehensive peace. Early in the Nixon administration, Soviet-U.S. dialogue in 1969 concentrated on developing comparable positions in Moscow and Washington from which the two powers might persuade their regional friends to break the stalemate by producing statements of changed position. These efforts failed because the political foundations for peaceful relationships did not exist.

As those efforts flagged, the attention of such individuals as Moshe Dayan, Anwar Sadat, and Henry Kissinger turned in late 1970 to whether an interim agreement around opening the Suez Canal might be possible. The thought was that such a step might change perceptions on both sides and open the door to a larger negotiation. With the help of U.S. diplomats, Egypt and Israel exchanged views intensively in 1971 on such an interim arrangement, but that approach also foundered for lack of political support for the compromises required.

In 1972–1973, Egyptian President Anwar Sadat tried persistently to engage active Soviet and U.S. involvement in the peace process in order to add weight to the political scales in favor of negotiation. In the end, he judged that neither nation was interested in investing heavily in ending the Arab-Israeli conflict; he concluded that military action was his only recourse. The October 1973 war was not a classic military attempt to reconquer lost territory. Its purposes in Sadat's mind seemed to be political—to win enough militarily to erase the humiliation of the 1967 Arab defeat, to press the big powers to focus on the conflict, and to persuade the Israelis they were not invincible. Even though Egyptian forces were being badly mauled at the end of the war, Sadat proclaimed victory, and that "victory" became the operative political fact in the Middle East.

Sadat told Kissinger he could now begin negotiations with Israel, and the result was a major U.S. commitment through the unique diplomatic format of the Kissinger shuttles. Although that mediation produced three interim agreements in 1974 and 1975—two between Egypt and Israel and one between Israel and Syria—they were far more than agreements on disengaging forces. The U.S. secretary of state moving back and forth continuously among the parties created a relational context for those discussions that enabled Israelis, Egyptians, and even Syrians to make their judgments in the knowledge of how their negotiating partners on the other side would react. Kissinger's constant effort to explain each side to the other created a fabric that began to weave thinking on both sides together at least in limited ways even though they were not sitting in the same room.

The philosophy behind the interim agreements of 1974–1975—"step-by-step diplomacy," as the process was called—was to carve out of the conflict problems that could be negotiated with implementable results. Although each agreement was written with the disclaimer that it was not an eventual peace, each agreement contained within it partial steps toward peace. The disengagement of military forces tangled up at the end of the war provided a rationale for beginning Israeli withdrawal from lines occupied in 1967; Arab commitments to resolve differences in negotiation rather than by force were first steps toward a commitment to peace.

Insofar as it remained a step-by-step process of building one interim agreement on another, the peace process relied on a cardinal principle: In negotiating an interim agreement, the parties would not try to resolve issues such as final boundaries or normalization of relations that could only be dealt with in a final peace treaty. Negotiations dealt with technical issues, but the larger purpose was to nurture a new perception— that negotiations starting down the road toward peace were indeed possible and that the parties could work together in that context. For that moment, the parties suspended demands to know the exact destination in hopes that a process was indeed beginning.

In 1976, as the United States looked toward a presidential election when little would be done in the Arab-Israeli arena, Kissinger and others (including Cyrus Vance, who would become the next secretary of state under President Carter) reflected on the step-by-step process. I believe it is fair to say that even if President Ford had been elected and Kissinger had remained secretary of state, they would probably have concluded that shuttle diplomacy and interim agreements had just about run their course. This was true simply because it was difficult to envision further interim steps that would not be almost as difficult as final peace itself.

In 1974, we had studied an Israel-Jordan interim arrangement to involve Palestinian-populated areas in the peace process. Circumstances— including leadership changes in Israel and the United States and an Arab summit that declared the PLO, not Jordan, to be the "sole legitimate representative of the Palestinian people"—made that step unviable. Still, the question of how to involve Jordan and the Palestinians in the peace process remained active because doing so was essential to building Arab political support for continuing the process.

Against that background, the Carter administration launched an almost year-long effort to develop terms of reference for a resumed broad Middle East conference in Geneva. That effort ran into the obstacles of inter-Arab politics and Israeli resistance to talking with the PLO, and by fall it seemed to be losing momentum.

At that point, I pictured Anwar Sadat as concluding in frustration that the U.S. diplomatic effort to achieve agreement on terms of reference for the Geneva conference did not address the main roadblock to negotiation: lack of trust in Israel and among Israel's U.S. friends that any Arab partner would negotiate peace with Israel and implement an agreement faithfully. In November, Sadat made his historic visit to Jerusalem to remove those political, psychological, and human barriers to peace by dramatizing that Egypt could accept Israel as a state in the Middle East, recognize it in the fullest political and human sense of that word, and make peace with it.

In the immediate aftermath of that historic visit, the effort was to translate it into agreement to begin an international conference. As other Arab states rejected Sadat's move, the exercise became an Egyptian-Israeli negotiation that eventually brought the leaders of those two nations to Camp David with President Carter and the negotiating teams of each party.

Many observers, especially Arabs, see the Camp David accords as producing a separate Egyptian-Israeli deal with little regard to other

Arab interests, particularly those of the Palestinians. Whatever the judgment about who "won" at Camp David, it is accurate to say that the intention of Egyptian, U.S., and at least some Israeli negotiators was not to produce a separate deal. "A Framework for Peace in the Middle East Agreed at Camp David" must be read as a document written with serious intention of making an Egyptian-Israeli negotiation the next step in a process that would bring into being a Palestinian self-governing authority and eventually negotiations on the final status of the West Bank and Gaza involving Israelis, Palestinians, Jordanians, and Egyptians working under U.S. mediation. Syria was also included in the vision of a comprehensive peace.

In the view of at least Carter and Sadat, the agreement to negotiate a peace treaty between Egypt and Israel was a subset of that larger process and was in spirit very much tied to its continuance. During negotiations on the peace treaty as we discussed the ultimate normalization of Egyptian-Israeli relations, U.S. and Egyptian participants repeatedly stated that the quality of normalization would depend on the quality of the continuing peace process because Egyptians would accept a normal relationship with Israel only if they felt their actions were vindicated by progress toward realization of the Palestinian right of self-determination and success by other Arabs in regaining territory lost in 1967.

Whatever one may think of Sadat's policies and achievements, the impact of his visit to Israel must be examined thoughtfully. In addition to changing the political climate in Israel, Sadat also helped Carter consolidate U.S. public support for the peace process by his skill in dealing with the U.S. Congress. By 1981, he had received in Cairo more than two-thirds of the members of Congress.

The results of Camp David were a treaty of peace between Egypt and Israel and Egypt's ostracism by the rest of the Arab world. As evinced by the exchange with my Jordanian friend, we did not succeed in persuading Arab leaders to support an open-ended political process. Negotiations on an agreement for a Palestinian self-governing authority were pursued through the Carter administration and then put on the back burner by the Reagan administration while it pursued an anti-Soviet "strategic consensus" in the Middle East. In late summer 1982, George Shultz as the new secretary of state enabled President Reagan to make a speech attempting to revive the peace process, but for much of the next year the administration devoted most of its energy to the crisis in Lebanon.

In the 1980s, the debate focused on an implicit difference between two approaches. Those at the top of the Reagan administration held the view that the situation was not ripe for negotiation but that when the parties themselves had put their houses in order, the United States would do what it could to help narrow the gap between them. On the other hand, those who had participated in the peace process in the 1970s recognized that the parties in the Arab-Israeli arena were unlikely to create a ripe moment unless some third party was actively engaged in helping the situation to ripen. They acknowledged that the odds would normally be against success, but they felt that an active, ongoing political process could change relationships gradually even if it produced no new formal agreements for a time.

When the administration engaged actively, it focused on developing a mechanism for negotiation between Israel and Jordan; the Palestinians would somehow be blended into that negotiation with the ultimate purpose of resolving the Palestinian problem "in association with Jordan." Although the ultimate aim was a comprehensive peace, efforts focused on steps toward an Israeli-Jordanian-Palestinian negotiation that were politically sustainable in Israel and on persuading Palestinians they could gain recognition from entering negotiations that would justify their recognition of Israel. Any active effort to respond to Palestinian political needs was left to Jordan.

At the end of 1988—almost a year after the beginning of a popular uprising in the West Bank and Gaza and four months after King Hussein had discontinued Jordanian legal and administrative ties to those territories—the Palestine National Council and PLO Chairman Yasser Arafat changed the context for negotiation. After years of refusing to accept Israel, they accepted the partition of the land west of the Jordan River into Israeli and Palestinian states. Many Israelis were skeptical that the change reflected a real recognition of Israel; most of the world treated the move as historic. It raised questions about whether Israel itself would accept a two-state solution in that land and a full and normal relationship with the Palestinian people as neighbors and as equals.

As several chapters in this book have stated sharply, this change in the Palestinian position brought into focus what had been obvious for some time—that the core of the conflict is a conflict between two peoples embedded in a larger state-to-state conflict. As those chapters suggest, approaches to resolving intercommunal conflict may not be the same as those techniques of negotiation familiarly used in resolving state-to-state conflicts. The change in the Palestinian position brought to the fore the question of what instruments and political approaches can help reconcile two peoples so as to negotiate the practical elements of a peaceful relationship between them.

As the administration of President George Bush turned its attention to the Arab-Israeli conflict within weeks of his inauguration, it was possible to cast the problem in the following way: Mr. President, you have a choice between two ways of looking at the Arab-Israeli peace process. One would describe your primary problem as finding a vehicle and formulations for beginning a negotiation between Israel and the Palestinian movement. In March and April 1989, that vehicle will take the form of a proposal by the prime minister of Israel to negotiate arrangements for holding elections in the West Bank and Gaza to choose Palestinians to negotiate with Israel. Another approach—not to the exclusion of the first—would be to see the primary task in the peace process not just as beginning negotiation but as changing the Israeli-Palestinian relationship. If the task is viewed this way, the problem is one of changing the political environment, changing perceptions, re-shaping debate in Israel, and helping both the Israeli and Palestinian peoples conclude that a peaceful relationship between them is possible and should be attempted.

The experience of the 1970s when the peace process produced five agreements argued for the larger approach, whether efforts to begin a negotiation around a proposal for elections succeeded or not. Palestinians had to be persuaded that the prime minister of Israel would negotiate seriously and fashion elections that would be the first step toward an ultimate Israeli-Palestinian peace. If negotiations began, many feared that the Israeli government intended to drag them on without results as long as possible. If the attempt to negotiate failed, governments would be seeking an alternative. Before that moment, the choice between these two ways of looking at the peace process would depend in part on whether leaders understood that the problem between Israelis and Palestinians is not one of state-to-state conflict and that the instruments for reconciling two peoples are not limited to the traditional instruments of force or negotiation.

For me, thinking in terms of the overall relationship between two peoples provides a conceptual context within which the tension in the peace process can be resolved. A relationship between Israelis and Palestinians exists; despite the intensity of interaction in many places and on many levels, the relationship is not a constructive one. That relationship is itself a political process of continuous interaction between communities—between significant elements of whole bodies politic. The main obstacle to improving that relationship is not the absence of technical solutions; the main obstacle lies in the fear, misperception, suspicion, anger, grievance, and even hate the two peoples hold in varying measure toward each other. Those obstacles to a constructive relationship will not be removed by negotiating a change in one practical aspect of the interaction, although that may be useful; the obstacles will be removed only by identifying them and by designing steps within the political process itself to change each people's perception of the other.

Only by intervening in the political process of continuous interaction that is the heart of the overall relationship do we resolve the tension—"square the circle"—between the vision of a changed relationship and concrete steps for beginning the change.

It is at this point, having set the peace process in a political context, that I find it useful to step back from the present Arab-Israeli-Palestinian stalemate to see what we can learn both from broader changes in the Middle East and from global change. Reflecting on changes in how the region and the larger international context have interacted may enable us to come back to the peace process with a wider perspective and a larger array of instruments than are included on traditional textbook lists of the instruments of statecraft.

A Changing Middle East in a Changing World, 1960–1990

Interaction between the peoples of the Middle East and the world powers was not new in the years after World War II. What became apparent increasingly in those years was that the nations of the region and the world powers on the global stage began to experience profound change as that interaction continued. Politics in the region became more complex; politics in the larger world became more complex; and the interaction between the two arenas became more intertwined. Two sets of observations suggest what was involved.

A More Complex Regional Environment

The increased ability of regional actors to influence the course of events or to block the big powers' ability to do so has made conducting relationships among nations in areas like the Middle East more complex both for big powers and for regional states. Many more variables, possible alliances, relationships, and potential consequences of policy had to be taken into account.

Middle Eastern states became stronger and vigorously pursued efforts to establish independence of action and to wrest a share of influence and resources from the established powers. States in the Middle East steadily loosened political ties to former colonial powers and tried to reduce dependence on the industrialized states. Dependence on Western-sponsored security arrangements gradually diminished.

As states in the Middle East established greater capacity to act independently, they found resources in the international arena for enhancing their influence. Some of these were old techniques in a new global situation; others were new.

Middle Eastern leaders had long been accustomed to exploiting big-power rivalries. As the cold war deepened in a nuclear age and Moscow and Washington competed for influence in the Middle East, especially after the mid-1950s, each of the states in the area manipulated superpower rivalry to expand its own influence.

They also found new international organizations to use in enlarging their political strength. The nonaligned movement, the Arab League, the Organization of African Unity, the Organization of the Islamic Conference, the Organization of Arab Petroleum Exporting Countries as well as the Security Council, the General Assembly, and the committees of the United Nations all provided contexts for gathering political support. The strength of the Palestinian national movement in the 1960s and especially after 1967, for instance, was enhanced by putting the Arab-Israeli-Palestinian conflict squarely into the context of nonaligned support for liberation movements against the vestiges of colonialism. An appeal to the principle of self-determination, a broad diplomatic campaign, and violent actions by elements of the PLO led to widespread awareness of the Palestinian cause and to recognition of the PLO.

In the 1970s, the rapid rise of oil prices, the global energy crisis, and the large accumulation of capital reserves thrust Arab oil-producers into central and unanticipated roles on the world economic stage as the price increases dislocated both industrialized and developing economies. They also provided an Arab source of financial support for Arab states and movements wary of dependence on big powers.

In addition to the enhanced capacity of regional states to act independently toward the big powers, a range of new phenomena operating outside the limits of the traditional state system posed new constraints on the actions of those governments as well as on the big powers. Within states, populations became more able to affect governments politically. With urbanization, masses could be more readily mobilized for political purposes. We saw what could happen in the streets of Baghdad, Cairo, Alexandria, Tehran, and Tel Aviv and what happened when people turned to guerrilla action in Algeria or Lebanon. Increasing numbers of educated business, professional, and technologically trained individuals sought a voice in setting political directions.

Many states experienced fragmentation within their societies, making them more difficult to govern. The disintegration of the national compact and of central authority in Lebanon raised questions about whether and how a state can be reformed from ethnic diversity once acceptance that there should be rules of the political game has broken down. In Israel, the majority shifted from a population with European roots toward one with roots in Arab and Oriental countries. The opposition Likud party grew until it ended the Labor party's dominance. Today, the polity is split evenly between the two major blocs, while a wide spread of small parties is eroding the major blocs.

As part of loosening ties with colonial civilizations, leaders experimented with ideologies from neither East nor West that could rally politically sensitive groups, often across national boundaries. Many people identified with ethnic or religious groups that took inspiration and even direction from centers beyond the states where they lived.

Nonstate actors became significant. The Palestine Liberation Organization, embracing four million Palestinians in and beyond the Middle East, formed a "state within a state" in Lebanon. It sometimes intimidated Arab governments because it provided an issue that could be used within states to rally masses against governments.

A Changing Global Environment

While Middle Eastern leaders saw the world from perspectives of a changing setting for the affairs of a changing region, leaders of the big powers saw accelerating change in the global environment in which they operated. Observations they gleaned on the world stage eventually affected their thinking about relationships with Middle Eastern states.

For most of this postwar period, the cold war and the intense competition between the Soviet Union and the United States provided one important set of lenses through which policymakers in those two nations looked at the world. From the mid-1950s on, the Middle East increasingly became one more arena in which the Soviet-U.S. rivalry played itself out. From the outset, economic and military assistance were primary vehicles in the competition for influence. The United States was concerned that Moscow would extend its influence by supporting radical political movements; Soviet officials saw the United States as using alliances with traditional regimes to maintain a military presence in the vicinity of Soviet borders. By the mid-1960s, both powers became concerned that their support for regional friends could draw them into an unwanted direct confrontation.

As the United States and the U.S.S.R. moved toward nuclear parity in the 1960s, leaders began to think of new ways of conducting relations in a nuclear world where the strongest components of military power could not be used. President Nixon and National Security Adviser Kissinger attempted to develop a relationship with the Soviet Union in which negotiation could substitute for the use of force in the settlement of disputes. Senior U.S. policymakers were actively searching for new ways of building a total relationship between two societies and of building into that relationship means for resolving disputes, including sanctions against violations of agreement. Despite that attempt, well into the 1970s and 1980s the superpower rivalry led the two powers to measure their ability to cooperate on some effort to begin an Arab-Israeli negotiation not so much on its merits as on judgment about whether it would leave one or the other in an advantaged position in their continuing contest for influence.

Détente did not founder in the negotiating room but in the political arena outside the negotiating room. Détente foundered because actions of each side convinced the other that it did not intend to build a genuinely cooperative relationship. Actions in Angola, Ethiopia, and the Middle East, military deployments in Europe, and finally the Soviet invasion of Afghanistan undermined efforts to build sound political foundations for a new relationship. Whatever political trust might have been enhanced in attempts at negotiating arms control was undermined by unilateral acts in other areas that appeared to be efforts to gain unilateral advantage. The complex intertwining of actions and perceptions blocked building a more constructive relationship. It is important for colleagues in the Middle East to realize that U.S. diplomats engaged in the peace process in the 1970s were working shoulder-to-shoulder with others in the U.S. government who were deeply involved in trying to change the superpower relationship. Thinking about how to change, develop, and conduct sound relationships in the world reflected continuous cross-fertilization between the regional and the global perspectives.[1]

The period when Moscow and Washington were testing each other in a new relationship was a period of increasing fluidity on the global stage. The U.S. effort to withdraw from Vietnam became partly enmeshed in big-power relations and negatively affected Soviet-U.S. ability to cooperate in the Middle East. Beginning with the Sino-Soviet rift in the late 1950s, big-power blocs very slowly but steadily loosened, and the U.S. opening to China in the early 1970s contributed further to the erosion of a bipolar world and to uncertainty in the Soviet-U.S. relationship. By the time President Carter took office in 1977, it was common to talk in some contexts of five centers in the big-power world: the United States, the U.S.S.R., China, Europe, and Japan. Though that fact did not by itself directly affect U.S.–Middle Eastern relations, big-power policymakers thought more and more about how to work in a world with multiple centers of power.

Since World War II, principles governing international behavior—codified in the Charter of the United Nations and associated documents—have intruded slowly but gradually into the internal lives of sovereign states. Although governments still jealously guard their relationships with their peoples as their own province, at the same time many have subscribed to international agreements beyond the UN Charter such as the Helsinki Final Act that legitimize international judgment on governments' treatment of their citizens. In addition, private groups such as Amnesty International carry weight in publishing their reports on the status of human rights.

Most nations have been ambivalent in applying these principles. Some of the newer nations, such as fundamentalist Iran, challenge them as extensions of Western values. Other actors, such as the Palestinian movement, have embraced such principles as self-determination and tried to hold Western governments to account for not applying the principle. Principles are often ignored by big powers when it serves their interests, but the norms still exert influence in various ways. They were used in internal debate within the United States by those who opposed continuing the U.S. military intervention in Vietnam. They were used in the Organization of the Islamic Conference to attack Soviet intervention in Afghanistan. The considerable efforts made by most states to justify their actions in terms of those principles suggest that there are increasing costs attached to violating these norms.

In the 1960s and 1970s, we became increasingly aware of significant nonstate actors and of issues that cut across national boundaries. Particular attention was given to the multinational corporation that built allegiances and defined interests across national boundaries. In addition, we paid more attention to issues such as energy pricing and availability, food and population, and environmental issues that could not be dealt with by single governments acting alone. These observations caused leaders increasingly to think in terms of complexes of related problems and to think in terms of significant elements of whole bodies politic interacting rather than only governments dealing with governments.

In that context, those of us working in Washington had for some time in a variety of ways experienced the interaction between policies and actions of other governments and actors on the international stage and the domestic politics of our own and other countries. Three widely different examples make the point.

Embassies in Washington at least since the early 1960s have learned to spend a lot of time in the Congress, especially in building constituencies for their economic and military assistance programs. The Israel lobby is well known, but Egypt, Saudi Arabia, and Jordan also increased the effectiveness of their representations to the Congress, working both through their embassies and with private consultants. Middle Eastern leaders appear regularly on U.S. television.

During the crisis of the U.S. hostages in Iran (1979–1981), U.S. policymakers were advised by non-U.S. observers how to construct a scenario of events that might enable those Iranians who wanted to release the hostages to build political support for that move among Iranian constituencies. The elaborate scenario involved sending a UN commission to Iran to hear Iranian grievances and ended with steps to transfer the hostages into the hands of the Foreign Ministry, which would release them to the UN after a Security Council meeting on the commission's report. In the end, domestic Iranian groups were able to thwart completion of that scenario, but the eventual release of the hostages through Algerian mediation depended in part on casting a complex legal and financial transaction in ways that would enable Iran's leaders to claim that Iran's demands had been met, while U.S. leaders had an agreement that would stand up in U.S. courts.

On the global front, the United States in the late 1960s and early 1970s found the North Vietnamese leaders appealing to those in the United States who opposed continuation of U.S. military involvement in Vietnam. The Soviet government launched an extensive campaign to divide NATO and to split some NATO allies from the United States by appealing to members of the peace movement in Europe. From 1986 on, Soviet leader Mikhail Gorbachev resorted repeatedly to unilateral proposals to change U.S. and other perceptions of Soviet character and intentions. His speech at the UN General Assembly in December 1988 seemed aimed directly at a U.S. audience that still questioned the sincerity of his reforms in the Soviet Union. Conversely, in 1990 and 1991, the moves of his military to suppress the independence movements in the Baltic states began to undermine the high esteem in which he was held after he won the Nobel Peace Prize.

The net effect of these and other similar experiences was to give leaders and people alike reason to reflect on the limits of familiar ways of thinking about the world and acting in it. Whether they drew correct conclusions is a separate issue; the basic point was that some recognized the need for new ways of thinking and acting. That realization was not simply rooted in analysis; it stemmed from the painful experience of recognizing that the old ways of doing things did not always work or produce expected results.

Emerging Limits on Instruments of Policy

As part of their experience in a changing region in a changing world, the experience of U.S. policymakers in the Middle East, as on the global stage, also drew attention to emerging limits on the traditional instruments available to them for influencing the course of events. Leaders have traditionally thought in terms of economic, military, diplomatic, and public-influencing instruments for carrying out their policies. My purpose here is to suggest some of the conclusions U.S. policymakers— at least instinctively—drew in some way from their experience about the present utility of those four instruments. Many of these observations echo those in earlier chapters.

Economic

Experience with economic development and security assistance demonstrated the limits of economic instruments both in achieving economic and social development and in influencing political institutions or policies. Essentially, we learned that leaders could not meet the development needs of whole societies with economic instruments alone.

In the early 1960s, practitioners and academics alike searched for strategies of economic development and assistance. These were the years of the large economic aid consortia and substantial development programs and of such village-level programs as the U.S. Peace Corps. Quickly, political factors intruded. Some experience in the 1960s and more in the 1970s made it increasingly clear that failure of political and bureaucratic policies can become just as serious an obstacle to economic growth as inadequate development planning or resources.

In the East-West context, the superpowers used economic assistance to influence the political orientation of aid recipients. Policy conflicts between donor and recipient apart from economic development became embroiled in the domestic politics of each and made it difficult to sustain the development relationship. In Egypt, for instance, food assistance first was a central part of the Kennedy administration's effort to achieve a cooperative political relationship. The United States also hoped that enabling Egyptian President Gamal Abdel Nasser to concentrate on his country's development would cause him to turn away from adventures in the Arab world that often put Egypt at cross-purposes with the United States. As the U.S. Congress reacted negatively to some of Nasser's policies, Presidents Kennedy and Johnson could no longer sustain congressional support for a multiyear food commitment. In the case of Israel, Arabs repeatedly asked why the United States could not use its substantial economic aid as a lever to press Israel to move toward a just resolution of the Arab-Israeli conflict. An important part of the answer lay in the intimate political relationship between the Israeli and U.S. bodies politic.

In more conventional arenas of trade and investment as well, as Robert Hormats points out in an earlier chapter, both the United States and the Middle East learned the limits of economic leverage. The oil embargo of 1973–1974, the rapid rise of oil prices, the accumulation of oil revenues in the Arab oil-producing countries, the investment of those revenues in industrialized economies, the participation of Western and Japanese companies in their development programs—all these brought about sophisticated new interrelationships.

What we learned from this experience was that a number of factors limited the use of economic instruments: Economic assistance strategies were often not broad enough to encompass the political policies necessary to remove political, bureaucratic, administrative, and legal obstacles to their success. It also became apparent that economic aid could not be used in most cases as leverage to achieve political objectives. "Aid without strings" became a slogan in the nonaligned world. Aid donors learned that political objectives are often of an order of magnitude much greater than the components of any economic or military assistance program. Governments do not barter their positions on issues fundamental to their security and to their futures for a certain item of military equipment or a specified increase in the level of economic assistance. Increasingly, policymakers in Washington and Middle Eastern capitals became aware that pressure lay not in the use of economic instruments but rather in making clear the consequences of actions for a total relationship. Even those who imposed the oil embargo had to recognize that their ultimate security and economic well-being depended in some measure on the targets of the embargo.

It also became apparent that economic instruments eventually ran into economic limits. The oil embargo and price increases had the potential of undermining the stability of economies in which oil producers invested their revenues for the sake of building their economic futures. They also had the consequence of stimulating energy policies in consuming countries that could over time reduce demand, lower prices, and undermine the producers' economies. By the mid-1980s, oil producers and economists looking back over the previous decade's experience concluded that the way supply and price increases had been managed had produced an oversupply that led to declining prices and intense demands on declining revenues. The oil weapon had become hostage to overambitious development plans within their societies and to conflicting economic demands for revenue among the oil producers themselves.

Military

Policymakers came to recognize increasingly the limits of military power in resolving disputes and changing relationships. In their relationship with the Soviet Union, U.S. leaders recognized that nuclear weaponry would not provide a means for deciding conflicts. In Vietnam, they experienced the limitations of conventional military power in dealing with a strong nationalist movement and a jungle insurgency.

In the Arab-Israeli conflict, despite Israel's military preponderance, it became apparent to both sides that the conflict could not be resolved militarily in the foreseeable future. Many Arabs concluded that Israel is here to stay. Israelis after four major wars and especially after the 1982 invasion of Lebanon realized they could not force Arab acceptance or forge political alliances by military force. While maintaining a deep suspicion of the Arabs, many Israelis have pressed face-to-face negotiation as a means of resolving their conflict.

In Lebanon, the United States contrasted its experience of landing the Marines in 1958 and again from 1982 to 1984. The earlier landing took place in the context of an energetic diplomatic effort to work out a political solution. In 1982–1984, the Marine landing was not accompanied by a comparable political effort, and policymakers learned that military forces could not resolve a problem involving the breakdown of political authority.

Policymakers also learned during this period that active arms races through several generations of sophisticated weaponry have increased the cost of each successive war. The moment is on the horizon, as General Tamir points out, when Middle Eastern states will also have to consider the consequences of dealing with nuclear weapons. Although it was conceivable in 1967 and 1973 that Israel could have gone on to inflict devastating damage on Arab military forces, Israel was unlikely to have been able to maintain permanent occupation over significant heavily populated areas of Arab states. The evolution of nonstate military organizations has demonstrated the difficulty of controlling and defeating them with conventional military force. The U.S. Sixth Fleet in 1983 demonstrated the difficulty of identifying terrorist targets for punitive military action.

Diplomacy, Negotiation, and Mediation

U.S. policymakers increasingly recognized the limits on traditional diplomacy in resolving disputes in the Middle East. I have already described how efforts to resolve the Arab-Israeli conflict moved from attempts to start a comprehensive negotiation to the shuttle diplomacy of Secretary Kissinger, the Camp David meetings, and the Egyptian-Israeli peace treaty.

In the Iran-Iraq war, mediation efforts were mounted by the Arab states, by members of the Islamic Conference, and by the United Nations, all to no avail through much of a decade. Conventional mediation failed because Iranian leaders, at least, had not committed themselves to a negotiated settlement and held to the political objective of bringing down the Iraqi regime. Iraq tried a number of military and economic strategies for increasing Iran's costs in the war as a means of precipitating a decision to negotiate, again to no avail for much of a decade. When UN mediation did produce a cease-fire, mediators found it difficult to move on to a final peace.

Policymakers learned from this experience that many conflicts are deeply rooted in social, political, and ideological causes and cannot be dealt with in the narrow framework of diplomacy. The Arab-Israeli conflict is not just a conventional war to achieve state interests but also a conflict between two peoples, Israelis and Palestinians. When a conflict between whole peoples becomes enmeshed in a state-to-state conflict, it is difficult to resolve the conflict among states in the conventional way before the political environment is changed so as to make resolution politically permissible.

Communication and Information

As the role of publics in foreign relations grows, some of the traditional tools for influencing and communicating with foreign populations remain weak, while newer instruments are growing stronger. In the United States, communication with publics in other states has often been considered the weakest of what have traditionally been regarded as the four major instruments of statecraft. Information programs—such as those of the U.S. Information Agency—are considered long-term, diffuse measures not very effective in dealing with acute problems.

That is because we are not yet thinking seriously about the potential of the dramatic political act conveyed to another public through the technology of the communication revolution as a highly effective instrument in changing perceptions. We still think it is a violation of the principle of not interfering in other countries' internal affairs to consider trying to reshape political debate; we have not thought through the fact that influence across borders is a fact of modern life. By merely existing, the Palestinians are a constant factor in Israeli policy debate; by either acting or not acting, the United States influences the peace process. Naomi Chazan, for instance, has explained the intimate and inextricable interaction between the external environment and internal political and social change in Israel. The question is not whether our acts should influence other bodies politic but what effect they will have. For some reason, many leaders in the United States cling to a view of international affairs that assumes politics stop at the waters' edge and some abstract international system provides the dominant framework beyond.

Advances in technology and development have made larger segments of societies aware of issues in foreign affairs while also increasing the ability of foreign governments to communicate with these newly mobilized publics. Foreign policy, in the United States and elsewhere, was earlier the sole province of diplomats. But the changes mentioned earlier— particularly social mobilization—combined with exponential increases in the volume and scope of communications to increase the number of people who will respond to major developments in foreign affairs. In the United States, for instance, the war in Vietnam ended the belief that foreign policy could safely be trusted to the experts. Congress—to the delight of some and the dismay of others—now strives to become a full partner with the executive in the formation and oversight of foreign policy. The same advances in communications technology have greatly increased the ability of governments to send messages to foreign populations. Borders have become more porous than ever, as people, messages, information, and materials flow back and forth at an accelerating rate.

In general it appears that the older, less sophisticated forms of communicating with foreign publics remain awkward and ineffective. Blatant propaganda is usually transparent. The benefits of tools such as cultural and educational exchanges are uncertain and long-term. More sophisticated approaches to foreign populations—sensitive to their concerns and often appealing to specific population segments—can play a growing role. For instance, the potential for direct communication by foreign political leaders grows as television extends their reach.

As these instruments of statecraft seemed less and less effective in their familiar forms, some of us began to reflect more and more on the potential of political instruments for changing relationships. Experience in the 1970s demonstrated their possibilities, but it was only in the 1980s that we barely began to think systematically about them.

The Concept of Relationship Among Nations

These observations about a changing world and the diminishing effectiveness of the familiar instruments of statecraft have led me to two further thoughts about how nations relate today: First, as I have already said, relations between nations today are increasingly a continuous political process of complex interaction among policymaking and policy-influencing communities on both sides of a relationship. Second, we need a concept for describing how nations relate large enough to encompass that continuous political process of interaction between whole bodies politic. The total interaction—the overall relationship between nations—is worthy of study in its own right.

To capture the totality of this dynamic interaction, I have come to use the concept of *relationship*.

The word *relationship* has disadvantages. At first hearing, it is such a commonplace word that we hardly notice it. But when we stop to think about relationships that sustain us as human beings, we begin to feel the power and depth of the concept. We also recognize that thinking about relationships causes us to think somewhat differently from the way we think about "us and them" or "I" and "you." Thinking as "we" produces a recognizable shift in mental gears.

Relationship does not translate easily. Soviets use "interdependent relations" or "comprehensive pattern of relations." Chinese have a strong concept of interpersonal relationships, but when they use the same word in the phrase "international relations" it does not have the connotations I am suggesting. Even in English, specialists in international relations bridle at hearing a word normally reserved for personal interdependence applied to whole nations. "States are different," they object.

Commonplace words, however, often acquire new dimensions only when we imbue them with new ideas. Perhaps the problem in accepting any word in this changing context is that we still think of states and power politics; we are not yet looking through lenses that focus on the political—even human—process of continuous interaction between significant elements of whole societies.

The fact is the world is changing: The concept of state institutions acting rationally does not realistically explain how this world works; the old instruments of statecraft are not the effective tools we need to work creatively in this world. Thus, we need a new vocabulary. After searching for a meaningful word and not finding a better one, I have decided to fall back on one we all understand and to use it in this new context, jarring as that may be to some ears. It does capture what needs to be said.

The very commonness of the concept may be the key to its usefulness. It is not a grand theory of international relations. It is an idea that human beings understand. It is a context in which human beings bring together, apply, and test in their intercourse with other human beings all the insights about life that help them understand and act. Those insights may have been learned from experience, from books, from parents and teachers, from the laboratory. Relationship is the context in which we humans integrate them. If we are increasingly in a world where people are more involved in the political process of interaction among whole bodies politic, then using a human-oriented word may provide a sounder basis for action in the real world than can abstract theories about state institutions.

Three other points about *relationship* are important: First, relationships may be good and bad—conflictual or cooperative, immature or mature, destructive or constructive. There are different levels, kinds, or qualities of relationship. Second, relationships are dynamic. Not only do they reflect kaleidoscopic shifts among internal or external factors that affect them, but they may change in character over time. They regress or mature and contract or enlarge their capacity to accomplish what needs to be done. A good relationship may sour, a bad relationship improve. Third, an overall relationship will involve many different interactions—or relationships—among subsets of people or groups. That different use of the word may cause some confusion, but as with many rich words, context normally will make the meaning clear.[2]

In sum, I have come to this concept by experiencing the proliferation of interactions among nations on many levels—well beyond any aggregate of government-to-government transactions. As my colleagues and I saw the effectiveness of conventional instruments of influence diminishing, we began to think of influence as lying in the ability to conduct that political process of continuous interaction effectively.

Although we did not articulate the point this way until the late 1970s, one can trace the beginnings of present perceptions at least back into the experience of the early 1960s in U.S. relationships in the Middle East. In effect, we were coping with the fact of political interdependence before the term came into common use again at the end of the decade. We began to recognize the web of relationship and learned that breaching one part of the relationship risked tearing the whole.

Egypt and the United States began to grapple with this factor as an integral element in their relationship in the Kennedy administration. We began feeling our way toward a new relationship by agreeing to put differences over the Arab-Israeli conflict "on ice" so as to develop our bilateral relationship. Then, the conflict between our policy objectives in places like the Congo and Yemen made it politically difficult to sustain key elements in the relationship, such as economic assistance. The U.S. Congress became increasingly reluctant to fund assistance to Egypt, and President Nasser in one particularly insulting speech told the United States to "drink the waters of the Red Sea." By 1967, the effort could no longer be sustained. In the 1970s, the situation reversed dramatically when close cooperation in negotiating Egyptian-Israeli peace opened the door for Egypt not only to one of the largest U.S. economic assistance programs in the world but even to provision of military equipment.

Even the Israeli-U.S. relationship—uniquely close since the 1940s—began to change character in the late 1950s and 1960s. The Israel lobby became much more intense and effective. Its pervasiveness became obvious—to the point where a president's programs in the Congress on issues not directly related to the Middle East could be threatened by the lobby if it was displeased with some aspect of his policy toward Israel. When in 1984 Israelis formed a deeply divided "national unity government," questions arose about whether the lobby was responsive to a harder Israeli line than that held by the prime minister of Israel, thereby complicating constraints on his action rather than adding support for his interest in pursuing a Jordanian-Palestinian negotiation.

It is in the concept of relationship that I find a framework large enough to embrace the totality of the interaction between two bodies politic. Only in a context that large do I find the opportunity to change conflictual relationships between peoples to peaceful ones.

Two Views of Foreign Relations Contrasted

As I began to think about the potential for political action that lies in focusing on the overall relationships among nations, I began to wonder what underlay the strong resistance among many policymakers to thinking this way. I found myself asking whether we were working from different assumptions about how the world works, so I set about trying to identify systematically the assumptions underlying two approaches. Before launching into that description, I want to be clear about what I am and am not doing.

I am conceptualizing assumptions I believe underlie different approaches to policymaking; I am not writing from the literature of international relations. I have looked at actions and tried to identify assumptions that seem to underlie them; I have not conducted scientific psychological tests to reveal policymakers' thinking. Mine is a common approach in the world of practice where policymakers often find themselves trying to figure out where others are "coming from."

After defining assumptions that seem to underlie different approaches, I have asked myself whether they have roots in the academic literature on international relations. Our perceptions of how the world works influence how we act. Those perceptions are formed both in the universities and in experience. If our theories of international relations define concepts in the minds of future leaders that are not accurate in explaining our world, those theories need to be reexamined, but that is not the main purpose of this chapter. My concern here is to address policymakers at the most basic level—questioning assumptions that do not fit today's world.

My personal experience leads me to believe strongly that it does make a difference which approach a policymaker follows. At least it makes a difference that we recognize openly when and why we are pursuing different approaches. My purpose in presenting these thoughts for discussion is to examine with U.S. and Middle Eastern colleagues the extent to which these approaches are adequate for the conduct of foreign relations in the closing years of the twentieth century and beyond. I will not hide my own strong view behind a facade of academic theorizing.

I am going to be somewhat arbitrary in contrasting elements of two different approaches to foreign relations. I sharpen this contrast in order to make the two approaches more vivid. In my mind, the distinctions represent two different real-world postures that one can identify at given moments in different policymakers, especially if one compares across cultures. At the same time, I quickly acknowledge that most policymakers will probably combine elements of the two approaches, whether consciously or not. Although I have cast each approach in its pure form, I know that normally neither will often be seen in that form and that in practice, we will see elements of the two approaches falling across a spectrum. I am casting these approaches in an "either/or" form to make a point, but in the end I realize that a "both/and" approach is more realistic. The world does not neatly shift from one paradigm to another in a short period of time, and practitioners act from one combination of assumptions in one situation and from a slightly different mix in another.

Despite some arbitrariness, setting up the contrast between these two approaches seems a useful way of making clear the real choices policymakers face. These choices involve assumptions about how policy is made, changed, and implemented both at home and abroad. By articulating these choices, I hope both to make them conscious choices for policymakers and to provide an analytical framework for understanding what might be added or subtracted from an approach at any given time.

Finally, although I have my own clear preference, I recognize that each approach may have its appropriate uses. For instance, one approach may have its roots in the need of the analytical community to isolate discrete elements of relationships among nations and policymaking so as to study them in depth. The other may reflect the untidy world in which policy is made and carried out. A problem arises only when we lack an integration of insights from analytical study into a conceptual framework that embraces the full range of human experience with which policymakers must cope.

Because I have already described the two approaches to the peace process as they have been debated in Washington—for instance, in 1985 following the Hussein-Arafat agreement or in early 1989 among advisers in the incoming Bush administration—I simply want to make one point in preview of a more detailed discussion. There is a sharp real-world difference between an approach that sees foreign relations as a series of discrete moves and one that sees relations as a continuously changing kaleidoscope in which moving one piece can make all the others fall into place differently.

This second approach is one that relies not on action and reaction but on reaching out through multiple actions to lay foundations for the forcing political acts that change a key element in the political environment and make all the other elements fall into a new pattern. This is an approach that does not stop with the analytical judgment that the situation is not ripe for movement but asks what can be done to help it ripen. This is an approach that assumes the political environment can be changed so that what is not possible today may be possible tomorrow. It is an approach that assumes trying and failing once or twice can leave a political leader in stronger control than if he or she simply drifts with events—if the leader uses the attempt wisely.

I would like to contrast these two approaches by making seven points. For economy in communicating, I will call one the "mechanistic approach" and the other the "organic (or process) approach." It is no secret that the latter underlies the view of the peace process as a political process.[3]

First: Whereas the mechanistic approach focuses on the individual policymakers as the source of foreign policy decisions, the organic approach focuses on policymakers interacting with their political environments.

The mechanistic approach tends to cast policy in terms of decisions. It tends to focus on the analytical components of a decision, the influences that affect the decisionmaker, the stages of decisionmaking, the written statement of the decision, and a series of discrete steps for implementing the decision. In this view, a decision is clearly made and a specifically defined course of action flows from it. The decision may be reviewed in the light of reactions, and adjustments may be made. As one senior adviser in the Carter White House once said to me with some frustration: "The President should make his decision and disengage so his lieutenants can carry out that specific decision without his further involvement for a time. The problem with Carter was that he constantly followed the implementation, and as the situation changed, his assumptions evolved and he refined his decision before it was fully implemented."

The organic approach looks at the policymaker as one human being interacting with his or her milieu. This point has several aspects.

The policymaker's judgments reflect one human mind and personality that must continuously "process" multiple inputs—all the analysis, opinion, action, reaction, influence, advice, and feeling swirling around a complex of issues. The person's psychological makeup is an extremely important factor because (to use the current U.S. vernacular) it provides the "program" by which an "internal computer" "processes" those elements of the environment that must be dealt with.

Those dealing with the policymaker in this person's complex milieu must look not only at the decision but at the whole complex of influences that impel or constrain. A leader must consider the impact of policy on other leaders and also on the political environment within which those leaders make policy.

Many levels of influences affect policymaking. The total political environment includes the inner circle of advisers, legislatures and lobbies, bureaucracies and agencies that implement policy, the press and other media, political parties and other elites, popular movements and other vocal subgroups, overall public opinion, and external constraints imposed by other states. It also includes ideas in the air—how a leader conceptualizes the issues and defines a sense of direction and how opponents do so.

The total environmental influence on policy and which parts of the political environment will be most influential will vary from polity to polity, from leader to leader, and between issues and over time. In the United States, legislative constraints are often formidable. In Israel, coalition politics are crucial. In the Arab world, other Arab states impose key constraints on policymakers.

The difference between the two approaches was captured for me when I went to work on the National Security Council staff in the White House in 1961. A senior colleague told me: "Remember, policy is not made on paper. It is a constantly changing mix of people and ideas." For one working at the policy level in the White House, it was clear that the president was the key figure in that constantly changing mix of people and ideas, but he was part of the mix. Today I would call that "constantly changing mix" a political process. I see making and implementing policy as a complex and ongoing interaction between the policymaker—a personality continuously in flux—and the person's constantly changing political environment. In the mechanistic approach, the focus is on the decisionmaker. In the process approach, the focus is on the entire policymaking system—the individual human being interacting as policymaker with the political environment. Those who focus mainly on leaders tend to see international relations in terms of rational government-to-government interactions. Those focusing on the whole complex of interactions tend to be impressed with a wide variety of exchanges taking place between whole polities at many levels.

Second: Whereas the mechanistic approach tends to see situations in terms of their static elements, the organic approach sees the fluidity of each situation. The individual thinking in terms of process sees each situation constantly in flux as one watching a shifting kaleidoscope.

When those taking a more mechanistic view assess the policies of a foreign leader, they study such factors as state interests, capabilities, and constraints seemingly built into the political or cultural structure. Among those static elements, they will look for potential levers for influencing policy change. In their assessments, one will often hear that "there is no room to maneuver." The picture is one of conflicting interests and power balances determining policy, and leaders are normally seen as limited in their capacity to change their environment. In January 1974 after the first Egyptian-Israeli disengagement agreement, one U.S. scholar said to me: "Egyptians will always be Egyptians. Israelis will always be Israelis. If you think you can change any of that, you're wrong." Four Arab-Israeli agreements later, I was skeptical of his views, but that is not the point.

Practitioners who think about process tend to focus on the constantly changing situation. Theirs is the language of political maneuver. They take no situation as a given but look in each situation for those variables that account for change. They ask not whether a situation can change but how it will change and how they can influence the course of change. They recognize that it is change which is inevitable and that it is good politics to be the one who shapes the course of change. The difference is between the leader who will accept the intractable elements in a situation as given and immovable in the near term and the leader who recognizes the obstacles in a situation but asks what he or she can do to chip away at them and begin removing them.

Third: Whereas the mechanistic approach tends to see international relations as a linear series of episodes, organic-oriented policymakers see it as a continuous process with too many variables at work at any one time to think of a simple straight-line progression of events.

The mechanistic approach emphasizes discrete events and episodes. Problems or opportunities arise, starting a decisionmaking cycle that puts into motion a number of possible diplomatic, military, or economic instruments. Reactions follow, and further decisions are made that produce new actions. The policymaking cycle begins when a problem comes to the attention of leaders and ends when a decision is made and implemented.

The organic approach emphasizes a continuous process of making and revising, implementing and making midcourse corrections in policy, both within and between states. Just as one state's policy is constantly being reshaped by the leader working within her or his environment, a relationship between two states is continuously being molded and recast through constant interaction at all levels. A decision is no sooner made than a new development changes the situation before it can be fully implemented. The process moves too quickly and is affected by too many influences to be described as a progression of episodes.

One consequence of considering whole polities interacting is that a diplomat stymied on the road to negotiation will, in pursuing the organic approach, step off the diplomatic path and look for other routes to take around the obstacles. Those thinking of process are just as likely to look for the Sadat-like forcing political act as they are for the verbal formula when they seek a way to open the door to negotiation.

Fourth: Whereas the mechanistic approach focuses on a series of actions and reactions, the person pursuing the organic approach thinks in terms of a longer sequence of interacting developments, each of which becomes possible because of what has preceded. The distinction is made concrete if one thinks in terms of the planning tool the policymaker uses: The mechanistic approach relies on the options paper describing a decision on a course of action; the policymaker thinking of process will think in terms of a political scenario laying out a complex of interacting steps.

In the mechanistic context, foreign policy analysts prepare lists of options for the policymaker to review in deciding on the "next step" in a diplomatic plan of action, including their estimate of the other side's probable reaction. The image often used is the chess game, proceeding one step at a time through a series of actions and reactions. If the "next step" fails to occur, the planned course of action may grind to a halt.

In the imagery of process, relationships among nations bear less resemblance to a chess game than to a complex dance, with many dancers moving together. The interaction is continuous, multiple, simultaneous, and mutually dependent. The policymaker, like the choreographer, is concerned not only with the details of the next step but also with the whole configuration and where it is headed. This person tries to realize a vision of how a sequence should develop and where he or she wants it to go, recognizing that there are probably several ways to proceed at each stage. A less elegant image in contrast to the chess game that ran through my mind during my last years in government was that of a game of squash or racquetball with four players on a five-sided court with six balls in motion at the same time.

The instrument often used in laying out such a sequence of steps is the political scenario. Someone has to describe in advance—and then to choreograph—such a sequence. A scenario has two purposes: First, it is a working document that permits planners to lay out a series of steps and to understand the responses and new situations each will generate and the further moves that may become possible. Identifying what will be required in the later stages may then permit going back and building preparatory elements into earlier stages. Second, if two parties work together or with an intermediary, a scenario can become a repository for assurances by each side that follow-on steps will take place if promised prior steps are taken. Whereas a traditional options paper may provide several actions through a course of events leading into the future, a political scenario will focus on what in the political environment needs to be changed before new steps can be taken and will concentrate on bringing about those changes through interacting steps. The focus is not so much on the options for the next step as it is on visualizing the larger, reciprocal process.

In this kind of process, the role of a third party is not so much to resolve problems as it is to help the parties come together in agreeing on a scenario for moving toward a solution. The metaphor of a choreographer coordinating a dance can be contrasted with the traditional metaphor of a broker mediating a business deal. One seems organic; the other, more mechanistic.

One other difference between the two approaches on this point is apparent in the two views of a negotiating process. The mechanistic view sees negotiations as prepared for analytically and then staged by agreeing on arrangements on terms of reference and format. The process view sees negotiation as only one later stage in a long process that involves political maneuvering around the fundamental issue of whether to negotiate at all. In this view, precipitating the decision on whether to negotiate may be more difficult than reaching agreement if negotiations begin. Whereas a mechanistic approach tends to see negotiation itself as the way problems are resolved, the organic view sees negotiation as only one stage in a larger political process.

Fifth: Whereas the mechanistic view tends to react to problems or opportunities, the organic approach emphasizes seizing the initiative to develop new situations and opportunities.

Those taking the mechanistic view analyze a situation to determine whether the "time is ripe" for an initiative. Questions frequently heard are "Is this the right moment?" or "Is progress possible?" These policymakers seem tempted to focus on the intractability of a situation and to decline to act if they judge the obstacles to progress too great to be removed.

In contrast, because process-oriented policymakers see both policy and relationship as constantly changing, they believe continuous engagement in the process gives them the best chance of influencing the course of change. Beyond that, their attitude is one of looking for ways to promote change. They are less inclined to wait for the "ripe moment" than to enter the process to make the moment more ripe. They ask, "What can we do now to change the situation to improve our odds?" Their aim is to contribute constructively to the continuous reshaping of a situation as a means of influencing not only their own constituencies but also the constituencies of leaders in other states with whom they must deal.

This may be the most dangerous generalization of all because creative statesmen have long acted with a vision of the future and played the chess game aggressively with a strategy to force the opponent to do as their interests require. Nevertheless, in my view there remains a difference between a statesman playing chess and a politician working in the middle of a messy situation to reshape it and to make it somewhat more manageable.

Sixth: Whereas the mechanistic approach thinks of the policymaker as a senior diplomat working with the support of a professional staff, those holding the organic approach think of the policymaker as a political leader operating in the political arena and using more the art of the politician than the craft of the diplomat.

The mechanistic approach thinks about diplomatic proposals and negotiating formulas; those shaping process think in terms of "forcing (or precipitating) acts" in the political arena designed to reshape the political environment. Whereas the object of the former's action is the foreign leader as decisionmaker, the leader pursuing the process approach will also target the constituencies of foreign leaders in an effort to reshape the political environment within which they operate.

Traditionally, diplomacy has been the realm of diplomats directed by political leaders. Diplomats normally devise formulas, present proposals, make statements through diplomatic channels or in public, and analyze the reaction. Their primary target is their counterpart responsible for the actions of other governments.

Those who pursue the process approach target a larger audience: the political environment of the other leaders, in addition to the policymakers themselves. They identify and try to loosen constraining elements in the political environments of the other leaders.

A dramatic example of the organic approach in the past was President Sadat's visit to Israel in November 1977. The Israeli government called the points in his negotiating position nonnegotiable, but Israel responded warmly. Why? Sadat brought a message of readiness to accept Israel as a neighbor and to make peace. By that political act, Sadat changed attitudes in Israel and helped create a political environment that ultimately led to a peace treaty. Sadat's "forcing political act," which delivered a message to all segments of the Israeli polity, reshuffled perceptions and created pressures demanding response from the Israeli government.

Seventh: Whereas the mechanistic focus falls on the other side's objective interests, those pursuing the organic approach also take into account the psychological and political concerns of the people on the other side as part of their nation's interests.

In the mechanistic approach, the objective is to bridge the gap between divergent interests, whereas the policymaker focusing on process will think of the psychological barriers that must be removed and the human needs that must be met in a political environment before a negotiated solution will win political support.

Traditional diplomacy focuses on such objective interests as military security, economic benefit, resources, alliances, borders, and juridical status of relations. In looking at approaches to a solution in terms of negotiated agreements, an adherent of the mechanistic approach focuses on writing an agreement that will accommodate the interests of each side. Solutions are often found in terms of artful verbal formulations that in fact often rely on ambiguity rather than on solution.

The proponent of process will go behind the objective statement of interest to find the deeper human concerns and will try to address them through a variety of possible solutions, not just those that can be written into an agreement. Those who take this approach recognize that, at times, psychological concerns—such as needs for identity, acceptance, participation, psychological security, and face-saving—can be as vital as objective concerns. They also recognize that these political and psychological issues can obstruct communications and block progress on other issues.

Sadat's impact on Israeli policy and politics did not stem from the objective content of his speech to the Knesset. His impact came instead from the act of visiting Israel and from his willingness to address directly the most deep-seated fears and longing of the Israeli public for genuine acceptance by their neighbors. If Sadat had taken the mechanistic approach, he could have sent the proposal by diplomatic channels to Israel where it might well have been dismissed out of hand because objectively it contained nothing new. Instead, he took an approach designed to change the political environment by introducing a forcing political act to which all actors on the stage had to respond.

The Arab-Israeli Peace Process in the Future

It is a thesis of this book that experience among nations around the world teaches new concepts and new vocabularies for dealing with problems such as the Arab-Israeli conflict. Some of us have learned those concepts and vocabularies while working in the Arab-Israeli peace process. Others have learned similar lessons more recently from pondering the political approach reflected in Soviet President Mikhail Gorbachev's actions and his "new political thinking." All of us will reflect for some time on lessons from dramatic changes in Eastern Europe in 1989— vivid examples of change swelling from the bottom up rather than being dictated from the top down.

That the world of Arabs and Israelis is indeed changing pervades earlier chapters in this book—pictures of an intercommunal as well as a state-to-state conflict, recognition that military power and economic pressure operate under more complex restraints and do not offer sure answers, vivid pictures of each policymaking community as heavily affected by the policy-influencing communities around it, an analysis of the peace process as far exceeding the dimensions of state-to-state diplomacy, and an emphasis that contradictions about a nation's sense of identity can undermine its diplomacy.

If the Arab-Israeli peace process is to be reconstituted and revived, we must put it in the context of the larger political process that embraces the overall relationships between Israel and its neighbors. One way to make this point concrete is to suggest that the instrument of policy analysis and planning is not the terms of reference for a negotiation but a political scenario of interacting steps designed to change the political environment and to open the door to changing relationships.

A political scenario has three uses: First, it begins by identifying the fundamental obstacles to a changed Israeli-Palestinian relationship— the deepest causes of Israeli fears of a Palestinian neighbor and the politics through which those fears are expressed as well as the underlying reasons for Palestinian reticence to take the political offensive in trying to precipitate a serious Israeli-Palestinian peace process.[4] Alongside that list of obstacles would be identified steps by either side that would begin to erode them and to build confidence that it is possible to develop a peaceful relationship. Second, those steps need to be laid out in an interactive sequence, starting with steps that could be taken without much further political preparation and leading to steps that can be taken only when prior steps have been absorbed and assessed. Finally, in the hands of a third party, such a scenario can be a vehicle for discussion and a repository for promises that one side will take a step provided the other will respond with a constructive step of its own. In short, the aim is to design an interactive complex of actions that respond to each other and build on each other to change perceptions and to open the door to new areas of cooperation.

My purpose here is not to detail a plan for reconstituting the peace process; I have done that elsewhere.[5] My purpose here is to make a more fundamental point: The peace process will not produce results in building a peaceful relationship between Israel and its neighbors until it is understood as a series of negotiations on specific technical steps embedded in a larger political process designed to change the political environment. The purpose of this chapter is to cast the peace process in a global perspective so as to paint a fuller picture of what the process can be—and what it must be if it is to move Israelis, Palestinians, and other Arabs toward peace and resolution of their conflict. Putting the peace process in a global context also generates insight for conducting other relationships in other places. The peace process both teaches much to a changing world and is affirmed by what is happening in a changing world.

A Middle East Peace Process
After the Gulf War

The Gulf war of 1991 focused attention on the larger political agenda of the entire region. The challenge is to conceive a political process large enough to encompass that large complex of disparate issues—a Middle East peace process.

Addressing that large political agenda as a whole does not imply that items on that agenda are linked in some formal way. It does imply that many objectively unrelated issues are related in the minds of human beings because they are seen as evidence of the real character and intentions of another party. It does imply that dealing justly with one issue can change the political environment so as to make it possible to address other issues that may be technically unrelated.

If the larger purpose in moving toward peace is to change hostile and destructive relationships to constructive ones, then changing the perceptions of each party of the other's character and intent is fundamental to making peace. That is more likely achieved if we think of the larger political process in which overall relationships are gradually changed rather than in terms of a series of technically unconnected negotiations on issues as different as arms control, justice in economic development, the identity of peoples, and the holy places of three great religions.

The Agenda

The political exchanges surrounding Iraq's invasion of Kuwait in August 1990 and the war that followed in 1991 called the world's attention to a broader agenda in the Middle East. Before war began, it was possible to discuss a political scenario for dealing with that agenda as a possible alternative to war. After war began, it was necessary to discuss such a political scenario in the context of ending the war and launching another attempt to build a wider and more just and lasting peace across the entire region. The substance of the agenda to be addressed might be sketched out under five points such as the following:

First: The territorial integrity, sovereignty, political independence, and national identity of every state in the Middle East must be acknowledged and respected.

The most immediate application of this point was total Iraqi withdrawal from Kuwait and restoration of the territorial integrity and sovereignty of Kuwait. The principle to be affirmed is that existing borders must be respected or be changed only through processes based upon genuine mutual consent. In the larger region, this suggests that Syria should not define a greater Syria and Israel should not define a greater Israel, to mention two other examples. (The special case of Israelis and Palestinians is discussed under point five.)

Respect for national identity raises a less concrete issue. Within the context of restoring the territorial integrity and sovereignty of Kuwait, the nature of the government of Kuwait should be left for broadly based political processes involving the leaders and people of Kuwait to decide. The principle of self-determination should be applied. The thought is that national identity reflects the total cultural and human experience of the people in the nation-state and government must be responsive to who the people are and want to be.

This is a delicate issue in a region of traditional monarchical regimes. The purpose is not a mindless demand that these governments suddenly be democratized; the purpose is to suggest that orderly and productive change over time will depend on the ability of each nation's people to reach into their own political experience in order to fashion a government responsive to their needs.

Second: Each state in the region has the right to live in peace with security against threats or acts of force.[6]

Security assurances must provide the most realistic guarantees possible against attack in all directions. A most obvious and immediate application of the point would be provision for a UN force on the Iraq-Kuwait border, as has existed on the Iran-Iraq border since the end in 1988 of the war between those two states.

In addition to meeting pressing needs emerging from the Gulf war are concerns about blocking potential future aggression. The problem in the Middle East seems quite different from that in Europe during the cold war. Whereas lines in Europe were sharply drawn between two blocs that threatened each other, the threat in the Middle East has tended to shift. Nowhere has that been clearer than in the Gulf: In the 1980s, Iran seemed the greatest threat and Iraq the force most useful in confronting that threat; at the beginning of the 1990s, Iraq was the threatening power and itself faced a possible threat of dismemberment by its neighbors. What state (or bloc) will be seen as the primary threat in the mid-1990s and later?

The problem of providing security guarantees in such a shifting situation has yet to be addressed seriously beyond the thought of trying to establish a new protective balance of power. In the early aftermath of the war, a continuation on a much smaller scale of some combination of the forces that fought Iraq might be possible as an instrument for assuring that Iraq's other borders—with Saudi Arabia, Jordan, Syria, and Turkey—are not crossed in either direction. The Gulf Cooperation Council is another possible vehicle for marshaling a force. Any of this could be done under a United Nations umbrella. Beyond the early postwar situation, the challenge will be to establish a political authority for security forces that will not be just a continuation of the coalition against Iraq but an authority capable of shifting focus as the threat shifts.

Beyond the issues involved in providing security for borders was a collection of issues involving arms control in various forms. Basic were concerns among arms suppliers to find ways to limit the flow of so-called conventional arms to the Middle East, while respecting the needs of governments to provide defensive security for their peoples. A corollary was the possibility of building incipient understandings on limiting force levels into whatever peace agreements might emerge over time. Beyond this fundamental level were the international efforts to limit the proliferation of chemical, biological, and nuclear weapons. Dealing with these problems involved, in part, the development and acceptance of inspection systems far more intrusive than previously known.

Third: As it is possible to move toward resolution of disputes, the underlying grievances, fears, and concerns as well as the concrete claims of each party must be considered thoughtfully and responsively.

The argument here is for addressing the causes as well as the symptoms of conflict. It is an argument for the broadest possible approach to resolving disputes—not just by negotiating claims and counterclaims but by trying to deal with the issues that deeply divide people in the larger political arena. It is an argument for an organic, political approach rather than continuing a more mechanistic approach of bargaining over how to split the difference between conflicting claims. Such an approach is an essential foundation for trying to develop over time a political process for changing relationships in the region.

Examples emerging from the agenda surrounding the Iraqi invasion of Kuwait included the following:

• Iraq stated that it needed two Kuwaiti islands to assure access to the sea. One could imagine the UN Security Council affirming Iraq's right to access to the sea and charging a UN peacekeeping force to assure that those islands not fall under the control of any party threatening that right.

• Iraq raised the question of the maldistribution of oil income in the Arab world. In doing so, Saddam Hussein attempted to exploit the genuine resentment of people in the Middle East who felt they had not shared in the benefits from oil production—who saw small ruling families investing oil profits in the Western industrialized countries rather than in the Middle East. Whether Saddam Hussein spoke out of conviction or from cynical motives, he tapped strong Arab feeling. In response, one could see bringing to fruition the initiative to create an Arab Bank for Reconstruction and Development funded by voluntary contributions from oil producers, including Iraq.

• Iraq expressed its resentment at Kuwait, in part, by charging that Kuwait had pumped oil from reserves that are rightfully Iraq's. Rather than dismissing that as a cynical claim, one could see addressing that claim under the auspices of the World Court or an international commission to assure that any possible grievance is fairly heard.

Fourth: All legitimate claims and debts must be settled by peaceful means in accordance with the United Nations Charter and in accordance with the principle that all serious grievances be heard.

Before Iraq invaded Kuwait, discussions were in progress over repayment of Iraqi debts to Kuwait and Saudi Arabia incurred by Iraq to meet the costs of its war with Iran. In addition to the legal merits of the case, mediators as well as the parties will need to take account in some way of the Iraqi feeling—however justified—that Iraq's prosecution of that war provided a shield defending the other Arab states of the Gulf against an aggressive Iran. In Iraqi eyes, that shield permitted other Arab oil producers to build profits free from threat. The issues in a settlement even before the invasion of Kuwait might have been more political than financial.

Iraq's occupation of Kuwait added the complex issue of Kuwaiti claims for reparations to compensate for the destruction and looting of Kuwait. Closely related was the question of how long the embargo on Iraq's export of oil would be maintained after Iraq's military forces withdrew from Kuwait. It was conceivable to maintain that embargo for a period of time while other Arab oil producers continued to pump oil at high levels and, by some formula, donated a portion of their income to rebuilding Kuwait as a way of assuring it compensation. They would, in effect, force Iraqi payment by channeling profits that Iraq would otherwise have received to Kuwait.

All of these issues needed to be resolved—not just in financial negotiations but in a settlement broad enough to provide a foundation for gradually rebuilding some constructive relationship between Iraq and its neighbors. Another example from another part of the region was the difficult question of how to compensate Palestinian claims for property lost when Palestinians left their homes in 1948 while taking into account in some way Israeli claims for Jewish property lost as Jews felt forced to leave Arab countries at the same time. Again, the debts needed to be resolved in a way that gave each aggrieved party a sense that its grievances had been heard and responded to. The calculation of what was fair might only be made in the context of shaping the relationship that aggrieved peoples were willing to try to build with each other, looking to the future.

Fifth: New contexts for resolving conflicts in the region must be created.

During the 1990–1991 crisis, Iraq called for resolution of the Israeli-Palestinian conflict in the context of ending the Iraqi occupation of Kuwait. Practicality argued in the eyes of many that the two issues could not be formally linked because of their different characters and different time lines. At the same time, the fact was that the two situations became intertwined in many Arab minds—not always without reason. The issue became not so much whether the United States and its allies should agree to an international conference to deal with the Israeli-Palestinian conflict as a condition for Iraqi withdrawal from Kuwait. The issue was how to resume efforts to move toward an Israeli-Palestinian settlement—efforts begun long before Iraq invaded Kuwait—in such a way as to contribute to a constructive political environment in the Middle East for dealing with that issue as well as a range of other important issues.

Discussion of this question gave rise to thinking about whether the traditional international conference for negotiation could provide the most fruitful context for the larger political task of changing relationships. That leads us to a larger discussion of the political process of moving toward more peaceful relationships.[7]

The Process

Those who addressed this agenda either before or after the war had a choice between two approaches: One was to take each of the issues and put it into its appropriate negotiating channel or diplomatic forum. The other approach—additional to the first, not exclusive of it— was to step back and bring the total complex of issues, negotiations, and diplomatic tracks into view and to try to understand their interactions in the larger political environment of the Middle East. The image was not so much of an organist at the console with control over the playing of each note from the score or the choreographer of a ballet designing each move in relation to all other moves on the stage. The image was of minds at work in the midst of an enormously complex situation with a sense of larger purpose and of the full range of human and technical capacities for nudging that situation in a constructive direction step by step, dealing with the unforeseen and making midcourse corrections at each turn.

Several ideas emerged from the early discussion of this problem. One reached back into history to recall the Congress of Vienna in Europe after the Napoleonic wars that attempted to reestablish the rules for the peaceful interaction among states. A second turned creatively to the more recent example of the Conference for Security and Cooperation in Europe (CSCE)—an effort since the 1970s by thirty-five nations in Europe and the Atlantic Community to deal with a wide range of issues, from human rights to avoiding surprise attack. What commended the CSCE model were the capacity to deal on separate tracks with a diversity of issues and the opening increasingly to involve citizens and not just government in changing political relationships.

The suggestion here is to learn from these other experiences but also to turn to one born in efforts to deal with conflict in the Middle East. As this chapter has suggested, the Arab-Israeli peace process as the experience grew became not just a series of negotiations but negotiations embedded in a larger political process. Troops were disengaged following a war. Political relations were restored. Confidence-building measures between disengaging military forces were arranged to prevent another surprise attack. Mutually agreed measures for assuring compliance were put into place with little friction. Force limitations in certain areas were implemented. An oil embargo was ended. Joint economic commissions were formed. Disengagement agreements were superseded by a peace treaty. A sequence of negotiations was designed for bringing a Palestinian self-governing authority into being and then for shaping a long-term relationship among Israelis, Jordanians, and Palestinians. Attempts were made to relate global powers to the process. Peace was addressed both in its juridical and state-to-state forms and in the form of normalization of relations between peoples.

The Arab-Israeli-Palestinian process remains uncompleted. Comparing thinking in 1971 about what is possible with thinking in 1991, one can hardly say that nothing has changed. Not as much changed as many of us had long ago hoped, but the possibilities for peaceful relationships have been enlarged. Even more important, the range of instruments available for changing relationships peacefully has been significantly expanded. Some of the new ways we have learned to think about peaceful resolution of conflict have been affirmed by what we have seen on the global stage.

In 1991 the challenge was to consider how in the wake of war the lessons of the Arab-Israeli peace process could be drawn on to build a larger peace process for the Middle East.

Notes

1. For a fuller discussion of this point, see Harold H. Saunders, "The Soviet-U.S. Relationship and the Third World," in Robert Jervis and Seweryn Bialer, eds., *Soviet-American Relations After the Cold War* (Durham, N.C.: Duke University Press, 1991), chap. 6.

2. This description of the concept of relationship also appears and is developed more fully in Harold H. Saunders, "An Historic Challenge to Rethink How Nations Relate," in Vamik D. Volkan, Demetrios Julius, and Joseph V. Montville, eds., *The Psychodynamics of International Relationships—Vol. 1: Concepts and Theories* (Lexington, Mass.: Lexington Books, 1990), chap. 1.

3. These assumptions were defined through extensive conversations with Thomas Smerling, who worked with me in 1985–1986 on a Bush Foundation leadership fellowship. As we defined them, he tested them against the literature of international relations while I tested them against political and diplomatic practice. A version of this analysis and a table presenting the differences in summary form appeared in "International Relationships—It's Time to Go Beyond 'We' and 'They,'" *Negotiation Journal*, vol. 3, no. 3 (July 1987), pp. 245–274, published as a work in progress. I developed this material further in "Beyond 'Us' and 'Them'—Building Mature International Relationships," an unpublished draft monograph written in 1987–1988 with the support of the United States Institute of Peace in collaboration with the Kettering Foundation.

4. I have discussed at length these deep-rooted human obstacles to peace in *The Other Walls: The Arab-Israeli Peace Process in a Global Perspective* (Princeton, N.J.: Princeton University Press, 1991 printing with new introduction, epilogue, and appendixes).

5. Ibid., chap. 9. And see Harold H. Saunders, "Reconstituting the Arab-Israeli Peace Process," in William B. Quandt, ed., *The Middle East: Ten Years After Camp David* (Washington, D.C.: Brookings Institution, 1988), part 4; and Saunders, "The Arab-Israeli Conflict in a Global Perspective," in John D. Steinbruner, ed., *Restructuring American Foreign Policy* (Washington, D.C.: Brookings Institution, 1988), chap. 8.

6. The wording of these first two points is intended to be compatible with that of UN Security Council resolution 242, passed after the June 1967 Arab-Israeli war on November 22, 1967. It states in part (format and italics not reflected here): "The Security Council, . . . emphasizing the inadmissibility of the acquisition of territory by war and the need to work for a just and lasting peace in which every State in the area can live in security, . . . affirms that the fulfillment of Charter principles requires the establishment of a just and lasting peace in the Middle East which should include the application of both the following principles: withdrawal of Israel armed forces from territories occupied in the recent conflict; termination of all claims or states of belligerency and respect for and acknowledgement of the sovereignty, territorial integrity and political independence of every State in the area and their right to live in peace within secure and recognized boundaries free from threats or acts of force."

7. These thoughts on political settlement are placed in the context of a fuller discussion of the Gulf crisis in Harold H. Saunders, "Political Settlement and the Gulf Crisis," *Mediterranean Quarterly,* vol. 2 (spring 1991). The *Quarterly* has given permission for use here of those portions of this chapter that may appear verbatim in both places.

About the Book

Well before events in the Soviet Union and Eastern Europe dramatized the rapidity with which a new political world is evolving and before the Gulf War sharpened the focus on the Middle East agenda, scholars and policymakers alike were searching for different concepts for addressing the intractable problems facing the Middle East. Even though the region shares such goals as negotiated resolution of conflict, stability, and prosperity, their attainment eludes traditional diplomacy. Historical, cultural, and religious factors continue to be major determinants of national behavior, often in ways incompatible with the assumptions of Western political culture.

This book is organized around the premise that conventional political and diplomatic concepts cannot fully explain the situation in the Middle East and that the usual instruments of statecraft do not reliably attain their intended goals. A wide spectrum of thoughtful perspectives is provided by the contributors, who include eminent scholars from the Middle East and the West, military analysts, bankers, economists, journalists, diplomats, politicians, and statesmen. Their essays challenge many foreign policy assumptions about the role of military and economic power, the relationship between larger and smaller states, and the nature of conflict and peace. In the wake of the Gulf War, these insights create building blocks for a regional peace process. Reflecting both Middle Eastern and Western perspectives, the book provides a well-balanced and refreshing analysis that will be valuable to scholars, students, journalists, diplomats, and businesspeople interested in this volatile region.

About the Contributors

Meron Benvenisti served as director and author of the West Bank Data Project. He is the author of *Conflicts and Contradictions*, wrote the cover story for *The New York Times Magazine* (October 16, 1988), "Two Generations: Growing Up in Jerusalem," and contributes to scholarly journals.

Naomi Chazan is chairperson of the Harry S. Truman Research Institute of Hebrew University. She is the author of *Decolonization in West Africa* and *The Human Factor in the Israeli Technical Assistance Program in Africa* and contributes articles to scholarly journals in Israel, the United States, and elsewhere.

Anthony H. Cordesman is national security consultant to ABC News and is adjunct professor of national security studies at Georgetown University. He serves as legislative assistant for national security to Senator John McCain. He is the author of *The Gulf and the West, The Iran-Iraq War: 1984–1987, The Lessons of Modern War*, and *Weapons of Mass Destruction in the Middle East*.

Stanley Hoffmann is Douglas Dillon Professor of the Civilization of France at Harvard University, where he has taught since 1955. He has been the chairman of the Center for European Studies at Harvard since its creation in 1969. He is the author of many books, including *Dead Ends* (1983) and *Janus and Minerva* (1986), and is the co-author of *Living with Nuclear Weapons* (1983) and *The Mitterrand Experiment* (1987).

Robert D. Hormats is vice chairman of Goldman Sachs International in New York. He served on the National Security Council staff from 1969–1977 and in the State Department as deputy assistant secretary (1977–1979) and assistant secretary (1981–1982) of state for economic and business affairs. He was also deputy U.S. trade representative with the rank of ambassador (1979–1981).

Ahmed S. Khalidi and *Hussein Agha* co-edit the Arabic fortnightly magazine *Strategic Review* and the Arabic edition of the *Journal for Palestine Studies*. They write extensively on Middle Eastern political and strategic issues jointly and individually. Most recently, Dr. Khalidi wrote "Middle East Security: Arab Threat Perceptions, Peace and Stability," which was published in *Middle East Security: Two Views.*

Rashid Khalidi is associate professor of modern Middle East history, Center for Middle Eastern Studies, at the University of Chicago. He is the author of *Under Siege: PLO Decisionmaking During the 1982 War* and many important monographs and articles on Arab politics, the Palestinian question, and Soviet policy in the Middle East.

Judith Kipper is guest scholar at The Brookings Institution and senior program associate with the Council on Foreign Relations, where she directs the Middle East Forum. She is a consultant to the Rand Corporation and to ABC News. She was resident fellow at the American Enterprise Institute when this project began.

William Green Miller is president of the American Committee on U.S.-Soviet Relations. He has contributed articles to many publications, including *The Middle East Journal, Final Report*, and *Common Security.* He edited *Perspectives on the Middle East, 1983* and *Toward a More Civil Society: The USSR Under Mikhail Sergeevich Gorbachev.*

Robert J. Pranger is managing editor of *Mediterranean Quarterly* and adjunct professor at American University. His many publications include *Ideology and Power in the Middle East, Nuclear Strategy and National Security, Detente and Defense, Defense Implications of International Indeterminacy*, and other monographs and articles.

Harold H. Saunders directs the International Programs of the Charles F. Kettering Foundation. He was a member of the National Security Council staff (1961–1974) and served at the State Department (1974–1981) as deputy assistant secretary and assistant secretary for Near Eastern and South Asian affairs and as director of intelligence and research. He was resident fellow at the American Enterprise Institute when this project began and later became a visiting fellow at The Brookings Institution.

H.R.H. Crown Prince El Hassan bin Talal oversees development planning, the education system's restructuring, and development of science and technology for Jordan. He is the author of three books—*A Study on Jerusalem, Palestinian Determination: A Study of the West Bank and Gaza*, and *Search for Peace.*

Avraham Tamir is a general (ret.) in the Israel Defense Forces, where he began his career in 1948. General Tamir oversaw security arrangements between Israel and Egypt, Syria, and Lebanon and was a member of Prime Minister Begin's delegation to the Camp David summit.

Ghassan Tuéni is the editor and publisher of the Beirut daily newspaper *An Nahar.* He is the author of *Une Guerre Pour Les Autres* and has contributed to newspapers and journals in Europe and the United States. He served as Lebanon's ambassador to the United Nations and has held other senior positions in government.

Index